George Augustus Sala

Rome and Venice with other Wanderings in Italy, in 1866-7

Salzwasser

George Augustus Sala

Rome and Venice with other Wanderings in Italy, in 1866-7

1. Auflage | ISBN: 978-3-84605-244-0

Erscheinungsort: Frankfurt, Deutschland

Erscheinungsjahr: 2020

Salzwasser Verlag GmbH

Reprint of the original, first published in 1869.

ROME AND VENICE,

WITH OTHER

WANDERINGS IN ITALY, IN 1866-7.

BY

GEORGE AUGUSTUS SALA,

AUTHOR OF

"AMERICA IN THE MIDST OF WAR," ETC.

1859.

"Ecco torno il Francese:
Vedete poi l' esercito che sotto
La ruota di Fortuna era caduto,
Creato il nuovo Rè chi si prepara
Dall' onta vendicar che ebbe a Novara."

Ariosto.

1866.

"Noi siamo padroni delle acque di Lissa."

Admiral Persano to General de la Marmora.

LONDON:
TINSLEY BROTHERS, 18 CATHERINE ST., STRAND.
1869.

LONDON:
ROBSON AND SONS, PRINTERS, PANCRAS ROAD, N.W.

TO

SHIRLEY BROOKS

This Volume

IS VERY CORDIALLY DEDICATED.

NOTICE.

The Letters forming this volume, with the exception of those headed respectively "On Travelling and Travellers in Italy," and "Roma Urbs," appeared in the columns of the *Daily Telegraph*, between the month of April 1866 and the month of February 1867. They are now republished by permission of the Proprietors of that Journal. That which now sees the light again, under the comprehensive title of *Rome and Venice*, is scarcely a fourth part of my original correspondence from, I think, nearly every province of continental Italy, save Calabria. Sicily I did not visit; and for many reasons, at which I have hinted "in another place," I have cancelled all record of my experiences in the Tyrol with Garibaldi—the Washington of Italy: "first in war, first in peace, first in the hearts of his countrymen," but whose reputation has been shamefully maltreated, within these latter days, in England, simply because he is old, and has failed in two attempts, and because he is too noble and too pure to tell lies, or to disguise his horror and hatred of the cogging and shuffling of diplomacy, and the wickedly impudent impostures of priestcraft. My readers, and especially my critics in the amœne sphere of journalism (how we all loathe one another, to be sure!), may be reasonably congratulated on the excision of three-fourths of my primary mass of matter. The whole would have made a work as intolerable as one of Prynne's,—"all rind and no fruit." The piteous entreaties of my terrified Publishers notwithstanding, I had resolved to produce an actual book of "Travels in Italy;" but better sense prevailed, and I held my hand at the present excerpt.

G. A. S.

CONTENTS.

ROME AND VENICE

IN 1866-7.

ON TRAVELLING AND TRAVELLERS IN ITALY.

THERE are two ways of doing everything—the poetic and the prosaic. There are some persons so richly endowed with the imaginative faculty that they have been able to invest the commonest and meanest things of life with an aspect of poetry, or with nobility of thought and language. Thus the sublime Siddons, at the dinner-table, astounded the little footpage, who had handed her a glass of ale by mistake, with an outbreak of blank-verse :

"I asked for water, boy ; ye've brought me beer."

And I have heard of a man, of the highest literary attainments, but whose pecuniary difficulties were continuous, who would borrow half-a-crown in the Spenserian stanza.

Although I have turned a verse occasionally, as husbandmen turn a sod, I think I can conscientiously aver that I have not one tittle of poetry in my soul, and that I never wrote, and (what is more) have never striven to write, anything of the nature of lyricism. But I do not affect to despise an art of which I am ignorant, or to undervalue a gift of which I have been deprived. The grapes are not sour. They are only as far beyond my reach as that sumptuous bunch of hothouse "sweetwaters," at a guinea a pound, which tempts my eyes, while it derides my pocket, in the central avenue of Covent-garden Market.

There are few things easier of accomplishment than to sneer at poets and poetry; and for smartly sour railing, the poet-hater may be commended to old Stephen Gosson, who, falling foul of Homer, tells the story of Mithecus, who was an excellent cook among the Greeks, and as much honoured for his confections as Phidias for his carving. But when he came to Sparta, thinking there for his cunning to be accounted a god, the good laws of Lycurgus and customs of the country were too strong for his diet. The governors banished him and his art, and all the inhabitants, following the steps of their predecessors, used not with dainties to provoke appetite, but with labour and travail to whet their stomachs to their meat. "I may," says Stephen, "well liken Homer to Mithecus, and poets to cooks; the pleasures of the one winnes the body from labour, and conquereth the sense; the allurement of the other draws the mind from virtue, and confoundeth wit." It is, I apprehend, very facile to be thus censorious. He who has no palate can say very cutting things about Francatelli or Jules Gouffé; the man who can neither whistle "Wapping old Stairs," nor hum "God save the Queen," is usually ready to sneer at Mozart and Beethoven as "Tweedledum and Tweedledee;" and if you would hear a good set homily on the nasty, filthy, selfish, idle, health-destroying habit of smoking, you should listen to the moralist whose stomach would be turned by three whiffs of the mildest of havanas.

Never was there a more terrific Rhadamanthus than he who sits in judgment on the things which he does not like, or which he cannot do. An author may be a very pungent satirist, but no poet: which may be one of the reasons, perchance, why the greatest poets have often been so scurvily treated by writers of satire: nor have I ever been free from a lurking suspicion that the eminent Juvenal may at one period of his career have essayed to write either eclogues or epics; that his performances were not very favourably received at fashionable dinner-tables or by the critics of the public baths, and that, soured and disappointed, he avenged himself on the Theseid, and "took it out," as the vulgar saying goes, of poor hoarse Codrus, whose chief faults, it is possible, were to have a wife and a large family, and to suffer from chronic bronchitis.

For myself, I can say with candour that I should like very much to be a poet, just as I should like to be Baron Rothschild, or the Marquise de Caux, or Mr. Millais the painter, or a Prime Warden of the Fishmongers' Company. Providence has decreed that I am not to be anything of the kind; but it is still free to me, I conjecture, to regard the man of millions with admiration and without envy; to go into ecstasies every time I hear Patti sing; to dwell with ever-recurring delight on the "Huguenot" and the "Order of Release;" and to dine at Fishmongers' Hall whenever I am asked, or my liver will endure clear turtle and Steinberg Cabinet.

I said there were two ways of doing everything—the poetic

and the prosaic; or, if you prefer to vary the terms, the refined and the vulgar. It can be no secret to such readers as I possess that I am a Vulgarian, and that I have never swerved from vulgarity of thought and coarseness of style during the twenty years in which I have been writing for a livelihood. *Me Bœotum in crasso jurares aere natum.* You might swear, finding me anywhere, that I was born in the gross atmosphere of Cockaigne; although for a man to be a cockney it is by no means necessary that he should have first drawn breath within the sound of Bow bells. He may have a cockney soul. The inmost utterances of his heart may misplace their *h*'s. Yet it has often struck me that one of the lower animals—say a dog or a pig—coarse as may be its appetites, gross its manners, and unintellectual its organisation, may have more and better opportunities of judging the qualities of things which are of the earth earthy, than the Colossus, stalking along sublimely, his head in the clouds, and his nose upraised, in the direction of the Milky Way.

It is the ascertained business of a very few persons, in every age, to study the stars,* and of a smaller number still to understand anything of that which they study; whereas the common and petty things of life intimately concern millions upon millions at every hour of the day. Granting, then,

* "Count me not, then, with them who, to amaze
The people, set them on the stars to gaze;
Insinuating, with much confidence,
They are the only men that have science
Of some brave creatures; yea, a world they will
Have in each star, though it be past their skill
To make it manifest unto a man
That reason hath, or tell his fingers can."
JOHN BUNYAN, Prologue to the *Holy War*.

for the sake of argument, that a cockney and a vulgarian has four short legs—the Colossus has two long ones;—that his nose, instead of scenting the planets, is the rather disposed to sniffing for foxes, or for truffles underground; and that his eyes lie naturally close to the earth, it may be conceded, perhaps, that he is sometimes enabled to arrive at a tolerably accurate estimate of the external phenomena of terrestrial nature, and that he may occasionally turn up little specimens of vegetation, or shells, or pebbles, which the Colossus—his nose still among the stars—has never seen, cannot see, will not stoop to see, and, in his sublime ignorance, tramples under foot, and crunches into powder. A persuasion that such may be the case, and an idea that the scent-hunting hound, and the truffle-grubbing swine, may in their generation do good service to that cause which we should all have, Titans and Troglodytes, at heart,—the increase of the sum of human knowledge,—are my sole apologies for republishing the papers which form this book.

For it appears to me that, from the poetical standard, Italy as a country and the Italians as a nation have been done, literally, to death, and that distance has led such enchantment to the view taken of the Peninsula, that the eye of appreciation has grown, occasionally, somewhat weak and watery: a circumstance which has led not unfrequently to the confusion of hawks as hernshaws, and to the acceptance of clouds as whales. China, I surmise, is a land about which almost every traveller has told lies. Spain and Russia are countries which no travellers save Ford in the first, and Mr. Sutherland Edwards in the second case, seem to have understood anything worth noting. Germany is a country which is not worth travelling in to understand, for its only tolerable products, its literature and its wines, can be studied or drunk at home; but Italy is a region about which every traveller that ever visited it has dreamed dreams.

The Italians themselves have, perhaps, been at all times the greatest visionaries with respect to their own country; and within these latter days the regeneration of Italy—may it be permanent!—has been chiefly the work of a statesman (Count Cavour) whom his enemies declare to have been no more an Italian than a Shetlander is an Englishman. I hasten, however, to quit this section of the argument; for, were I to continue the discussion as to who is and who is not a good Italian, patriotically considered, I should have Mr. Swinburne battering me with a fiery torch, and telling me that out of the pale of Mazzinism there was no political salvation; while, if I dared to hint that my own beau-ideal of a patriotic Italian was the late Daniel Manin, I might be reminded that the illustrious Venetian in question was by no means an advanced democrat, that he was an uncompromising advocate of a "strong" government, and that as a lover of moderate freedom he enjoyed to the last the esteem and admiration of the Emperor Napoleon III.

French travellers in Italy have, perhaps, dreamt fewer dreams concerning the Peninsula than have the Germans or the English. But their theory as to things Italian is decided enough. A Frenchman's political views of the country are very simple, and seldom vary. He is of opinion that Italy should be free; but he questions the expediency of her being united. *His* dream is one of a federal Italy governed by native sovereigns, all to be petted, patronised, and protected by the grand French nation. He would remorselessly drive out the Teutonic invader,—indeed, he has driven him out over and over again; nor would he install himself as an armed occupant in the invader's place.

The first Napoleon might, by a stroke of his pen, have united the whole Peninsula under his sceptre; but he held his hand. He was crowned King of Italy, it is true; but his kingdom comprised only Lombardy and Venetia, with some part of Piedmont, and later the "department of the Tiber" and the "department of Thrasymene" were decreed, under exceptional circumstances—those of the impossibility of bringing an impracticable priest to terms—to be integral parts of the French Empire. He dreamt the federal dream, and made a kingdom, here, for his brother-in-law, and a grand duchy, there, for his sister. Rome excepted, he never held, nor professed to hold, Italy as a conquered country, as the Spaniards had held Naples, and the Austrians Lombardo-Venetia. He wished Italy to have her own princes, her own usages, her own judges and magistrates, and her own troops. He exacted merely that social barbarism should be abolished, that the Code Napoleon should supersede the antiquated system of mediæval jurisprudence, and that all the Italian governments should be amenable to French influence.

It need scarcely be said that in the tail of the last sentence lies the sting. In my own opinion (and I trust that I am not singular in it) both the first and the third Napoleon have done an immensity of good in Italy; but as I shall frequently have to revert to their Italian work, I shall not enlarge upon it now.* But had the Bonapartes converted the Italian into a perfect angel (which they have certainly failed in doing), the non-Latin nations would still fiercely denounce the influence of Bonapartism in Italy, and continue their stale tirades about "the insatiable ambition" of the conqueror of Marengo, and the "occult designs" of the victor of Solferino. The non-Latin nations have, I take it, a clear right to talk in that way; but those who are of the Latin race have as clear a right to talk in *their* way, and to regard the influence of Cesarism in Italy as much more beneficial than detrimental: — beneficial as being calculated to establish a temporary *mezzo termine* between the peril of a return to the stupid and cruel despotism

* During my sojourn in Italy (I admit the time was one of tremendous political excitement, and that the national vanity was intensely mortified not only by the defeats of Custozza and Lissa, but by the contemptuous cession of Venetia by the Austrians, not directly to the Italians, but through the intermediary of France: a scornful flinging away, as though the Kaiser were saying, "Here, give this dog his bone; and let your General Lebœuf hand it to him; for I will not"), I heard, saw, and read, in conversation, in public orations, in caricatures, and in journals serious and trivial, at least five hundred times the Emperor Napoleon III. compared to Tartuffe, to Timour, to Ignatius Loyola, to Herod, to Commodus, to Amurath, and to Judas Iscariot. In a satirical paper of large circulation, published in Milan (the *Spirito Folletto*, I think it was called), I noticed one very large cartoon, which was simply a blasphemous travesty of the magnificent Road-to-Calvary picture by Rafaelle, now at Madrid, and known as the "Spasimo di Sicilia." It was Italy who was staggering and fainting under the weight of the Cross; Rome and Venice were the Holy Women; and the Emperor Napoleon was the Roman centurion on horseback, who sternly orders the procession to move on. This abominable picture was exposed, surrounded by admiring crowds, in the Piazza del Duomo, on the bookstalls by the theatre of La Scala, and at a dozen shops in the Corso Vittorio Emmanuele—three of the most public resorts in Milan.

That same evening (an exquisitely beautiful one in August) I strolled far away through the suburbs of Milan, past the great Naumachial circus built by Napoleon I., past the Piazza de' Armi, towards that famous triumphal monument of marble begun under the viceroyalty of Eugene Beauharnais, and dedicated "*alle speranze d'Italia indipendente*," by Napoleon I., and of the Hapsburgs and the Bourbons on the one hand, and, on the other, the equally dismal danger of rabid Red Republicanism.

The necessity for French influence and protection in Italy must one day—and at no very distant one—cease to exist. But every new nation must remain, for a certain time, in leading-strings; and in the Italian case which is, the advocates of French influence may argue, best?—that the guide should be a nurse of a kindred race, and who has already helped to suckle the bantling and place it in

---

terminated by the Austrians, who dubbed it the "*Arco della Pace*," and covered its sides with tawdry bas-reliefs, and fulsome inscriptions in bad Latin, crying up the virtues of the Emperor Francis, the gaoler of the Spielberg. It was thus decorated when I first went to Milan, many years since. But when I revisited the arch that August evening in 1866, it had changed its aspect; it bare record of the events of 1859, and the inscription beneath the architrave ran, Englished, thus:

NAPOLEON III.
AND
VICTOR EMMANUEL II.
ENTERING, THEIR ARMS COVERED WITH GLORY,
EXULTING MILAN,
TORE FROM THIS MARBLE THE IMPRINT OF SLAVERY,
AND WROTE, INSTEAD,
THAT ITALY WAS FREE.

Where would "*Milano esultante*" have been in '66 but for that "entrance with arms covered with glory" in 1859? Where would Italy have been now, without the help of Napoleon? Could Victor Emmanuel have won Solferino and Magenta alone? Without the aid of France, the Piazza de' Armi of Milan would be full at this day of white-coated Austrians, exercising "in squadrons and platoons, with their music playing chunes;" the adjoining Castello would be full, as of old, of political prisoners; and any caricaturist venturing to lampoon the ruling powers would be very summarily taken to a guardhouse, strapped down upon a bench, and scourged—it would matter little if the offender were man or woman—within an inch of his or her life. But "exulting Milan" had forgotten the *cavaletto* and the *bastone* in 1866; just as those liberated Fenian convicts the other day were no sooner freed from picking oakum at Millbank and wheeling bricks at Chatham, than they went home to Ireland and set about abusing the British Government.

the way of walking; or an Austrian corporal, brandishing handcuffs and willow-rods, or a ranting, raving Red Republican, with Pianori's dagger in one hand and Felice Orsini's fulminating bomb-shells in the other? I must be pardoned on this head for quoting one Italian authority on Italy, when I entreat all English admirers of this beautiful and interesting land to read M. Cimmino's novel, *I Congiurati*. Therein—from the testimony of an *Italiano italianissimo*—they may form some idea of the infinite mischief and misery inflicted on the cause of Italian independence by secret societies and assassination plots; by Mazzinism, in a word, which has never ceased to retard, instead of accelerating, the great cause—that of the creation of a new and healthy member of the European family.

I don't say that I agree entirely with the ordinary French traveller who pins his faith to Cesarism in general, and M. Thiers' Italian notions in particular; but I do say that a nation which has been more or less enslaved and held captive to the foreign bow and spear for fifteen hundred years has some need of guidance and protection ere she sets entirely up for herself as a great European power. Perhaps in a dozen years or so we shall have no kings in Europe at all, and then the Republic of Italy may form an important section of the United States of Europe. In the mean time Frenchmen will continue to opine that united Italy, with an army thrice as large as she needs, with finances in a state of chronic disorder, with a clergy continually plotting to overthrow the newly-built edifice of freedom, and with a canker-worm at her very heart in the shape of Rome, and its Pontiff more impracticable than that Pius whom

Napoleon I. took into custody, is, if not a failure, a mistake, and that the next European convulsion will crumble the newly-built edifice to fragments.

With regard to Italian literature, the French know well-nigh nothing about it. They sat patiently by while an Italian, the late M. Fiorentino, learned the French language in order that he might translate Dante for them. They wouldn't read the *Inferno* when M. Fiorentino had published it; and at the present moment it is probable that the only notions entertained by the majority of educated Frenchmen touching the works of Italy's greatest poet are derived from the dráwings of M. Gustave Doré. Every Italian above the rank of a shopkeeper speaks French; and not one out of every score of French travellers I met in Italy during nine months could speak twenty words of Italian.*

With respect to art, the average Frenchman's Italian creed is as simple and as invariable as his political one. He regards artistic Italy as a mine, and he extracts as much precious metal from it as ever he possibly can, nor will he pay even for smelting the ore if he can help it. The English tourist goes to Italy to buy ancient pictures, or

* Nor, much as they vapour about "La Diva," and much as they profess to admire Rossini, and much as they sneer at us as a nation incapable of appreciating classical music, do I think that the French have any sincere love for, or any profound comprehension of, Italian music. The Théâtre des Italiens in Paris has always been an exotic, which would have died long ago but for a large subvention from the Government; whereas in England private enterprise and the coöperation of the people have, during a period of a hundred and fifty years, maintained one and sometimes two vast theatres for Italian opera in London. In George the Third's time, even, we had two—the King's Theatre and the Pantheon. Again, there is scarcely a provincial town in England in which, periodically, the very best Italian artists have not been heard. When did Grisi or Mario, Alboni or Lablache, visit Tours, or Abbeville, or even Bordeaux?

modern copies; the wiser Frenchman sends the clever young *alumni* of the Ecole des Beaux Arts to the Villa Medici, to copy the pictures on the spot, and bring them home to Paris. In art, the Frenchman is the worst customer the Italian can have. He purchases little; but he observes, imitates, and borrows everything he can lay his mind and hand upon. When he was all-powerful in Italy, he stole. Napoleon would surrender a principality, but he would stick like grim death to an antique cameo. He would part with a kingdom, but a manuscript by Lionardo, or a picture by Rafaelle, was not to be rescued, under compulsion, from his insatiate maw. "*Galli, semper crudeles, rapaces, barbarorum omnium Italis infestissimi.*"

The cruelty and the barbarism may be doubtful; but of the artistic rapacity of the French there can be no doubt. I have an old catalogue of the contents of the Museum of the Louvre, dated 1812; and it is half droll, half melancholy, to follow page after page of the records of impudent plunder. The Venus de' Medici and the Apollo Belvedere, the Transfiguration and the Communion of St. Jerome—nothing came amiss to these "cracksmen with a taste." But they did not destroy: they only stole. If they were obliged to bombard a city, they built it up again. Of the long Austrian sway in Italy, no architectural trace is visible now but fortresses and barracks; whereas, although French domination in the Peninsula endured only from 1804 to 1815, in hundreds of cases, while travelling, when your eye lights on a good road, a well-built bridge, a commodious hospital, a solid quay, a handsome modern theatre, you will, asking, "*Chi l' ha fatto?*" receive the answer, "*Napoleone Primo.*"

The veneration still shown by the Italians for the memory of the first Napoleon,* and which is so magnificently expressed by Manzoni in the *Cinque Maggio*, differs very widely from the feverish and fantastic *cultus* accorded to the Corsican by that French people whom he subdued, but whose vanity he flattered by the ephemeral gift of military glory. There can be little doubt that Napoleon's heart was constantly and chiefly in Italy, and that he loved Milan more than he loved Paris. In his desolate captivity, Italian was the tongue he liked best to speak; and in Italy his exiled kindred found a home and a respectful welcome. He did great things for Italy, and he would have done infinitely greater and better ones; but his life was short, and the task was long; but the occasion was fleeting, and judgment difficult: as many men have discovered since Hippocrates' time. He succeeded, however, in abolishing feudalism in Italy; everywhere he reformed the criminal code—save in Tuscany, where it was scarcely susceptible of reformation, and in Rome, where the priests baffled his efforts to reform anything. If his gendarmes were somewhat unscrupulous as to the number of brigands they shot (Fra Diavolo was among the number), there is abundant contemporary testimony to prove that, for a time, he extirpated brigandage from the Alps to the Adriatic, and that during his sway there were rooted out those hideous pests to society the *bravi*, or professional assassins, who, for at least eight centuries, had publicly pursued their abhorrent trade throughout Italy. If his gendarmes did nothing else, they blew out the

* A gold piece of twenty francs is habitually called by the peasantry in north and central Italy "*un marengo.*"

brains of Saltabadil, and Sparafucile, and Spaventoro. And let this especially be noted: that so soon as Napoleon fell, and Italy once more reverted to the Pope, the Bourbons, the Austrians, and those pale Grand-Dukes, always trembling, always ready to invoke the aid of Austrian bayonets, brigandism and bravoism revived. Finally, let it be remembered, and to his imperishable honour, that the Republican General, the First Consul, the Emperor, the King of Italy, the "Chief of Banditti," as he has been called by high Tory critics, inexorably decreed the abolition of that abominable and inhuman outrage to, and desecration of Humanity, which for ages had been common all over Italy, and the audible evidence of which only lingers at this day in ROME, where it counts yet a few miserable victims among the choristers in the private chapel of the Supreme Pontiff of the Roman Catholic Church.

And now, not without perturbation, I approach mine own countrymen who have travelled, or who travel, in Italy. I think they may be divided into three grand classes: the solemn, severe, and classical travellers; second, the canting and gushing ones; third, the idiotic plagiarists.

Addison justly enjoys a considerable degree of renown as a classical traveller in Italy. He drags in quotations from the ancient poets, it is true, *à tort et à travers,* in all parts of his interesting work; but now and again he allows the mellow humour of Sir Roger de Coverley to peep from beneath the ambrosial curls of his periwig, and gives us some very lifelike and unaffected touches of Italian manners. Sterne, perhaps, might have written, an he would, the very best book on the social habits of the Italians that has appeared in the English language—a book as shrewd and trenchant as that of the President de Brosses in the French; but Sterne's incurable laziness and perversity, "his essential cussedness," as I once heard an American phrase it, prevented him from doing anything thoroughly; and he teases us only with such delightful but disappointing fragments as the bit about Radicofani, and the Italian lady with whom he went to the oratorio at Milan.

The Head Master of English classical travellers in Italy is, without a doubt, the Reverend John Chetwode Eustace, who made the tour of the Peninsula with his patron Lord Brownlow, and in whom may be summed up nearly all the merits and demerits of all the chaplains who have ever made the grand tour with noble lords. To his really sound learning, and genuine love for antiquities, the compilers of Murray's Italian handbooks have been very largely indebted; and, although Eustace was a Roman-Catholic priest, his four weighty volumes are generally regarded by the most orthodox Anglicans as a standard of all that is decorous and right-principled in Toryism. Mr. Eustace went to Italy while the French were dominant in the country, and it will be very easily understood that, as a faithful child of the Papacy, he does not approve of the late Napoleon Bonaparte. "Banditti" is the mildest term he has to bestow on the French armies. When at Verona, he noticed that the French were "detested as the most cruel of the many barbarous tribes that had invaded the devoted country."

You may be aware that at Verona there exists, quite intact as to its outward walls, and even susceptible of use as to its interior, a magnificent Roman amphitheatre, capable of holding twenty-two thousand spectators. For many ages it has been far too large for any purposes of recreation to which it could be put by the Veronese; but from time to time some sort of *funciones*—to use the convenient Spanish term—have been held within its gray old walls. Now it was an Emperor Joseph patronising a bull-fight in the arena where an Emperor Gallienus had gazed on the combats of gladiators and wild-beasts; now a Pope made a journey hither, and gave his benediction to the closely-packed thousands in the forty-five ranges of seats.

Mr. Eustace is inclined to be tolerant towards exhibitions of this nature; but those wretched French, during their stay in Verona, having erected a wooden theatre near one of the grand portals of the amphitheatre, and caused several farces and pantomimes to be acted there for the amusement of the army, the Reverend Mr. Eustace is "down" upon them immediately. "The sheds and scaffolding," he writes, "that composed this miserable edifice were standing in the year 1802, and looked as if intended by the builder as a satire upon the taste of the Grande Nation that could disfigure so noble an arena. The Veronese beheld this characteristic absurdity with indignation, and compared the invaders, not without reason, to the Huns and the Lombards."

I have no doubt that they did, and to the Goths, Ostragoths, and Visigoths likewise; the modern Veronese being a dirty, lazy, good-for-nothing lot, generally speaking, who find it convenient to excuse their own sloth and uncleanliness by declaring themselves to be the lineal descendants of ancient Romans, cruelly oppressed by successive hordes of barbarians; but within my own time I have known the "noble arena" of these ardent classicists desecrated by all kinds of "miserable edifices" with the full consent and concurrence of the Veronese, who flocked to the edifice, and paid their *soldi* to see the show. I have seen a horse-riding circus in one corner, and a company of *zanni* and pantomimists in another, and Dr. Dulcamara, in his red coat, powdered wig, and top-boots, drawing teeth, and selling vials of the elixir of love in the centre, where Hercules' pillar used to stand. And perhaps there was not much desecration in any of these harmless buffooneries, and they were preferable, in the long-run, to the Austrian Emperor Joseph with his bull-fight, and the Roman Emperor Gallienus with his gladiators and wild-beasts.

Eustace, in a solemn "Preliminary Discourse," has laid down something like a code of rules for the guidance of travellers who intend to visit Italy in the true classical spirit. "Virgil and Horace, Cicero and Livy, should be the inseparable companions of all travellers; they should occupy a corner in every carriage, and be called forth in every interval of leisure to relieve the fatigue and to heighten the pleasure of the journey." This is excellent advice; and, indeed, the majority of educated travellers are given to carrying a copy of Horace (Firmin Didot's exquisite little red-lined edition is at once the most portable and the most legible); but in these rapid railroad days, when we have so frequently to change trains, a Murray's guide-book ordinarily supersedes Virgil, Cicero, and Livy.

Very admirable is Mr. Eustace's advice to "diligent travellers" to learn a little of the language before they go to Italy; and very aptly does he quote Bacon's famous reminder that he that travelleth into a country before he hath some entrance into the language, goeth to school, and not to travel. After this, according to Mr. Eustace, the traveller should study the history of the different revolutions of Italy, not only before, but during the decline and after the fall of the Roman Empire. "The republican part of Roman history," he goes on to say, "is considered as purely classical, and as such is presupposed in the first paragraph."

Eustace wrote before those sad sceptics Niebuhr and Sir George Cornewall Lewis had disturbed the learned world with their doubts, else he might have added that much of the republican part of Roman history was considered to be not only "purely classical," but purely mythical. He wrote, too, before the days of Sismondi, or at least before that illustrious historian had published his great work; so the student of Italian history is commended to the Abbate Denino's *History of the Revolutions of Italy*, and to Roscoe's *Lorenzo the Magnificent* and *Leo the Tenth:* both books quite worthless as authorities now.

The young traveller, too, may read Addison's *Dialogues on Medals* (and very delightful reading they are, written with the untiring felicity of that graceful author); numismatically, the *Dialogues* are not worth a brass farthing. Mr. Eustace's model traveller may then turn his attention to architecture, and is counselled to con Dean Aldrich's *Elements*, "translated by Mr. Smyth, of New College;" and, if they are accessible to him, he should peep into Stuart's *Athens*, and Wilkins's *Magna Græcia*. Then as to sculpture: "Some acquaintance with anatomy is a desirable preliminary to the knowledge of this art;" therefore the tourist would do well to attend a few anatomical lectures before he starts. To cultivate his taste in pictorial art he should read (shade of my grandfather's pigtail!) Du Fresnoy's *Art of Painting*, and Sir Joshua Reynolds's "well-known" *Discourses*. At music good old Mr. Eustace shakes his head gently, but gravely. Italy, he admits, is the first country in the world for music, both with regard to composition and execution; yet "young travellers ought rather to be cautious against its allurements than exposed by preparatory lessons to their dangerous influence." When Mr. Eustace penned this, Mrs. Billington was the great *prima donna assoluta* of Italy. The model traveller must take maps with him—D'Anville's map of ancient, Zannoni's map of modern, Italy.

Touching the time selected for travelling, and the route to be taken, the traveller is advised to pass the Alps early in the autumn, and first proceed to Brussels; thence to Liège, Spa (*gare à la roulette!*), Aix-la-Chapelle, Cologne, Bonn, and along the banks of the Rhine to Coblentz, Mayence, and Strasburg; there cross the Rhine to Mannheim; traverse the Palatinate, the territories of Wittemburg, Bavaria, and Salzburg; enter the defiles of the Tyrol, or Rhætian Alps; and, passing through Innspruck and Trent, turn to Bassano and to Mestre, whence he may send his carriage by land to Padua, and embark for Venice. From Venice he may go by water up the Brenta to Padua, and visit Arequa, and then pass onwards to Ferrara and Bologna; then follow the Via Emilia to Forli, thence proceed to Ravenna and Rimini, make an excursion to San Marino, and advance to Ancona, whence he may visit Ostia. He will then continue his journey by Loretto and Macerata to Tolentino; thence, over the Apennines, to Foligno, Spoleto and Terni, and so follow the direct road through Civita Castellana, to Rome. He should reach Rome in November, and devote the whole of December "to a first contemplation of the Eternal City, and the consideration of its most striking beauties." He will then proceed to Naples, where the months of January, February, and March will be delightfully employed. In the week before Easter he must be back in Rome. April, May, and June will be given to a leisurely survey of Tibur, Ostia, Antium, Mount Soracte, Præneste, and the Sabine mountains. The tumuli of the Alban mount may be reserved for the hot months of July and August; and in September it will be time to turn towards Florence, between which and the other Tuscan cities the winter is to be agreeably divided. In the beginning of the next February our indefatigable traveller is to pass the Apennines to Modena, Parma, Piacenza, Lodi, Cremona, Mantua, and Verona. Thence Peschiera and the Lago di Garda are to be explored. After that he may direct his course by Brescia and Bergamo to Milan. Having taken a trip to the Lago di Como and the Lago Maggiore, he may shape his course by Vercelli and Tortona to Genoa. He will then take the road of the Maritime Alps by Savona to Nice, after which he will turn inland to Turin; and I wish him joy of his inland tour, for he will have to go over the unutterably-abominable pass of the Col di Tenda.

But for geographical authorities to the contrary, one might think that the Sea of Galilee washed the shores of Nice, and that it was over the Col di Tenda that the demoniac pigs passed. The scenery is magnificent, but every village is one huge hoggery, and every cottage a sty. "Mount Cenis, the termination of the traveller's classical tour, then rises before him in distant perspective." It will be observed that the Reverend Mr. Eustace does not say one word of getting in or out of Italy by the way of St. Gothard or the Splugen, the Simplon or the Stelvio, or even the minor passes of the Tonale or the Bernardina. The reasons for his reticence: Napoleon was, at the time of Mr. Eustace's visit to the Peninsula, very busy indeed in making roads through the peaks, passes, and glaciers; but he granted rights of membership in his Alpine Club only to himself and to his soldiers. I wonder even that he left Mont Cenis pass and the Cornice road open to Mr. Eustace, and that the good ecclesiastic was not obliged to make the coast of Italy by long sea, say from Gibraltar to Genoa, or from Malta to Venice.

Most of us have heard of a celebrated musician who, ere he sat down before his pianoforte to compose, was accustomed to dress himself in his Sunday best, to have his hair frizzed and powdered, and his handkerchief elaborately scented. Numbers of wax-candles were disposed about his room, and a diamond-incrusted snuffbox, filled with the choicest Macabaw, was placed at his elbow. Then, with laced ruffles at his wrists, and jewels on his fingers, he felt himself *en train* for the cultivation of counterpoint and thorough bass, and proceeded to invent tremendous sonatas. It is difficult to rise from the perusal of a book on Italy by an English traveller without being reminded—the tremendousness of the result apart—of the musician who combined composition with coxcombry. The majority of English tourists seem to think it essential to dress themselves in their very finest intellectual clothes before they pass the Alps;

and nine out of ten of them, as I have before hinted, either gush or cant. The poets may be exempted from this category, since gushing and canting are perfectly admissible in poetry, so long as they are relieved by beauty of language. We do not expect a poet to be logical, or even rational. We only want him to be eloquent.

Byron gushes tremendously in *Childe Harold* about the Coliseum and the Dying Gladiator; but he gushes milk and honey; or the conduit of his thoughts runs with rich burgundy in lieu of water. In his letters, however, to Murray, and in his conversations with his friends, Byron showed that he had a very shrewd, practical, and even humorous appreciation of Italy as a land inhabited, not by poetical abstractions, but by substantial human beings; and there can be little doubt that, had Lord Byron chosen to do so, he might have written one of the best prose works on Italy or the Italians with which it was possible to endow his country's literature.

The *Italy* of Samuel Rogers, again, must be criticised not as a book of travels, but as a purely poetical rhapsody, less high-flown than Byron's, but still rose-coloured and myrtle-tinged and orange-flower-flavoured in an elaborate degree; yet was Samuel Rogers, poet and banker, one of the dryest, 'cutest of men; and it is clear that he knew all about Italy and the Italians, and could have written in prose most admirably about them. The monkeys are said to forbear from speaking articulately lest their rich relations, mankind, should force them to work. Sam Rogers piped seemingly sweet poetry, lest his countrymen should insist on his telling the truth in prose.

And why on earth should not the truth be told about this country? Why could not Madame de Stael, hard-headed, clear-sighted daughter of Necker as she was, tell us real Italian things, instead of gushing and canting as she has done in *Corinne?* Because the Apollo Belvedere and the Transfiguration are in the Vatican, and the Venus de' Medici is in the Tribune of Florence, is all Italy, from Calabria to the Susa, to be hallowed ground? Why, there is a splendid Murillo in our National Gallery; and in the British Museum there are numerous exquisite examples of Greek statuary; but the possession of those art-treasures does not blind us to the fact that St. Giles's is very near Great Russell-street, Bloomsbury, and that St. Martin's Workhouse is just behind Trafalgar-square. If a man goes to Italy, and discourses upon his return about the filth and the barbarism to be found in many of its parts; the half Joey-Grimaldi, half mumbo-jumbo buffoonery and mummery into which the rites of the Roman Catholic Church have degenerated in Rome and Naples; if he discusses Italian cookery, and alludes to the really important fact that the sausages of Bologna are very much superior to our best Cambridges,—he is told, forsooth, that he is a Philistine, that he has no soul for art, and that he is indifferent to the charms of historic associations.

As to being a Philistine, I scarcely know what the term, intellectually used, means, or how it applies. The shallow and conceited sciolist who devised the sneer, in order to insult writers whose minds and views were broader than his, may plume himself mightily on his device; but twenty years hence, I fancy, we shall trouble ourselves no more about what a literary Philistine may have been, than we trouble ourselves now about "Della Crusca," or "Rosa Matilda," or that "Satanic" school about which poor Southey made such a pother.

As for having no soul for art, whether a man has a soul for anything is a fact known only to his Maker and himself; and by his acts and deeds only are we entitled to surmise whether his soul is as broad as the beam of the Great Eastern, or so small and narrow that, as some old writer whose name has escaped me puts it, it is just but a pinch of salt that serves to keep his body from stinking.

And, finally, touching the sanctity of historic associations, didn't Julius Cæsar invade England? and am I thereby to be debarred from talking about a grocer's shop in Snargate-street, Dover, or the *table-d'hôte* at the Lord Warden, or the slipperiness of the Admiralty pier? Wasn't Constantine the Great born at York? and am I for that reason to be forbidden to refer to the Doncaster St. Leger? Every country is full of historical associations. Every country in Europe; scores of lands in Africa and Italy bear the indelible stamp of the Romans. In the market-places of dirty little Moorish villages in Barbary you will find battered stones, two thousand years old, with the inscription, "*Hic Cæsar transebat,*" dimly legible upon them. Julian the Apostate had a palace in Paris; Pontius Pilate, they say, died at Marseilles (although others stand out for the shores of the Lake of Lucerne); am I in consequence to be warned off from the jewellers' shops of the Rue de la Paix, or the flower-girls of the Cannebière, or the Bedouin *douars* of Algeria? Every country has a history; every country is old; but the actual modern condition, manners, and circumstances of every land need close and careful study and record, which will be all the more trustworthy if it be constantly compared with the conditions, manners, and circumstances which have gone before.

It seems to me in the highest degree disastrous that for a real and life-like picture of Italy and the Italians in the last century we should be constrained to go to the smirched pages of the profligate adventurer Jacques Casanova. Yet, with the exceptions of that which Stendhal (Beyle) has written concerning Italy, and Storey the sculptor's admirable pictures of Roman life, I do not know a single book in which a tangible Italy, and breathing, vascular Italians, are so vividly depicted as by the diverting vagabond whose voluminous memoirs are at once half the pride and half the shame of autobiographical literature. No doubt that Casanova has told an infinity of lies about his amours, and about the illustrious and the celebrated personages with whom he claims to have rubbed shoulders; but there is, notwithstanding, an amazing quantity of truth in his writings—truth which, perhaps, he told in spite of himself, and to a great extent unconsciously. Be it as it may, he has painted with Mieris-like fidelity the Italy and the Italians of the eighteenth century. But Casanova in his entirety is so infamous, that a man dare scarcely place his volumes on the shelves of a library; the sale of the Memoirs is prohibited by the French police, although it is tolerated throughout Belgium and Germany; and in England discreet booksellers announce in a whisper to the collectors of *facetiæ* that they have a copy of Casanova on hand. It would be a futile task to publish an expurgated edition of the rascally *magnum opus*.

As well might one strive to treat Jean Jacques Rousseau as Dr. Bowdler treated Shakespeare, and bring out an edition of the *Confessions* for "family reading;" but it might be feasible, I imagine, to collect in a single volume the marrow of Casanova's descriptions of the cities he visited, and his observations on the men and the manners of his time, kicking Casanova himself and his scoundrelly amours entirely on one side.

I.

THE AUSTRIANS IN VENICE.

I WAS very tranquilly and happily enjoying the spring-time of the year 1866 in the fair city of Seville, in Andalusia, revelling in oranges, sweet lemons, early peas, and other luxuries (including that inestimable one of not doing more than I could help), varying existence by occasional trips upwards to Cordova and downwards to Cadiz, and meditating a trip to Lisbon and Madeira, when, moved by the instigation of the Father of Evil (as the old indictments for high-treason used, in somewhat stronger language, to say), the heart of the Prussian Otto Von Bismark Schönstein, count of that ilk, was stirred up to wrath against the Austrian Graf Mensdorf-Pouilly; and, these two statesmen pulling the strings of the respective royal and imperial puppets they held in the hollow of their hands, William of Prussia began to shake his fist fiercely at Francis Joseph of Austria, and the Emperor Napoleon III. became (good soul!) infinitely concerned at the prospect of the peace of Europe being disturbed.

In consequence of Bismark, my journey to Portugal and to the Canaries was adjourned *sine die;* an inexorable telegraphic message informed me that war was imminent, and that I was wanted near its probable scene of outbreak; so, with a heavy heart, I retraced my steps; came back to Madrid, mooned for the last time on the Puerta del Sol, and watched Dona Isabel de Borbon, with her covey of niños and niñas, "robust infantes and infantas" all of them, roll by in their gilded coaches, drawn by fat sleek mules; and so passed the Pyrenees, grumbling, and came through Bordeaux to Paris, whence, growling like a bear with a sore head (I saw that identical bear, sore head and all, in Long-acre yesterday, escorted by two foreign persons of brigand-like aspect, and in blue blouses, and followed by a troop of ragged children), I went down to Calais, and abode at an inn, even at Dessein's Hotel, as that delightful George Borrow says, when it seems to occur to him that he has been talking a little too freely about the Caloros and Rommany chals, and that it behoves him, for the sake of the Society, to be a little biblical.

Dessein's was very dull; but I had to stay there for the best part of the week, waiting for messages and letters and a travelling-companion. I read Sterne, of course, conscienciously—a copy of the *Sentimental Journey* lies on the coffee-room table—and pleased myself in fancy by selecting places in the court-yard, where the *désobligeante* might have stood, where the Franciscan might have accosted the clergyman, and where the little French captain might have come dancing in from the street. On being informed that the inn formerly kept by Sterne's M. Dessein was in quite another part of the town, and was now converted into a museum, I was much abashed, and retired to my room, there to smoke tobacco.

"This Indian weed, now withered quite,
Though green at noon, cut down at night,
Shows thy decay;
All flesh is hay:
Thus think, and smoke tobacco.

The pipe, so lily-white and weak,
Does thus thy mortal state bespeak;
Thou art e'en such—
Gone with a touch:
Thus think, and smoke tobacco.

And when the smoke ascends on high,
Then thou beholdst the vanity
Of worldly stuff—
Gone with a puff:
Thus think, and smoke tobacco."

I was very low in spirits, in consequence of Bismark, and the non-arrival of my messages and travelling-companion, and I learned the whole of the quaint old poem by heart, and Ralph Erskine's paraphrase of it, too, out of a ragged copy of the *Gospel Sonnets* which I had picked up, together with a Moorish door-knocker and a rusty dagger, at a rag-shop at Toledo. How on earth did that book of the old Scots minister get to Toledo? Perhaps it was found in bygone days on the person of a wandering heretic by the familiars of the Holy Inquisition, and that the heretic was roasted for having it. No; that was scarcely so, for the *Gospel Sonnets* are prefaced by a poem in praise of smoking; and the Spaniards are too fond of smoking, for the merciless Inquisition even to have burned a sincere lover of the weed.

Messages, letters, and travelling-companion came at last, and we went straight through Paris and Chamberi, over Mont Cenis (which was almost impassable in consequence of Bismark—I mean of the snow-drifts, and had to be traversed in sledges) to Milan, and so, by Peschiera, to Venice. Here I begin the excerpts from my Diary.

Venice, April 20.

The Italians are certainly a strange people, and, according to our received notions, not at all business-like. It may be asked, "What *is* business?" Alexandre Dumas the Elder has answered the question very wittily and pithily—"*Les affaires: c'est l'argent des autres.*" Business is other people's money, and business-like habits are the systematic process by which we make that money our own. The English, who have been so signally successful in the acquisition of wealth, have always understood, as a first principle, that all matters appertaining to business should be plain, prosaic, and altogether divested of imagination or fancy, or of that picturesqueness which is apt occasionally to trench on Bohemianism. The foreign merchant will smoke in his counting-house, whereas to the English trader the consumption of tobacco during office-hours is scandalously unbusiness-like. The foreign banker shuts up his *caisse* while he eats his breakfast, indulges in a nap, or strolls off to the casino to take a hand at piquet. It would be horribly unbusiness-like—it would be within an inch of the commission of an act of bankruptcy—for an English banker to do such a thing. If you call on a Continental man of business it is not unlikely that you will find him in an elegantly-furnished *salon*—that you will see pictures on the walls, china on the mantelpiece, and flowers on the table. Not unfrequently abroad, when I have gone to draw a bill, I have stumbled into the *boudoir* of Madame instead of the *bureau* of Monsieur; and more than once I have mistaken the *cuisine* for the *caisse*. Who would be liable to fall into such errors in Birchin-lane or Tokenhouse-yard? The sound of a grand pianoforte or the smell of *compote de pigeons* would be as astounding in purely city regions as a salute of a hundred and one guns, or the odour of orange-blossoms. Business men in England require business environments. For them, consequently, have been devised the hideous paraphernalia known as "office furniture"—funereal desks and stools, and leathern-covered tables, and with no gayer ornamentation to the walls than is comprised in a Stationers' Almanac, weights and scales, a letter-rack, or a placard full of inhospitable platitudes to the effect that you should call on a man of business only during business hours—that you should confine your conversation exclusively to business, and that having done your business you should go about your business as soon as possible.

The mention of office furniture and mural decoration brings me at once to the position with which I started—that the Italians are far from business-like in their habits. Would you believe that the walls and ceilings of the waiting- and refreshment-rooms at the Milan terminus of the Lombardo-Venetian Railway are covered with colossal fresco paintings, illustrative of fanciful allegories and fantastic passages from the works of such unbusiness-like people as Dante, Boccaccio, and Ariosto? That these frescoes are exquisite in conception, grand in design, and beautiful in execution will avail very little, I am afraid, as an apology for their thorough violation of established business rules. What can the author of the *Divine Comedy* have to do with locomotives and goods-wagons? What connection is there between the *Decameron* and a viaduct? between *Orlando Furioso* and the permanent way? We men of business well know how railway waiting- and refreshment-rooms should properly be decorated. Nothing should be seen there but monstrous sign-boards, or framed-and-glazed advertisements having reference to breakfast cocoa, corn-flour, lists of bedding, felt roofing, Sydenham trousers, and Benson's clocks. Art should have its place, but a business-like place, there: such as in the information that the Chinese colour tea for the English market, that no vent-peg is required for Barlow's tap, and the pictorial emblazonment of Allsopp's Pale Ale, and Dunville's V.R. Whisky. No doubt the man of business, after cooling his heels for half an hour in one of these vestibules, will enter his train a wiser if not a sadder man. He will have learnt the all-important truth that Epps's cocoa is a breakfast beverage, and acquiesced in the futility of "giving more;" nay, from attentive study of the Kamptulicon and the Eureka, the Revalenta, the Anthropoglossos, and the Kalos Genesis, he may pick up a little Latin and more Greek; the value of which to business men, whose classical training has ordinarily been neglected, can scarcely be exaggerated.

The Milanese have got their frescoes, nevertheless; and among the series on which I gazed with rapt attention this April was one which has since furnished me with a theme for these remarks. It was a noble allegory of VENICE. There she was: the patriarchally aged, yet the ever young—stately, superb, the beautiful Queen of the Adriatic. Over her rounded limbs fell in rich folds the ducal robe of purple velvet lined with ermine. On her fair hair rested the Cap of Estate and Maintenance—the princely diadem she wore for eleven hundred years. Around her were the lions which are still the delight of St. Mark's Place. Behind her throne soared the two columns with St. Theodore trampling on the crocodile, and the Winged Lion conning his eternal Evangel. At her feet were strewn thick the gems and the rich vessels, the drugs and spices, the infinite merchandise, which of old time were brought by her argosies from the ends of the earth. And in the foreground stood the shawled and turbaned Turk, the Jewish merchant in his gaberdine and high cap, the negro glistening and brawny, and gaudy as his brethren who in bronze and marble bear up the mighty architrave of Doge Pesaro's tomb. They all—Turk, Jew, and Pagan—were come to pay obeisance to the Sea Sultana. This, with the Piazzetta for a background, was the allegory of Venice. It pictured the Silent Sister, the Niobe of nations, as she Once was, and as the Italians in fond, yet half-despairing, imaginings hope that she will be again. But when is the day of her deliverance to come, and when are the tears which, with but twelve months' intermission, have flowed for half a century, to be dried? She waits and waits, and the Italians wait too, clenching their hands and grinding their teeth; and meanwhile the waiting-room at Milan is thronged with tourists and pleasure-seekers.

There is not a better waiting-room, nor, indeed, a better railway terminus, in all Italy than at Milan. The Turin station is handsomer in an architectural sense, but Lombardy beats Piedmont in the internal arrangements and decorations. Fees to porters are not only prohibited, but the prohibition is rigidly enforced by the inspectors.

Ten days elapsed. I went down with my head full of the fresco through Bergamo, and at Desenzano saw the last of the kingdom of Italy and the Italian flag. Heaven help her out of all her troubles, for they are many and sore enough, and threaten to be sorer. And then I came to Peschiera, the Austro-Veneto frontier, the which Peschiera I consider to be, with the exception of Fenchurch-street in the City of London, and Jersey City in the State of that name, U.S.A., the most abominable railway station with which in the course of my wanderings about this sublunary globe I have ever met. The place is like an ill-kept station-house, out of which a herd of drunken devotees have just been turned to make way for the captured belligerents of a Patrick's-day shindy. The platform is beset by a loitering mob of Austrian soldiers and *douaniers*; the refreshment-room, both as regards its fare and its cleanliness, is about on a par with a Hottentot kraal; and a male and female gorilla would be disgusted at the "accommodation" for ladies and gentlemen.

I am wasting time, however, in disparaging this vile excrescence to the Quadrilateral. Peschiera—not Peschiera the fortress, but Peschiera the railway station—is on its last legs. It is to be pulled down very shortly. Under the wise and enlightened policy of the Government the passport nuisance has been abolished in the Austrian dominions; and the little hutch at Peschiera, through whose aperture the police commissary used to blink mistrust at you through his green spectacles, has been closed for good and all, and looks like a stopped-up rat-hole. Luggage is no longer examined at Peschiera, but is merely *plombé* till you reach Venice, where the examination is all but nominal. In another six months or so, it is to be hoped, Peschiera will be numbered among the dead ducks on whom, according to Mr. Andrew Johnson, it is useless to expend ammunition. Yet how soothing to the spirit it is to shake your fist at an extinct or an expiring nuisance! When, as an old traveller, you remember how you have been worried and bullied, and teased and harried, at this same Peschiera—how needlessly impertinent questions have been asked you; and how hands with nails, with a mourning border a quarter of an inch long, were thrust into the middle of your clean linen, and pawed the leaves of your favourite books—you are apt to regret that shut-up passport hutch, and that now useless luggage counter, with a sensation of relief akin to that with which you look on a despotic schoolmaster's tombstone. The ruffian cannot any more cane little boys because his breakfast bacon was ill-toasted, or because his wife scolded him overnight. He is shut up, and is as impotent a pedagogue as the bygone despot of Corinth.

Pending the good time coming, they still keep you waiting a whole weary hour at Peschiera; and as fifteen minutes would amply suffice for the transference of the luggage from the Italian to the Austrian train, I conjecture that the delay is due to a laudable desire to benefit the Hottentot kraal of a refreshment-room. It is Erquellines or Verviers over again. I intend to write a book some day on the "Average number of hours wasted by continental express trains." Without going deeply into the calculation, I am sure that the average would not be much under five-and-twenty per cent. You have another hour's stoppage—or fifty-five minutes, a pretty close imitation of one—at Verona. The train halts at the Porta Vescova. You have no time for a run to see the Roman amphitheatre; but you may be regaled in an apartment scarcely superior to the Peschiera kraal, where the viands and the mode of serving them irresistibly remind you of the establishment of that *restaurateur* on Holborn-hill, who used to supply the hungry with "a devilish good dinner for threepence-halfpenny," consisting of leg-of-beef soup, bread, and flies. The refreshment tariff at Verona is slightly in excess of Monsieur Francatelli's.

There is not, however, much to be gained by grumbling at the state of things here, or at Vicenza, or Padua. If the stations are wretchedly provided with anything in the way of comfort or luxury, and contrast miserably as regards architecture and pictorial embellishment with the gay and tasteful edifices in regenerated Italy, you may console yourself by the reflection that they are all very strongly fortified. The Verona station, indeed, is a complete citadel; and goods-sheds and signal-houses are curiously mixed up with moats, bastions, and lines of circumvallation. It is impossible to cross the frontier or to be half an hour in the Austro-Venetian territory without becoming aware that the Austrian "autograph" —as Mr. Thackeray used to call the double-headed eagle— has got a very tight grip of the country, and that there is a remarkably opinionated conclusion in his duplex brain that he means to keep that country as long as he can. As he is a very powerful eagle, strong on the wing and adamantine in the talons, the contingency of his giving up his Venetian quarry is, to say the least, remote. It is not impossible.*

That England should abandon the Ionian Islands seemed, for many years, a contingency more remote; but a compact body of importunate persons in baggy breeches tired out our patience at last, and we gave up the Sept-insular Republic to

* This was written in the spring. In the summer came Sadowa, and the Austrians gave up Venice. But would they have surrendered it had Custozza been the only battle fought?

the discontented Ionian deputies and placemen; not to the Ionian people by any means, who, misgoverned and overtaxed by Greece, are now mourning over the withdrawal of the British, and howling for them to return. I dare not presage that any Venetian would regret the departure of the Austrians from Venice, or would be unpatriotic enough to pray for their return; yet I have read that some degenerate Venetians, after their ten years' servitude to France, welcomed Ferdinand of Austria in 1815 as a saviour and a deliverer; and that even during their brief spell of Republican independence in 1841, under the heroic Daniel Manin, there were Venetians who murmured, and Venetians who did not agree with the late Dr. Pangloss in his notions of universal optimism.

The Kaiser Francis Joseph, who, rightly or wrongly, conceives that he has as clear a title, both by treaty and conquest, to his Italian dominions as we have to Lower Canada—and when we talk so glibly of the claims of races to be governed by rulers of their own blood, we should do well to remember that we have in North America little less than a million of Frenchmen, and Roman Catholic Frenchmen too, under our rule—will doubtless stick hard and fast to Venice and the Quadrilateral until those territories shall be wrested from him by the upheavings of a great European war or a greater European revolution; or until, as is just possible, the ingenuity of diplomacy exerted in that long-threatened European congress on which we threw cold water a few years since, but in whose assembling we must soon acquiesce, shall suggest some convenient arrangements satisfactory to all parties, by means of which Italy shall gain her heart's desire, the *amour propre* of Austria shall be gratified, and the ruler of France assured that the thorough independence of Italy "from the Alps to the Adriatic" will not open the door to the "party of action," that is to say, of anarchy. In the mean time it would be unreasonable to expect that Austria should do very much towards beautifying or developing the resources of the country which, in the opinion of liberal Europe, ought to be taken from her at the first favourable opportunity. A tenant-at-will has little temptation to improve the acres he is cultivating, but out of which he may be turned to-morrow. To fortify your house against those who come with sticks and staves is one thing, but to repaint it inside and out, and have the gas and water laid on, and the roof seen to, and the front drawing-room new-papered in white and gold, when, for aught you know, and within a couple of years, John a'Nokes may be declared the rightful owner of the messuage which now pertains to John a'Styles, and the brass door-plate now bearing the name of F. J. Hapsburg replaced by one inscribed V. E. Savoy-Carignan, is quite another thing.

The Austrians, therefore, have concluded to keep their powder dry in the Venetian territory, and are ready to execute any necessary repairs in the way of bombproof casemates, curtains, ravelins, and demi-lunes; but they think it no part of their duty to sweep and garnish the country, socially speaking, when, at very brief notice, they may be forced to quit, and be sued besides for dilapidations and mesne profits. The money they can muster is expended in works to keep the Italians out, and not in beautifying the cities, which they occupy, in hopes of pleasing the Italians when they come in. The Austrians indeed complain that, as it is, they have done a great deal too much for the internal improvement of Venice;

and were they even ready, politically, to surrender the city, they could not do so equitably without reimbursement for the enormous outlay they have incurred in building bridges, embanking canals, and preserving palaces from tumbling to pieces.

Thus, while on the Italian side of the frontier traces of energy, enterprise, and go-aheadism meet you at every step, the posts no sooner begin to be striped with the Austrian colours than you find inertia, stagnation, and neglect. The only traffic is in munitions of war and convoys of provisions for the forty or fifty thousand armed men who are kept idling in the provinces from which Austria, oppressive as may be her taxation and never-ending her exaction, does not derive one kreutzer of profit. Venetia is, in every respect, a dead loss to the Government of Vienna; and the few thousands of Italian conscripts who are annually squeezed from a reluctant and disloyal population are hurried off to distant garrisons, and are not in their entirety half so useful to the Empire as a couple of regiments of Swiss mercenaries would be. The railway passenger traffic is languid and unsatisfactory. In free Italy few signs are more encouraging than the alacrity with which the people, properly so called, flock to the railway stations; but between Peschiera and Venice not many persons are to be seen in the trains beyond English tourists and Austrian officers and *employés*. Small need is there, then, to decorate the gaol-like walls of the stations with frescoes. Were any such painted, and were they designed to harmonise with the aspect of affairs around them, such productions would be, I trow, of the dismallest nature.

Suppose I draw a fresco in imagination. There might be

an Allegory of Venice—not clothed in purple and ermine, but half-naked, and in rags. An Austrian *bonnet de police* is on her golden locks, instead of the cap of Estate and Maintenance. A neat pair of handcuffs must be substituted for the ring with which she was wont to wed the Adriatic. An Austrian sergeant with a stick keeps watch and ward over her. You may introduce the Doge's Palace in the background, but in the basement is an Austrian guard-house, and a park of very ugly field-pieces are planted in the Piazzetta, prepared to blow the caryatides of Sansovino at the Zecca opposite into shivers at the slightest notice. Her Grand Canal is still dotted with gondolas, but among them please not to forget an Austrian gunboat lying off the Lido, and the mail-packet of the Austrian Lloyd's getting her steam up for a trip to Trieste—Trieste the thriving—which has put the commerce of Venice into her pocket. She has little to hope for from the opening of the Suez canal. Trieste will profit by it; *Brindisi may profit a great deal more;** but the port of Venice is well-nigh dammed up; her tide has little scour, and it would take millions to dredge a channel deep enough for ships of burden. Danish men-of-war, they say, once came up to Holborn-bars. When they besiege Middle-row again we may see East Indiamen unloading at the Dogana. These hints may suffice for the Allegory of Venice as she is—stay, we may throw in the island of San Giorgio Maggiore, whose convent is said to be full of political prisoners.

It is quite time to have done with allegories and other figures when you come to Venice itself, and find it miserable, silent, impoverished, and forlorn. Of its unequalled struc-

* 1866.

tural beauty, of its glories of architecture and painting, nothing short of such a sack as Alexandria suffered under the Arabs, and such destruction as Carthage under the Romans, could rob Venice. But beyond her palaces, her churches, and pictures,—and of these last even nearly all that could be with any show of decency removed from the walls have been stolen or sold,—Venice is as empty as Napoleon's grave at St. Helena. She is a despoiled sepulchre, desolate, deserted, and despairing.

This wondrously-beautiful spring-time should be the beginning of a prosperous invasion of pleasure tourists; but even of these there is a lack at Venice. The Holy Week is gone and past, the benediction to the City and the World has grown stale, and the *forestieri* should be rushing up from Rome and Naples; yet the hotelkeepers of Venice sit with aching hearts and blank faces, wistfully gazing on the virgin pages of ledgers. Last year, although there was no cholera, and the mosquitoes were few, there was no influx of travellers. This year, when the political horizon is still further troubled, the army of tourists may be still more meagre. If the plain truth must be told, Venice has become rather a bore to travellers of the calibre of Messrs. Brown, Jones, and Robinson. They have been spoilt by the Alpine Club and by Paris, and its new Boulevards and Grand Hotelism.

The beauties of Swiss scenery can be appreciated by travellers of a very low intellectual calibre. A healthy lad or lass can take alpenstock in hand, and tramp about Chamouni and the shores of the lake without incurring even the perils attendant on over-adventurous investigation of peaks, passes, and glaciers. The exercise one gets during the "regular Swiss round" is as bracing and invigorating as that enjoyed in riding to hounds, or footing it over the Brighton Downs; and while the chest is opened, the lungs are cleared, the muscles animated, and any number of reefs shaken out of the liver, the eye is pleased and the mind delighted by the contemplation of the most romantic and sublime scenery in the world. You have no need to have read Payne Knight, or Louis Viardot, or John Ruskin, to be able to understand Mont Blanc. The Grands Mulets and the Mer de Glace would interest the merest clodhopper. This is the reason why Switzerland is with travellers an universal favourite. You can't wrangle about the conflict of styles in a precipice; the *odium theologicum* has nothing to lay hold of in an avalanche. The merest Philistine may be wonder-struck by a mountain; whereas in the Campo Santo at Pisa, or in Giotto's chapel at Padua, he is gravelled at once. Switzerland is easily accessible; delights girls and children as well as matrons and old men, and, to all save idiots, is cheap.

To travellers of even more mediocre mental capacity, Paris is Paradise. Paris and the Grand Hotel, Paris and the Louvre, Paris with its boulevards, its shops, its Bois de Boulogne, its innumerable theatres, its inexhaustible gaiety, its cafés, its restaurants, its perpetual round of brilliance and excitement—Paris is the place, almost the only place, for those who travel for pleasure. I have passed through this gay metropolis three times within the last six months, although my stay in it each time has not exceeded a few hours. Last January I came to Paris from the north of Germany, on my way to Spain. It was about nine o'clock when we drove through the blazing streets from the Place

Lafayette to the Rue St. Honoré. The carriage turned down one of the narrow streets off the boulevard—the Rue de Grammont, I think. A white-jerkined cook, just emancipated from his *bain-marie* pans, was smoking a cigar at the street-corner, and ever and anon *dancing a lightsome jig by himself*. We reached an hotel, but had scarcely been in our room ten minutes, ere a little glazed card was thrust underneath our door, with the address of Monsieur Alphonse, "*coiffeur de la maison.*"

Could you wish for a completer epitome of Parisian life than that which we saw in a twenty-minutes' drive? It is all cooking and dancing, and fiddling and smoking, and the barber always ready to friz your hair. No wonder that Brown, Jones, and Robinson adore Paris. Hampstead, according to the middle-aged gentleman in *Pickwick*, is the place for a wounded heart; but since the Second Empire, Paris has become not only the universal amuser, but the universal consoler. Doctors tell their patients to run over to Paris, as they used to tell them to run down to Tunbridge Wells. It is rather too hard to expect that when Brown, Jones, and Robinson, with their wives and their sweethearts, snatch a brief holiday, they are to spend it at school. You would not like to pass your honeymoon looking out of one of those cheap undertakers' omnibuses which are half mourning-coach and half hearse, and which carry the body in the boot. A gondola, when the picturesqueness of the thing has worn off, is not much better. Brown, Jones, and Robinson can scarcely divest themselves of the idea that the contractor-general for the Venetian gondolas is Mr. Shillibeer.

Again, it is not to be denied that Venice is damp, and

that the brighter is the weather the more abominable is the stench emitted by its narrow canals. At low-water the stones of Venice—that is to say, their sea-stones—remind Brown, Jones, and Robinson unpleasantly of the Fleet-ditch. Sanitary regulations notwithstanding, the canalazzo rolls a very large tribute of dead dogs to the Adriatic. At the best of times, the back-streets of Venice are not much superior to a succession of Cranbourn-alleys; and on a wet day, the Venetian billiard-tables being impracticable to those who play the English game, and there being no club, Brown, Jones, and Robinson are with difficulty restrained from cutting their throats or jumping into the canals.

A cheery, healthful, youthful tourist taking his pleasure wants amusement. The tomb of all the Capulets is not a place for recreation; and Venice is the family vault not alone of the Capulets, but of the Montagues, and many other noble families to boot. You grow tired at last of sitting outside a café on St. Mark's Place, and listening to the Austrian band playing schottisches and mazurkas. After a week in Venice, Brown, Jones, and Robinson come to know all the officers in the Austrian garrison by sight. The perpetual passing and repassing of those fair-haired, tight-waisted men in white coats, with their eye-glasses and their jingling spurs, grow as irritating at last as the sight of the man tying his shoe was to the gamester. If you have managed to scrape any acquaintance among the Austrians, not a single Italian will speak to you; if you know any Italians, they will bore you to death about the woes of Venice.

Brown, Jones, and Robinson did not come to Venice to be bored. They very soon grow aware that not only a special taste and a special aptitude, but a special education, and that too of no common order, are needed before the beauties of Venice can be properly appreciated, or her pictorial and architectural wonders enjoyed. They engage a *valet de place*, and go through the usual round of sights; but when they have seen the ducal palace and the churches, the Arsenal and the Academy, the Museum and the Armenian convent at San Lazaro; when they have tried all the cafés, and find that only one kind of ice is sold in them until midsummer; when they have seen the pigeons fed in St. Mark's Place, and admired the equitation of the solitary horseman at the Giardino Pubblico, and have been rowed about in a gondola till they have caught a toothache,—they are apt to find Venice slow, and to long for some city where there are carriages and theatres, and balls and concerts, and where the people are not trodden under the heel of the Austrian "autograph."

The Rev. Mr. Eustace found Venice slow, and, moreover, he failed to admire St. Mark's. "The five domes which swell from its roof, and the paltry decorations" (those glorious mosaics!) "which cumber its portico, give it externally the appearance of an Eastern pagoda." Again: "A person accustomed to the rides, the walks, the activity of ordinary towns, soon grows tired of the confinements of Venice, and of the dull, indolent, see-saw motion of the gondolas. He longs to expatiate in fields, and to range at large through the streets without a boat and a retinue of gondoliers." Which shows that Mr. Eustace did not know his Venice. A lady may go out shopping in the streets of Venice for half-a-dozen hours without stepping into a gondola.

II.

FROM TRIESTE TO VIENNA.

Trieste, May 1.

I WAS once supercilious enough to laugh at the Spaniards for announcing in their humbler fondas the advent of an "arrogant *olla podrida*" ten days beforehand. I might have been taught a little humility had I remembered the old gentlemen at the London clubs, who put their names down for early slices of the roast sirloin of beef which is to be ready at 6.45 P.M., and are furious if the undercut of fat they have built their hopes upon be gone. Why should not mankind speculate on an *olla* of ten days hence, and invest in beef, so to speak, for the account? But what do you think of a railway train which is a coming event, and casts its shadow before? How would your worships' patience square itself to the necessity of waiting from Saturday until Monday for a *Schnellzug?* Yet this was my case when, landing the other day from the Austrian Lloyd's steamer at Trieste, I hoped to go upstairs without delay to Vienna. Nobody cares about staying long at Trieste. It is the Swindon of Austro-Levantine Europe, the junction from which innumerable routes diverge, but at which you merely gulp down a basinful of soup, and then scamper away to Germany, or Italy, or the East.

And Trieste is, besides, something else that begins with "Swin"—to wit, the most swindling place in the way of hotel charges I ever entered, or, grumbling and plundered, left. The armed rhinoceros and I have by this time become brothers as regards toughness of epidermis. You might tan my skin like old John Ziska's, and beat the "Wedding March" upon it; and the ordinary extortions of landlords run off me as water off a duck's back; but at Trieste, I confess, I found that my hide was not impervious. I was flayed, and felt it. "Everything at Trieste," quoth by way of consolation the Italian Commissionaire, "is *carissimo*." I was indignant that so endearing a superlative should be applied to this den of rapacity; but I sullenly agreed that the place was abominably dear. "The reason," continued the Commissionaire, "is obvious. Trieste is a free port. Free ports are always dear." So I was fain to content myself with this fiscal paradox. 'Tis very odd; but so it is. Free ports are always dear, just as communities which are said to be irremediably bankrupt are always steeped to the lips in luxury and extravagance.

There are only two express trains a-week from Trieste to Vienna, and the ordinary train is said to be so very slow and sure as to give you time to visit the Grotto of Adelsberg, and inspect the antiquities of Gratz ere you reach the capital. The Germans prefer it to the Schnellzug, as it makes many stoppages, and remains at intermediate stations long enough for comfortably consuming those four substantial meals per diem in which Teutons delight. Those four meals a-day are, I am inclined to think, at the bottom of the deep hatred which the Italians bear to the Austrians. "The Venetians have no heart," said a genial German with whom I once travelled from Trent to Roveredo. "You are half starved in

Venice. During twenty-three hours out of the twenty-four you can get nothing but water, ices, and wafers."

A general tendency to abstinence is really remarkable in Venice, when the eating and drinking customs of the people are compared with those of the convivial and *bon vivant* Germans, to whom heaps of *Butterbrod* between regular meals are no more than a few *cigaritos* to the smoker who is waiting for a pipe or a *puro*. But even the promise of abundant *Butterbrod*, and solemn stoppages for the four traditional meals—even the charms of Adelsberg's wondrous caves, with their dome of stalactite and their glancing spiracles of stalagmite—even a laudable desire to inspect the famous Old Hat preserved in the Landhaus at Gratz, and worn by the Kaiser when he receives the allegiance of the inhabitants of the Duchy of Styria—even a wish to turn off to the quicksilver mines of Idria, and see the glowing cinnabar roasted, and the glittering mercury running away in rivers, or to halt for a while at Laybach, and moralise upon the doings of that defunct congress of kings and emperors and plenipotentiaries which met forty-five years ago to settle the affairs of Europe for ever and ever, and whose solemn protocols are now so much waste paper—even these inducements were powerless to make me forget that, for a great many reasons, I was due in Vienna, and that I was bound to hasten to the Kaiserstadt. It was rather an Irish way, I own, of making haste, to wait three days for the express; but for that I had my reasons, too—reasons connected with a crutch and a cut shoe—and so I put my name down for the *Schnellzug*, and was flayed by the innkeepers, and blown down by the north-east wind, and blown up again by the south-east, until six o'clock on Monday morning last.

It is one of the delights of Trieste that you always have one of the above-named winds as a companion. The south-easter is a Greco-Levantine wind, no other than the terrible sirocco. It comes fraught with intolerable heat and clouds of choking sand. The north-easter is the no-less-celebrated "bora," the "burrasca" of the Italians, and the "bourrasque" of the Provençals. It is said to be generated in the crannies of the mountains surrounding the desolate plain of the Karst—of which more anon—for even winds, like railway companies' accounts, must be concocted, and it comes down to Trieste and blows your head off. It blew all my louis d'ors into Austrian paper money. It blew up the innkeeper's bill to the dimensions of the Nassau balloon. How the late Dr. Reid, ventilator-general of the Houses of Parliament, would have enjoyed a "bora"! According to "Murray," it will blow people into the canal, upset wagons, and overturn ships of large tonnage in the inner port. In fact, it is almost as powerful as the historical wind at the Escorial, which once lifted up an ambassador from the Low Countries, with his coach-and-six and his entire retinue, and would not set him down again till he was converted to the true faith. I have seen it gravely stated that if you lean against this rude and blustering railer he is absolutely strong enough to support your reclining form; from which I conjecture that Boreas must be of kindred to the fog you could cut with a knife. I don't know whether this tremendous blast ever blows upwards as well as laterally, but if such were the case, when the time came for *sus. per coll.* to be written against my name, I think that I should like to be hanged with my feet upon a "bora."

For a fourteen hours' journey, and that, too, of very comfortable and accelerated travelling, you have twenty minutes at Steinbruck for breakfast, but at the other stations the train never stops more than from three to six minutes. The run from Trieste to Vienna may be safely backed as the most astonishing in Europe. I was about to say in the whole world, but I recall the awful passes of the Cumbres and the first ravishing sight of the Valley of Mexico at Rio Frio.

The route through Illyria and Styria to Vienna has a threefold interest: you see so many changes in the earth's surface, and so many varieties of man; and finally you mark so many gradations of speech. The geographer, the geologist, the naturalist, and the artist, may take their fill of mountain scenery, varied strata, complex vegetation, and wonderful effects of aerial perspective. Nature is of all hues, and all her caprices find record here; now justifying our Telbins and Pynes and Hollands; now proving that Cooke and David Cox were in the right; now causing you to pin your faith to Linnell, and now to Eugene Isabey; and now forcing you to admit that the only true art-prophet was good old Sam Prout. I would that more artists lost their way between Gratz and Laybach; but these gentry are a perverse race, with mental horizons painfully contracted, and are no more to be weaned from beaten tracks than from hackneyed books for subjects. Switzerland and South Wales; it is always South Wales and Switzerland in Suffolk-street and Pall Mall, just as at the Academy it was always

Gil Blas or *Pepys's Diary*, as now it is the *Idyls of the King*.

To him whose delight is in man, his manners, his vesture, his habitation, and his language, this strange country is not less rife with matter for observation and thought. At Trieste you leave a very Babel of tongues, a very Salmagundi of humanity; and the money-changers write up their willingness to cheat you out of your gold and silver in Greek more or less Attic, in Russ more or less sweet-flowing, in the stubborn Teutonic black letter, and even in the quasi-cufic, quasi-cuneiform Sclavonic character, all darts and wedges and isosceles triangles. The railway clerk from whom I took my ticket demanded "*fiorini settanta-due;*" the employé who gave me my baggage certificate told me there were "*achtzehn gülden fünfzig kreuzer*" to pay—by the way, he marked "sixteen" on the certificate and cheated me out of two florins—whereas the driver of the omnibus from the hotel was a Dalmatian, in a "snowy camise and a shaggy capote," like a "dark Suliote"—if the Suliotes wore shaggy capotes, which they do not—and the porters who carried my trunks to be weighed were unmistakable Sclaves, with flowing tawny hair, blue eyes, and high cheekbones. We had as travelling companions a Greek of the Hellenes, a Greek in a braided jacket, baggy silk breeches, high boots, a fez cap, and an umbrella—why will they always spoil their picturesque Oriental costume with a Sangster's Best?—and a Greek of the Rayahs, attired in the latest Parisian fashion. The custom-house officer who searched our luggage—for, as Trieste is a free port, they are very inquisitorial in their quest for tobacco, salt, gunpowder, playing-cards, and prohibited books—was a fat, good-humoured *Tedesco*, an adept in the admired Austrian custom of pulling off the cap to everyone he met. The Austrian of the lower classes rarely bows. He uncovers with both hands, and as though he were offering you his head with all that was inside it. To complete the ethnological hotch-potch, we passed as we left the terminus a whole regiment of Hungarian infantry drawn up in battle array; pudgy little men in blue tights and blucher boots. The lower extremities of a Hungarian soldier always resemble, to my mind, those of the industrious sporting gentlemen whom, with a parti-coloured kerchief round their loins and scantily clad as to their upper anatomy, you meet steaming along suburban roads in England, walking against time, or Deerfoot, or somebody, or something, for five-and-twenty pounds a-side.

The odd concourse of different nations at Trieste is accidental, and due to the fact that the great *entrepôt* of the Levantine mercantile navy is on Italian soil, and in the possession of a German power. As you advance into the interior, it is less a mixture than a succession of races which becomes apparent, and the succession is graduated and natural. The pure Triestinos are Italians—Venetians, in fact—settled "over the way," swarthy, black-haired, dark-eyed, vehement, and much gesticulating. Beyond Nabresina, where the rail from Udine and Venice joins the main line, the Italian element begins to disappear, and by the time you reach Adelsberg it is entirely eradicated. The guide-posts and police prohibitions no longer appear in the two languages, and the railway guard speaks nothing but German.

It would seem as though Nature herself, the European settlement of the Congress of Laybach notwithstanding, had determined to erect a barrier between the stern north and the sunny south; for north of Adelsberg commences that Neutral Ground of geographers, the wild and desolate expanse called the Karst. It is an immense tract of gray limestone, worked of old time to good purpose by the Venetians, and known as Istrian marble. It starts here, at the east of the Alpine spurs, and stretches away down Dalmatia and Albania into Greece. I never saw a more hideous region: it is more terrifying even in its barrenness than the great stony desert of the north of Spain; for there at least the stones are broken, and heaped in wild disorder about the landscape, offering all kinds of fantastic shapes, replete with changes of light and shade. The Karst is one huge piecrust of limestone. It is furrowed, riddled, and pierced into caverns, clefts, gully-holes, rock basins, valleys that have no outlets, and rivers without any perceptible sources or reservoirs. But there are no *débris*. The covering is hard, homogeneous, and as gray as Napoleon's greatcoat. All life seems to have been suddenly become petrified; or I may best explain my meaning, perhaps, by saying that everything seems covered by a crust of stone snow. The Karst is just the place where you might imagine the limeburners in Nathaniel Hawthorne's weird story had set up their kiln, and where the remorseful gentleman who had committed the unpardonable sin tried to calcine his heart by means of strong caloric, but tried in vain. I should not like to walk barefoot over the Karst in November. That awful Bora lives on the Karst when he is at home. On this barren plateau he lashes himself into a rage, and after howling up and down for a time, and sending any carts or country people spinning that come in his way, rushes down to Trieste to blow up the natives. For that is the way, my merry friends. Be sure you get up your passion in the parlour. Then you can rush down-stairs foaming to the kitchen, and kick the servants. But that dear old Mother Nature of ours is not always in her high tantivies in this howling wilderness. She can smile sometimes. In a few out-of-the-way corners of the Karst the vine and olive grow, and yield fruits of Italian sweetness and savour; nay, successful attempts have been made to cultivate the Marasca cherry, the brother to the wild red cherry of the Dalmatian hills, and from which is made the exquisite *liqueur* called Maraschino—the real nectar of Olympus. Ladies—albeit repudiating our harsh potations—can rarely resist it; and it was of Maraschino that Hebe took too much.

But why am I lingering on this blasted heath, or rather quarry, where the wondrous pass of the Semmering Alp awaits me? On goes our train through enchanting mountain scenery, now stern and sublime, now soft and smiling. You shall be carried by towering viaducts over such valleys as you have never seen before—valleys such as you thought had no existence off the stage of the opera. Here is one with a babbling brook, and a tiny flossy skein of a waterfall, and a pretty church half hidden among chestnut-trees, and a hoar old donjon keep at the top of a high hill, and dozens of pretty white cottages, nestling amid trellised vines—the vines are grown here *à l'Italienne*, and not in the hard-hearted, spiky, hop-pole, French fashion—and everything, down to the painted effigy of the Virgin in its little penthouse, in the foreground, brings back to my mind the happy valley in the second act of the *Night Dancers*. Ah! here is another valley, with such *châlets*, such a village inn, and a real water-wheel. I seem to see Amina in her nightgown coming over the rustic causeway, to hear the candlestick come washing into the torrent. There is poor Elvino with his hair dishevelled, and his stockings down, and that artful wicked Lisa, and my lord the Count, with his dyed moustache and his intolerable travelling-cap with the gold band. Stay! see; there is Doctor Dulcamara—scarlet coat, top-boots, flaxen perruque, and all—who drives up to Pöltschach Station, in that identical gig with the white horse. He dismounts and hands Nemorino—the station clerk, indeed—a little black bottle. Down in that green nook I see Signor Lablache in the *Gazza Ladra*, come creaking over the bridge in all the majesty of podestal pride; and there, beyond in the antique village, a ruddy farm damsel, in the shortest of petticoats, is milking her kine, and a love-lorn swain notches her name on the roof-post, while the thievish magpie runs away with the spoon. They come again, those happy operatic days, when one paid so delightedly the half-crown for the gallery at the opera, and listened with bliss to Rubini and Grisi, though their voices had to travel a quarter of a mile to reach us. Talk of Italy and Switzerland! Bah! they have become as prosaic as Norwood or Twickenham. The only picturesque places left in Europe—I except Spain, which is in Africa, you know—are Styria and Illyria.

When your train stops at some station you find the same picturesque diversity—real notaries in black gowns and snowy falling bands—the very notaries who sit at rickety little tables in the *Sonnambula* and the *Elisire d'Amore*, and draw up the marriage contracts; real monks, with shaven crowns and sandalled feet and hempen girdles—and I am glad to admit that the Austrian friars are the cleanest I have seen for a long period; Tyrolese sharp-shooters and jägers, Uhlans and Pandours in all manner of wildly martial garb—for the Government of the Kaiser seems to have as many nationalities in its military pay as the Government of India; to crown all, a "bold peasantry their country's pride," very comely and contented in appearance, with an abundance of gold and silver ornaments quite surprising in a country where a specie-currency is unknown; working men wearing shaggy jackets with half-dollars for buttons, parti-coloured gaiters and hats with streaming ribbons; their wives and daughters in the most coquettish of bodices, the brightest and briefest of petticoats, stockings of gay hues, and variegated cloaks.

Alas that there should be a reverse to this rosy picture; but the interests of truth compel me to state that it was only on the platforms that the pretty villagers in their coquettish costume were visible, and that by the roadside in all the cultivated tracts they were to be seen in the fields bent double, ragged, with foul clouts tied about their heads, hoeing and weeding, digging and delving, and bending under baskets of manure like beasts of burden. When I saw, as the train stopped for a moment at a station, a young girl about fifteen experiencing some difficulty in drawing a bucket from a well —and when I observed a grim, gaunt man, presumably her father, aiding her by the administration of a thwack across her shoulders with a cudgel that looked big enough to fell a bullock—I confess that my operatic reminiscences began to fade away in a despondent haze, and the sad conviction followed, that the condition of the female agricultural population is much the same all over continental Europe—and insular Europe too, for that matter.

It was my lot, ere the day was out, to witness a change in the aspect of the scenery and the condition of the atmosphere for which I was no more prepared than for the appearance of a waterspout or the downfall of a shower of red-hot scoriæ. You will be pleased to recollect that this was the 22d of April—midspring—and that we were in about the latitude of Lyons. At Trieste, abating a touch of the "bora" on Sunday, the temperature had been well-nigh oppressive. So late as ten o'clock that morning we had journeyed through a really southern clime—for miles and miles by the blue and waveless Adriatic, and through teeming regions of vines which, in some cases, covered the very slopes of the railway cuttings and embankments, through groves of figs and olives, and fields of Indian corn. It needed but the orange to have made me think I was back in Andalusia. We got to Gratz about three in the afternoon, and plunged with an almost appalling suddenness into the depth, or rather the height, of winter. Mountains capped with snow—for these we were prepared; but the entire country was a mass of snow, the rivulets were frozen, the tiny lakes were sheets of solid ice, the snow lay thick in the village streets and on the roofs of village houses. There was snow on the church-spire, and snow on the cart-tilts in the farmyards—not snow having the appearance of a passing storm, but snow that looked as though it were an old friend, and had come to stop. The air was piercingly cold. And then sleet, and then snow, came down, and continued falling until evening.

Under these hyperborean circumstances did we cross the Semmering.

I have had my snow this winter, as the unhappy prisoner-boy Josephs, in Mr. Charles Reade's wonderful novel, had his castigations—by instalments. Returning from blazing sunshine—the south of Spain—I found all the northern country between Avila and Burgos as white as the top of a wedding-cake. This was about the first of April. "Well," I said, "here at last is an end of winter." It was warm on the shores of the Bay of Biscay, and warmer at Bordeaux, and for one day in Paris I broiled. Then, going into Italy, we had a smart fall of sleet at Chamberi. "It is nothing," I said; "I come to thee, Savoy; and thou art generally shrouded in sleet or in a Scotch mist." But we had not reached Lans-le-bourg, in our passage over Mont Cenis, ere a grim winter—almost as grim as that which overtook us on the Semmering—clutched us by the throat. We were transferred from the diligence to a sledge, and were going down to Susa merrily enough on runners—we never bumped but one of our lady-companions declared that we had met with an avalanche, which in her opinion was a kind of ditch—when we were fairly caught in a snow-drift, and had to be dug out of it with pickaxes and shovels, and set running again by the introduction of rollers underneath our sledge-irons. Turin was still weeping bitterly for her fugitive Sovereign, her recreant court, and her diminished house-rents—that is to say, it was pouring cats and dogs, which it usually seems to do at Turin. At Milan we had the usual allowance of humanity—smiles and tears; more of the last perhaps than of the first; but it was April weather, anyhow, and to complain would have been unreasonable. In fact, one or two good soaking wet days a-week seem to do the incomparable Duomo at Milan all the good in the world. The white marble turns, under the moisture, to a myriad varieties of hue; the wet searches all the little cunning crannies of the sculpture and tracery; and when it dries up, and the sun comes out again, the thousand-year-old fabric shines forth with a fresh glory spick and span new, as though its first stone had been laid but yesterday:

> "My heart leaps up when I behold
> A rainbow in the sky;
> So was it when my life began;
> So is it now I am a man;
> So be it when I shall grow old,
> Or let me die."

For the "rainbow in the sky" Mr. Wordsworth might very well have substituted the Duomo of Milan. It is a joy for ever.

At Venice, I have already told you, we had the brightest phases of the golden *primavera;* and we had done with the hateful winter, I thought, for good and all. I had left all my furs and winter gear behind at Venice, and had indulged in day-dreams of white ducks at Vienna. But I reckoned without my host—and the Semmering.

After all, the combined influence of rain, sleet, and snow, under which we accomplished the passage of the great Alp, may not have been without a beneficial effect. The adverseness of the circumstances to anything like sight-seeing rendered it impossible for me to inflict on you a detailed account of our sensations at the head of the Pass, the middle of the Pass, and the tail of the Pass. Rejoice, therefore, at my impotence to give you a yard and a half of fine writing about the Semmering. That it is awful, majestic, and sublime I make no doubt. Not being able, however, to see anything but snow and rain and the steam of the engine from the carriage window, I went to sleep. So I have slept over other Alps—over the Brenner and the Stelvio, over the Cordilleras and the Sierra Morena. Where is the use of keeping awake if you can't see anything from the window?

When you wake up, and have hooked your travelling-lamp to the padded head-rest, you may consult your "Murray," your "Baedecker," or your "Guide Joanne" at your ease; and discover that at the head of the pass the engineers have constructed a tunnel four thousand feet long through the mountains, at a height of nearly three thousand feet above the level of the sea, and that this is the loftiest railway in the world. All astonishing as it is, the old post-and-carriage road made under the Kaiser Karl VI. soars even higher. It passes by artful zigzags right over the mountain, and directly above the railway tunnel attains a height of three thousand two hundred feet. These zigzags, forming in their integrity an angular spiral, caused an old traveller to remark that the road over the Semmering was the only one which enabled a man going before you to see the nape of your neck. By others the line has been called the Retrospective Railway; and if Lot's wife were among the passengers one might expect to find all the telegraph-posts converted into pillars of salt.

So by Gloggnitz and Wiener-Neustadt we came, about half-past nine at night, to Vienna, and found the atmosphere soft and balmy as that of a spring night should be.

III.

THE KAISER.

Vienna, May 5.

I MADE one of a party, while in Vienna, bound for a stroll in the gardens of Schönbrunn. The Kaiser and the Kaiserin are in residence; and while they are in the palace the private apartments are not shown to the public. Otherwise you are free to wander as you will about the imperial domicile. No policemen warn you off the premises. The possessor of all this splendour has seemingly arrived at the sensible conclusion that beautiful things were made to be looked at, and that although a thing of beauty is a joy for ever, it is shorn of half its interest when its contemplation is confined to a select few. So the gardens and the conservatories, the aviaries, the menagerie, the fish-ponds, the artificial ruins, and the statues, are all very much at the service of that public who, in the origin, paid for them; and as soon as the imperial family go back to Vienna, one of the gorgeous flunkeys will take you through the rooms in which they eat and drink and sleep. Well, we took our fill of what was visible; and, unhindered by minatory notices, our carriage-wheels were permitted to crunch the gravel of drives on which it would have been high treason in England to impinge.

When we had seen the Gloriette and the Schönbrunn

—the Beautiful Fountain itself—and watched the exquisite effect of the sunlit green spring foliage chequering the marble form of the Hebe, who is perpetually dispensing to thirsty sight-seers an element much purer than the nauseous lime-impregnated stuff which passes for water in the hotels of Vienna—when we had seen the wild beasts, including the African lion, who was in a rage as usual because his cage was too small; and the grisly bear, who was curled up into a ball in the sun and sleeping tranquilly through the European crisis; and the fox, who was wide awake and sitting on the top of a tree-bole, looking remarkably like the busts of Count Bismark; and the Bengal tiger, who, in consequence of the heat of the day, had retired to an inner apartment, and only allowed one brindled paw to be visible across the threshold of his den—when we had seen the golden eagle, troubled in his mind and plumage by conscience or by fleas; also a very frolicsome ostrich, who was executing in his paddock the precise "Sahara waltz" which has furnished Mr. Carlyle with such a very valuable figure of speech; a peculiar crane, just imported, whose particoloured head, with a quantity of yellow hair, presumably false, behind, reminded one strongly of the last new thing in bonnets; a most horribly ragged, morose, and depraved-looking vulture, clad apparently in an old door-mat, who was exhibiting such feats of strength with his beak in the way of twisting and widening the interstices between the wires of his cage as made the likelihood of his coming out for a walk among the ladies and children rather a proximate and imminent one than otherwise—when we had seen all these things, we halted for a time to rest ourselves under one of the cool and shady archways of the inner peristyle of the palace.

Suddenly we saw a carriage rapidly coming towards us up the long, smooth, gravelled road. An officer on duty made a courteous sign for us with his hand to move a little on one side—quite as much, I think, with the view of preventing our toes from being crushed as with that of preserving the illustrious inmates of the carriage from the contact of the vulgar. Up came the carriage, awakening a hundred echoes from the archways. It was a simple equipage enough: an open calèche, black and yellow—the Austrian colours—lined with drab; and the coachman and footman in liveries of the same hue. It had two occupants, both in full uniform—an officer in white and an officer in light blue. He in light blue was the Emperor Francis Joseph. No guard turned out, no drums beat to arms. The Kaiser and his aide-de-camp alighted at a narrow side-door; and I, going on my way, saw them no more.

A very different Kaiser was this from the gay, gallant young man who, nearly twenty years ago, was called from the camps of Italy to fill the throne vacated by the harmless but inane Ferdinand. Four months ago I saw King William of Prussia driving *unter den Linden* in an equipage well-nigh as simple as this. There can be no mistake about King William's age. He looks what he is—a stubborn, stiff-necked, obtuse, but withal genial and kind-hearted old gentleman; his mind thoroughly made up, and he himself quite easy in it. But I declare that Francis Joseph, who comparatively speaking is a mere boy to William I., looks, by a dozen years, the older man. He is a comely

Kaiser, quite the gentleman in appearance, and should be slim to dapperness, with an alert, vivacious mien; but, ah! how weary and worn and wretched he looks, how furrowed with premature wrinkles, how grizzled with untimely gray! What a life of ceaseless worry, care, anxiety, must be his! He cannot retire to an inner apartment like the royal Bengal tiger, and allow only his Kaiserlich-Königlich paw to be visible. He must always be in evidence. He must be always giving audiences. All day long he is being bored by somebody—by generals, by ministers, by courtiers, by suppliants; and all the while the timbers of the ship of state are creaking and yawning, and the ship itself is rolling and pitching after the manner of that much distraught barque which lay all the day in the Bay of Biscay, O! Her pitchy seams are rent; the dismal wreck to view strikes horror to her crew; but no sail in sight appears.

Instead of a sail, the Medes and Persians are at the gate; Bismark is gnawing at the wire fences of the Silesian border; the Italians are boiling and bubbling up at Pizzighettone like the "*tenere pece*" in the Arsenal of Venice described by Dante; the Bohemians are beginning to murmur about Panslavic unity and the dynasty of George Podiebrod; the Hungarians, instead of crying as they did to Theresa, "*Moriamur pro rege nostro!*" are squabbling in interminable consonants about "legal continuity;" Austrian credit is exhausted; there are half a million men in white to be boarded and lodged at the Kaiser's expense every day; the forced paper currency is at fifteen per cent discount; and the Emperor Napoleon declines to avow his intentions. Surely this is enough to silver the hair and furrow the cheeks of the amiable and well-meaning middle-aged gentleman in the sky-blue tunic, whom I saw step from his carriage at the side door, and, leaning on the arm of his aide, plod wearily up the staircase of his grand palace, not to enjoy rest or healthful occupation, but to be badgered, and baited, and teased out of his life by telegrams, and despatches, and rumours, true or false, to the effect that everybody is arming against him, so that in sheer self-defence he is compelled to arm against everybody too, and throw his half-million of white-coated men—with never a penny in hard cash to pay for their coats or their pumpernickel, or their daily kreutzers of pay—into the *mêlée*.

Would you lead such a life even to be king and kaiser, and imperial, and royal, and "apostolic," and receive the allegiance of the Estates of Styria with that celebrated Old Hat upon your head? Better to wear the most battered of wideawakes, and, a knapsack at your back, go tramping up and down the Rhineland, with a second-class return ticket from London-bridge, grumbling because the gasthof-keepers charge you ten silbergroschen, instead of eight, for a bottle of Liebfraumilch. Better the workman's jacket, the peasant's blouse, than that perpetually buttoned-up sky-blue tunic, with a white-flannel tunic as tightly buttoned up by way of a change.

It is the doom of honest and inoffensive Francis Joseph to appear without cessation in the guise of a fire-eater. For twenty years he has been in full uniform. There is a story in Irving's *Wölfert's Roost* of a piratical Dutchman who came in a storm, and lived in a storm, and went away in a storm. Two-thirds of the story would apply closely enough to Francis Joseph. With boyish hand he was made to pick up the sceptre—as heavy and well-nigh as unpleasant to wield as a red-hot poker—which the fatuous Ferdinand had suffered to slide from his grasp. The echoes of Windischgrätz's cannon, the trampling of the terrible Ban Jellachich's chargers' hoofs had scarcely died away when he found himself, in full uniform, installed in a Burg whose approaches had been but half cleared from the barricades of red republicanism. He has always worn that full uniform. What time, what opportunity has he had to go into mufti? The non-military section among his subjects murmur at this eternal apparition of the drill-sergeant. They remember that Ferdinand—common-place, chip-in-porridge, as he was—used to stroll about the Graben and the Kohlmarkt in the plainest of plain clothes. It was a distinguished characteristic of the monarch, now "retired from business," that he never wore gloves. The Viennese, who are in general the slaves of a more than Chinese etiquette, admired this touch of Bohemianism in their Kaiser. With even greater admiration they recall the days of the old Emperor Francis, who was renowned for wearing in the street a particularly shocking bad hat—not the Styrian one, but a weather-beaten beaver—the brim of which was quite worn away under the attrition of continual responses to popular salutes.

But these pleasant *bourgeois* days are fled. The Emperor is always in sky-blue. The Archdukes, whose name is legion, are always in sky-blue or milky-white. It is a buttoned-up, leathern-stocked age. The costume and the customs of the barrack prevail; but the fault is scarcely with the well-intentioned Sovereign, who would like to reduce his army, encourage literature and the arts, and reign constitutionally; but who came to the throne in a muddle, and has continued to reign in a muddle; who inherited nothing but empty grandeur, whited sepulchre, Chinese etiquette, half-a-million of soldiers in white coats, debt, discontent, disunion, and bankruptcy. It is not Francis Joseph's fault. "*C'est la faute de la fatalité*," as M. Bovary observed.

I came back to Vienna to find the Prater full of rumours, and the Kohlmarkt ripe with *on dits*, and the courtyard of the Archduke Charles Hotel crammed with quidnuncs, all asserting the most disastrous things. I pass by the reported proclamation of war between Prussia and Austria, between Prussia and Saxony, and between Austria and Italy. Of such proclamations we have verbatim accounts at least half-a-dozen times in the course of every day. I pass by the "joint note" of protest said to have been presented to Prussia by England and Bavaria. England and Bavaria! Eagles do not habitually consort with tom-tits. I give, for what it is worth, the story that the King of Italy, being lately at an entertainment offered to him by the Municipality of his Lombard capital, said in proposing the health of the Podestà, "Gentlemen, you have given me a ball at Milan. Next year I hope to return the compliment by giving you a supper at Venice." I don't think this story very trustworthy. The King of Italy is not in the habit of uttering "buncombe" under any circumstances; and he is too honest and sensible a gentleman to plagiarise or to parody the famous sarcasm of the daughter of Alexander VI. to the seven young nobleman she had poisoned: "*Messieurs, vous m'avez donné un bal à Venise; je vous rends un souper à Ferrare.*" The imaginative journalist who concocted that Milan story had probably just risen from the perusal of Victor Hugo's *Lucrèce Borgia*.

As to the repeated statement that Garibaldi has been written for and telegraphed for to Caprera, that he is by this time in Florence, busy enrolling volunteers, one cannot afford to treat *that* with ridicule. It is as likely as not, and likelier. The grand old man in the red shirt has been used as scurvily by the King he made as was blind old Belisarius by the Emperor he saved. Thank God that Garibaldi has not yet had to beg for the obolus. But he who conquered Southern Italy, and who gave up the Dictatorship as calmly as though he had been a one-armed commissionaire intrusted with a parcel; he who, while generals and placemen gathered greedily round the rich spoil, went quietly off to Caprera to live on five *soldi's* worth of polenta and a little goat's-milk cheese—just as when, installed in splendour at Stafford House, he told one of the superb flunkeys who came to inform him that breakfast was ready, that he had breakfasted two hours before—the meal being a morsel of bread and a drop of stale beer, the remnants of the last night's repast—he, whose only requital for services such as never before were rendered by subject to Sovereign was to have his ankle smashed and his name vilified—Giuseppe Garibaldi is too much of a whole-souled Christian to bear malice, or to sulk because he has been ill-treated.

"As for my life, it's the king's," says Jack, in Dibdin's ballad. Garibaldi has shown a hundred times already his willingness to lay down his life for Italy; and if he is wanted, he will be ready, no doubt, until the end and until that epitaph be written over him to which so few aspire and which fewer still deserve, "Well done, thou good and faithful servant."

Nor are rumours less numerous from the interior of Germany, nor are some dry facts of a sufficiently ominous nature wanting to back those rumours up. Poor ex-Emperor Ferdinand, who for many years has been passing a quiet, humdrum, harmless existence in the Hradschin Palace, at Prague, spending his vast wealth in gifts to the poor and donations to churches and convents, has suddenly waked up, they say, to the disagreeable consciousness that Prague is in Bohemia, that Bohemia is unpleasantly close to Saxony, and that the Saxon lamb is unmistakably menaced by the Prussian wolf. Ex-Emperor Ferdinand has begun to opine that the Hradschin at Prague is no longer a safe and comfortable retreat for a monarch retired from business, undeniably pious and charitable, but somewhat weak-minded. The very name of Vienna is abhorred by the ex-Kaiser, who still sees, they say, in imagination the sanguinolent phantom of red republicanism roaring round the Burg, and hears Windischgrätz's big guns, and Jellachich's infinite troop-horses. To the Kaiserstadt he will not return; but he is packing up to leave the Hradschin, and intends to settle at Linz. Eight large fourgons, padlocked, bolted, and barred, and crammed with jewels, stars, crosses, and crucifixes of gold and silver, are waiting, it is asserted, at the Prague railway-station, ready to be sent South when the evil day arrives. Poor old gentleman—who only wants to say his prayers, and to be tucked up comfortably at night and have a hot posset to send him to sleep!

The King of Saxony is said to be in a quandary even

more dire than that of ex-Kaiser Ferdinand. The language used by Count Bismark to this respectable second-rate Sovereign would seem to be akin to that delicately qualified by Emilia in *Othello* as terms such as a "beggar in his drink" would not have used towards his "callet." I suppose it is the right sort of thing to do—to be passably civil to the Great Powers, but to bully the small Germans like pickpockets. Besides, it is the way of the world. When the Baron Front de Bœuf made that prodigious haul of prisoners, he discriminated in the usage to be shown to his captives. The noble Athelstane and the Lady Rowena were conducted to comfortable apartments, and treated in a manner befitting their rank; but Isaac of York was flung *sans cérémonie* into the deepest dungeon beneath the castle moat, where the baron presently waited upon him, and proposed, with the aid of two heathen blackamoors, to broil him upon a gridiron, unless he counted out on the dungeon-floor a thousand pounds of silver. Bismark has used no more ceremony towards the King of Saxony than the Norman baron did towards the Jew of York. He has made no secret of his determination to seize upon Saxony. The King is said to have already sent away his entire treasure—eight millions of silver dollars, all the uncut Peruvian emeralds, the large oval sardonyx, the famous green diamond, Rafaelle's "Madonna di San Sisto," and the priceless rarities of the Green Vault. Forewarned is forearmed, and the King of Saxony is resolved not to fall unprepared into the net of the Prussian fowler.

IV.

A FLIGHT FROM VENICE.

I CAME down from Vienna to Trieste, and thence returned to Venice—always in consequence of Bismark, whose conduct was now growing outrageous—at the end of May; and on Thursday evening, June 14, at half-past six o'clock, I left Venice to follow Garibaldi and his fortunes. It was time. The overt act of violence committed by the Prussians in Holstein left no doubt of the imminence of war; and it was thought likely in Venice that the Italian forces massed at Piacenza and Bologna might at once cross the frontier, and commence operations without waiting even for the launching of Victor Emmanuel's proclamation, and his manifesto to the Cabinets of Europe. There was no need, it was argued, for any solemn declaration of war between the Kaiser and the Rè Galantuomo. They have been always at war, as the knights of Rhodes were with the Turks. The kingdom of Italy has never been recognised by the Power which was driven out of Lombardy in 1859, and which the Italians hope to scourge out of Venetia in 1866. With a denial of the existence of the sun at noonday, which would be droll were it not pitiable, the official gazetteers of Austria always speak of the united country they hate and fear as *Il Regno di Sardegna*, or *L'Italia Sarda;* while the Italian Parliament is the "Assembly of Piedmont, sitting at Florence." What is there in a name, however? The Emperor of Austria calls himself, on his silver coinage, "King of Lombardo-Venetia;" and behold, in the capital of his empire, not a single silver coin is to be seen.

It was time for me to go. The internal terrors of the Ritter von Toggenburg, Luogotenente of Venice, had grown too desperate for continence, and he was arresting people right and left. Over a hundred domiciliary visits and as many arrests had taken place, in Venice itself, on Wednesday night. At Padua, too, there had been disturbances; and some fifty political prisoners, caught up by the Austrian police, had been sent under a strong guard to the capital to join their fellows in misfortune at San Giorgio Maggiore, and, perhaps, to be subsequently transferred to Goritz or the Spielburg. Toggenburg met them at the station, and doubtless experienced much innocent satisfaction at seeing them coupled together. Finally, a number of Venetians of position and influence—professors, medical men, advocates, artists, noble ladies even—had been summarily ordered by the Government to banish themselves from the Venetian territory. They were scarcely allowed time to pack up a few necessaries. They were not permitted to enter Italy by Bologna or by Peschiera, but by a refinement of cruelty were forced to take the long and wearisome route by Verona and Bolzano, through the Tyrol into Switzerland. Even the Pass of the Brenner is now closed and guarded by Austrian artillery. Some of the involuntary emigrants were coerced into making a promise that they would not seek a permanent refuge either in Switzerland, Italy, or England—the atmosphere of free countries is evidently mephitic to the olfactories of the Cavaliere Toggenburg—which promise, so soon as they are well out of the clutches of the double-headed eagle, it is to be hoped those involuntary emigrants, with all convenient despatch, will break, like so much pie-crust.

In favour of foreigners, it was stated, an exception was to be made. Twenty-four hours' grace had been granted them to get out of Venetia into Italy. On the strength of this assurance, having my passport duly viséd by the police in Venice, I took a ticket to Padua, whence a branch line has just been opened to Rovigo. At the last-named place a diligence was to be in readiness to convey us to Ponte Lago Oscuro. There the Po was to be crossed to Ferrara, and thence we could take the Italian rail to Bologna. Nothing could be more satisfactory than this theoretical itinerary. In practice, however, it was quite another thing. On arriving at Padua I received the grim intelligence that all the bridges on the new branch line—it was only opened last Monday, and these said bridges were regarded as triumphs of engineering skill—had been broken down; that there were no means of conveyance across the Po; and that the Austrian engineers were busy making preparations for inundating the surrounding country. Under these circumstances, nothing was to be done but to go on to Verona, and sleep there.

We reached the fine old city, now converted into a frowning fortress, garrisoned by thirty thousand men, at midnight. It is a long drive from the Porta Vescova to the city gates, and when we reached them they were closed for the night. Only after infinite trouble, and the thrice-performed rite of exhibiting our passports—first to a gendarme, whose lantern went out; next to a German, who was drunk, and was for leaving us out in the cold; and last to a Croat sergeant, who could speak neither German nor Italian—were we allowed to make our way to a most infamous hostelry, called La Colomba d'Oro, where I remained until six in the morning, a prey to bugs and anxiety as to how I was to proceed on my journey. So soon as the clock struck six, having heard overnight that the military authorities might perhaps grant permission to foreigners to proceed by rail from Verona to Peschiera, and knowing that the through train from Venice was due at Verona at ten, I made the best of my way to the quarters of the Commandant della Piazza. The urgency of the case making me bold, I penetrated into a guard-room, where there was an Austrian officer in bed, who, being awakened from a sweet sleep, doubtless about the *butterbrods* and *bierhallen* of Vienna, swore at me. Nothing disheartened, I woke another, who was civil, and directed me to the office of the commandant of the place, a very fierce old Austrian gentleman in a suit of whitey-brown holland, covered with decorations, who, early as it was, had begun his day's work and his day's allowance of cigars. I told him I was a foreigner, and wished to leave the Empire—at which he nodded his head—and enter the kingdom of Italy, at which he bent his fierce old brows—I should have said the kingdom of Sardinia. Be it as it might, however, the commandant of the place could do nothing. I must apply, he said, to the commander of the army, the Archduke Albert.

So off I went to his Imperial Highness's quarters, a pretty villa, near the Porta Nuova, called the Casa Peris. It was not yet seven, but the Archduke had been up an hour past, and was away inspecting his troops in the citadel.

Whatever faults the Austrians may have, the credit at least must be given them of being very early risers. The Archduke, a stout aide-de-camp told me, would be back at eight, and then his adjutant-general might give me what I required.

So, to while away the time, I strolled along the great square of Verona, and its narrow streets and picturesque market-places. The city is in a most deplorable condition. Stagnation, and the concomitant of stagnation, rottenness, have marked it for their own. It is bad enough to see palaces going to ruin, it is worse to see ruined shops, or such mean stalls as are yet tenanted, seedy and forlorn, and scarcely any stock to show. I do remember an apothecary I saw on Friday morning in Verona, and I am sure that Romeo must have seen him in the neighbouring city three hundred years ago. There he stood, a pinched and disconsolate starveling, at the door of his *farmacia*, and behind him was his beggarly account of empty boxes. But not even a customer came to ask him for a trifling draught. The Austrians have their medical staff abundantly supplied, and stand in no need of the services of Veronese apothecaries. At Trieste, it is true, they have put forth an appeal to the public at large for patriotic donations of lint, bandages, and lard for ointment, but they have not had the conscience to ask the Venetians for such succour. They have been content with the infliction of the twelve-million "loan."

It was half-past seven, and I went into a *caffè*, the grandest one in Verona, but like everything else in this war-begone town, pitiably neglected and dilapidated. Waiters without braces, slipshod, unshaven, and dirty; coffee-cups without saucers and without spoons, looking-glasses cracked across, columns split up the shaft, and chairs with three legs —it was all of a piece. There is nothing new, nothing tidy here but barracks and fortifications. The brand of Cain—of the Austrain corporal's cane—is on everything. To anyone who has known Verona in its good days—to anyone who has turned over the pages of the sumptuous edition of Rogers's *Italy*, with its exquisite illustrations by Turner—the actual aspect of this historical and artistic place is most miserable. You can scarcely believe that you are in Italy. From one end of the town to the other there is the smell of the Austrian cavalry stable, and the guttural jabbering of the Austrian guard-room, and the white-coated Croats swarm like a plague of lice. Only on the Piazza stands, defiant of time and laughing at the little ways of men, the old Roman amphitheatre, well-nigh as complete now as when, eighteen centuries since, the gladiators fought, or the Christians were thrown to the lions in its arena. Black and seared and scarred it is, like some great brand which has been thrust into the furnace only to make it harder; but it is yet solid and entire, with its huge portico, its *podium* for the senators, its *gradus* for the mob, and its exterior *baltei* and *præcinctiones* and *vomitoria.* The vaults in the basement of the outside walls have been let out—as though they were arches on the Greenwich Railway —to those who carry on petty trades. There are blacksmiths' forges, and cobblers' stalls, and butchers' shops burrowing in this one of the few unrivalled monuments left of the grandeur of Imperial Rome; but, its degradation notwithstanding, the old amphitheatre still looks superb, and frowns down with infinite contempt on the biggest of the barracks which the Austrians have built up in its vicinity.

Half-past seven A.M. is perhaps not too early in the morning to drink coffee, or, perhaps, if case-hardened and your stomach will bear it, to indulge in the matutinal weed. You may read the newspaper, too, appropriately over your coffee and cigar; but it is a little too early, I think, to wear white-kid gloves and strut about with an eye-glass stuck in your optic muscles.

In goodness' name, for whom do these white-coated captains and lieutenants dandify themselves? Women are said to dress for one another: not to please the eyes of men, but to strike envy to the hearts of their own sex. So I suppose it is in mutual rivalry that the German officers are such tremendous bucks. In most European countries defective sight is held to be a disqualification for military services; but to judge from the number of eye-glass wearers—many of them mere boys—I saw before eight o'clock in the *caffè*, nearly half the garrison of Verona must be purblind.

At eight I went to the Archduke's again. I had retained since six, as a guide, an Italian lad, who was a kind of ostler at La Colomba d'Oro. I think he must have been half-witted. In any case, he was so desperately afraid of the Austrian soldiers that he could not approach a corporal without assuming the posture of adoration, or pass a sentry without quivering like an aspen. This lily-livered wight being rather an impediment than an assistance, I dismissed him in peace, and prosecuted my further inquiries alone. But my second journey to the Archduke was as fruitless as the first. I was told that I must go to the police, as a preliminary measure, to have my passport viséd. The police-office is in the Piazza dei Signori, a mile and a half away. Thither I sped, to find it surrounded by troops, who with difficulty allowed me to pass into a crowded and dirty room full of Prussian shoemakers, French milliners, and Swiss couriers, all begging and praying for their passports to be viséd.

I had to wait in this den a full hour, and watch the resuscitation of the whole hideous machinery of the passport system, which, I had thought, was happily abolished for ever. But it is astonishing how soon the memory of the bad returns, and how easily we fall into the way of doing evil. Give me but a fortnight to drill my men, and I would undertake to furnish you with any number of sworn tormentors or familiars of the Inquisition. Grubby registers were consulted; fresh entries were made; you were teased with trivial questions; the old muttering and mumbling, and reading signatures upside down; the old stamping with greasy blue ink, and scrawling illegible nonsense on honest paper, and countersigning, and numbering, and sanding, and blotting, and smearing took place; and after every man had got somebody else's passport, and an amicable scramble for a distribution of property had taken place, we scampered back to the Archduke's for the final permission. Arrived at the Casa Peris, we were allowed the *entrée* of the back-stairs; and, after being repulsed at the doors of many military departments, from the "Train Commando" to the "Hydrographisches Bureau,"—the Inundation Office, I suppose,—we found, in a garret, Hauptmann von Somebody, and Oberlieutenant von Something else, breakfasting heavily on beefsteak and cabbage. The Hauptmann turned his back upon us, and the Oberlieutenant, taking our passports, and flinging them on one side, ordered us peremptorily to wait "down-stairs."

As the staircase was barely wide enough for two persons to pass one another, "down-stairs" would only mean the coal-cellar; but beefsteak and cabbage are holy things, and will not bear interference. Not being able to find the cellar, I chose the second-floor landing for an ante-chamber, and sitting down on the stairs, cooled my heels there until the Hauptmann and the Oberlieutenant had finished their breakfast. The capacity of the human stomach as a receptacle for beef and cabbage is extensive; but it has its limits. Being full, the satiated functionaries addressed themselves to our little business. Then the Adjutant-General, and finally, I suppose, the Archduke, had to be consulted, and we received our passports and a magic slip of paper attached to each—a *lascia passare,* or permission to proceed by rail from Verona to Peschiera. The Prussian shoemaker was especially overjoyed, and seemed to be thankful as for some special deliverance. I do not know that there exists in war any particular prejudice against shoemakers—it is our tailors, perhaps, whom we are more disposed to kill so soon as the battle-trumpet sounds; but this man was a Prussian as well as a shoemaker, and he had seemed all the morning haunted by an uneasy expectation of being fallen upon and massacred by the Austrians, merely because he was a countryman of the abhorred Bismark.

The landlord of the Colomba d'Oro, having presented us with *his* permission to quit the Austrian territory in the shape of receipted bills,—whose amount, so far as my own was concerned, led me to the conviction that the Clarendon in Bond-street is not such a dear hotel after all,—we started in the hotel-omnibus for the railway-station. It was by this time past ten; but the landlord, as he took from us seventy *soldi* apiece omnibus fare, gave us a solemn assurance that the time-bill had been altered, and that the train did not start until eleven. The man knew perfectly well that he was telling a lie; but seventy soldi a head, when you have an omnibus-load of a dozen, are something in these times; and, besides, he had an ulterior object. A little Venetian, who had carefully concealed from the authorities the fact that he was one, and had somehow procured a French passport, remarked solemnly, as we left the Colomba, "In this same omnibus shall we have to travel to Peschiera." We tried to think him a false prophet; but his prediction turned out to be true. When we reached the station, the porters laughed in our faces, and told us that the train had left a full hour before. Nothing was to be done but to return to the Colomba d'Oro, abuse the landlord, hear him tell more lies, and then fall to a-chaffering with him for the horsing of the omnibus to Peschiera.

The war is not yet a day old, yet things seem to have gone back a dozen years already. Here were the good old times of haggling and bargaining with *vetturini*—of threats, recriminations, and vows of good faith as false as dicers' oaths—come back as though by magic. At last, for the hire of a rickety omnibus, drawn by two miserable spavined jades, —one of them by Rosinante out of Galloping Dreary Dun, the other brother to the celebrated candidate for the Cow-cross Stakes, on which Petruchio rode to his marriage with Katharine,—we agreed to pay about double the first-class railway-fare between Verona and the frontier. But we were lucky, as it turned out, to obtain any conveyance at all. An interdict had been placed on all the diligences and post-chaises. Nothing, in fact, save military baggage-wagons, was allowed to circulate.

By two o'clock we were at Castelnuovo, and soon afterwards came in sight of Peschiera. The drive along the shores of the Lago di Garda is exquisitely beautiful. On this, a lovely day in leafy June, the water looked so blue, the distant mountains were so glowing in purple and orange tints, the sails of the fisher-boats glanced so snowy white, the tall pines spread their velvet-green canopy of foliage so witchingly, that the temptation to leap from the omnibus, produce a sketch-book and a box of moist water-colours, and fall to limning on the spot, was well-nigh irresistible. On reflection, however, it appeared that a better time might be selected for taking sketches on the Lago di Garda. In numerous convenient eyries on its banks, Austrian soldiers are posted, and more than one sketching civilian has been fired at lately, on the assumption that he was "taking plans" of the fortifications of Peschiera. The anathemas of the Old and New Societies of Painters in Water Colours rest on the fortifications of Peschiera!

The Austrian engineers are doing their best to ruin the Lago di Garda. The foreground they have spoilt already. As we journeyed onward we could feed our eyes on one side with all the luxuriant beauty of the lake; so calm, so blue, so sunny, so happy. On the other, the bowels of the earth were being ruthlessly dug up, and hordes of soldier-slaves in white coats were heaping the sods into breastworks and strengthening them with fascines. Most hideous did their picks and mattocks and wheelbarrows look on the border of this Paradise. It was as though you saw Death digging his first grave in a snug corner of Eden, and waiting with a leer for our dear brother departed. On one side, then, you saw horrid, ugly, devilish War; on the other, the inestimable beauty and repose of the Peace of Nature, which is as the Peace of God, and passeth all understanding.

Over moats and drawbridges we rattled into Peschiera, which really is so very paltry a town that to fortify it seems not like gilding refined gold, but locking up a brass farthing in a silver casket. I suppose, however, that the strategic position of Peschiera makes it of importance as a fortress. I do not believe in fortresses myself, holding that there was never a citadel so strong but that sooner or later it fell, and that the final cause of all strongholds is to be taken. We were very glad to get into Peschiera, and gladder still to get out of it. Half an hour after our departure the Austrians locked up the place for good and all, and neither natives nor strangers are now allowed ingress or egress. On the whole, I think I would rather be a cabin-boy on board a South-Shields collier than Podestà of Peschiera.

After another examination of passports and a new bargain-battle with the *vetturino* who was to take us to Desenzano, we entered omnibus number two, and had another two hours' drive to the frontier of the kingdom of Italy. I suppose we were favoured with the very laziest driver ever whelped. He was not even to be moved into activity by the offer of a collective *buona mano* of enormous extent, but lolled on his box in a calm state of semi-somnolence, sucking the butt-end of that whip the other extremity of which we should have so dearly liked to apply to his own shoulders. My companion in the *coupé*—for it was a double omnibus—was a fat German gentleman whom I shall always remember from his having presented me with one of the most execrable cigars ever manufactured. He was very friendly, and at great pains to assure his fellow-travellers that he was not an Austrian; but I have a shrewd suspicion that I had met him before as a seller of meerschaum pipes in the Rauhenheim Strasse, Vienna. His stock of Italian was limited to one word, "*Subito*," which he dinned without intermission into the driver's ears, who only slept the sounder. The German gentleman's warnings of "*Kein trinkgeld, kein trinkgeld,*" were quite thrown away on this dense oaf, whom not even the promise in his own language of a bribe could arouse.

The frontier line between the dominions of Francis Joseph and Victor Emmanuel is marked on the Austrian side only by a post painted in the imperial colours, black and yellow, and an oval signboard with the word *grenze*. I do not know, as a general rule, anything more insignificant to outward view than the actual frontier line between two States. You may play at hopscotch over it all day long without fear of the resentment of hostile armies. It is only by common accord to quarrel that certain points on the line have been fixed upon as objective; and it is only on the general's map and at the green-table of diplomacy that the frontier assumes its real importance.

At this *grenze* the last inspection of our passports—I think it was the ninth that morning—took place. The drowsy driver was just preparing to lunge into Italy, when a gendarme seized the horses' heads, and another asked us half insinuatingly, half menacingly, if we knew anything of a "Signor Bianchi." Nobody knew him, of course; our passports were all scrupulously *en règle*, so there was no more to be said. In another moment we were in Lombardy,—in the Regno d' Italia. "*Bianchi hat etwas gethan,*" said the German gentleman, with a look of great wisdom. It was clear that Bianchi was wanted, and that the Austrians would have been very glad to get hold of him. I wonder whether the little Venetian who had contrived to procure a French passport was Bianchi. Small blame to him if he concealed his identity. There are certain critical moments when it becomes a moral duty to swear that black is white.

The jolly Italian *doganieri* at the King of Italy's custom-house fifty yards on just took the trouble to ascertain from our papers who we were, and made a perfunctory examination of our luggage; that is to say, of the luggage of my companions. It is certain that the writer of this brought nothing into the world, and it is equally certain that, were a hostile bullet or an Austrian rope to send him out of it presently, he would leave nothing behind him but a race-glass and an Italian dictionary, and some socks and pocket-handkerchiefs. That is all I have at present. I have put off the old Adam, and begun the world afresh, and the plunder of my effects would not fatten a flea. The inspection over, we shook hands all round, including the *doganieri*; and if I for one did not join in the shout of "*Viva Italia!*" which arose from our wayworn group, it was because I was adust, and, being a foreigner, afraid of taking liberties.

In the picturesque town of Desenzano, which stands in

need of a little pulling down and building up again—and it would be as well, perhaps, if the Desenzanian housemaids made the beds before five in the afternoon; for the sight of mattresses and sheets hanging out of window at that hour, in order, I suppose, to air them, and bake the fleas in the afternoon sun, is not pretty—at Desenzano, I say, we found the railway train waiting, and at nine o'clock on Friday evening we were in Milan.

It was at this moment difficult to know where I could find Garibaldi. It was not known with certainty at Milan. His movements are rapid and secret. He had left Como, the head-quarters of the Garibaldini, I was told. He had gone to Lecco, to Bergamo, to Cremona, or even farther south to Bari and Barletta, at which last point his son Menotti and another considerable force of volunteers is stationed, ready to go—no man can tell whither, and no man should know whither, till the right time comes. On Saturday morning, however, I took the train to Camerlata, and thence drove in a carriage to Como, on the shore of the lake. Six thousand volunteers were in garrison at Como, and, to my great satisfaction, I found that Garibaldi had returned from his tour of inspection, and was at Como too.

NOTE. I have very scrupulously suppressed the description of all that I saw of actual hostile operations between the Italians and the Austrians in Venetia and in the Tyrol in the months of June and July 1866. I am not a "military critic;" and I imagine, were I to venture on military criticism, that my remarks would be equally offensive, both as to form and to foundation, to soldiers and to civilians, to Italians and to Austrians.

V.

FERRARA.

August 5.

I ARRIVED in this interesting Italian town early on Sunday morning, in company with seven young Italian noblemen, my intimate friends. Our mission was one of State; indeed, we formed the *personnel* of an embassy sent by the most serene Republic of Venice to the equally illustrious Don Alfonso d'Este, Duke of Ferrara. I may mention that our train comprised the gallant Don Apostolo Gazzella, the grave Giacopo Liverotto, and that lively little dog Maffeo Orsini, who sings such rare drinking-songs, and has a face so beardless and so buxom, that you might easily mistake him for a woman. From this you may judge that we were all very gay cavaliers indeed, and made a very lively appearance as we swaggered past the old Castello and down the Strada de' Mercanti, the velvet and satin of our doublets rustling, the plumes swaling in our bonnets, and the hilts of our rapiers glancing in the sun.

I know not whether it was the choice Lambrusco we had quaffed at our collation at the sign of Le Tre Corone, or some foregone predisposition to mischief which possessed me, but as we were passing the Ducal Palace I must needs, and in spite of the remonstrances of my companions, clamber up to the plinth of one of the columns of the gateway, and, standing on tiptoe, make a dash with my dagger at a big letter B cut in stone, and which was indeed the first letter of my Lady Duchess's name sculptured beneath her coat of arms, the which was displayed by the side of her husband's, in the midst of the architrave. Some of the young gallants laughed at my madcap freak, but the grave Giacopo shook his head, and opined that it was likely to prove a bad business. If I remember aright, I had met the Duchess before, in the gardens of the Grimani Palace at Venice, one night during the carnival, and had had a few words with her.

The news of the mischief I had wrought soon reached the ducal ears, and about an hour before dinner I was arrested by a man in black, named Rustighello, was heavily fettered, and thrown into the deepest dungeon beneath the ducal coal-cellar. Later in the afternoon, a guard of halberdiers conducted me to a splendid apartment in the palace, where I found the Duke and Duchess. They also seemed to have had words. The countenance of Don Alfonso wore a very evil expression, and the Duchess had apparently been crying. I heard her mutter, as we entered, that the Duke was her fourth husband, and that he had better take care. To my astonishment, I was not ordered to immediate execution. I was received, on the contrary, most affably. The politeness of Don Alfonso was exquisite. He was good enough to inquire into the history of my early life, and was so obliging as to offer me a commission in the Ferrarese army; but I thankfully declined the honour, having no reason to complain of my then employers, the Most Serene Republic, and my state of life, that of a captain in the Venetian Heavy Horse. The Duke, however, vowed by Hercules—one of his Grace's ancestors—that I should drink with him. Rustighello, who was a kind of butler as well as sheriff's officer, brought in a flask of Asti *spumante ;* and the Duke, who was in a sportive humour, insisted that my Lady Duchess should fill the goblets for us. This she did, her hand trembling strangely the while. Don Alfonso looked toward me, and I wished him luck, and I felt quite nice; for it is, after all, rather the proper kind of thing to do, to drink with a live Duke. His Grace did not say anything about t'other bottle; but, with a wish that what I had taken might do me good, bestowed on me a paternal benediction, and, scowling at the Duchess, went out for a little walk.

I observed that, as that scoundrelly catchpole Rustighello followed his master, he opened his curiously-slashed sleeve and laughed in it. No sooner had the pair quitted the apartment, than the Duchess rushed to the door, locked it, and informed me, in a rapid recitative, that the Duke was a villain, that I had been poisoned, and had not ten minutes to live. At the same time she forced on my attention a small black bottle, containing a quantity of Old Doctor Jacob Townsend's sarsaparilla, and telling me that it was an antidote, bade me drink it. I was at first reluctant to obey her, for there was no end to the naughty fibs told by that woman, but eventually, feeling as though I had a quantity of red-hot watchsprings underneath my waistcoat, which were beginning to uncoil themselves, I swallowed the mixture; it was very nasty, but made me quite well again. The Duchess then implored me to leave Ferrara by the next train for Bologna, and with a wish that she might never see me again—a wish cordially reciprocated by the undersigned—attempted to kiss me. I successfully resisted the indelicate attempt, and glad to be well out of this improper place, went for a stroll in the Piazza de' Signori.

There, at the Caffè Tofana, I met Gazzella, Orsini, and the rest, who told me that through the kind offices of a Spanish gentleman of their acquaintance, named Gubetta, they had been bidden to a hot supper that very evening, at the Princess Negroni's. Her excellency lived on the first-floor over the chemist and druggist's shop, next door to the Ducal Palace. They proposed that, although uninvited, I should join them. The linkboy of the Corriere della Mattina, they said, would pass me in. Now, I know that I ought at once to have driven to the station, and taken a ticket for Bologna; but hot suppers were always my weakness, and, in an evil moment, I consented to wait on the Princess.

We went, and had a very good time. There were *beccafichi*, there was pigeon pie, and a delicious Nesselrode pudding, which, however, had slightly too strong a flavour of bitter almonds. The best *chefs* will sometimes err. Francatelli has been known to nod. We were joined at supper by several beautiful young ladies, in low-necked dresses, who subsequently entertained us with music and dancing. Apostolo Gazzella, who has a rich bass voice, gave us "Mynheer van Dunk," and Maffeo Orsini sang a comic song with a roaring chorus. I have forgotten its name, but it was something about the way to be happy. Everybody had proposed everybody else's health, and we were almost ripe for "Auld lang syne," when, in the distance, the sounds of a chant, which was anything but a comic song, became audible. The voices came nearer and nearer, and I could make out the words, "*Nisi Dominus ædificat domum,*" to which succeeded some most unpleasant extracts from the Burial Service.

The young ladies in low dresses had all disappeared, and the wax-candles went out one after another, leaving a disagreeable odour behind. Presently the great folding-doors of the saloon flew open, and there appeared on the threshold my Lady Duchess, dressed all in black, attended by seven Capuchin monks, all in white, who, ranged in a row, were singing "Down among the dead men." The Duchess came forward and explained, that as we had once given her a ball at Venice —she alluded to that little misunderstanding at the Grimani Palace—she had deemed it her duty to return the compliment by offering us a supper at Ferrara. She went on to inform us that there was a pound and a half of strychnine in the pigeon pie, and three-quarters of a pint of prussic acid in the Nesselrode pudding. That abominable pudding!—I had partaken twice of it. Then, directing the monks to draw on one side a little, she showed us that, in addition to board, she had provided lodging for us in the shape of seven patent coffins, adding that if we wanted washing, the seven monks could supply us with any quantity of holy water. I made bold to remark, in the most pointed manner, that her accommodation was insufficient, seeing that we were eight in number, and seeing that only coffins for seven, with Capuchins to follow, had been provided. Whereat she screamed, and, bundling my young friends out of the room, once more produced the black bottle, and prescribed the mixture as before. I indignantly refused the antidote, and remarking that I considered her a highly offensive person, not to be permitted to go about any longer poisoning the junior branches of the nobility with impunity, informed her that I proposed to despatch her with the carving-knife, and without further notice. This I presently did, and, as she gave up the ghost, she told me that she was my Mother. Upon this, with a disagreeable consciousness that several Pharaoh's serpents were in a state of combustion at the pit of my stomach, I sang a brief song, in the minor key, on the subject of maternal love, and expired. At which the curtain fell, and life's brief candle was blown out. I forgot to state that my mother's name was Mademoiselle Tietjens—that is to say, *Lucrezia Borgia*.

Now I do most conscientiously assure my readers that, although I alighted from the through train from Milan to Ferrara on this Sunday morning, in the company only of a lively little lieutenant of Garibaldini on leave from Creto di Bona, and who was anxious to air his red shirt on a tour through Venetia—although I myself was clad in garments not more romantic than a travelling-suit of brown holland and a straw hat, and carried a perfectly modern carpet-bag in my hand—and, finally, although I drove from the station to the inn in a hack-cab, whose driver was slightly elevated with perfectly modern rum—I did, during the whole of some six hours' sojourn in Ferrara, experience all the sensations, and see in imagination all the things to which I have alluded above. To be sure, I was full of the Borgias when I came hither, for I had seen some of the golden tresses of the beautiful wicked daughter of La Vanozzi and Alexander the Sixth, which are preserved at Milan, and a learned English medical friend had been talking about some original letters of Donna

Lucrezia which he had discovered in the municipal archives, and which he proposed to translate and publish.*

But it was the town itself that took me back to the sixteenth century, and the days of daggers, doublets, and mortal doses. They have done wisely to erect the railway-station so very far from Ferrara itself. The enormous Campo di Marte intervenes between modern civilisation and the wholly mediæval city of Lucrezia Borgia; she walks in all the Piazzi; her shadow is on every wall. Rustighello and Gubetta are lurking round every corner, dogging your footsteps to destruction. Pray, can you tell me why there are, to this day, so many doctors' shops in Ferrara? Can you give me a reason why the "Spezeria dei Fratelli Forzadura"—what a name!—is a dark cavern, through whose shadows loom ghostly-looking jars, containing, no doubt, aqua Tofana, laurel-water, powdered glass—for flesh wounds——and Scheele's preparation, highly concentrated? Can you tell me why the Vicolo delle Catene—Chain-lane—should run out of the Strada Oscura—Dark-street; and why the Contrada dell' Agonia—Agony-road—should be so very near the Piazza de' Martiri? The whole place reeks of poison and carving-knives, and masks and fetters, and man-traps and spring-guns. Don't tell me that this is all idle fancy. Go and look at Ferrara, and you will at once confess that it is the abode of horror and the cave of despair. Bologna, with its interminable porticoes, is gloomy enough; but Ferrara is the very quintessence of the Tenebra in architecture. The Castello strongly resembles the City Prison at Holloway, em-

* Mr. William Gilbert has since published his elaborate vindication of the terrible Duchess of Ferrara.

browned by the dust of ages, and the Albergo del Pellegrino is as like Newgate as one pea is like unto another. Ferrara, in one sense, may be said to rival the Escorial, for it is one huge gridiron of window-bars; and, curiously, the huge cathedral is dedicated to San Lorenzo.

The heat of the sun being positively scorching on Sunday morning, I could not walk half-a-dozen paces without being reminded of the savoury saint, *muy buen asado y tostado*, with whom I made acquaintançe last January in Spain. Ferrara is one cage. Ferrara is barred by an undying statute of architectural limitations. The windows of the palaces and public buildings are all barred. Those of the private edifices are closely grated. The fanlights over the doors are protected by iron rods; the pleasant view of internal courtyards and orange-trees—Seville oranges, doubtless, and very bitter—is intercepted by heavy trelliswork. I saw a cobbler at work, although it was Sunday morning. He was working behind iron bars, like Mr. Benjamin Webster in the Bastille. I saw a woman selling peaches and ripe figs behind bars. The butchers' shops were simply twin brothers to the dens of the wild beasts at the Zoological Gardens; and the clerk at the Post-office was asleep in the corner of his cage, and had to be stirred up like the hyæna with the long pole of an umbrella, before he would answer questions. Why all these bars? Are the mammas of Ferrara apprehensive that their daughters will elope with the officers of the garrison, or their housemaids run off with the baker's man? Is the city inhabited only by usurers, and do they fear that their strong boxes may be invaded by some Italian Manteuffel? Are the houses full of starlings that "can't get out"?

Ah, no! Ferrara is bolted and barred up, and put, like the Koh-i-noor, behind a wire fence, because the people are all so terribly afraid of Lucrezia Borgia. She fell in love with the Camerine, at the Pellegrino, on Wednesday afternoon, and by Saturday night he died of the cholera-morbus. She asked the Archbishop of Ferrara to dinner on Friday, and on the same evening his Grace was a cold corpse. They said it was indigestion; but it was only Donna Lucrezia. For only a wink—a mere wink of disparagement—that unhappy captain of the National Guard died of the colic the day before yesterday; and the wretched landlord of the Caffè Tofana, who ventured to observe to the notary that we lived in ticklish times, was laid hold of by Rustighello and his followers, and was hanged, they say, in the great tower of the Castello this morning. Donna Lucrezia's brougham is always standing before the Spezeria of the Brothers Forzadura; and she is strongly suspected of impregnating by wholesale the cavours and virginias of the governmental tobacco-shops with opium and cocculus indicus. This is Ferrara. It smells of the cord, the dagger, and the poison-vial. The legend beneath the city arms is, "*Guai se ti sfugge un moto.*" If you doubt my word, go and look at it.

Darkness is not an indispensable concomitant of horror. There was light enough, you know—although it was but darkness visible—in that terrible place which Milton drew and whither Dante went. Thus Ferrara seemed ten times more horrible to me, because on Sunday morning the sun shone so brightly on its grim houses and dismal rows of dungeon bars. Shone! The sun rather blazed, pierced you with flaming glaives, came down upon you in a vulgarised

Danaëan shower—red-hot coppers in lieu of new Mint tokens. The dogs flatly refused to venture out in the sun. The very cats were chary of basking in it, and, peering from beneath archways, put one paw forward into the blaze and then drew it back again, broiled—the very converse of boys who test with one foot the temperature of the stream in which they yearn to bathe. Shadows of deepest blue did the barred projections of the casements cast on the walls, whose laminæ of lime had been cracking and scaling off for centuries beneath these pitiless rays. There was scarcely a soul abroad. Now and then you saw something living glide along close to the wall, pelted by the sun's darts, and disappear. If it was green, it was a lizard; if it was gray, it was a rat; if it was black, and wore a cassock and a shovel-hat, it was a priest.

The common object of myself and the little lieutenant of Garibaldini was forthwith to cross the Po, and proceed through Rovigo and Padua to Vicenza, where my companion had business with the commissary of the King, Mordini. But to enter the Venetian territory, even the portion evacuated three weeks since by the Austrians and now occupied by the Italians, was a thing easier said than done. There is a bran-new railway from Pontelagoscuro, on the Po, to Vicenza; but the Austrians smashed the bridge over the Po to pieces ere they left, as a parting token of their affection for their quondam subjects, and, kindly leaving the rails untouched, took away all the locomotives and most of the carriages. A railway without locomotives is as unsatisfactory as mustard without beef. As Rome was not built in a day, so are things in Italy never done in a hurry; and it does not appear to have yet occurred to the railway authorities that they might get a few locomotives down from Piacenza or Bologna to replace those stolen by the Austrians. In any case, they have not taken any such steps, and the railway from Ferrara being thus quite useless, the jolly old diligence, cumbersome, uncomfortable, and barbarous, has been brought out again, and looks as fresh as the paint of the year 1836, and the dirt of the year 1846, and the dust of the year 1856 can make it. So it is, hey! for the good old wheels whose tires are always coming off, and the good old delays, stoppages, and breakdowns, and the good old rope harness, and the good old postillion in a mountebank's jacket, who winds the good old airs on the cracked bugle-horn, and comes round at the end of every stage, holding out his hat, and craving coppers like a common beggar. There are coincidences in this world. A Tory Ministry, I perceive, has snatched the reins of power in England; and the *diligenza* is to the fore again at Ferrara.

This truly Conservative slow coach was full on Sunday morning, and we were bound to seek some other means of conveyance into the Veneto. I was very anxious to get out of Ferrara; for, to tell truth, the plenitude of druggists' shops had begun somewhat to alarm me, and I was not at all easy in my mind about a certain *cotelette di vitello, con zucchette,* on which I had just breakfasted at the restaurant adjoining the station. The damsel who waited on me was far too fair, and there was slightly too much of the red gold in the auburn of her locks. Let it be assumed, for the sake of argument, that, in a purely platonic spirit and before I ordered the veal chop, I had winked at that young woman. Just imagine the consequences, supposing her to have been married, and her maiden name something beginning with a B. "*Son le Lu-*

crezie rare a provar," says the page in *Maria di Rohan;* yet may this young woman have been Lucrèce.

The *diligenza* in default, the most obvious vehicle was a gig. Respectability would seem to be very rife in this part of the country, for almost everybody drives a gig. The *vetturino* who drove us from the station to a most cut-throat-looking little hovel in the suburbs, which was his own livery-and-bait stable indeed, offered to drive us to Vicenza, a distance of forty-five miles, "like the wind," and with two fiery, and most valiant horses, "*freschi e valorississimi cavalli,*" for—how much do you think?—a hundred and eighty francs. "Otto Marenghi,* Eccellenza, is the last price," quoth the *vetturino*, throwing up his hands. "It is the just and exact sum which a man of honour and of heart should ask for such a journey."

I remembered in this conjuncture an anecdote I once heard, of a gentleman who was accosted by one of the itinerant dealers in fine art who hang about the Royal Exchange and Bartholomew-lane, with those wonderful daubs in oil, surrounded by Dutch-gilt frames, representing the Eruption of Mount Vesuvius, Tintern Abbey by Moonlight, and similar subjects. For mere curiosity's sake, he asked the dealer how much he would take for a pair of landscapes. The dealer, probably assuming that his customer had just bought largely

* As I have already said, the gold Napoleon is called throughout Northern Italy "*un Marengo.*" It is curious to mark how indelible is the stamp impressed by the first Napoleon on the customs, and even the thoughts, of a people by whom perhaps the Bonapartes have been and are more scurrilously abused than by any other nation in Europe. No language is too foul for an Italian to use when he speaks of the Emperor past or the Emperor present; yet there is scarcely an element in the modern civilisation or the modern freedom of Italy which has not been rooted into the land by the strong will of a Bonaparte.

into the Funds or drawn his January dividends, replied, that as a particular and personal favour he would part with the two pictures for seventy guineas. "I'll give you thirty shillings," said the gentleman. "They're yours, sir," cried the dealer, in quite a transport of delight, and he subsequently acknowledged that there was a clear profit of fifteen shillings on the transaction.

So when the *vetturino* told me that eight Napoleons was the lowest price he could possibly take, I told him that I would give two, and no more. Eventually—that is to say, after infinite haggling and chaffering—we struck a bargain for forty-five francs, between which and the upset price of a hundred and eighty-three there was, it will be admitted, a slight difference. Most things in Italy, indeed, must be purchased on the principle followed in a Dutch auction. You must bid downwards, or you will be unconscionably swindled. I told a tailor at Milan the other day to make me some white waistcoats, for which, foolishly omitting to make a bargain beforehand, he charged a price so ludicrously extortionate, that I offered him just one-half, threatening in case of his refusal to accept it to complain to the British ambassador in Florence, and all the tribunals in the Kingdom of Italy. He accepted the composition quite cheerfully, and I daresay, had I persisted, would have submitted to a still further reduction. A born Italian, I doubt not, would have got the things even cheaper than I did.

The complaisant *vetturino* had covenanted that he should not be obliged to start till the afternoon heats were over. So till five o'clock, and till it had cooled a little, we went to the Pellegrino,—infamously filthy, like all Italian inns away from the great cities,—and lay down on a sofa in a darkened room, vainly endeavouring to chase away the flies, and to slake our thirst with lemonade and peaches. If I had carried the cholera away with me from Ferrara, I should, I daresay, have ascribed my mishap to the wicked wiles of Lucrezia Borgia, which is the way of the world. It is always the salmon, and never the wine. The terrible Duchess has done it all. We quite forget the lemonade and the peaches.

VI.

FROM FERRARA TO ROVIGO.

August 6.

In the Campo di Marte, at Ferrara, were parked a hundred of the heaviest pieces of field-artillery. This was the first sign I had seen, since leaving Milan, of Italy being in the midst of war. Let me mention that for the gig with which the *vetturino* originally contracted to supply us had been substituted a carriage with four seats; and we had now two additional travelling-companions—a merchant of Bologna, and a captain of artillery belonging to the royal army. They were excellent company—civil, intelligent, and communicative; indeed, a sulky Italian is almost a monstrosity. I was not sorry to have an opportunity of conversing with an officer in the regulars; for, on the *toujours-perdrix* principle, I found myself growing rather weary of the eternal self-laudations of the Garibaldini, their bitter complaints against La Marmora and the Ministry, and their incessant abuse of France and Napoleon. They are very courageous, enthusiastic, and sincerely patriotic fellows, these Red Shirts; but it is certain that they do brag and bluster to an almost incredible extent—that they quite forget that but for Magenta and Solferino, and the ally whom they vilipend so vehemently, the Austrians would still be in Milan, and the Monsignori still in the Legations; in fact, that but for their present bugbear, the Emperor Napoleon, there would never have been a kingdom of Italy at all.

"We want no foreign aid," scream the Garibaldini; "we have been long enough in a state of pupilage. We can even do without Prussia. We will march to Vienna alone. *Faremo da noi.*"

Now, "*Faremo da noi*" is a very terse and piquant expression; only, if my memory serves me correctly, the people of this beautiful peninsula were in the habit of screaming for at least half a century, "*Italia fara da se.*" It was found eventually that Italia could not do anything for herself, and that France had to do it for her. Ingratitude, I suppose, is a political crime, whose prevalence is universal. The present generation of Englishmen is, perhaps, not sufficiently grateful to the good Tory statesmen who, according to the Tory journals of the present day, abolished the corn-laws, emancipated the Catholics, and carried parliamentary and municipal reform. It may be that we have forgotten who our real benefactors were, and that we are under quite a mistaken impression in supposing that the Liberals, and not the Conservatives, conferred on us the constitutional benefits just mentioned. But Italy cannot plead a long lapse of time as an excuse for her ingratitude to France. 1859 is not so long ago, after all; and in 1859 the Frenchman, now denounced, maligned, and scorned, was hailed as a liberator and acknowledged as a protector. It is barely possible that ere long Italy will be forced to incur a fresh debt of gratitude to France, and will as swiftly ignore it, as she has ignored all previous claims.

The captain of artillery told us that some of the cannon

we saw in the Campo di Marte had been at Borgoforte, and had done good service there. It was a grand affair—a "*giorno di festa,*" he said. The guns were splendidly served; and at night the rockets whizzed about in the beautiful blue sky in a manner which might have made the fireworks purveyors of Mabille and the Château des Fleurs frantic with envy. With pardonable pride he pointed out the mathematical accuracy with which the guns were ranged—"*benissime allineati,*" as he said. There did not seem, indeed, to be the deviation of an inch from the straight line in front, or in the intervals between. The guns were burnished until they shone like gold. Pretty little penthouses were built over the touch-holes, to protect them from dust or moisture. With hairbreadth exactitude the ammunition-wagons were disposed behind. Wheels, bolts, chains, limbers, powder-chests were all fitted with exquisite nicety, and kept in scrupulous tidiness. These hundred big guns had really a prim, toyshop air. Murder became Quaker-like, and the accessories of slaughter were finished with the patient elaboration of a Chinese rice-paper miniature.

After all, there is nothing like pipeclay, and pipeclay's twin-brother, apple-pie order, to which red tape, who is sometimes disowned by the family, is cousin-german. As an example of neatness and orderly arrangements, few things can surpass a battery of artillery. Have you never seen such a battery trotting by, the horses keeping time exactly to the cheerful strains of the band? It is true that the drivers, perched on those ammunition-chests, must have rather a hard time of it, and should be earnest reformers so far as concerns a redistribution of seats; but how charming is the spectacle, how coquettishly natty the details, how daintily agreeable the whole effect! Spurs seem to jingle, chains to clank, guns to gleam, buckets to wag, the very drivers even to bump, in cadence. You talk about "lumbering"* cannon; yet these huge engines of destruction seem to be moved as easily as though they were children's perambulators.

What a pity it is that when the time arrives for all these pretty things to be put to their proper use — that of destruction — all the mathematical accuracy, all the toyshop primness, all the Quaker-like neatness, all the sparkling, coquettish, natty features of the regiment and the battery disappear!

The final cause of war is Anarchy, and on the battle-field the old Anarch reasserts himself, and makes ducks and drakes of the entire business. Chaos turned into a shambles—that is a battle. Your Dirk Stoops and Vandermeulens, your Horace Vernets and Geromes, your Bellangés and Armitages—famous battle-painters were all these; yet do I question whether any one of them ever drew a fight which resembled, even in a remote degree, the actual occurrence. A battle on canvas is to a battle in the real field as the brigands in *Fra Diavolo*, with their velvet-jackets and steeple-crowned hats, gay with parti-coloured streamers, are to the verminous varlets who captured Mr. Moens. A battle is a Row, with no police to stop it; and it is, besides, a row from which, even in the most heroic conflicts, a great many of the combatants run away.

It cannot be expected that the historians should tell the whole truth about a battle. They write, usually, many years

* I don't mean "limbering."

after the thing has happened, at a long distance from the spot, and with sources of information as to its scenes which are, to say the least, imperfect. M. Adolphe Thiers, writing *The Consulate and the Empire* in his luxurious library in the Place St. Georges, can have at the best but a very dim and uncertain notion of what Austerlitz and Wagram were really like. Even Mr. Carlyle, wonderful word-painter and picture-builder as he is, has not added much more to our stock of knowledge about Fontenoy than we already possessed in the brief, dry, poignant, sneering half-page in which Voltaire, in the *Siècle de Louis Quatorze*, sums up the great rout of the English Guards. And I hope that those who desire to know what a battle is like will not seek instruction at the mouth of Mr. Kinglake. A battle is a shindy. A battle is Donnybrook Fair, interspersed with long, dreary, dusty, hungry, thirsty intervals of waiting. Wait, wait, wait! The soldiers in a battle have to wait as long as Mariana in the Moated Grange. She waited until she wished that she were dead. The soldier often waits until a ball comes whistling by, and he falls dead without his wishes being consulted at all.

Perhaps the only artist ever fully qualified to paint battle scenes was Salvator Rosa. The inextricable muddle and imbroglio of his composition, with which his critics so bitterly reproached him, were precisely suited to the delineation of that greatest of all muddles—a battle. And Salvator's most peaceable characters all look as though they wanted to fight. In his rare religious pieces he has drawn the angel Gabriel in the likeness of a swashbuckling sergeant, and has made of Mary Magdalen a penitent baggage-wagon woman. He would have painted Custozza or Bezzecca to the life.

Do you know the mishap that turned the fortune of the day at the first-named combat against the Italians? It was not Durando's stupidity; it was not La Marmora's obstinacy. They are but scapegoats. It was not the Archduke Albert's chivalrous powers. All the Austrian archdukes are chivalrous and valiant, and the greater number of them are donkeys. The battle of Custozza was lost through a muddle. The huge overloaded wagons, drawn by the slowest of white oxen belonging to the Treno-Borghese—a very picturesque name for a very clodhopping concern—or Italian civil land-transport corps, got between the advanced guard and the main body of the King's army. The Austrian cannon began to thunder, and the dunderheaded wagoners of the Treno-Borghese, terrified out of their few wits, cut the traces and decamped. The Italian army was literally cut asunder by an impassable barricade, and the Austrians were enabled to gobble up an entire corps, without their comrades on the other side of the wagons being able to rescue them.

Precisely the same thing occurred five years ago, in America, at Bull Run. The Federal wagoners in the rear lost their senses, cut the traces, skedaddled; and the Federal army, which otherwise might have made an orderly retreat to Alexandria, was thrown into hopeless confusion, and compelled to stampede.

Very nearly the same thing took place on the 21st of last month, with the Garibaldini, at Bezzecca. The commissariat wagons, whose march from Storo had been delayed until the army was half-starved, came up in an endless string of beef, biscuit, and wine carts, exactly at the wrong moment, wedging up the road between Triano di Sotto and Bezzecca, and nearly succeeded in converting the Garibaldian movements into a scandalous rout.

All this, I trust, is not foreign to my original thesis that no real picture of a battle has yet been drawn or written. Do not look for such a picture from the pencil or the pen of a professional soldier—even were his name Napier. He has the honour of his calling, the prestige of his corps to maintain; nor is he, as a rule, at all anxious to let civilians know how many base and mean and grotesque elements are mingled with those which are grand and heroic in a battle. As for the common soldier, as has been admirably pointed out by Erckmann-Chatrian in the *Conscrit de* 1813, he sees less than nothing, unless, indeed, he happens to get killed, and then he sees something, but of a nature which he is not permitted to communicate. Putting this and that together, one is inclined to arrive at last at the conviction that the very best account of a battle the world has yet seen is the narrative of the onslaught on the Swedish fort by the Dutchmen in Knickerbocker's veracious history. It is meant to be a burlesque, but it reads terribly like truth for all that. Tipsy sergeants, bawling trumpeters, and abusive trulls; black eyes, ensanguined noses, and luckless musketeers, tumbling about, their falls broken by quagmires "prepared for them by nature, or some kindly cow;" cursing, swearing, calling names, dram-swigging, and running away; these are the chief components in Washington Irving's inimitable piece of drollery; and who shall deny that they form features very prominent indeed in every battle?

I have already warned you that the historians, with all their learning and eloquence, and the professional soldiers, with all their honourable candour, are but faintly to be trusted in this respect. They are averse from spoiling a noble thing; they shrink from marring the recital of an honourable action by the introduction of details painful, often ludicrous, but true.

For example, there is now lying a prisoner in the hospital at Brescia, and *with no less than seventeen wounds in him*, an Austrian captain of foot by the name of Rucciëka. Mark his name well. It is worth remembering. This gentleman fought like a Paladin—or perhaps much better than Paladins ever fought—at the Caffaro. Garibaldino after Garibaldino did he engage in single combat, smoking all the time; and ever and anon he would call out to his orderly, not for help, but for a fresh cigar or a new lucifer-match. At length, hacked, maimed, riddled, slashed, with bullets and sword-gashes and bayonet-thrusts, his own sabre broken, and the last cartridge for his revolver spent, he was overpowered by numbers and made prisoner. His very clothes were on fire, and I have seen one of the visiting-cards taken out of his portmonnaie by his captors. It is scorched to an oval form by the heat; but the neat copperplate inscription, "Hauptmann von Rucciëka" is yet visible. The *coup de grâce* was given him by a Garibaldino, who thrust his bayonet into him; but the blow being given with all his force, and the weapon being clumsily fixed to the barrel, it remained in his body like the matador's rapier in a bull's neck. Captain Rucciëka, disdaining to be carried to the rear, with seventeen wounds in him, walked proud and defiant to the last, with the bayonet sticking in him—where do you think? Why, just where the lumbar vertebræ of the spine should end and the caudal vertebræ—even were we Niam-Niams instead of men—should begin. They were afraid to pull the bayonet out till a doctor came, and he walked several hundred yards with the murderous thing stuck into that portion of the human frame where the back changes its name and is called something else.

Now where is the historian who would condescend to record this ungenteel but still more heroic fact, although candid army surgeons will tell you that at least five-and-twenty per cent of the wounds in a battle are, through no cowardice on the part of the sufferers, in this unromantic region? I am glad to say that the brave Captain Rucciëka is doing well, and in a fair way towards convalescence. The two rough soldiers who undressed and put him to bed knelt down by the side of his pallet and kissed him on the forehead. The Italian governor of Brescia has placed his carriage at his disposal against the time when he shall be fit to take an airing. The Italian ladies of Brescia have sent him so many jellies, and so many packets of cigars, that he might open a pastrycook's-shop, or a *bureau de tabac*, when he gets well. He, the poor captive captain, is more honoured by his enemies than John of France was by the Black Prince, or our own hero, Sir William Williams of Kars, by Mouravieff; and when I last heard of Captain Rucciëka he was sitting up in bed at Brescia, all blood and bandages, but with his seventeen wounds healing kindly. He was reading the *Neue Freie Presse* of Vienna, and smoking furiously; which is a fact for Mr. Pope and the United Anti-Tobacco Association to put into *their* pipe, and smoke too. I hope the Kaiser will make Captain Rucciëka a colonel. I hope he will send him the star of something studded with diamonds. But, fifty years hence, will any historian venture to allude to the circumstance of his walking a hundred yards with a bayonet wagging to and fro in the small of his back? I very much doubt it.

August 7.

I am glad to own that for many of the reflections on the actual aspect of war set down in my last I am indebted to my friend the artillery captain, a most judicious gentleman, of long experience and considerable information, and destitute, besides, of many of those prejudices which we are led to consider as well-nigh inseparable from professional soldiering. He had travelled much, and made many campaigns. He had been in the Crimea, and at the Tchernaya. He rendered full justice to the pluck and steadiness of the English army, but he declared that their *pas de charge* was a world too slow, and that, owing to the pedantic formality of their movements in a charge, they always lost twice as many men as the soldiers of the French and Italian army.

"In mechanics," he said, "you cannot have too little friction; for war you cannot have too much. And, by the bye," he continued, "when next you go to war, tell your quartermasters' people to *mark their mules*. Through rejecting the simple plan of branding their *bât* animals, the English must have lost in the Crimea hundreds of thousands of francs. Everybody stole the English mules—Frenchmen, Turks, Tartars, *ed anche noi Italiani*. I tell you that the Crimean war was one great carnival of plunder. I do not think your own officials steal. They are honest by nature and by choice; but they allow all the world to steal from them, and that is just as bad."

I could not but sit corrected under the artillery captain's strictures; and I remembered, with an uneasy twitch, a dashing young commissariat officer of my acquaintance, who bade fair to fulfil the most sanguine of the hopes we had formed in his regard, but who was so unfortunate as to be out a trifle in his accounts, to the extent of eleven thousand gallons of rum before he had been a month in the service. But there is no need to tell the story of Crimean mismanagement over again. I may just hint, however, that some of these days we may go to war once more, and then, perhaps, the authorities may attend to such minutiæ as marking their mules. I know that the hint is one exceedingly impertinent on my part, in the peculiarly invidious position I occupy; for, not later than last Thursday, I heard a young English gentleman, with very pink cheeks and without any beard, and who had just been gazetted to the proud post of ensign in a marching regiment, allude at a public *d'hôte* to the correspondents of the English press who were with our forces in the Crimea as "those cursed newspaper scribblers who went about poking their noses into what didn't concern them." But for the efforts of these "cursed scribblers," the number of brave soldiers who were starved and frozen in the Chersonese, and the number of beardless and pink-cheeked young ensigns who rotted with dysentery in the hospitals of Scutari, might have been considerably larger, I imagine.

I did not fail to compliment the captain on the very noble behaviour of the small detachment of regular artillerymen detailed to aid Garibaldi in his mountain operations, who, with weak numbers and very few guns, have saved the Red Shirts over and over again from thorough and disgraceful discomfiture. Indeed, I saw so much of the courage, skill, patience, and cheerfulness of the Italian artillerymen during my brief campaign in high latitudes, that I always feel inclined to raise my hat when I pass a private in that most plucky corps. The unprejudiced captain took the compliment, and I subsequently saw that he appreciated it by insisting on calling very late that night at Rovigo for a bottle of Lambrusco, and drinking the health of the "valorissimous British Army." But, on the present occasion, his candour rose superior to flattery.

"We do what we can," he said; "but it is certain that we brag tremendously. *La blague* is at the bottom of all bravery. All soldiers brag. The Bersaglieri do; so do the Zouaves. So do the Kaiser-jägers and the Uhlans. So, I daresay, do the Prussian Guards. We artillerymen crow over the line. Do your Highlanders and riflemen crow over your line? But *la blague* has its advantages. It keeps a regiment together. It is better than all the drums and all the flags in the world. It encourages the waverer, and makes the coward ashamed to fly. We are most of us cowards when we begin. Real courage consists in doing that which you are devilishly afraid of. *La blague*, however, should be confined to the ranks. Among officers it is offensive and contemptible. With them reason should supply the place of boasting. For the rest, *la blague* is only one of the innumerable varieties of fiction. It is surprising how much lying there is, not only before and after a battle, but during its continuance."

I took occasion, furthermore, to express my admiration for the sobriety, honesty, and civility shown by the Garibaldini to the populations of the villages through which they passed; but on this point the unprejudiced captain met me with a degree of scepticism which was, to say the least, mortifying.

"Where were you?" he asked.

"At head-quarters," I replied.

"Good," he continued; "you did not see the five thousand men who lagged behind, who spread out like fans as they straggled out of the ranks; who built themselves comfortable huts in shady copses; who went to bed for a couple of days in barns and haystacks; who sought out every remote farmhouse, every solitary cottage, every sequestered tavern; who ate and drank, and beat the tavern-keeper when he asked for payment; who kissed his maid, and kicked his wife; who drove off his cows, and stole his poultry, and smashed his crockeryware as a parting benediction. There are always about five thousand men, more or less, according to the strength of the main body, hanging about the skirts of every army, regular or irregular, with which I have ever been acquainted. I like the Garibaldini. I would put on a red shirt myself if it were not my trade to wear a blue coat. But the Garibaldini are not angels, and no army, save the Angelic Host in your *Paradise Lost*, ever marched without a fan-like fringe of stragglers and plunderers. They seek out very quiet country places for their depredations, where they steal, and break, and kill; there are no newspapers printed, and no gentry or priests to remonstrate. You, at head-quarters, see only the good and true men, who are always to the fore; who march though shoeless, who charge although starving, and who get shot or stabbed without complaining. When the battle is over, the stragglers and plunderers come to the front gaily. They are rosy, well-fed, strong, and full of spirits. They mount on the guard-room benches and tell lies. 'I killed the Croat corporal,' shouts one who never killed anything bigger than a *gallina*. 'I should have the epaulette for saving the colonel's life,' screams another; on the battle-day he was busy swilling up the milk in a dairy. And so on, and so on. And so it is with all the armies in the world. War would not be war else. Do you think that, if I were suddenly to empty the audience at the Scala at Milan, or better, the congregation at the Duomo any Sunday morning, into a bag, and shake them well up together, there would not be a great many rogues among them? And do you think that all the shaking in the world would turn the rogues into honest men? An army is an audience, an army is a congregation, and neither better nor worse than other flocks of human sheep."

Thus far the unprejudiced captain of artillery. You are not to suppose, however, that the visible aspect of war, or the merits or demerits of soldiers on the march, wholly furnished matter for our conversation as we four drove from Ferrara to Pontelagoscuro, on the shores of the broad and bright river Po. The merchant from Bologna had a great deal to say about the stagnation of commerce and the financial embarrassments of the Government; but still he deprecated the conclusion of an armistice, and wished the war to continue, at any sacrifice, until a peace could be negotiated on secure and honourable bases. The little Garibaldian lieutenant, who had been hopping about like a parched pea in a fire-shovel on his seat while the captain had talked of the five thousand plunderers in the trail of the Camicie Rosse, was of course for war—war to the knife—war to the fork, the spoon, the salt-cellar, and the pepper-castor—war to the last *lira* and the last *ragazzo*—war to extermination—war to spiflication. "*Guerra! guerra!*" There is a chorus, for men's voices, with this title, and to a most exciting tune, in a well-known Italian opera. We all joined hands and sang "*Guerra! guerra!*" till we were hoarse, and the *vetturino* turned round on his seat and yelled "*Guerra!*" too; and even the horses, who were by this time growing rather distressed, snorted fiercely and caracoled in a warlike manner.

To give them rest, and slake our own thirst, we halted at a roadside inn and partook of some *birrone di Marzo*. After the beer, and on calmer reflection, being asked for an opinion, I stated that were I an Italian I should be of the opinion of these gentlemen; but that, happening to be an Englishman, I was on the side of peace, and thought that the best thing they could do was to accept it, and, saying grace before meat, be thankful for the Veneto and all other good things. The captain of artillery, who wound up the discussion, said that he was partly of my mind and partly of that of the lieutenant and the merchant, but that there was a casting-vote at his disposal, and that he gave it in favour of continued war.

"I give it," he said, "as a soldier and as an Italian. It is all very well to talk of the blessings of peace, but we have not conquered Venetia; and although we are to have it, Austria flings it to us as a marrowbone is flung to a dog. It is all very well to talk about our having fought bravely, and of the honour of our arms being intact; but everybody knows that we were beaten at Custozza. Everybody knows, now, that we were beaten at Lissa. Everybody will soon know that Garibaldi's campaign has been virtually a failure. I want war, and I am content to abide by the terrible chance of war—alone, poor, and matched against a formidable enemy—because I am proud, vain if you like, of my profession and my country."

I will give the captain's concluding words in his own language.

"*I Tedeschi*," he said, "*dicono che noi siamo stati bastonati da loro, e questo mi fa mal al cuore.*"*

There was nothing to add to the captain's argument. It was forcible enough and logical enough. It was far more cogent than the little Garibaldino's denunciations of La Marmora as a traitor, and of the Emperor of the French as first cousin to Pontius Pilate. It is certain that the Austrians are going about saying that they have thrashed the Italians, and one cannot be angry with a brave and sensitive people for wishing to retrieve their reverses in one supreme conflict. Pending which we came to Pontelagoscuro.

* "The Austrians say that we have been thrashed by them; and that they should have any reason to say so pains me to the heart."

VII.

PASSAGE OF THE PO.

August 8.

I LEFT you at Pontelagoscuro. It was from this same Pontelagoscuro that I was repulsed by the Austrians on the 14th of last June, and bidden to make my way back to Verona, there to crave permission of the Archduke Albert to quit the "empire." How time and circumstances do alter cases, to be sure; and into what remarkably small mincemeat has the "empire" been chopped! How sulkily did I then wend my way back to Padua! How eagerly am I pushing thitherward now! In what a desperate hurry had I been to get out of Venice! To-day I would give my ears to find myself once more on that bridge which traverses the Lagoons. Padua is but twenty miles from Venice; yet Venice, until the armistice merges into peace, is as good as a thousand miles away. I should be thankful even for permission to enter that Verona, to be forced towards which I deemed in June such a crying injustice.

With that slow, cruel, pigheaded pedantry which, above all things, distinguishes the Austrian Government, they still cling to Venice, although they know that its dominion has passed away from them for ever, until the very last moment that the deliberations of the plenipotentiaries at Prague will permit them to occupy it. I daresay that Toggenburg is carrying it with a high hand, even now, at the Luogotenenza, and that Alemann is denouncing all kinds of dreadful penalties against such Venetians as may presume before the hour strikes, and the last Austrian Lloyd takes away the last Austrian official, to fancy themselves free. Read the last proclamation of the military governor to the population over whom the continuance of his sway may now be reckoned by days. "Large purchases of coloured stuffs," says the military governor, "have recently been made. Taken in themselves these purchases have no signification; but the undersigned thinks it his duty to inform the inhabitants that if these stuffs—*stoffe colorate*—are made use of to serve any purpose of political demonstration, those displaying them will be punished with the utmost rigour of military law."

General Alemann knows as well as that he himself wears a white coat upon his back that these *stoffe colorate* are simply so much green, red, and white silk or bunting, wherewith is formed the Italian tricolor, and that thousands of fingers—some of them the fairest in Europe—are at this moment busied in fashioning national flags to be hung out from every window on St. Mark's Place, and from every balcony on the Grand Canal, so soon as a good perspective view is obtained of the Austrian back fading away beyond the channel of Malamocco. But till this blissful consummation arrives, General Alemann affects wholly to ignore the fact that Venetians are no longer bond-servants to the Tedesco. The officers will swagger about the *caffès*, the savage Croats will scowl from the windows of the palaces, the marines will mount guard on the Lido for many days to come. I have no doubt that the *Gazzetta Ufficiale di Venezia* continues to enregister the *sovrane resoluzioni*, by which his Imperial Royal and Apostolic Majesty has been pleased to confer fifth-rate decorations upon tenth-class Government clerks; and that until the very day before Victor Emmanuel makes his entry into Venice the kingdom of Italy will be referred to as the "Stati Sardi." After that I should think the editor of the *Gazzetta*, a renegade Italian, who made friends long since with the Mammon of Austrian unrighteousness, will clear out with all possible despatch. Otherwise it might be found that one of those tall masts before St. Mark's might be capable of holding something else besides a banner in a state of aerial suspension. *Ballare in campo azzuro* is a very pretty locution, which, to the able editor in question, might come to have rather a woful meaning.

I suppose that it is not entirely the fault of the Austrians if they are unable to yield with grace or make the best of a bad job. It is said that they intend to blow up the fortifications of Verona, dismantle Mantua and Peschiera, and altogether do as much mischief as ever they possibly can to the territory they have been compelled to surrender. I should not be surprised to learn when I reënter Venice that, in addition to plundering the Biblioteca Marriana and the archives of the Frari, they have stripped the arsenal of Dandolo's sword, Cristoforo Moro's armour, Mahomet the Conqueror's spurs, and Angelo of Padua's needle-pistol. I should learn without astonishment that a captain of artillery had come down on the Accademia delle Belle Arte, and carried away Titian's Presentation of the Virgin and Paolo Veronese's great pictorio-architectural "machines." The Austrians are quite capable of these or similar vandalisms. They belong to the essentially military mind, the guard-room ethics, and the barrack-yard sentiment of the Tedeschi. Even now the more excitable of the "Party of Action" in Italy are beginning to ask whether a fresh *casus belli* may not very soon arise from the probable refusal of the Austrians to give up the iron crown of Lombardy, which they carried away from Monza in 1859, and which is now at Vienna or Comorn.

I don't think they will give up the iron crown, and I don't think that the Emperor Francis Joseph will cease to call himself on his coins and in his public acts "King of Lombardo-Venetia." "What's in a name?" and he may plead, in the last particular, that before the King of Piedmont came to that tremendous fortune which the Emperor Napoleon and Joseph Garibaldi bestowed upon him, he used to call himself King of Cyprus and Jerusalem, in addition to Duke of Genoa and Savoy, Marquis of Monferrat, and Count of Pignerol. Now he is only King of Italy. The possession of the iron crown, and "Lomb: Ven: Rex" on the obverse of a florin, will not whistle Francis Joseph's Italian kingdom back again; but the childish retention of vain symbols and empty titles will only afford an additional proof of the Austrian inability to comprehend the logic of facts, and the surly dudgeon in which they take their expulsion from Venetia.

I will wager that, if by any underhanded intrigue or cunning sleight-of-hand the thing be possible, the Kaiser will avoid, in the treaty of peace now in preparation, the formal recognition of the rival whom he hates and despises as "King of Italy." Hatred and contempt are precisely the feelings with which respectable, Conservative, well-buttoned-up, tightly-strapped Austria regards that free-and-easy upstart, Young Italy. The Hapsburgs are no more able to forget than are the Bourbons. It is impossible that a respectable, Conservative, well-buttoned-up, tightly-strapped Austrian general should not remember, even to the gnashing of his teeth, that not seven years ago the people of Lombardy did not dare to call their souls their own, and that less than a month since a Venetian who ventured to speak ill, write ill, or think ill of the Government might be clapped up at once in San Giorgio Maggiore, or sent, handcuffed, to write a new edition of *Le Mie Prigioni* at Goritz or the Spielberg. It is but natural that men who have been accustomed for so many years to hector and domineer over an enslaved population, to trample them under foot, to gag and chain them, to meet discontent with the bayonet and remonstrance with bombshells, should feel sore when they are compelled to meet as equals those whom they were wont to treat as serfs—to hang, and shoot, and imprison, and flog, according to their good pleasure. The Austrians feel for the Italians the mingled anger and scorn which a South-Carolinian planter might feel were he to find himself elbowed on the side-walk, and sued in the courts of law, by the "buck-nigger" whom he bought for so many dollars from the auction-block. The Italians feel for the Austrians the deep and vindictive loathing with which an emancipated New-Orleans quadroon might regard the quondam master who used to send him, for a trifling fault, to the whipping-house.

The exacerbation of feeling on the part of the Austrians is aggravated, at present, by the knowledge that they have lost Venetia, not by a fight, but through a fatality—that Custozza and Lissa were of no use to them—and that, but for their haughty and purblind stupidity, they might have conciliated Italy last May, sold Venetia to her for as many millions as ever they chose to mention—there is not an Italian but who would have pawned his shirt to pay the covenanted price—and dissociated her from the unnatural alliance with Prussia. Now it is too late; and Austria must be bitterly aware that she is mastered diplomatically by the foe whom she has undeniably beaten in the field. There would seem to be no reason why, a sensible peace once made, and a definite frontier agreed upon, Italy and Austria should not become as good friends as England and France. Every country must have neighbours, and powerful ones too; and I set little store by the assertion that the Austrian fortresses in the Tyrol and the Austrian fleet at Pola will be a continual menace and a continual peril to the Italians. They will be able to pit Verona and the Quadrilateral against the Tyrolese fortresses, and they must construct a port in the Adriatic to keep Pola in check. This done, why should they not shake hands? Politically they might well do so; but socially many years must, it is to be feared, elapse ere the Italian looks upon the Tedesco, or *vice versâ*, with aught but sour and malevolent hostility.

The social sores on either side as yet are raw. The generation of Parisians who had seen the Highlanders mounting guard at the Louvre, and the Scots Fusiliers encamped in the Bois de Boulogne, really entertained a lively and personal hatred towards Englishmen. If Blucher wanted to blow up the bridge of Jena, it was principally because the misfortunes of Queen Charlotte and the theft of the Great Frederick's sword were, to him, outrages of yesterday. So, I apprehend, we must not expect to see Austrians and Italians walking about, yet awhile, arm in arm. The Italian whose father lay for long years in an Austrian dungeon, whose brother was tried by court-martial at Brescia and shot, whose sister was tied down to the *cavaletto* and scourged—the Austrian officers standing by grinning, and smoking their cigars—and who has himself been imprisoned, exiled, and ruined in purse by the Austrians, is not very likely to regard a person of that nation in a very Evangelical spirit; nor, on the other hand, must we expect much cordiality or good-fellowship on the part of the Tedesco towards the foreigner who was so recently his thrall, and whom he has been for nearly fifty years accustomed to coerce with gyves, and gags, and rods, and halters.

It has been the misfortune of the Italians never to have known the real people of South Germany—easy-going, good-natured, warm-hearted creatures, as all those who have inhabited Vienna must, in common justice, admit them to be. Had the Kaiser planted a few colonies of Viennese *bourgeois* or Lower-Austrian peasantry among his Italian subjects, the result might have been different; but, as it was, the Lombardo-Venetian saw the Austrian only in his most repulsive aspect—in full uniform, and with a frowning countenance, his sword by his side, a cane in his hand, an orderly-book under his arm, and the handcuffs jingling in his coat-pocket. Nor was the Italian visible to his Austrian master under an aspect much more favourable.

I was much amused some years ago by a Viennese, with

whom I travelled over the Brenner to Trent, telling me that the Italians were a people "without heart." Poor Viennese! it was not possible that the warmth and impulsiveness of the Italian heart should be revealed to him. He saw only the Italian in opposition—the seditious, scowling, conspiring malcontent, who wouldn't listen to the Austrian bands, who wouldn't smoke the Austrian tobacco, who wouldn't sit down in the Austrian caffès, who wouldn't ask an Austrian to dinner, but who was always ready to plot and to rebel, and not unfrequently went to the extremity of stabbing an Austrian soldier in his sentry-box. All of which is, I take it, a very strong argument against the system of forcing standing armies down anybody's throat, and in favour of the nations of the earth knowing each other a little better by means of railways, telegraphs, newspapers, and other sensible intercommunication. At present, however, we have to deal, not with theories, but with facts; and the fact is, I am afraid, as indubitable as it is melancholy that neither the Austrians nor the Italians will retire from the conference-chamber at Prague in that placable and mutually-forgiving mood which so well befits honourable adversaries, who have submitted their differences to the arbitrament of the sword. The Austrians will continue to gnaw their fingers at the knowledge that but for Königgrätz they might have held out in the Quadrilateral for unnumbered months, and that "*Dicono che siamo stati bastonati da loro*" will continue to rankle in the Italian mind.

Even during the brief continuance of the war, it was easy to see that on neither side did there exist that frank and courteous feeling which should obtain among soldiers for foemen worthy of their steel. The prisoners have, it is true, been treated with humanity; but, with this exception, hostilities have been carried on in a savage, surly, snarling spirit. The proclamations both of the Austrian and the Italian generals have been unusually personal and abusive. The Austrian press has tried to throw ridicule on the Italian army, and spoken of the Garibaldini as little better than footpads; while in Italy the army has been hounded on by the journals towards a kind of crusade against ogres and cannibals. The Austrians have been accused of deliberately shooting at the poor drowning wretches with whom the waters of Lissa were covered after the sinking of the Rè d' Italia; and the Italians exulted over the statement that the hands and arms of some of the Austrian dead at Custozza were found to have been bitten through and through by their enraged enemies. This surely is not war, or the manner in which war among civilised nations should be carried on; although it quite bears out a doctrine I venture to hold personally—that the most civilised of your warriors, directly he has got on his war-paint and danced his war-dance, becomes as brutal and savage as any Choctaw or Potowatomie that ever screeched or slew his fellow-creatures.

There is at Pontelagoscuro on the Italian side—both sides are Italian now, but I make the distinction for convenience' sake—a very remarkable construction, resembling a Burlington-arcade of colossal size, and in a most dilapidated condition, which had been lifted bodily, say by means of a balloon, out of Piccadilly, and set down in the middle of a swamp shelving to the shore of the Po. Beside this arcade, and two or three hovels scattered about, there is no other village of Pontelagoscuro; or perhaps the real Pontelagoscuro is on the opposite side. The whole affair is, however, to me, hopelessly obscure.

I saw in Russia once a village, termed of the "Wendish" order; that is to say, the houses were built in a circle, the windows and doors looking towards the centre, and with but one narrow porch by which admission to the interior of the hamlet could be obtained. This peculiar mode of construction dated, I was told, from the time of the Teutonic Knights, who were a kind of Christian highwaymen, carrying the Bible in one hand and a centre-bit in the other, and accustomed to sacking a village first and converting its inhabitants to the true faith afterwards. But I never yet saw a village built after the model of the Burlington-arcade. There are some caffès, and wine-shops, and fruiterers, and old-clothes stores in the arcade, and the entrance towards Ferrara is made grand by means of a gate of terra-cotta and in the Renaissance style, with an inscription informing the world that it was erected A.D. Sixteen Hundred and Forty-eight by the munificence of Cardinal Donghi and the Monte di Pietà.

Mystery! what could Cardinal Donghi have had to do with the national pawnbroker? On reflection, however, I remembered that the Mons Pietatis is in Italy an inscrutable institution, whose attributes seem to be universal, and its powers, like those of M. Ledru Rollin's Republican commissioners, illimitable. It gives "secret consultations," it portions orphans, pensions generals, and grants annuities to deserving widows. The Monte Napoleone at Milan is a kind of Lord Chancellor combined with the Society for the Relief of Distress. In fact, there would appear to be no end to that which My Uncle in Italy is able to do. But from the fact of there being a bridge at the river-end of this arcade, and of all vehicles as well as foot-passengers being compelled to pass through it on their way to the Po, I was led to the conclusion that such things as tolls haply formed part of the Donghian scheme of munificence, and that the cardinalitian portico was only a highly-ornamental kind of 'pike. Let me not quit Arcadia without mentioning that the front of the archway was decorated with some very handsome frescoes, as sharp and glowing as though they had been painted yesterday. The artist who executed them had indulged in one very curious freak of imagination. Gates in his day were generally prisons as well, but the Cardinal, doubtless a good-natured ecclesiastic, had not desired his architect to build a dungeon for the incarceration of those who neglected to pay toll. The Bishops of Antwerp were not so merciful. They had not only a prison, but a chopping-block, for those who strove to pass that 'pike without paying, and were empowered to cut off the right hands of those who evaded the toll on their bridge across the Scheldt. The artist at Pontelagoscuro was, however, not to be balked in his notion of the proprieties. He has painted on a convenient space of the wall a most symmetrical dungeon-window, closely barred, and through the bars you can just see the dim outline of a human face. Thus has one barbarous Thought risen superior to Time, and kept breast-high above the waves of centuries.

We found no fewer than three bridges across the Po. They were all of rough planks laid across boats, and were, indeed, the bridges used by Cialdini for the passage of his army across the river in his march on Borgoforte three weeks ago. Although the biggest of guns had been transported by means of these boat-bridges, we were fain, in obedience to the orders of a sergeant's guard stationed at the end of the arcade, to alight from our carriage, and traverse the particular bridge pointed out to us on foot. The carriage was sent, at a snail's pace, by another. Arrived at the opposite bank, we found the only road blocked up by an enormous railway-carriage, which eighteen white oxen were striving to drag towards the railway, which is finished, but not in working order, from here to Rovigo. A railway-car in a dusty road, and with a string of oxen attached to it, and any number of Italian teamsters screeching and gesticulating round it, is about as manageable an object as a stranded whale would be in Hanway-yard, or an elephant in the box-entrance to the Adelphi Theatre. Except the one road just spoken of, all this part of the shore of the Po is at this time of the year one fat, soggy swamp, as treacherous as a rice-field in South Carolina, and not at all practicable for wheeled vehicles. The probability, therefore, of our passing the night on the agreeable brink of this bog, which was not in the least Italian, but rather Dutch in appearance, did not seem at all remote. Our captain of artillery, however, proved equal to the emergency.

"When there are none to give orders," he remarked pithily, "it is I who take the command;" and so saying, he leapt into the very midst of the eighteen white oxen and the screeching and gesticulating drivers. It was a word here, a blow there, and a kick for whoever was nearest. He smote Pietro on the back; he cuffed Gaetano on the cheek; he sent

Angelo sprawling; he called Beppo *carogna;* and he said uncomplimentary things about Giuseppe's, I hope deceased, mother. Still, somehow, after about a quarter of an hour's frensied effort, he did manage to get that railway-carriage, its oxen, and its teamsters out of the way, and rejoined us, smiling and calmly triumphant, mopping his manly face with his handkerchief. What became of the huge impediment I do not know. I should not wonder to hear that it had rolled, bullocks and all, into the Po, never to rise again.

It made one very savage, amidst all this delay and discomfort, to see, a few hundred feet away, the beautiful, bran-new railway-bridge wrenched from its standfasts, and smashed and crumpled up, as though it had been stricken by lightning. But no bolt from Heaven had ruined that noble structure—only a few tons of gunpowder, and the monstrous wickedness and stupidity of man, had sufficed to turn a monument of labour and ingenuity; and what should have been a guarantee of peace and goodwill, into a shapeless structure. The bridge has been destroyed, I am told, for "strategical reasons." May all "strategical reasons" go to the Devil, their father, who had the begetting of them, say I. For "strategical reasons" the world is to be thrown back, forsooth, half a century, and anarchy, ruin, and pauperism are to prevail where there should be prosperity and tranquillity. For "strategical reasons" an inconceivable old Austrian blockhead, named General Kuhn, is going about the Tyrol, hammering out loopholes in all the walls of all the churches, convents, villas, and farmhouses he can get at; planting cannon in every vineyard, and quartering soldiers in every cottage, and declaring, with a sneer worthy of his master, that, although he has heard of a thing called an armistice, and although such another thing as a peace may spring from it, he has as yet received no official notification of the fact, and meanwhile he intends to go on hammering out loopholes and planting cannon.

How long is the world to continue under the sway of these mischievous old dodderers, with stars on their breasts and cocked-hats on their heads? For how much longer is some bloodthirsty, brainless old dotard—be he Italian or German—to prevent honest men from going about their lawful business? We had an association for putting down garotters. Who will start an association for putting down generals of brigade, and hanging generals of division who go about Europe robbing and murdering, and cutting down standing crops, and blowing up bridges, with an associate society for sending to penal servitude those sovereigns and diplomatists who are proved accessories before the fact? We have a society for the protection of young women and children; but where is the organisation for the protection of peaceable men against the aggravated assaults of Methusaleh grown sanguinary? It would be a different thing if these murderous old gentlemen showed signs of military genius. But they prove themselves at the supreme moment asses. They make the most lamentable blunders. They get thrashed like sacks. They are knocked into cocked-hats, and then, always for "strategical reasons," they devastate the whole country round, and turn smiling fields into a desert.

There was some grim consolation in the appearance of the late Austrian custom-house on the Po, which, for reasons equally strategical, was occupied by Cialdini twenty-one days since in his advance. Over the frontier sign-post with the legend of *Dominio Veneto* had been daubed the words *Regno d' Italia* and the *Imperiale Reale Dogana* had been very rudely transformed into a custom-house of his Majesty Vittorio Emmanuele. The Imperial and Royal Eagle had lost both his heads, and his claws, and his tail to boot, and, torn down from his escutcheon, lay prostrate in the mire, a most woful bird, while from the heraldic firmament in which he lately shone now blazed the cross of Savoy. Instead of the black-and-yellow banner, now flaunted in the evening sun the Italian red, white, and green. The Imperial and Royal Post-office and the Imperial and Royal Tobacco-shop were transformed into the *Regie Poste* and the *Regi Sale e Tabacchi.* I confess I did not look upon the change from anything like an optimist point of view. I am not "Italianissimo." I have had enough to do with the brawling and wrangling of nationalities over the world not to be "issimo" in anything. I only want to plant my cabbages and eat my soup in quietness.

I was glad to witness the Teutonic collapse here, and to read the first chapter of the "Finis Austriæ," because I know that wherever Austria is dominant, there the drill-sergeant and the corporal with his stick, and the blockhead general with his loopholes, and pride, ignorance, intolerance, and cruelty, will prevail; but I cannot see that a millennium is imminent on the banks of the Po because the double eagle has been superseded by the cross of Savoy. Jack goes up, and Tom comes down, that is all. The King of Italy's custom-house officers were already at work, spying into our trunks and poking into the carriage-lining with their spiked sticks in their own obsolete and idiotic manner. The Austrian monopolies of salt, tobacco, and playing-cards had given place to Italian monopolies of the same nature: and ere long I will wager the towns of the Veneto will be in the full enjoyment of the Royal Italian Lottery and the Royal Italian paper money; nor, I fancy, will they find the Royal Italian taxes one whit less onerous than the Imperial and Royal Austrian imposts. The people of the liberated provinces, so far as I have come—for I am many miles from the Po as I write this—do not, either, seem to be optimists as regards their emancipation. There was an immense amount of cheering and shouting, it is true, at Rovigo and at Padua; Garibaldi's Hymn is ground on every organ, and yelled in every grog-shop; but underneath all this there is a strong substratum of philosophy—the philosophy of the people, who really don't care a *centesimo* who is uppermost, but content themselves with extorting as much money as ever they possibly can, in exchange for their services or their wares, from all those who pass through their part of their country. I think that if they show any preferential feeling in their swindling, it is towards cheating their liberators more than they were wont to cheat their tyrants. The tyrants had rods, and beat them when they extorted too much.

One's sympathies, therefore, were pretty equally balanced upon entering the *Dominio Veneto*. Anger with the Austrians for smashing the railway-bridge was equipoised by deep disgust at finding a new custom-house set up, and a fresh tribe of *doganieri* plying their mischievously-imbecile vocation. But as we proceeded through the low, fertile country to Rovigo, anti-Austrianism reasserted itself, and far preponderated over every other sentiment. The Tedeschi seem to have been determined to leave behind something that the Venetians should remember them by. For "strategical reasons" they have turned half this luxuriant region into a howling wilderness. I will say nothing of the acres upon acres of Indian corn and clover they have cut down for forage. Cavalry horses and artillery mules must be fed, that is certain, and fresh green-meat is very good for the animal stomach at this season of the year. Thus, too, it may have become necessary to carry off the wheat-ricks and to grub up the flax, the hemp, the olives, and the vines. But what had those poor mulberry-trees done, that they should be so ruthlessly cut down? Surely the silkworms had not been anti-Austrian. Surely the cocoons had not whispered sedition against the Kaiser. Whole plantations of mulberries had, however, disappeared, and an equally clean sweep had been made of the tall straight poplars, double rows of which should line the roads. It is a crueller act to cut down these trees than to rob a poor man of his beer. The Austrians have robbed the dusty, footsore, panting wayfarers of the inestimable blessing of shadow. To cut down a tree which gives shade in a hot country is constructive murder. The Spaniards cut down their trees, through hatred of the Moors who had planted them. A just Providence punished them for their ignorant malice, and where the trees are cut down the rain comes no more, and there is a dust instead of greenness.

I was less grieved to mark between Pontelagoscuro and Rovigo the ruins of no fewer than four formidable forts, with huge earthworks and circular moats, erected by the Austrians as outworks, and blown up by them ere they abandoned this untenable portion of Venetia. The great heaps of dust and clods and shattered masonry were very hideous to view, and were the graves, I have no doubt, of many millions of florins and hours of fruitless human labour; but it is at least good to look upon a ruined fort, as upon an abominable thing which is gone, and which haply may never be replaced. They have not yet rebuilt Sebastopol, and peaceful omnibuses ply over the site of the Bastille.

VIII.

THEATRE AT ROVIGO.

August 12.

Between supper-time and our taking coach again to Padua, there was, after all, something to be done; and to my surprise I found out that there was such a thing as "life" in Rovigo at that very witching hour of night when, if graves do not exactly yawn, the inhabitants of Italian country towns certainly do. As a rule, there is nothing under this firmament duller than provincial existence in Italy. It is duller than a *table-d'hôte* dinner in Switzerland, where half the guests are English, and the other half are Americans, and both coldly stare at one another in grim silence, to the horror of the one representative of the Latin race present—a conversational Frenchman, who, after vainly endeavouring to engage the gentleman from New Hampshire on his left in sociable talk, and offering the *charmante miss* on his right a beautifully-peeled peach in a spoon, the which is frigidly declined, shrugs his shoulders in agonised despair, and, turning savagely to the waiter, who has become habituated to Anglo-Saxon taciturnity, and has grown idiotic thereby, says, in a voice which echoes through the dreary dining-room, as that of a disappointed ghoul might through a family-vault, "*Donne-moi un verre de chartreuse, parbleu! si tu ne veux pas que je meure du spleen.*" It is duller than a literary and scientific conversazione at Wimbledon, or the first reading of a new domestic drama in the green-room of the Theatre Royal Cumberland Market; the influenza being rife at the time, the popular dramatic author having an impediment in his speech, the stage-manager being asleep, and the walking gentleman not on speaking terms with the leading lady.

For my part, I have never been able to understand how it is that three-fourths of the town population of Italy escape every year from being bored to death. Ennui should properly make among them ravages more fearful than those of the cholera. After sunset, in Italy, there is literally nothing to do but to go to the *caffè*, smoke, drink lemonade, and talk politics. I suppose these constitute the *dolce far niente* we used to hear so much about, and to envy, in cold, overworked England.

Italy is the home of the lyrical drama; but at the season of the year when English people usually go abroad they are nearly sure to find all the Italian theatres closed. Italy is the land of music; yet one of the rarest things to be heard in the peninsula is the sound of a tolerable band. For the Austrians, politically, I think I have an affection about as passionate as that which Mr. Thaddeus Stephens might be supposed to entertain for Mr. Andrew Johnson; yet, on one ground, I do most sincerely regret that Milan is no longer occupied by the Tedeschi, and that the last days of their sway in Venice are at hand. At least the white-coated oppressors fed the Italians to repletion with first-rate instrumental music. Now that the tyrants are gone away, the delicious strains of their bands are heard no more; and the deprivation is felt with fuller force under actual circumstances, when all that Italy has to show, in the way of military music, is away with the army at the front. At most, now, do you hear the tinkling of a cracked mandolin, as the airs in the *Trovatore* are being pinched into fits, or you are reminded by a tin platter being thrust under your nose for coppers that the *virtuoso* who has been tootling during the last twenty minutes on the kerb-stone and on the flageolet, or the hoarse-bawling woman in the large crinoline who has been giving to "*Qual cuor tradisti*" the intonation of a Leith fishwife and the expression of a Seven-Dials last dying speech crier, expects reward for their performances.

Italy may be the land of song, but her singers seem to fly a good many hundreds of miles away before they can properly tune up. I do not think, in fine, that I can give a more convincing proof of the prevailing dulness of provincial Italy, than by noticing the fact that from one end to the other of this delightful country there is but one public garden —the Giardino Pubblico at Milan. Many of the *caffès* have gardens attached where you may dine and smoke; but the garden I mean is that delightful combination of the park, the caffè, and the casino—a sprightly Luxembourg grafted on to a reputable Cremorne—which flourishes in the environs of every continental town, even to the fifth-rate ones, except in Italy. Here it is supposed that the blue sky and the balmy air, the delicious sunsets, the vines, the olives, and the figs, are to supply every material and intellectual want. If the ladies lack amusement, they have religion and they have love to fall back upon. If the gentlemen desire recreation, are there not caffès by scores, and any quantity of iced lemonade and cheap cavours, and the never-failing amusement of talking politics?

But one cannot be perpetually telling one's beads, or going to mass, or twirling one's fan, or setting one's veil at the young men. You grow tired, at last, of swilling lemonade, sucking up essential oil through convoluted tubes, and declaring that La Marmora is a traitor, and that Persano ought, forthwith, to suffer the fate of Admiral Byng. You may read the newspapers; but the whole of the *Perseveranza* may be perused in about fifteen minutes. The *Pungolo* does not take five; the contents of the *Lombardia* may be mastered in about eighty seconds, and the *Sciolo* is not worth reading at all. The real leading-articles are roared, over lemonade, from the lips of yonder leather-lunged patriots. Leather-lunged patriotism bores you at last. There are other countries in Europe besides Italy. If they would only talk, for instance, about the Danubian Principalities, or Spanish finance, which, I perceive, is cropping up again in a promising manner! but no, La Marmora and Persano, Persano and La Marmora, form the invariable staple of discourse. Bother La Marmora and Persano! If the first lost his head at Custozza, why does he persist in walking and talking without it, like King Charles in the nursery-saw, or St. Denis in the *Acta Sanctorum*? I am truly sorry that the good ship Affondatore went down; but one's grief might have been mitigated had Persano been on board the ill-fated craft, and sunk, full fathom five, for ever.

Rovigo, although it was talking politics until it was purple in the face, offered a splendid contrast, so far as the reproach of dulness extends, to the rest of Italy. Late as it was, the Théatre Royal Rovigo was open. The glad intelligence was brought us by the artillery captain, who had ordered the supper. "Go there for half an hour, my children," he said, "until the repast is ready. As for me, I shall lie down on this sofa and sleep. Sleep is a thing to be taken when you can get it." And with this remark—worthy, perhaps, of being enshrined beside Molière's apothegm as to the expediency of taking your property wheresoever you find it—the artillery captain lay down, shako, epaulettes, pouch, sabre, and all, and began to snore.

The little Garibaldino lieutenant and I went off to the theatre. The hardened Austrians had capped the climax of their many crimes by cutting off the gas in the side thoroughfares prior to their departure; or perhaps the gas company of Rovigo, being in the equivocal position of the donkey between two bundles of hay,—or, worse, of the donkey between two empty panniers,—and not quite certain as to whether the next quarter's bill was to be sent to Francis Joseph, Vienna, or Victor Emmanuel, Florence, had cut off the supply themselves, and were waiting to see what should turn up, and whether King or Kaiser was to be the responsible party. Behind the spangled gauze and coloured fire of the great transformation-scene now taking place in the Venetian provinces, there are a good many persons who have conscientiously adopted this line of tactics. Pending a settlement, the street leading from the inn of the Iron Crown to that where the theatre is situated was as dark as a mass-meeting of liberated Africans with the candle gone out.

We found, however, a patriot with a lantern, who showed us the way, and cast a merry light upon our path, and was very anxious to know from the Garibaldino lieutenant what had been the achievements during the war of a certain Pastrucci Gaetano, native of Vicenza, who was a high private in the ninth regiment of volunteers. In vain did the lieutenant hint to him that out of thirty thousand men it was rather too much to expect him to know every individual Red Shirt, and that the acts and deeds of Pastrucci Gaetano were entirely beyond his ken. "Not know Gaetano!" cried the patriot with the lantern; "you *must* know him, *Signor Tenente*. Gaetano from Vicenza. *Sicuro!* Why, his brother keeps a barber's-shop in the Sotto-Portici. Gaetano! he is one of the most spirited young men of our city." We repeated, however, that this member of the sprightly youth of Vicenza was quite unknown to us; whereupon the patriot turned off the light of his lantern in dudgeon and left us. Were you never asked whether you had met a Mrs. Cæsar Dodge in New York, and did an American never ask you if you happened to be acquainted with a Mr. Sydney Smith in London? I believe there are five hundred Cæsar Dodges in the New-York Directory; it is certain that you might fill the smaller concert-room at St. James's Hall with Sydney Smiths; and at the Garibaldian roll-call the Pastrucci Gaetanos are, I have no doubt, as thick as leaves at Vallombrosa, or as fleas at the inn adjoining that shady place.

The Theatre Royal Rovigo exteriorly much resembles a county bank in an English town, real marble, however, being substituted for stucco. On the squat Doric pediment is graven the inscription, "Societas MDCCCXIX." Society has done a good many things and seen not a few changes since the year '19; and one felt inclined to ask to what order of society the Rovigan theatre was dedicated—whether it was genteel society or middle-class society, society liberal or society despotic and ultramontane. The portico was draped in the Italian colours, and on either side a *bersagliere* sentinel stood on guard, while the further safe custody of the building was confided, as a compliment to patriotism, to the freshly-improvised National Guard of Vicenza, who were in a kind of Robinson-Crusoe costume, wearing military forage-caps and scarlet-facings to their blouses, but adhering otherwise to the waistcoats and pantaloons of civil life. They were very proud, however, of their new muskets and bayonets, and marched up and down with a janty elasticity pardonable in citizens who for the last half century had been accustomed to the unpleasant sight of tawny-faced persons in white coats, and of Teuto-Sclavic extraction, mounting guard with muskets and bayonets over them.

The very first thing done by a liberated foreigner is to dress up as a sentinel and mount guard. No sooner is he released from the despot's sway, than he takes up with an employment which, ostensibly, is the most senseless and wearisome in the world. The majority of civilian Englishmen being put to stand sentry for two mortal hours would, before they were relieved, either go raving mad, or, throwing their musket and bayonet over the nearest wall, go round the corner to see what o'clock it was. Our rifle movement would soon become unpopular, I fear, if mounting guard were among the duties imposed on volunteers. But foreigners seem to like it. Give them a shako and a cartouche-box, and Brown Bess with a spike at the end of it, and they are happy.

At Milan just now there are no regular troops, and all the sentries at the public buildings are supplied by the National Guards; that is to say, hundreds of clerks and shopkeepers are taken away from their legitimate business every day to mount guard over that which cannot run away. Surely theatres have not wings. Surely a post-office is not the nimble stag. We have nearly got rid of the sentinel nonsense in England, although we are still absurd enough to keep a squad of grenadiers grinning into vacancy under the porticoes of the opera-houses as they grinned lately in front of the British Museum. But abroad this pitiable delusion obtains as strongly as ever. Wherever there is a vacant niche a sentry-box is popped into it, and a human being set to waste his time. National-Guardism at Rovigo I can understand. It is but since yesterday that the Venetians have been allowed to carry arms at all. National-Guardism anywhere I can appreciate and applaud when it means drill, rifle-practice, and marching out; but I refuse to acquiesce in the use of a multitude of sentries and a plenitude of guard-room benches.

I have a shrewd suspicion that the reason why mounting guard is so popular abroad is because, *under the pretext of doing something, it affords such a capital opportunity of doing nothing.* Saunter up and down with a stick over your shoulder for two hours, or sit on a bench for two hours more, twiddling your thumbs, gossiping, dozing, or ogling the milliners' girls, and you will run some risk of being called a lazy fellow. But put a forage-cap on your head, shoulder a gun, and saunter in a measured manner, and you are on guard; you are serving your country; you are a patriot and a soldier. Standing sentry is, in fact, only the *dolce far niente* put into uniform. I am afraid that the Latin races are not to be weaned from this sad propensity for idling in a military manner; but I would suggest, as a middle course, that every sentinel should have a barrel-organ at one end of his beat and a mangle at the other, and be expected to grind alternately with keeping guard. For the use of the warriors who twiddle their thumbs on the guard-room bench, sewing-machines might be provided. At least they would be kept out of mischief. Do you know to what thumb-twiddling on guard-room benches has led in Spain? To *pronunciamientos* and revolts, to drumhead court-martials and judicial massacres at the Principe Pio, to despotism and Narvaez.

It was evidently a gala-night at the Rovigo theatre. The *fioraje* were in great force, and thrust bouquets into your button-hole whether you would or not. The flower-girls of Italy are nuisances nearly as intolerable as the mosquitoes. If they were only pretty flower-girls; but, in most cases, they are hard-featured females, with hoarse voices, and of impudent aspect. You would not, for instance, care about having a rose thrust into your ribs by a free-and-easy pew-opener or an affable orange-woman. You delight in flowers, of course; the custom of presenting bouquets to strangers, ostensibly for nothing, but really for the sake of as many pence as the stranger can be pestered into giving, is a very pretty one; but suppose your floral *penchant* is for roses, and the *fioraja* persists in ramming down your throat pinks or geraniums which you abhor? Suppose that you have long since given up buying bouquets, and that the only flower you care about is a certain camellia, once white and blooming, but now lying in a very crushed and coffee-coloured condition between the leaves of a Walton's *Complete Angler*, in a deal drawer, a thousand miles away? It is the camellia you had the honour of purloining one night in the year 1849 from the young lady in white glacé silk, who subsequently had the bad taste to marry a collector of inland revenue. You have never cared for camellias since. Why should you be made to swallow them, or any other flower, and expected to pay for them too, on the grand staircase of the Theatre Royal Rovigo?

The house had a grand staircase—ay, one of exquisite marble, the panels and ceilings painted in fresco—and the theatre itself was a grand one to boot. Society knew what it was about in the year '19. Vases of evergreens and flowers which you were not expected to buy lined the corridor. Rich carpets were underfoot. An usher, in silk shorts, a lace frill, and a silver chain round his neck, came, with a low bow, to ask us where our places were. They were for the pit; no others were to be obtained, for it was a gala-night, and the house was crammed. Pushing aside a great curtain of crimson velvet with a heavy fringe of bullion, we entered the house, and I was astounded. I had been prepared for such a modest little temple of music and the drama as you might expect to find in an ordinary second-rate provincial town abroad, say at Amiens, or Cologne, or Gratz. But I found, instead, one of the handsomest theatres I had ever beheld. The theatre at Rovigo is certainly very little inferior in size to Drury Lane, and has no fewer than five tiers of boxes. Its architecture is stately, its decorations splendid;

the ceiling, above all, is really a triumph of the difficult and shamefully-undervalued art which Inigo Jones and Antonio Canaletto and Charles Lebrun were not ashamed to practise, but which in England, owing to Mr. Pope's genteel sneer against the sprawling saints of Serrio and Laguerre, is now accounted only a superior kind of plastering.

There was an enormous gas chandelier hung in the centre; but gas, that night, was fated to be at a discount in all Rovigo. The theatre was lighted *a giorno*, as only the Italians know how to light a theatre, with literally myriads of wax-candles, in whose mellow, shadowless radiance shone all the rank and all the beauty, and diamonds and epaulettes, and pearls and swords, and necklaces and gauze, and lace and embroidery, and white-kid gloves, of all that Rovigo could muster of fair women and brave men. Every box was occupied. The large one, right in the centre of the grand tier, was the Royal box, and there, in a gorgeous framework of velvet and bullion, Italian tricolors and wax-candles, sat, with a brilliant suite, M. Allievi, the King of Italy's commissary for the city of Rovigo.

"Pepoli, Allievi, Mordini e Sella
Mangian allegri alla stessa gamella."

This is an opposition distich, directed against the Marquis Pepoli, who is *commissario regio* at Padua, M. Mordini, who fills the same functions at Vicenza, M. Allievi, who is here at Rovigo, and M. Sella, who is at Udine. I am not quite sure that I do right in quoting the disrespectful couplet. But where are there not oppositions, and when will not your opposition have its distich?

The principal business of the King's commissary on this

eventful evening was to rise up in his box—not like Jack, but in an easy and *dégagé* manner, and bow. From time to time he was expected to smile. Then it was evidently thought the proper thing that he should lay his hand on his heart. Then he would make believe to peruse his programme for an instant. Then he would scrutinise somebody in the third tier through his *lorgnon;* after that he would repeat the agreeable performance of rising, bowing, smiling, and laying his hand on his heart. All this was hard work; but one cannot be King's commissary for nothing. That high office has its duties as well as its privileges. M. Allievi, in fact, was performing at the Theatre Royal Rovigo the duty assigned in old times to the King of England's portrait in the Grand Reception Hall of the Residenz at Herrenhausen, near Hanover. His Britannic and Hanoverian Majesty being away at Kensington, they used to stick his picture in an arm-chair under a canopy at Herrenhausen. Chamberlains used to stand by the side, and halberdiers mount guard over the precious effigy, which was saluted by the courtiers with multitudinous genuflections. Poor arm-chair at Herrenhausen, your occupation is quite gone now! Poor Hanoverian courtiers, you must hinge the knee now to a very different kind of king! M. Allievi had this advantage, however, over the painted simulacrum at Herrenhausen, that he could mop, and mow, and smirk, all of which he did with most commendable zeal.

As to what was going on behind the footlights, nobody seemed to care about that. It was a performance like *George Barnwell* or *Jane Shore* on the first night of a pantomime, entirely in dumb-show. It seemed, so far as I could make out, to be some description of vocal and instrumental concert; and a gentleman attached to the fire brigade standing by me whispered that had I come an hour sooner I might have heard some "delicious fugues." As it was, I could only make out that from time to time some ladies and gentlemen in full evening dress walked on to the stage in a ghostly manner, waved sheets of music-paper with deprecating gestures, and addressed themselves to a grand pianoforte, whereat sate, rapidly moving a pair of very large hands, a solemn man in black and a white neckcloth, over nineteen-twentieths of whose countenance a bushy beard might have grown, but who had mercilessly swept the field of his face with a razor, so that only the remaining twentieth was permitted to show, in the shape of a moustache like an overgorged leech—what the whole of his physiognomy might have done under more favourable auspices. Whether any "delicious fugues" were performed by the orchestra, or any thrilling solos and duets performed by the vocalists, I am unable to state. As at Her Majesty's Theatre, on the night of the great Tamburini-Colletti sedition,

> "Fal de ral tit sang fol de rol lol;
> But scarce had he done when a row began;"

so at the Theatre Royal Rovigo was there a row going on all the time. But it was a good-humoured row—a row of loyalty and exultant joy. *"Viva Italia!" "Viva il Re!" "Viva il Principe Umberto!" "Viva l' Esercito!" "Viva l' Indipendenza!"* These were the cries shouted forth with but brief intervals, and to each "sentiment," as the Americans would say, succeeded a deafening din of cheering, handclapping, and stick-rapping. The movements of the King's commissary became more and more like those of the lithe performers in that admirable entertainment known as the "Fantoccini." He was all nods, and becks, and wreathed smiles; but he was rewarded by the ladies waving their handkerchiefs at him, by one man in the far-off distance crying, "*Viva Allievi!*" and by an enthusiastic lady in the box above him dropping a bouquet in his direction, which, narrowly escaping the flame of a wax-candle, hit the *commissario regio* fortuitously on the nose.

Nothing could be nicer, and all went merry as a marriage bell; only the oft-repeated sentiments seemed to issue with a regularity rather too narrrowly approaching the mechanical from the stentorian lungs of a knot of gentlemen not very clean in appearance, and rather forbidding in mien, stationed in the pit just underneath the royal box. "*Gente della questura*, ban-dogs of the police," muttered the little Garibaldino lieutenant. "They would cry, '*Viva Francesco Giuseppe!*' just as loud to-morrow for fifty *centesimi*. Just wait a moment; I think I know that family in the second tier. We will see if I can't give them something else to shout about."

We were blocked up in the *platea*, where there was only standing room, and the little lieutenant was lost and unnoticed in the throng; but he managed to elbow his way out, and presently I saw him in a box, evidently the centre of the admiration of three very pretty young ladies and a tall mamma in diamonds rather camelleopardish, but still stately. Anon the unabashed Garibaldino came to the very front of the box, and swept the house with martial glances. "I am here," he seemed to say. "*Son Io.* I, the hero of Monte Suello, of Bagolino, of Rocca Pagano, and of Bezzecca. In stature I am a manikin; but in heart a Colossus. I salute you. Be good enough to return the compliment." They did, and in a manner which must have rather astonished the King's commissary, if it failed altogether to please him. The little lieutenant's was the first red shirt that had been seen at Rovigo. The whole house rose at him, and one huge thunderous cry was heard of "*Viva Garibaldi!*" To these succeeded shouts of "*Vivan' le Camicie Rosse!*" "*Viva la Guerra!*" The police-people in the pit tried to get up the stereotyped and governmental cries; but their hour was past, and when I had succeeded in reaching the corridor and dragging away the little lieutenant, who was sobbing for joy, and had already accepted in a maniacal manner about a dozen invitations to supper, bed, and breakfast, to say nothing of immediate ices and lemonade, the name of Garibaldi was still lord of the ascendant. As it was, we were accompanied back to the Iron Crown by a patriotic mob shouting "*Viva Garibaldi!*"

After supper, and when our *vetturino* had tackled to again, and we were jolting in the cold gray morning along the road to Padua, it was curious enough to contrast the brilliant and luxurious scene we had so lately quitted with the drifting mass of baggage-wagons, and tumbrils, and cannon, and plodding soldiers, on whom the dawn threw an uncertain and spectral light. We were in the trail of the great war-serpent again; and in the horizon there loomed, like an inky cloud, the bare possibility that after all these gay doings the Austrians *might* come back, and the Dominio Veneto not be won without more hard fighting. But the strangest thing to note in this strange evening was this—that the splendid theatre, sumptuously decorated, lighted *a giorno*, filled with rank and beauty, had been opened that night *for the first time during twenty years.* During the Austrian occupation it had remained a silent and deserted sepulchre. There are more silent and deserted theatres in Venetia which will spring up into life and splendour when the Austrian back is seen for good. Among them is a certain house at Venice called La Fenice. A gondolier took me thither last May. Ah, how damp and dreary and ghastly it seemed! May another gondolier take me once more to La Fenice this coming September, and may I see it lit up and filled with beautiful Venetians, and I will not grudge my oarsman double fare!

IX.

THE IDLE LAKE.

On the Lake of Como, between Cernobbio and the Villa d'Este, August 20.

HUMBLY emulous of the ubiquity of the bad halfpenny, this is where I have, for the moment, the honour to turn up. I am on the sweet shores of the Idle Lake, and I intended to remain here and hereabouts for a week, thinking that I might tempt some of those English tourists who, to the despair of the Continental innkeepers, are so slow in coming abroad this year—is it the cholera, or reform, or the smash of the limited-liability delusion, or the dread of another European war that keeps them at home?—to explore this most delightful region, to visit the exquisite *villeggiature* of the lake, to shake hands once more with Bellaggio, and kiss Como on her comely cheek. *Elle en vaut la peine.* Not that any panegyrics of mine are necessary to make English tourists in love with this enchanting district; they know the Lake of old. Did not the Reverend Doctor Stanhope, with his interesting family, here expend his prebendal revenues, shamefully neglecting his duties at the cathedral of Barchester? Still, well known as it is to the affluent, and the indolent, and the lovers of the picturesque, it is certain that as yet neither Dr. Stanhope nor Dr. Syntax has started on his autumnal tour Comowards. It is the worst year, the hotel landlords declare with a groan, that they have known for years. *Dove sono?* Where are they, those *forestieri?* The clean and comfortable hotels of the Lake shores present a beggarly account of empty bedrooms. At the *tables d'hôte* there is nobody but the host himself to dine. Padrones, who in times of prosperity are deadly enemies, are fain, in order to escape a Robinson Crusoe-like isolation, to strike up a sulky friendship, and play billiards and sip their coffee at each other's inns.

There was a courier who came with me in the train from Milan to Como on Friday. He was a big-whiskered courier, with much braid and very bright gold earrings, and looked as though he had served many milords. He had no sooner embarked on board the four-o'clock steamer for Colico than the Lake landlords smelt him. He had come, they doubted not, to make arrangements for the sojourn of his Excellency the Lord Smith, of the *pregiatissima, nobilissima, e gentilissima Signora* Lady Brown, his wife, and of the fifty *amabilissime Donzelle* the Ladies Robinson, his daughters. The noble family would want rooms—two suites of rooms, twenty suites of rooms, a flotilla of pleasure-boats, and a whole regiment of guides. The good time was approaching, the halcyon epoch of low bows and long bills. But the courier coolly mentioned to the captain of the boat that he was just then unattached, and on his way to Coire to visit his grandmother, who was sick of the rheumatism. As for the *forestieri,* he did not think there would be any to speak of on the Lake this year. I wonder the landlords, or the touts, or the interpreters, or the guides, *et hoc genus omne,* did not forthwith make as short an end of that bird of ill omen as Mrs. Helen Macgregor did of the wretched Morris in the

Scottish loch. They forbore to fling the courier overboard; but they left off treating him to coffee and cavours. The man at the wheel, who, although not to be spoken to, sometimes speaks, murmured against him as a *bestia propria*, and the captain peremptorily ordered him off the bridge. So fall the mightiest. I was glad to land at Cernobbio, and be quit of the company of this unattached Jonah; and it strikes me now that, with his blacking-brush whiskers, blue upper lip, and dark eye, he bore a strong resemblance to the late Benjamin Courvoisier.

It is not my intention at present to detain you on the Idle Lake, although worse quarters might be found during this latter part of August. I only mention, *en passant*, that I have arrived here, as a prelude to the information that I am going forthwith back to Venetia again. It has pleased the Austrian authorities—so, at least, I learn from a sure source—to allow civilians coming from Padua and Mestre to enter Venice. When I left Padua the feat was no more possible of accomplishment than would be the passage of the Niagara Rapids in a washing-tub. At present, however, they tell me the thing is to be done, and I must do it. So I shall once more return to Milan, and to Piacenza, and Bologna, and Ferrara, and Pontelagoscuro, and Rovigo, and Padua—in fact, I must travel round three sides of the square again to arrive at the fourth angle, and journey about a hundred and seventy-five miles in order to reach that which is over the way.

My next letter, I hope, will be dated from Venice. To-day I propose to conclude the narrative of my travelling impressions during that tour through Venetia which, for the fifth time in three months, I am about to recommence. Had I never read a line of Mr. Ruskin, it would be possible for me in the end, I think, to know all the stones of Venice, or at least of Venetia, by heart.

We came from Rovigo to Padua. It was early morning. Rovigo, as I have already remarked, had not shown any symptoms of a desire to go to bed. Padua, on the other hand, had evidently not been to bed at all, but had kept it up all night. Padua, I submit, ought to know better. She is an old, a very old, a venerable city, and is bound to take care of herself. She looked, it must be admitted, after her protracted orgie, shaky, not to say dissipated. These high jinks ill beseem the aged.

Do you remember that inimitable description of poor old Major Pendennis, as he appeared at early dawn after dancing attendance all night on Lady Clavering and her daughter at a great London ball? He presented a sight lamentable to view. His beard had grown during the small hours, and pierced bright and stubbly from his aged chin. His cheeks were sunken, his jaw had dropped. The parting of his wig was painfully unnatural, and there were dark rings of *bistre* round his bloodshot eyes. His nose was as sharp as a pen, and the crow's-feet in his countenance could be counted by scores. Flaccid was his white cravat, and dingily yellow looked the shirt-front yesterday so spotless. In a word, rouge, starch, patent varnish, tight-cingled girths, padding, pomatum, Rowland's kalydor and Bully's toilet vinegar, false teeth, and eau-de-Cologne, had all fallen through, and only seventy years and sciatica, and the palsy in perspective, remained. This was Major Pendennis; and this was Padua as I saw her under the pressure of Aurora's rosy fingers, otherwise the bright August morning sun.

The antiquity of Padua is, as you know, immense; and the city really looks its age. She is scarred; she is furrowed; her cornices and architraves have lost all their sharp lines; her walls crumble; the foliage of the old capitals of her old pillars has faded away, and the plinths of the columns themselves have settled down into the earth. Her old inscriptions are three parts illegible; her old gates are rusty; her old windows are boarded up. She is, in fine, a decrepit old place, highly interesting and respectable no doubt, but still belonging to the centuries that shall return no more. Padua yet boasts a famous university, but from its gates you expect to see issue only grave doctors in hexagonal caps and gowns of striped black-and-buff velvet, sages learned in the Taliacotian operation, and demonstrators of anatomy who had once given lessons to Dr. William Harvey. Padua is a city where mediæval shrews might be tamed; where Petruchio might ride to his wedding on a horse wind-galled, shoulder-shotten, far gone in the botts, and irrevocably attacked with farcy; and Grumio confer with the woman's tailor on the subject of slashed farthingales and bombasted kirtles: but Padua is not at all the kind of place in which to look for that frivolous and hysterical order of recreation known as "going on anyhow."

It was this mode of progression, however, in which Padua had chosen to move during the past three weeks; and I have little doubt that when I return I shall still find the incorrigible old place "going on anyhow." *Festa* had succeeded *festa*, and one illumination had followed close on the heels of another. Padua, in short, was still in the heyday of that ecstasy of delight which followed the departure of the Austrians: a people who at home—say at Vienna, or Gratz, or Brünn — are the jolliest, best-natured, and most placable to be found anywhere between Cape Cod and the Carpathian Mountains, but who, abroad, rarely fail in making themselves as nauseous as nicotine and as insufferable as asafœtida.

The King of Italy was at Padua, and there, or in the neighbourhood, his Majesty will remain, it is to be presumed, until the ratifications of the much-bungled treaty of peace are exchanged, and he can enter Venice at the head of the Italian army. It is not, I should opine, proposed to march the Italian dragoons and hussars and horse-artillery into St. Mark's Place; yet, by the aid of a flotilla of flat-bottomed barges, the invasion of the Lagoons by cavalry might be practicable. The spell which hitherto tabooed the entry into Venice of anything four-footed that was bigger than a poodle has been broken within these latter days by the Austrians. I hear that there are at present not fewer than three thousand troop-horses picketed in the Giardino Pubblico at Venice. The Uhlans pertaining to these chargers are likewise, I suppose, on the spot; but it may be asked what on earth General Alemann thought of doing with three thousand dragoons in the City of the Sea!*

I have an old book of Venetian costumes, drawn by one Cesare Vecellio, Titian's nephew, A.D. 1590, and the volume contains a curious view of the Piazzetta, with a bull-ring at the foot of the Campanile, and the citizens of the Most Serene Republic actively engaged in baiting the infuriated

* The report was utterly false.

animal. One bull, however, went far enough in those days; but three thousand dragoons in the Giardino Pubblico pass my comprehension. It is impossible to charge along the Riva di Schiavoni; for the Ponte della Paglia, and a dozen more canals and bridges, are in the way. St. Mark's Place would hold as many regiments of horse as the great winter riding-school at Moscow; but you must get your horses there first ere they can manœuvre, just as you must catch your hare before you can cook him. When I was at Venice in the spring, there was but one horse, a meek hack, let out at so much an hour in the Giardino. Ex-Modena used to ride him, before he went to Vienna to carry candles at the feast of Corpus Christi. Ex-Bordeaux would have a trot now and then. Janty Austrian aide-de-camps would bestride the one saddle-horse of Venice, and make believe that they were caracoling along the Prater. He was everybody's horse—a quiet, resigned-looking Dobbin, with a round nose, a switch tail, and a cold-boiled eye in which there was no speculation. Peace to his mane! He has gone to the dogs long since, I fear; and now three thousand fiery steeds neigh and prance where erst he so tranquilly hobbled.

I should have very much liked to stay in Padua, say a couple of days; for I love the picturesque city, with its shady arcades, and its steep flights of stairs, and its façades rich in storied sculpture and heraldic achievements of a proud nobility long since fallen into the portion of weeds and outworn faces. There was one capital impediment, however, to making any lengthened sojourn in Padua—and that was the absence of any place whereat one could stay. The presence of Royalty is usually effectual in raising house-rent; but there were no more houses, and no more rooms, and no more beds in Padua to be rented. There was nothing to let. All the hotels were full. After Rocca d'Anfò* I should not have been mighty particular as to the kind of accommodation to be found; but I did not hear of a stable, or a billiard-table, or a cupboard, or even a cottage-floor that was vacant at Padua and open to take in lodgers. And, talking of stables, will someone learned in the Italian language tell me the difference between a *stallaggio* and a *stallazzo?* Both are augmentatives of *stalla;* but I want to know the nice distinction between the *aggio* and the *azzo.*

Beds being unobtainable, there was nothing to do but to walk about Padua, and make believe that you lived there, and were something else besides a homeless vagabond. I confided my valise to an entire stranger—a *facchino* at the diligence-office—simply for the reason that he had *not* mounted an Italian cockade in his cap. All the other *facchini* were flaming in the tricolor, and, in the intervals of fardel-carrying, lurched in and out of the wine-shops grunting "*Viva Italia!*" or "*Viva Garibaldi!*" The uncockaded porter did not cry *viva* anybody, but stood with his arms folded, passing sad, waiting until a kind Providence should send him a traveller and the chance of earning a few *soldi.* He was an old *facchino* and a gray, and had been sweating under burdens, I daresay, for half a century. It did not much matter to him, perhaps, whether it was beneath the trunk of an English tourist or a German hauptmann that he perspired. When you have been carrying heavy loads on your

* In the Tyrol. For some weeks, during the campaign of the Garibaldini, my lodging was habitually "on the cold ground."

spinal column since the year eighteen hundred and sixteen you are apt to become indifferent to the nationality of your masters. Perhaps the *facchino* sympathised with the departed Tedeschi. Robespierre's landlord wept for him. Haynau was beloved by his valet-de-chambre. The Germans may have been more liberal in *trinkgeld* than the Italians in the *buona mano* to this uncockaded man. At all events, there was something about him that impelled me to confide to him, without exacting any security or guarantee, the precious depository of my other shirt, my socks, and that dictionary. "There is a man," I said, "who is verging on threescore and ten, who is poor and shabby, and yet has courage enough to avow his opinions, and to disdain to screech with the rabble rout. He will not prove a fraudulent bailee. He will not steal my other shirt, nor sell my dictionary to the Egyptians." Nor did he.

The King was lodged in the Great Place, and the entire frontage of the rooms he occupied was hung with crimson velvet and gold lace. In the principal streets the inhabitants had likewise testified their sense of the festal nature of the times by hanging their carpets out of the windows. An uninitiated person might have imagined that all Padua had got the brokers in, and was about to be sold up; but the general effect of this variegated display of tapestry was undeniably pleasing. Early as it was the flower-girls were afoot—barefoot be it understood—and made fierce lunges at the buttonholes of every passer-by. Shame upon me! the lovers of the romantic will cry, because I look on these bold wenches as nuisances, little inferior in nastiness to the ragged boys who turn *soubresauts* and the raggeder girls who sell cigar-lights in London streets. But an Italian flower-girl! she must be, from the romantic point of view, full of poetry, witching sentiment, and all that kind of thing. Only consider Lord Lytton's Blind Girl in the *Last Days of Pompeii.* What exquisite songs she sings; how we sympathise with her when her brutal mistress whips her with leathern thongs! Alas, were the truth known, I daresay that Pompeian blind girl was a slipshod slut who didn't comb her hair, and bored the life out of Glaucus and Diomed and the young Pompeian nobility to buy her stale bouquets.

I was not in a charitable mood when I made these reflections upon flower-girls in general and the *fioraje* of Padua in particular occurred to me. When you have been travelling all night, and fail to secure a place whereon to lay your head in the morning, the milk of your human kindness is very much given to turn to curds-and-whey. I was irritated, too, to find that the good shops were as yet closed, and that there were at least five hundred establishments open for the sale of bad wine, worse cigars, and postage-stamps; which last are very useful things in their way, but do not go far towards supplying a tired and hungry man with bed and breakfast. Nor does there lack something essentially unpleasant in the sight of the extreme alacrity with which the collectors of the internal revenue of the kingdom of Italy have swooped down on the newly-liberated provinces. We must have the tax-gatherer, I suppose, like the poor, with us always. It is our lot to be taxed from the cradle to the grave; yet might perhaps some means be devised, when a country is newly rescued from the grasp of the stranger, for gilding the pill a little, and making the taxes look like something else.

The Italians have not been at these pains, and the Venetians are told, rudely enough, that the first thing they have to do is to pay. They may shout as much as they like, and hoist flags and hang their carpets out of window; but they must part with their *lire* and *centesimi* nevertheless. The Liberators, it may be whispered, are sadly in want of ready cash. Liberty is proverbially hard up; and the first and not very agreeable results of the annexation of Venetia to Italy are an intimate acquaintance with a constitutional Government blessed with an enormous national debt—a Government which has been spending for the last five years on an average about seventy-five per cent above its annual income—which has had as ministers of finance a succession of gentlemen deeply versed in poetry, the fine arts, philosophy, and jurisprudence, but wholly ignorant of the simple rules of arithmetic as taught by the late Mr. Edward Cocker—a Government, in fine, which is pecuniarily about as deeply dipped as the Sublime Porte, and experiences an equal difficulty in making both ends meet.

However, the Venetians and all other Italians may hope for the best. Peace, retrenchment, economy, good management, will do a great deal in a very short time towards retrieving the finances of a magnificently productive country. Only, if it is to be peace, let it be peace in good earnest, and not another seven years' spasm of feverish agitation, with a congested army and an inflated navy, and a perpetual growl of "*Guerra al Tedesco!*" To render such a peace possible, plead the Italians, Italy must have its "natural confines," the Trentino, Ischia, and the rest of it. But suppose France had refused to make peace with us until she got back Guernsey, Jersey, Alderney, and Sark, which, as all the world knows, are bits of Normandy chipped off the French cake by perfidious Albion; and suppose England persisted in menacing France with war until the latter Power surrendered Brittany, which is palpably a part of the ancient Armorica—where the very cows speak Welsh, and where the female peasantry, after selling their luxuriant tresses to the Parisian manufacturers of chignons, cover the nakedness of their heads with Welsh wigs. Which is a fact not generally known.

I should have left Padua with but a sorrowful impression as to its hospitality — even to that hospitality, most cosmopolitan, which is to be obtained by paying for it—had not the Caffè Pedrocchi been open. The Caffè Pedrocchi is the stateliest coffee-house in Italy. It is one of the institutions of Padua, and as famous almost as its time-honoured university. It is a great many stories high, and is I know not how many hundred feet broad and long, and contains I have forgotten how many score apartments, large and small—some of them, especially the one called La Sala Chinesa, magnificently decorated. In fact, if you wish to see something "right-down handsome" in the way of Corinthian columns, chandeliers, plate-glass, marble tables, crimson-velvet settees, niches with statuettes, and mosaic pavements, you should visit the Caffè Pedrocchi. It is the Alhambra, the Alcazar of Padua; and the Padovesi are never tired of sauntering in its marble halls, and lounging on its marble staircases, and admiring its frescoed ceilings, and expatiating on the glories of its Sala Chinesa. Who Pedrocchi was, although there is a vague story about him in "Murray," I know not. There is a casino upstairs, which is opened only at the time of the Carnival, when a *ridotto* is held there. Now, what is a *ridotto?* or, if you come to that, what is a *casino*, taken in its signification as a place of popular recreation? A *ridotto* is, I believe, a land relative of a *regata;* and both are what the Spaniards term a *funcion*, and the Americans a "shake up and break down of the High She Quality." Have I made myself understood with sufficient clearness?

The most marked peculiarity of the Caffè Pedrocchi is this—that, like its brethren at Venice yonder, it never closes. From the 1st of January until the 31st of December—morning, noon, and night—all the year round, you can obtain refreshment at this large-hearted and indefatigable establishment. You may breakfast, lunch, and sup at the Caffè Pedrocchi; but at no time, I believe, during its existence—which dates from the invasion of Italy by Attila, King of the Huns—was ever anybody known to dine there. It was at Florian's, in the Piazza San Marco, that the discrowned royalties immortalised in *Candide* met; every one of whom had come to see the Carnival of Venice, and not one of whom had money enough to pay for his supper. The dethroned princes, I have heard, subsequently came on to Padua, and regaled on *demi-tasses* and *petits verres* at the Caffè Pedrocchi. Their score remains unpaid to this day. It was the then head-waiter's great-grandson who told me so. The unfortunate Charles Edward Stuart consumed a monstrous quantity of cognac on credit; and Theodore, King of Corsica, was shabby enough to fill the pockets of his threadbare surtout with cigars ere he took diligence *en route* for Gerard-street, Soho, and the London Insolvent Court.

These are shadows, vague and improbable enough if you please; but can any shadows I can conjure up vie with the real historical ghosts which yet linger on the threshold of this enormous tavern? But twenty days since, and the Austrians were here. Legions of white-coated phantoms seem stalking about the halls, now thronged by the jovial and gesticulating Italian officers. I hear guttural cries of "Kellner." I see spectral copies of the *Neue Freie Presse* and the *Wiener Zeitung* bestrewing the marble tables. Alas, poor ghosts! Their spurs are to jingle, their swords to clank, no more in this delicious land. The Tedeschi really liked Italy—the country, the blue sky, the soft climate, the golden groves of citron, the purple vines, the mountains and the lakes—the ices, the macaroni, the vino d'Asti, the picture-galleries and palaces, the *caffès* and the operatic music. They liked the Italian ladies very much indeed. The only hitch was that the Italians didn't like them.

Still, in this lachrymose age, when everybody is blubbering about something, I think we ought to squeeze out a tear for the Tedeschi. "*Laissez-moi pleurer cette race morte,*" said M. Victor Hugo of the Bourbons, taking out his pocket-handkerchief and weeping bitterly, while all France was clapping its hands for joy to think that the Bourbons had been kicked out. If you please, I will drop the silent tear over two niches on either side the bar or *comptoir* of the Caffè Pedrocchi—niches hung with crimson drapery of richest damask — niches which of old time contained the highly framed and glazed lithograph effigies of the Kaiser Francis Joseph and his pretty Kaiserinn; and now, in these niches, in lieu of their Imperial, Royal, and Apostolic Majesties, I behold the burly physiognomy and incredible moustaches of Victor Emmanuel, side by side with a most ungenteel-looking individual in a red-flannel shirt, by the name of Garibaldi. It is a world of ups and downs, and the Caffè Pedrocchi is not exempt from the common see-saw.

X.

PONTE D'ARANA.

August 24.

To think that I should have come to Ferrara again on my second journey of discovery through Venetia, and passed once more the noon-tide heats in a darkened room, waiting for a carriage to take me to Padua, and never have known that this was "*la citta bene avventurato*" of Ariosto, and "*la gran Donna del Po*" of Tassoni; that here the immortal Torquato himself had a commission *de lunatico*, consisting of one despot, taken out against him; that here was the retreat of that sweet bird of song, Guarini; that the walls of Ferrara were built in the sixth century by the Exarchs of Ravenna, who incorporated with the newly-founded city the bishopric of Vigovenza; that during the sixteenth century the Court of Ferrara was unsurpassed by any in Europe for intelligence and refinement—I had only remembered it for its propensity to poison people; that there were once so many English students in the University of Ferrara as to form, as they did at Bologna, a distinct "nation" in that learned body; that the Ferrarese school of painting numbered among its illustrations the accomplished Galasso Galassi and the gifted Dosso Dossi; that the high-minded Duchess Renée, daughter of Louis XII. of France, and wife of Hercules II., Duke of Ferrara, afforded protection and asylum to Calvin and Marot, and other lights of the Reformed Faith; and that in the ducal palace at Ferrara was educated the famous Olympia Morata, the queen of strong-minded ladies, "who here acquired that knowledge of the Gospel which supported her mind under the privations and hardships which she afterwards had to endure!" Twice had I been to Ferrara, and of all this I had known nothing.

Equally ignorant was I of the fact that in the north-east tower of the grim old brick castello, and in a dungeon several feet under low water-mark, Parisina and her guilty lover were put to death; for the details of which dreadful tragedy *vide* Gibbon's *Decline and Fall*, Lord Byron's poems, and Frizzi's history of Ferrara, *passim*. It was in a hole underneath the chamber called the "Aurora," "at the foot of the Lions' Tower, at the top of the street called the Giovecca, and on the night of the 21st of May, that first Ugo and afterwards Parisina were beheaded." The extreme severity shown to this unfortunate female has always surprised me. Even as the historian of fiction, in recording the circumstance that Mr. Sampson Brass, attorney, of Bevis Marks, was struck off the rolls, has remarked that there must have been something special and extraordinary in his culpability, seeing how many rascals yet remain unexcised upon those same rolls; so would it appear that in Parisina's case there must have been an extra and unpardonable degree of naughtiness which led the Sir James Wilde of the period to chop off her head for that which at least fifty per cent of the married ladies of Italy were then in the habit of doing, with complete impunity.

The fact is, that when I went to Ferrara I was quite unread in the history and antiquities of the city, beyond the highly-coloured episodes in M. Hugo's melodrama, a work of genius now generally held to be "unhistorical." I know all these things now; but it is too late to utilise my information, for it is not probable that I shall ever return to Ferrara. The air is not good. It smells of henbane and strychnine. We all of us experience a certain amount of vague and unaccountable terror at *something*. I confess that I am frightened at Ferrara. Nor, perhaps, should I have become acquainted with what I have set down above—notably for the information respecting La Stella d'Oro—had I not recently become the proud possessor of Murray's *Handbook for Travellers in Northern Italy*. The work cost me fifteen francs, and was in a dilapidated condition; but a "Murray" in a strange land is a thing of beauty and a joy for ever. I have had something more to do lately than to study "Murray." The instruction I have acquired has been purely of the *vivâ-voce* order. My recent education has been essentially un-Aristotelian, and based on the canons laid down by Lord Bacon. Everything has been done by induction. I have been taught botany as the young gentlemen at Dotheboys' Hall were taught it, viz. by being sent into a field to hoe potatoes. So soon as I have spelt a word, I have "gone and done it." I know that there is no butcher's meat at Salo, and that there are thieves who steal breastpins at Rocca d'Anfò.

In the interest of all travellers in the less-frequented parts of Italy, I must insist on the necessity of some guide or handbook, be it a "Murray," a "Bradshaw," or a "Baedecker." In other countries you may sometimes dispense with such assistance, or you make shift with the local guides; but in

Italy you *must* have a printed finger-post, and, preferably, that finger-post should be an Anglo-Saxon one. Only an Englishman writing for Englishmen can properly understand the requirements of his own countrymen and countrywomen, and direct them to where they can procure decent and comfortable accommodation, as the words decency and comfort are understood in the British Isles. *Away from the great cities the Italian inns are certainly the filthiest and most infamous which I have ever seen—not even excepting those of Spain and Mexico.* The Italian *albergo* seems to have changed very little indeed from what it was in the days of Cicero. The Roman "Caupona," according to Horace and Aulus Gellius, was patronised only by those who were destitute of letters of introduction to private houses; and the modern edition of the "Caupona" is patronised only by pedlars and farmers, and such unhappy foreign tourists as, being strangers in the land, know not where else to hide their heads. An Italian of rank or refinement is rarely to be found at a provincial inn. He has acquaintances in the neighbourhood. *Italians of the middle class, unless they have visited England, are absolutely ignorant of what comfort, cleanliness, or common decency mean.*

An innkeeper at Bergamo was insolent enough to tell me that the incredibly horrible nature of his domestic arrangements was thought good enough for Italians, and, by the same rule, ought to suit English people. But I told him that his inn could not have been intended for Italians, whom I respected as a noble and intelligent people, seeing that his house was fit only for skunks and swine, of whom I added, as a compliment, he was one or both. Whereat he looked as though he would have stabbed me, but ultimately subsided into a kitchen, there to fry in rancid oil some entrails—the famous *frittura*, indeed—which somebody had ordered for lunch.

I am afraid, however, that to the great majority of Italians such a sty as that of Bergamo would have been looked upon as a perfectly tolerable place in which to abide. I am afraid that they like dirt, darkness, stench, inattention, laziness, and coarse food badly cooked. What does your middle-class Italian want? His needs are simple. First, *alloggio* —that means a room, or half a room, or half, or a third of a bed, if it comes to that; anything, in short, where he can lie down and sleep, with or without taking off his clothes. Very little water, and the corner of a post-octavo towel, will serve his turn. In the morning he wants a cup of black coffee and a morsel of bread. Some, but by no means the mass of Italians, take the *collazione* or *déjeuner à la fourchette*, but many prefer to wait until five or six o'clock, when they dine heavily and indigestibly on macaroni or some other paste swimming in grease and gravy, or *minestra*, a stodge of *brodo* and rice; boiled beef, roast veal, tomatoes, *zucchetti*, and fried entrails. Without the *frittura* it is no dinner at all. This, with some excellent cheese and some delicious fruit, is the kind of dinner you get in nine out of ten provincial inns in Italy; but the revolting coarseness of the viands, and the gross carelessness shown in their preparation, are ill compensated by the piquant savour of Parmesan and the dulcet suavity of ripe peaches. If you asked for a *bouillon*, they would stare; if you wanted a cup of tea, they would either tell you there was none, or send round to the doctor's shop for some simples of noxious odour, apparently culled by the late King Nebuchadnezzar in his botanising days, and from them make a decoction fit to turn the stomach of an ostrich. The Italian, of course, does not require such luxuries. After he has fed, at five or six, he requires absolutely nothing more save the privilege of smoking whensoever he pleases.

It may be urged that strangers are bound to put up with the customs of the country in which they travel; but it is my duty to remark that directly the Italian innkeeper finds out that you are a foreigner, and especially that you are an Englishman or an American, he charges you four francs for the dinner, or six francs for the room, which a native would get for two. Over and over again have I been presented with a bill for twenty *lire* when I had had the lodging of a brute. I have put down ten francs and buttoned up my pocket, and after many "*Per Dios!*" and infinite shrugs and grimaces on the part of the landlord, the composition of ten shillings in the pound has been thankfully accepted.

They do not use you so in Spain. For comfort in the great cities you must pay extravagantly; but away from Madrid or Seville, at the miserable *fondas, ventas,* or *mesons,* where you can only obtain that which nature needs, you will find that "man's life is cheap as beast's." The twopence which the good Samaritan left at the inn for the wounded man would, translated into *reals* and *cuartos*, very nearly pay for all that a Spanish innkeeper can let you have. Moreover, you do not expect to find comfort or even adequate sustenance in the Spanish provinces; and when you get accustomed to the country you never venture on a journey without taking provisions with you.

But the case is different in "Bootia Felix." Italy is not half Moorish. Africa does not begin at the Alps, as it does at the Pyrenees. Italy should be as civilised and polished a land as any in Europe; but I repeat that in the provincial towns the customs of the people are atrocious. Liberty is a grand thing. The remark cannot be repeated too often; but first learn to live less offensively, and then go in as much as you please for liberty. The only clean and comfortable villages I have yet seen in Italy are those in the immediate neighbourhood of Milan, and on the shores of the Lake of Como.

These few words of warning will, I trust, suffice to impress on the mere tourist for pleasure—for he who travels by compulsion or on business must needs take things as he finds them, and be thankful they are not worse—the necessity of coming to Italy armed with some kind of guide-books which shall tell him where inns, fit for civilised Christians rather than savage Yahoos, to live and sleep in may be found. And where such inns are not to be found, let him avoid the town or district, however rich in pictures and antiquities, altogether. There is always a sufficient stock of professional travellers and antiquaries who do not mind roughing it; but I do not see that a peaceable and polished layman, accustomed to clean linen, wholesome food, three-pronged forks, and plenty of cold water, has any call, merely for the purpose of publishing an octavo volume, or telling his friends at the Sybarite Club that he has seen such and such a fresco, or "done" such and such a lion, to undergo the hardship of a Speke, a Livingstone, or a Burton.

Richard Brinsley Sheridan once pointed out to his son

Tom the inutility of going down a coalpit. Could he not *say* he had been down one? he hinted. The insinuation was immoral, and truth is precious; but the modern code of ethics accepted by society affords many convenient loopholes by means of which a man may evade an embarrassing confession without positively telling a fib. When you have been asked, for instance, if you know Bergamo, you may hum and hah, and dexterously turn the conversation into a different channel by remarking that the Pension Suisse at Bologna is an excellent house; and he who has been to Naples has a clear right, in equity, to lead to the inference that he is intimately acquainted with Sorrento.

Under ordinary circumstances trust to a guide-book that does not puff, and give all towns where the inns are not marked as "clean and good" a wide berth. Again, never be led by what your courier tells you, or patronise the hostelries which he most strongly recommends. This morsel of advice may seem to some superfluous; for in these days of railways and universal education it would appear as useless to travel with a courier as with a guard of halberdiers. Railways and universal education notwithstanding, there are still some thousands of miles in Europe to be travelled only by stage or post; and there are yet numbers of persons, male and female, of mature age and of ample means, who go abroad without a larger stock of foreign words than that in the French vocabulary of Albert Smith's old lady: "Garsong, donnez-moy —some 'am."

If you are so unfortunate as to be compelled to engage a foreign travelling servant, you will act well, as a rule, never to believe a word he says, and always to do the exact contrary to that which he advises you; but, in particular, mistrust his counsel concerning hotels. If you have no guide-book you are of course in his hands, and must go to the inn he selects as a fool would to the correction of the stocks; but have a guide-book, and he need not make a fool of you, nor you a fool of yourself. Couriers—the Italian ones especially—are almost sure to be in league with the landlord, who is generally an old courier and a great rogue; so Boniface and Sganarelle play into each other's hands. Nor are the inns kept by ex-couriers, although they never fail in being extortionately dear, always the cleanest or the best. Finally, let me entreat the traveller never to stay at the hotel where the diligence starts or where it halts. Coaching inns in England used to be good and comfortable; but the *albergo delle diligenze* in Italy is, with scarcely an exception, abominable in every respect. The *conducteur* of the diligence—usually a civil, specious, rascally fellow—will of course earnestly entreat your excellency to descend at the coaching inn. He is in the landlord's pay, and gets a regular commission on every traveller he brings. A middle-class Italian who has not travelled beyond the limits of his own country is a counsellor quite as pernicious. He, poor benighted being, knows that at the *albergo della diligenza* such bare necessaries may be had as *alloggio*, the *minestra*, the *frittura*, and the *vino del paese*—the common wine of the country, very like a beverage they used to sell at a gin-palace in Whitechapel, called "Imperial Black Stuff, very nobby," and apparently a mixture of logwood, vinegar, treacle, and blacking; and of anything beyond these he does not dream.

Therefore, by all means, carry your "Murray," your "Bradshaw," or your "Baedecker" as a precious burden; but if you lose it, or can find no bibliopole who sells handbooks, take care, ere you leave the clean and comfortable house in which you may be stopping in Milan, or Florence, or Venice, to inquire for the names of the hotels in the towns you propose to visit with which your Milanese or Florentine landlord is in "correspondence." He will know at once the kind of inn you require; and he will not dare to recommend an inferior one, hoping as he does that you will return, and apprehensive as he is that you will devote him to the infernal gods when you find that he has misled you.*

* I wrote this at Ponte d'Arana, a few miles from Padua; but of Ponte d'Arana itself I have nothing to say that is good. Well may they call it Ponte d'Arana, as my countryman said of Stoney-Stratford—for I was most terribly bitten by fleas there.

XI.

CAFFÈS.

August 25.

Not easily shall I forget an incident which I witnessed one evening just before I left Vicenza—an incident trifling in itself, and which, as things progress, will every day become more common, but which to me was a straw showing unmistakably the way the wind had begun to blow, and was eloquent as to the commencement of the new era, including new men, new measures, new clothes, and new brooms. There is a very handsome caffè at Vicenza, in the Piazza called de' Signori, the said Piazza being a miniature copy of the Piazza San Marco, with two tiny columns crowned with statues, and a Liliputian Ducal Palace, and a microscopic Broglio for the proud signori to walk upon in scarlet gowns, to the exclusion from the flags of meaner mortals, and a baby Torre dell' Orologio, or clock-tower, and three slender little masts for the banners of the Venetian Dominion to float from, and a brace of diminutive façades, rivalling, on the scale of two inches to a foot, the Procuratii Nuovi and the Procuratii Vecchj of the mother city, Venice. And everywhere that space can be found for a statuette or a bas-relief, the Lion of St. Mark, reduced to the proportions of a Maltese lap-dog, wags his little tail, and flutters his little wings, and shakes a little mane *en papillotte*, and cons his eternal hornbook.

The old Venetians were very fond of setting up in their

provincial towns minified copies of the Superb and Serene Place. Little columns, little piazzettas, little masts, little basilicas, are scattered all over Venetia; and even at Pola, and Istria, and Fiume, and other spots on the Ischian and Dalmatian shores, there linger reminiscences of Venetian architecture which might be carried away on a porter's shoulders, and ducal palaces that might be put into a pint-pot. These things are not to be laughed at, however. Though infinitesimal, they are beautiful as those tiny models of state-coaches and miniature broughams which skilful artisans in Long-acre construct, and which may be seen in shop-windows side by side with the mightiest coach-building establishments. At Vicenza, for instance, the pretty little tiny kickshaws on the Piazza de' Signori are mainly from the designs of Palladio and Scamozzi—illustrious architects who, after here luxuriating in carving cherry-stones and reducing bas-reliefs to the dimensions of postage-stamps, crossed the lagoons, and at Venice built staircases for giants, and stately houses for the senators of the greatest republic in the world, and tombs for doges supported by caryatides seventy feet high.

Genius the most colossal must disport itself sometimes in an infantile manner, and take delight in little things. I have heard of a grave historian, a famous novelist, and a fellow of the Royal Society, who were wont to indulge every Sunday afternoon, and on a lawn at Putney, in a game at leapfrog. Sometimes they admitted an epic poet and an eminent tragedian to their company, nor do I think it would have done the Lord High Chancellor or the Archbishop of Canterbury much harm to have joined that social circle. We *must* have an admixture of the funny, the playful, the nonsensical if you please, in the dismal course of daily life. The sages, scholars, and philosophers, who with such lamentable frequency go raving mad, are precisely those who have never made fools of themselves. It is good to be a young donkey sometimes, or a frolicsome kitten, or an impudent puppy. Your Eldon-like owl sits perpetually in the ruined keep at Arundel, looking unutterably wise; but everybody knows that he is really as blind as a bat, and is always running his head against wrong points of law. So I greet those baby Venices whenever I see them, and only regret that hydraulic engineers have been unable to bring up an Adriatic no bigger than the Serpentine to their doors.

Vicenza is not all Liliputian. It boasts a score of palaces as vast and sumptuous as any to be found in Venetia or Lombardy, and has, besides, a Palazzo della Ragione, or law-courts, a Pinacoteca, a Duomo—in which the Council of Trent held some supplementary sittings, and did much to embroil the world—and one of the handsomest pawnbrokers' shops I ever saw. It is three stories high, of the Doric, Ionic, and Corinthian in due progression, and inside is prettily decorated with subjects from Roman history, painted by Signor Fassola. I did not narrowly inspect these objects of art, having no intimate business to transact with the Monte di Pietà, so I am puzzled to know what events in the history of old Rome could be tortured into any connection with My Uncle. "Cornelia disposing of her jewels;" "Cæsar's wife entering by the back-door in order to be above suspicion;" "Vespasian remarking that thirty per cent from the poor was good money, and had no vile smell;" "Caligula's groom pawning the gilt oats of the consular horse;" or "Virginius consigning the urn containing his daughter's ashes to the care of Mr. Attenborough"—these are the only Roman subjects I can think of which suitably might adorn the avuncular palace at Vicenza. The roof, I may observe, is beautified by no less than four splendidly-carved columns of funnel form—ostensibly chimneys, but which I imagine to be spouts; and under the principal façade there is a lion's-mouth letter-box, with the directions, "*Consulte segrete,*" above it. What secret consultations can be needed in the course of negotiations with My Uncle? Are any of the noble signori of Vicenza in the habit of confiding to the letter-box their applications concerning the backing of tickets? One thing is certain. The king of beasts has a mighty capacity for swallowing; but you cannot "pop" a flat-iron in a lion's mouth.

Much more might I say about Vicenza; but I remember my own perhaps not over-discreet avowal as to the facilities for cramming which "Murray" gives you; and so, carefully eschewing the historical and the antiquarian, I will make my way to that *caffè* on the Piazza de' Signori, where I witnessed that incident which I was about without further digression to narrate—only, as often happens, some reflections more or less pertinent stood in the way. The little Garibaldian lieutenant who had been "ovated" at the theatre at Rovigo, and your humble servant, were using the *caffè* in question very late one night. Vicenza is holding incessant festival, after the manner of Padua, Rovigo, and Udine, and all other places in the *Dominio Veneto* freshly emancipated from the Austrian rule; and the *caffè* was crowded. The Venetians, ordinarily nearly as sober a nation as the Spaniards, have now been tipsy for three weeks—really tipsy, on alcoholic preparations. There is not a bottle of champagne to be had between Goito and Mestre. Patriotism has drunk it all up in toasts to the King, Garibaldi, and the unity of Italy. So much of the genuine old "black-strap" or *vino del paese* of last year has been consumed in patriotic liquoring-up, and so little promises to be made this year, in consequence of the general confusion springing from the war, that the market-price of ordinary wine has risen fifty per cent.

On this night I speak of, Vicenza was even more than usually thirsty. All the oranges and lemons of all the golden groves in Arcadia seemed to have been converted into *limonate* and *aranciate;* and if all the coffee which, with milk and without milk, and hot and cold, was frantically asked for came from the Antilles and from Mocha, it is certain that the West Indies are not yet ruined, and there is yet a land called Arabia Felix. As for the seltzer-water, I am afraid that the Austrians must have blown up by means of their own gases all the effervescing-drink manufactories before they evacuated this part of the country, for there is not a drop of seltzer or soda to be obtained north of Ferrara. I suppose the caffè-keepers at Vicenza and elsewhere are all making rapid fortunes. I do not envy them their new-found riches, but I may impress on them the expediency of cleaning their spoons, and of putting a smaller quantity of ground-rice into their cream, so soon as the régime of constitutional liberty and representative institutions has been settled on a firm basis. At present the chief characteristics of the Italian *caffès* I have seen are sloppiness and muddiness. They, indeed, resemble the penny-ice shops of the low London neighbourhoods on an extended scale; and this I say without wishing to cast the slightest reflection on the esteemed M. Gatti, who has, in his generation, by combating the beer-shop, and competing even with the gin-palace, done an immense deal of good in *London;* as much good, perhaps, as the multiplicity of *caffès* in Italy, and their absurd cheapness, has done harm.

This looks like a paradox, I admit; but it is one that will hold water. The Italian *caffès* are all too cheap, and their proprietors are all far too tolerant in permitting persons of the genus "loafer" to remain for hours together, consuming nothing more expensive than a cup of black coffee, price four sous, or a glass of iced water. You may also remain in an Italian *caffè* for as long as ever you like without taking anything at all, and neither landlord nor waiter will venture to drop a hint as to the propriety of consuming anything for the good of the house. Those of the guests who smoke—and nearly all do—bring their own tobacco, so the house makes nothing out of nicotine. All this may conduce towards sobriety; and in England, places where you might sit, smoke, gossip, and sip cold water or weak tea, without being compelled to get drunk for the benefit of a member of the Licensed Victuallers' Society, would be a boon well-nigh inestimable to the poorer classes. The penny-ice shops go a great way towards it; but the London proprietor of the penny-ice shop, looking towards his rent, taxes, and poor-rates, would naturally turn somewhat sullen if you did not order a penny ice say once in every half-hour. The end of the continual consumer of cheap lemons and vanillas might equal in horror that of the over-zealous teetotaller, whose stomach on post-mortem examination was found to contain nothing but tea-leaves and snowballs.

There should be a golden mean in everything. That mean is not to be found, so far as I am aware, in any country under the sun. In England the cheap *caffè* would be a blessing, and out of the palatial clubs of Pall-mall it is rarely to be found.* In Italy the cheap *caffè* abounds, and is open to all, and I look upon it as a kind of curse, and one of the chief causes of the backwardness, the laziness, and the general impracticability of the Italian people. They swarm into these *caffès*, where their outlay need never exceed a few halfpence, and there they pass at least half their existence, ruining their digestion with black coffee and blacker cigars taken on fasting stomachs, neglecting their business, wasting their time, and mag, mag, mag, endlessly magging, on one invariable theme—politics. Here they graduate in gesticulation; here they learn to blaspheme—and in blasphemy an Italian will beat an American, which is saying a great deal; here they learn to repeat the *canard*, to give the lie, to

* The London "coffee-shops," properly so called, although excellent in many respects, and provided with a store of newspapers and periodicals which many a continental *casino de' nobili* might envy, are for the most part dark, stuffy, and uncomfortable, and cut up into gloomy "boxes" little better than the compartments of a cellular van. The penny-ice shops—of which I am very glad to recognise the unpretentious value, from a temperance point of view—are rendered intolerable to grown-up persons by swarms of blackguard little boys and girls, restless, impudent, and precociously vicious; while at the West-end too many of the really handsome cafés on the Parisian model which have been started—I daresay with the most innocent and laudable intent—have within a very brief period become the resort of "fast men" and of more than questionable women. Those whose proprietors are determined to continue respectable in every sense are constrained to adopt a tariff so high as to be well-nigh prohibitory, in order to exclude "gay"—that is to say, abominable—company.

denounce their own Government, and malign those of other countries. Any other more solid information I do not see that they can acquire. One man just skims the contents of a little flysheet called by courtesy a newspaper, and spouts what he has read to half-a-dozen companions, and the rest screech and yell, and assert and deny, and thump the table till they make the cups and saucers dance. From time to time some patriotic gentleman may remember that he has his livelihood to earn, say breeches to make, or bellows to mend, or boots to cobble, or young lambs to sell—for Italy is really a democratic country, and there is a curious equalisation of rank in the *caffè*—and away he goes to take a short spell of work. But he speedily returns, to light more cavours and drink more thin swizzle, to mouth and rant more nonsense.

This, then, is my position: Your *caffè*-frequenter spends but little money; but he spends an enormous amount of time. Which is the most precious? The time, I think. He keeps sober, so far as alcohol is concerned, but gets most drunk in the way of gesticulation and argument. He talks much and learns little, if anything. Finally, the *caffè* is to him as a sort of garment which covers all manner of deadly sins. In England a man who is not an incorrigible drunkard or idler experiences a certain amount of shame if his friends meet him continually going in or coming out of a tavern. The public-house door, like the pawnbroker's, is, after all, a portal of ignominy, and of close parentage to the debtor's door. We even rally the decorous old gentlemen who are always wandering in and out of their clubs. But no shame attaches to the foreigner who, from morn to dewy eve, strolls backwards and forwards between his house and his caffè. It has many doors, they are all wide open, and you may float in and out unperceived. You may be only going to write a letter, to repose yourself after a long walk, to meet a friend, to keep a business appointment. In England the thoroughly idle man scarcely escapes detection at the hands of those who work. We know what tavern he "uses," or what club he haunts. But in Italy the idlers and the workers are so intimately mingled, that, seeing the *caffès* at all times crowded, you are puzzled to know when it is that the people work at all, and whether they were given to hang about *caffès* in the days when Palladio built, and Buonaroti carved, and Sanzio painted, and Ariosto wrote.

Pray understand that I exempt the *cafés* of France from these strictures. They are thronged only at certain hours of the day, *and they are not so cheap* as to encourage the loafer and the lotus-eater. The French *dame de comptoir* has a very keen scent for unprofitable customers; and the *garçon*, from a corner of his little eye, can very soon discern the *habitués* who sit long and order nothing. The necessity of "*la consommation*"—a terrible word—is a check on the stingy idler in France. I have heard a French waiter—in a third-rate café, be it understood—cry out when orders were languid, "*Consommez! il faut consommer, messieurs.*" An Italian waiter who ventured to utter such a remonstrance would be skinned alive by the indignant company.

Your Italian waiter is, under most circumstances, a shambling, shiftless creature, perfectly affable and urbane, but with a painfully-defective memory, and a general deficiency in the qualities we ordinarily expect to find in persons of his calling. He is much given to yawning, without taking the trouble to veil his sepulchral mouth with the palm of his hand; he is usually slipshod; and one end of his napkin, which is seldom clean, is tucked into the waistband of his pantaloons. He *will* not wear braces. You can see that he has a hard time of it, between the flies, which insects he is continually flacking away, and the *padrona,* who has a deuce of a temper, and the customers, who are constantly calling for *zolfanelli* wherewith to light their cavours, but are not over-generous in the bestowal of copper gratuities. If you put down say a two-franc piece in payment of what you have had, he brings you as much small change as the subdivisions of the Italian currency will permit, and they even comprise the *centesimo,* or the hundredth part of ninepence-halfpenny, which he places before you on a little electro-plated tray.

The Italians, who certainly take care of the pence if they do not trouble themselves about the pounds, and in their minor dealings are an unpleasantly thrifty race, generally shovel the entire contents of the tray into their pockets, and stalk away without further parley. They have an excuse for this niggardliness. Were they to give but a couple of cents to all who asked, they might give away their incomes, at the rate of five hundred pounds a-year, every day. There is no end to the beggars, licensed and unlicensed, who tug at your purse-strings in an Italian *caffè.*

To the waiters it does not appear to be the custom to give fees. Foreigners may fee them, but the natives only bestow on them a "*buon giorno*" or a "*riverisco,*" which are graceful salutations, soothing to the spirit, and costing nothing. Now and then I have seen a large-hearted Italian customer pick out from his trayful of small change the smallest coin discoverable, and hand it to the waiter with a glance of proud philanthropy, such as we might suppose the Chevalier Bayard might have put on when he handed the twenty-five hundred silver crowns to the two beauteous damsels of Breschia. The *bottega* has received the lowly copper with a shuffle of pleasure and a yawn of gratitude. I am sure the waiters are grateful for their scant allowance of halfpence; for I have always found the waiter whom I have fee'd, when I asked for a light for a cigar, insist on lighting it himself, and in his own peculiar fashion, which consists in placing the weed in the cleft of a long slender pole, and holding it up to a gas-jet. After a little dexterous twiddling, the end of the cigar is kindled to perfection, and the waiter then, with a friendly nod, and a yawn signifying that he is glad to have discharged his office and to be well out of it, hands you the cleft stick and the burning brand.

Surely these waiters are the laziest mortals alive, always excepting emancipated negroes and officers in the Light Cavalry. There is much latitude as to the way in which to summon an Italian waiter. You may cry "*Bottega!*" or "*Cameriere!*" although the latter would the rather signify a waiter at an hotel; and he will even understand "*garçon*," Italianised into "*garzone*." In Milan he comprehends the oriental call of clapping the hands, doubtless imported by the Spaniards, and used by them during their long occupation of Lombardy. I have likewise tried the Spanish sibilation "*Pss-Pss;*" but I do not think Italian waiters like that way of being called. Often the noise in the *caffè* is so great, that your voice is drowned by the screams of neighbouring politicians. The best manner, then, in order to attract attention is to hammer on the table with a knife, or bang a spoon violently against a glass. As a rule, the Italian waiter does not come when you do call to him. He looks over his shoulder, regards you sleepily, and says, "*Eccomi!*"—"Behold me;" or, as we should say, "Here I am." Two thousand years ago I suppose he said "*Adsum*" when the customer in the toga began to grow impatient. But "*Eccomi*" does not mean that he is coming. It means simply that he is still devoted to your interests, of course, but not disposed to stir an inch until you call him again. This you do, to which he responds, "*Subito,*" or, to save trouble, "*Subit,*" banging several trays on a neighbouring table to give you a proper impression of his alacrity of movement, and also, I presume, to waken himself up. But he does not come. At last you roar and hammer and bang, and, if you are of the Latin race, invoke Bacchus and the Madonna and several saints. Then does your waiter shuffle towards you, flacking the flies away, yawning, and smiling sweetly. It is impossible to be angry with him, his "*Commanda,*" or "What is she pleased to order?" is always put so affably, "she" being the pronoun used for the courteous abstraction of your "lordship," which, among Italian nouns, figures as the feminine substantive "Signoria." Besides, Italy is a country where time is of no account; and a *caffè* is a place where you are bound to waste as much of the great old dust-contractor's sand as ever you possibly can.

There is no rule without an exception. In the four emancipated cities of Venetia, the waiters neither yawn nor shuffle, nor flack the flies away. They run like the nimble stag; they leap like troutlings in a pool; they fly like Peter Wilkins; they are glib of speech; they give change with lightning rapidity; they rival American bar-keepers in the celerity with which they serve cool drinks—to be sure they only serve, and do not compound them; they are here, there, and everywhere, like Figaro in the opera. They never go to bed—at least it is unlikely that anybody in Vicenza has been to bed since the twenty-fifth of July. It is a marvel how they keep awake. Voltaire, you know, had become so entirely intellectual,—having brains even in the tips of his fingers, like the inhabitants of the Island of Ilicichi,—and drank so much black coffee, that when he had come to be about eighty-five years of age he had ceased to be able to sleep at all. He was always up and doing, always drinking black coffee, always writing, always sneering away religion and royalty, and the rest of it. He would have gone on, perhaps, drinking coffee and denying things, sleeplessly, to this day, had he not tumbled one evening into that great sound sleep which knits up the ravelled sleeves of everybody's cares—death.

I fancy the Vicenzan waiters must be kept up by means somewhat similar. The properties of coffee were, I believe, first discovered by an Arab farmer, who noticed that his camels, after browsing on the berries of a certain shrub, were unusually frisky and preternaturally wide-awake. What may be good for camels may serve the turn of waiters. Green tea is a capital thing to banish sleep withal; but it is too expensive in Venetia for ordinary consumption. I imagine that the hard-hearted proprietor of the *caffè* at Vicenza administers copious doses of double-distilled essence of coffee to his waiters every half-hour, otherwise I really do not see how they could keep up. But this sort of thing cannot last.

Reaction, collapse, must follow every kind of excess. Those high-pressure waiters must *crever* at last, and despair and die, as the sleepless old Arouet did.

And my incident? It is but a trifle—the barest bagatelle. I made its mention, at the commencement of this paper, only a pretext for telling my readers something about Italian *caffès*. In this one at Vicenza I lingered very late—far into the small hours, I am afraid; for until this moment so rapid have been one's movements, so troublous the times, and so confused one's impressions of travel, that I am not quite certain as to whether I lived anywhere at Vicenza, or whether I had merely the day occupancy of a room, after the manner immortalised in *Box and Cox*, and, being Box, was bound to walk the streets or haunt the *caffès* during the hours that Cox was slumbering on the pallet, which at 8 A.M. once more became mine. I can remember, vaguely, some hours of feverish tossing and perturbed day-dreams, among a colony of fleas, and some wretched breakfasts and wretcheder dinners at the Three Moors, or the Two Wheels, or the Iron Crown, or the Golden Star—I am sure I forget the exact name of mine inn at Vicenza; but I know I did not go to bed as Christian men should do, and that I haunted the *caffès* fearfully.

The performance at the Theatre Royal Vicenza was over. Like its brother at Rovigo, it had been closed for I know not how many years; but now the new era had commenced, and the new *impresario*—let us call him Angelo Scartaffacci—had reopened the establishment with a troupe that drew crowded audiences. Scartaffacci's prospectus was wonderful to read. "Long," he wrote, "has the noble and elevating dramatic art been crushed beneath the iron heel of the usurping stranger. Despotism has watched with a jealous eye the efforts of that grandiose profession whose aim is the portrayal of human passions, the delineation of human sentiment, and the inculcation of all that can delight, refine, and elevate the mind. Long has the tyrant, sword in hand, and the clerical censor, brandishing his scissors, forbidden the representation of some of the noblest masterpieces of human genius. The drama, like everything else in Italy, has been gagged, stifled, shackled by the accursed Tedesco. But the reign of liberty and progress has begun. The Stranger is no more—*Lo straniero non è piu.* Therefore the director and dramatic artist, Angelo Scartaffacci, has the honour to inform the intelligent and gentle Signoria of Vicenza that the performance will commence this evening with a grand drama, in four acts, translated from——*La Dame aux Camellias*, by Alexandre Dumas *fils*." Yes, there is such a thing as a bathos even in prospectus-writing, O Angelo Scartaffacci!

The performance of so much vaunted promise was at an end, and the audience came pouring into all the caffès for ices and cool drinks. There was no incident in this, you will say. But in *this* there was: that, amidst a great rustling and fluttering of silks and gauzes, there was inducted into this public coffee-house a party of no less than five elegantly-dressed ladies. Ay, there were mamma and her daughters, and there was grandmamma too, if I mistake not; and age was venerable, and youth ravishingly beautiful, of course. It was a radiant vision of bare necks and shoulders and arms, and dainty hands enclosed in white-kid gloves, and daintier feet in pink-silk hose and white-satin shoes, and wreaths, and veils, and bouquets, and fans, and bracelets, and flashing gems. For all escort they had but one weak-kneed little old gentleman in evening dress, a tall white cravat, and a sprinkling of powder on his head. They were soon surrounded by a bevy of Italian officers, who fluttered like moths around them; and then there were smiles, and bows, and tappings of fans, and waving of finger-tips.

This is my incident, pure and simple. There is nothing in it, you will say. Why should not a party of ladies come to a *café* and eat ices after the play? But to those who have known this country of aforetime there would be a volume in the sight I saw. No fact could be more significant of the thorough and definitive shut-up of Austria, and of the complete plucking of the double-headed eagle, than this apparition of Italian women of station, in full dress, and in a public coffee-house so lately the resort of Austrian officers. When the Tedeschi were here, an Italian lady who had so shown herself in the company of Germans would have been, both by her countrymen and her own sex, as bitterly scorned as would be a Mahometan woman who, casting aside *haick* and *serroual*, walked down the Rue Babazzoun at Algiers, with Balmoral boots, a porkpie-hat, and a chignon, arm in arm with a French sergeant of sappers. But such a thing would be impossible at El Djezzir. The very stones would rise and cry aloud against the unveiled one. As morally impossible would have been the appearance of an Italian signora in a *caffè* "used" by the Tedeschi. The times have altered. Those who scowled and made faces at John a'Nokes have no looks too bright, and no words too sweet, for John a'Styles. *Ojala!* May the galley row bravely into port! May the "Carnival of Venice" once more become the most enchanting air that ever was played on the fiddle; and may the new brooms, when they grow old, continue to sweep as deftly as they do now!

XII.

VENETIA.

Ponte d'Arana, Venetia, August 31.

Here we are on the brink of the piping times of peace—until war breaks out again somewhere else. The winter of our discontent is made glorious summer by the sun of Prague, and the "Empire is peace"—until next time—and the Paris Exhibition of 1867 will be its profit. Now has your helmet become a hive of bees, and you must live on prayers, which are old age's alms. Now is the time for the lute and the dulcimer, and the lady's chamber; and the traveller who gnawed mouldy bread and weevilly biscuit till he fell ill of dysentery blows up the head-waiter at the *table-d'hôte* because, for two days running, there has been no clear soup for dinner. Now do you, the homeless tatterdemalion, threaten to leave your hotel because there is a hole in the mosquito-curtains. Now do you, who went contentedly as tattered and torn as the man whom the shaven-and-shorn priest married to that all-forlorn maiden, who milked that crumpled-horned cow, immortalised in nursery anthology in connection with a dog, a cat, a rat, and some malt that lay in a house built by one Jack, shudder to be seen in the Giardino Pubblico in a wideawake, affect light-kid gloves in the Corso, and become very particular about the cut of your pantaloons. Pantaloons! last July you were nearly as destitute of pantaloons as Evan Dhu Maccoimbich.

Now do you, as is the way of the world, begin to forget that you were ever poor, ever hungry, ever dirty and ragged, and as full of sores as that just man of the land of Uz. Now, finally, is the time to lead the "gentle life"—by which I I mean that you can travel like a gentleman, order people about, give yourself airs, and be quite oblivious of those not very remote days when, from day to day, it was on the cards for you to be shot by misadventure, or hung for a spy.

With paper on which you can write, ink that will flow, a pen that will spell, a roof over your head, and the certainty that there will be something hot for dinner, and that the Austrians will not drop in on you before bedtime and steal your greatcoat, you naturally feel inclined for study and reflection of a light and elegant kind, to polish your sentences, and look up your dates and illustrations. It is impossible to be grammatical in time of war. Bellona has a standing feud with Priscian, and breaks his head whenever she comes across him. I must have written this summer many incoherent and ill-spelt letters; but in future —always until next time—you may look for literary efforts of the most elaborate nature. I proudly point to my last notice of Ferrara as a sample of what may be done in this line. It is true that to the initiated the exercitation in question may bear some slight traces of "cram;" and I honestly confess that all the literary and historical facts are taken bodily out of "Murray." But what of that? Murray's cram is the most digestible I know; and he enables you to quote Dante and Guicciardini and Frizzi, without having actually read a line of those admired authors. The sole inconvenience connected with this mode of study is that you are apt to forget all your cramming within twenty-four hours of your having crammed it.

I remember hearing of a gentleman, a barrister, accustomed to "getting-up cases" between dinner- and bed-time, who was invited to spend a couple of days down in Yorkshire, with a worthy squire, M.P. for a Riding, and a great authority on all agricultural matters. So, ere the invited guest stepped into the train at King's-cross, he provided himself with the volume of the *Encyclopædia Britannica* containing the article "Agriculture," and with Stephens, and Caird, and Jethro Tull, and *Our Farm of Four Acres.* With these invaluable treatises he crammed himself for a couple of hundred miles, and by the time the train reached York he almost ran over with deep drainage, subsoiling, liquid manure, rotations of crops, and sliced mangold-wurzel. His first dinner was a great success. His host was delighted. Never, he said, had he met with a person so thoroughly well-informed on agricultural matters. He insisted that his guest should prolong his stay to a week at least, and in an evil hour the barrister consented. The great county families were invited to meet him. There came the celebrated protectionist Sir Bos Bovis, Bart.; Mr. Sheepskin, the eminent conveyancer from Doncaster, who has made thousands of broad acres change hands; and old Lady Acres, of Pomona Court, who presents a new smockfrock once in every five years to the bold peasant who has been hedging and ditching for half a century, and has brought up a family of not less than nine children in the principles of the Church of England, and without receiving parochial relief. With these came the eminent philanthropist, Mr. Oates, of Titus Park, who, out of his great bounty, "built a new bridge at the cost of the county;" and the rector of Lambswool-Parva, with all the Miss Ramsbottoms. They were all eager to hear the brilliant London barrister, who knew so much about farming. Unhappily he had left the Encylopædia and Jethro Tull and the rest in the railway carriage, and in the course of three days, woful to relate, *the cram had all gone out of him.* At the state dinner he hadn't a word to say about pigs; broke down altogether on steam-ploughs; and, on going out the next morning on horseback, didn't know wheat from barley. I need not say that his reputation collapsed dismally, and that he ever afterwards eschewed the Northern Circuit.

I recalled this anecdote and meditated much upon it, when, sitting down at Como lately to write a letter about Vicenza, I found that I had left my much-prized "Murray" behind me at Milan. I have recovered it by this time, and brought it with me to Padua, and further still to Ponte d'Arana, on the very verge of the Austrian outposts; but on reflection I have thought it best to tell you only what I saw at Vicenza, without the aid of "Murray," and to leave the public at home to interpolate the cramming as condiment if they choose. This is an age of liberty, and I am not so unreasonable as the man in Mathews's *At Home*, who insisted that his neighbour should take mustard with his beef.

I found young Italy actively employed in sweeping Vicenza clean with the very newest of brooms. The peculiar virtues of unworn besoms have become proverbial. The principal energies of the Vicensi seemed to be devoted to the obliteration of all signs and symptoms which could by any means recall the memory of the late Austrian dominion. The Tedeschi themselves, their financial embarrassments notwithstanding, are a thrifty race, and, ere they vanished, they carefully removed all the governmental archives, all the plate and linen in the official residences, all the black-and-yellow flags which were wont to float so proudly over the public buildings, and so many of the ensigns and scutcheons bearing the effigy of Francis Joseph or the double eagle as were portable. But very many of the latter were too firmly fixed, or were cut in stone, or painted in fresco, and these the patriots of Vicenza had been during the last fortnight indefatigably hacking, hewing, rubbing, painting, and scraping out. Imperialism was at a discount. Royalty was in the ascendant, and the Kaiserliche Adler nowhere.

Watching the anti-Cesarean operation so ruthlessly performed on the bird of love, I could hardly persuade myself that I had not lately been reading *Paul's Letters to his Kinsfolk;* that this was not Paris in 1815, instead of Vicenza in 1866; and that all these scrapers and erasers were not rubbing out the symbols of the Bonaparte, and putting up the emblems of the Bourbon. Down with the eagle and up with the fleur-de-lys, or the cross of Savoy; it does not matter which. Death to the man who cries "*Vive l'Empereur,*" and let everybody, on pain of extermination, shout "*Viva il Rè!*" If one must needs shout, I prefer the *grido* of the French philosopher who cried "*Vive le Roi! ma femme et moi;*" or, better still, that shout of shouts, "*Vive nous autres! à bas les autres!*" in which I take it the whole philosophy of patriotism is composed. For there is nothing new under the sun, and *viva* anybody, seeing that we know he must die, and that probably to-morrow we shall denounce him as a humbug.

Meanwhile, the Vicenzesi went on scraping valiantly. Streets had changed their names. Garibaldi stood sponsor for some, the King and the Principe Umberto for others. Not a blind alley would condescend to ask Francesco Giuseppe to hold it at the font, or foreswear, on its behalf, the devil and all his works and the pomps and vanities of this wicked world. I had a godmother once, who thus went bail for me. She is alive, I believe, and I hope she does not suffer much anguish through the knowledge of the mess her godson has made of things generally, and of the fine market to which he has brought his pigs.

All being vanity here below, one could scarcely refuse the sardonic grin to see how very easily the King went up and the Kaiser went down. Take this police-office; for instance, "*I. R. Divizione di Sicurezza Pubblica*" was written up here on the plaster three weeks ago. There was a world of meaning in those two letters. "I. R." meant "Imperiale Reale"—Austrian despotism, Viennese bureaucracy, standing army, Quadrilateral, conscription, forced loans, spy system, Spielberg, priestcraft, bastinado, willow-rods, chains, courts-martial, white coats, anything you please. Under the "I. R." two million of people wept and groaned, tore their hair and beat their breasts, were scourged and imprisoned, and exiled, and hanged, and shot. And now comes a journeyman house-painter, at four *lire* a-day, and a tricolored cockade in his cap. He mounts a ladder and scrapes out the letter "I."

from the plaster. Hey, presto! the thing is done. Bastinado and white coats, spies and Spielberg, chains and bureaucrats, sink through the central trap, surrounded by lurid flames, like wicked Don Juan in the pantomime; and the genius of liberty, accompanied by flying spirits, dexterously supported by iron rods affixed to occult parts of their anatomy, stands on one leg in the centre of a revolving star, in front of a magnificent transformation-scene. How much used Mr. E. T. Smith's pantomimes at Old Drury to cost him? A pretty penny, I imagine; but here a few coppers and the touch of a trowel have sufficed to transform the Dark Domain of Despotism and Despair into the Radiant Realms of Regal Regeneration. Despotism has had its "I" knocked out, and the "*Reale Divizione di Pubblica Sicurezza,*" a strictly liberal and constitutional institution, remains. In many cases the workmen had not been at the pains of scraping out the objectionable letter, and had merely covered it with a coat of white paint, through which, yet damp, it loomed a ghastly blue, like an alphabetical ghost.

Wagon-loads of pictures of the King, the Royal Family, Garibaldi, Cialdini, and Medici, and "the rest of the loyal and patriotic toasts," must have come down from Bologna, or else the printsellers must have kept a large stock of prohibited portraits in reserve. I did not see any pictorial representations of La Marmora or Persano. I wondered what had become of all the Kaisers and Kaiserinns, of Benedek and Clam-Gallas, and of the archdukes whose name is legion. Hapless Erzherzogs! There are so many of them that the Austrian Government, hot in its new-born zeal for retrenchment, is about to cut down their handsome annual allowances by one-half. The nation, looking with dismay on the prodigious number of princes of the blood, insists on a pecuniary "reduction on taking a quantity." It will come to this, that at last an archduke will have to work for his living. Yet, three weeks ago, they, and Albrecht, "victor of Custozza," and Benedek—whom it is proposed to make Prince of Frindesland—and the rest, swaggered in their white coats and twirled their moustaches in a hundred *cartes de visite* in the Vicenza shop-windows. That wonderful transformation-scene has swallowed them all up.

XIII.

FINIS AUSTRIÆ.

Venice, September 22.

The cruel and unreasonable delay in the transfer of Venice from foreign to native rule is beginning to bear evil fruit. Every day a more bitter feeling is shown by the townspeople towards the Austrian soldiery—a feeling which, so far as the common soldiers are concerned, is reciprocated, and with interest. The flux of proclamations from the inexhaustible Director Frank—for police *avvisi* are continually appearing—seems rather to aggravate than to assuage public irritation. The Venetians urge, not without reason, that if the Austrians have ceded Venetia to France, they have no longer any legal *locus standi* in Venice; and that enactments respecting the police of the city should properly issue either from the French Commissioner or from the Venetian municipality. Again, when the Austrians plead that they only publish exasperating manifestoes and keep their patrols prowling about for the purpose of preserving public tranquillity, they are reminded that their own presence in the city constitutes in itself the sole obstacle to the maintenance of good order. If they would evacuate the place, or at least withdraw their troops to the forts until matters at Vienna were arranged, the chances of discontent and outbreak among the population of Venice would be very much reduced. As it is, the smouldering hatred with which the lower classes here regard the foreigners who, after formally surrendering their suzerain rights, still claim to be *de-facto* masters, may blaze forth any day in open revolt, and the wishes of the most bigoted *Austriacanti* who yearn for a little shedding of Italian blood may thus be gratified.

It is reported in town this morning that a serious riot took place in the course of yesterday afternoon on the quay called the Canareggio, a very poor and populous quarter close to the railway terminus, and one which—always substituting a waterway for a roadway—may be qualified as the Whitechapel of Venice, just as the Calle Larga Maritima, hard by to the Giardino Pubblico, may be described as its Ratcliff-highway. There was a row, then, yesterday, so they say, between the Austrian *polizei*, who are armed and accoutred in every respect as soldiers, and some gondoliers and longshore men. A good deal of bad language was exchanged, and thence a transition took place to blows, which is by no means usual, the bargee class in Venice being renowned for slanging much but hitting seldom. The gendarmes drew their cutlasses; one of the prowling patrols came up to help them; a round game of sword, dagger, and bayonet took place; and the end of the fray was the killing of one Italian, and the wounding of four. It is all but impossible to get at the rights of this story, and therefore I tell it under all possible reserve. There may have been a mere street-row on the Canareggio, and there may have been a really sanguinary riot. You must not expect to hear the truth about it from anybody. The *Gazzetta Uffiziale* will take care to preserve a discreet silence on the matter; the Austrian police, were you to ask them for any information, would return an "evasive answer"—equivalent to telling you to mind your own business; and any Venetian account of the transaction would be untrustworthy, from the deep-seated propensity in the Venetian mind to exaggerate and misrepresent everything in which the Austrians are interested.

There have been published about the alien rulers of Venice in the Italian papers, and within the last four months, a series of lies perhaps the most prodigious ever known since the immortal American bulletins of General Joseph Hooker. As a rule, I have been very cautious in repeating the stories I have heard; but if Homer, the original special correspondent who "did" the siege of Troy, occasionally nods, his humbler followers in prose may be allowed a nap now and then; and on two or three occasions I have been taken in by the circumstantial fibs told by the Italian press. For instance, there was a particular village in the Tyrol said to have been burnt by General Garibaldi after he had left Rocca d'Anfò. There never was such a village, and General Garibaldi never burnt it. Again, there were the three thousand cavalry horses reported to be stabled in the Giardini Pubblici at Venice. I went straight to the Public Gardens the last time I came to Venice, and found not a square inch of stable nor the ghost of a troop-horse there. It was only a lively lie on the part of some Tedesco-hating journalist.

Again, at Milan, the other day, I read in a very well-accredited Italian paper the story of a "deplorable tragedy" said to have occurred on a certain day at Verona, and to which I might have attached some degree of credence, had I not happened to have been at Verona on the very day in question, and to know very well that no such deplorable tragedy had taken place. Three little boys, the imaginative scribe set forth, had been brought by their fond parents on a visit to the fair city on the Adige, and were taken for a walk on the Piazza d'Armi, attired in mimic Garibaldino costume. The tiny redshirts were pounced upon by a squad of Austrian gendarmes, and forthwith arrested. Thereupon a stout Veronese butcher, standing with his arms akimbo at his shop-door, remarked in a taunting tone to the *polizei* that against mere infants they were very valorous, but that, were they confronted with real Garibaldini, they would take to their heels and run. The remark of the fabulous butcher was as inappropriate as it was uncomplimentary, seeing that, on the rare occasions when white coats and red shirts have been confronted, the Garibaldini it was, in most cases, and not the Tedeschi, who ran away. Let this pass, however. An Austrian gendarme, the scribe continued, maddened by the butcher's sarcasm, drew his bayonet and stabbed him *fuor fuori*— through and through. He died on the spot. What became of the three children is not stated. Perhaps they were cast into a fiery furnace, or forcibly enlisted into the Kaiser-jäger regiment, or taken to the Castello, there to expire under the bastinado. Now the whole of this story was a lie, pure and simple. No such disturbance took place, and no such deeds were committed.

I hope the encounter on the Canareggio, if not entirely disproved, may be reduced to harmless proportions. Hitherto the bad blood existing between the Austrians and the Venetians has shown itself more under a grotesque than a ferocious aspect. Coarse allusions to "*Cecco Beppo,*" the disparaging diminutive for Francesco Giuseppe of Austria, may be found scrawled on a few dead walls; and on the Canareggio, I am told, some provocative persons have, with desperate charcoal, written up "*Morte agli Austriachi*" on the wine-shop shutters; but these wall-scribblings, after all, are but effete and contemptible things. Wise governors would do well to take no notice of them. But wisdom in the government of the world, or in the government of cities or parishes, is not often to be found. I don't think that the personal comforts or the mental serenity of the Croats, or the Magyars, or the Czechs, or the Poles, who happen to be soldiers in the Austrian army and in garrison at Venice, are, to any appreciable extent, disturbed by the *graffiti* of a few desperate bargees.

The Austrian soldiers when off duty preserve a remarkably philosophic, not to say stolid, countenance, and seem to care a great deal less about politics than about procuring as large a quantity of beer, ripe figs, and tobacco as is consistent with the exiguity of their daily pay. Moreover, a large proportion of their number are wholly ignorant of the Italian language; and, could they speak it, their limited acquaintance with Lord Palmerston's "three r's" would render them incompetent to understand the libels indicted against them on the dead walls. I think we are apt to assume rather too much as regards the mental susceptibilities of private sentinels. I have heard of godly Scotch Presbyterian regiments in Malta whose souls were harrowed at having to present arms when a Roman-Catholic procession passed by; but I doubt whether the Onety-Oneth regiment, in the aggregate, troubles its head much about the religious bickerings of Peter, Jack, or Martin.

"He is risen," said the Czar Nicholas, issuing from his palace on the morning of Easter-day, and saluting with the customary embrace the grenadier on guard.

"So they say," replied the grenadier sententiously. Now it was his duty, as a soldier of the Orthodox Greek Church, to have responded, "He is risen indeed."

The Czar was appalled at the man's impiety. "Nephew of a dog—" he began.

"May it please your Majesty," urged the soldier, "I am number seventeen in company B, second battalion; I come from Yorghi-Karai in Krim Tartary, and I am a Mahometan."

The Autocrat passed on; but I even wonder that he did not forthwith issue an order of the day commanding all his Mahometan troops forthwith to embrace Christianity under pain of running the gauntlet in case of recusancy.

As with religion, so it may be with politics. The white-coated soldier who reads—if he can read at all—"Death to the Austrians" on the walls of Venice will not necessarily be lashed to frenzy. The insult may not be addressed to him. He is, as likely as not, the very reverse of an Austrian. He may be a Slav, a Magyar, a Polack, a Czech, an Italian Tyrolese, an Istrian, a Dalmatian. More than all this, in his heart of hearts, deep down under dense and dull layers of concrete ignorance, stupidity, and the mechanical apathy begotten of drill and heavy marching order and field-days and outpost duty (the whole consolidated by bullying and the stick), there may be an obscure kind of consciousness that he has no business in Venice, and that he is helping to oppress a nationality there.

More obscure, but still latent, may there be in that poor man-machine's mind the conviction that he himself is also, after a fashion, an oppressed nationality. They read out to him yesterday in the barrack-yard a general order, in which he was told that he loved the Kaiser passionately, that he was always ready to shed his blood for the good cause and the sacred rights of the House of Hapsburg. The Kaiser thanked him with all his heart; but ten minutes afterwards Fritz Schweinbein, sergeant, threatened him with the black hole for not turning out his toes properly while the general order was being read. What is the general order to him? what is the good cause? what does he care about the sacred rights of the House of Hapsburg? Somebody violated his sacred rights when they took him away from his old mother and the cottage where he was born, and cropped his head and made a soldier of him. Piet and Jan, who essayed to revindicate their sacred rights by running back to their cottages, were caught and put into the dark dungeon. Piet they laid across a truss of straw and larruped with cudgels, and Jan they shot. The survivor does not run away; he will turn out his toes when the sergeant tells him; he will fire off his gun or shove with his bayonet when the Hauptmann gives the word, because he has been taught to do it, because he does not know any better, because he cannot help himself, because he does not wish to share the fate of Piet or Jan. As for the Kaiser, whom he never saw, and of whom he knows no more than the Welsh school-child who told the examiner that the King of England was an "old man who lived in London in a house of gold, and ate taxes," I don't think the Kaiser's love for his soldiers, or the soldiers' love for their Kaiser, enters much into the actual state of affairs, which sends armies raised by merciless conscriptions to fight in quarrels to whose merits nine-tenths of the fighters must be utterly indifferent.

The persons who are really annoyed at the taunts of the Venetians, at the denunciations and libels, at the seditious cries of the barcaroli and the wall-scribblings of "*Morte agli Austriachi*" and "*Vogliamo Vittorio Emmanuele per nostro Rè*" are mainly *Austriacanti,* foreign sympathisers with the expiring dynasty, and as a rule more Austrian than the Austrians themselves. Have you not frequently been aware of people who were good enough to trouble themselves much more about your private affairs than you yourself were in the habit of doing? There is more than one English exquisite of the "haw-haw" order, more than one dignified lady akin to that distinguished member of the Tite-Barnacle family, who opined that the disasters of Catholic Emancipation and the scandal of Parliamentary Reform might have been averted had George Barnacle only possessed the firmness of mind to "call out the cavalry," and who are now inconsolable to think that the Austrian domination in Venetia is really about to cease, but who rejoice with unholy glee over every day of its unnecessary protraction, and who would like to see the Venetians bullied, gagged, and if possible scourged, until the very last moment allowed by the Law of Force. These are the ladies and gentlemen who are so very irate at the natural restiveness of a population who feel that the hour of their enfranchisement is at hand, and who resent, as a wanton insult, the parading of bilboes and shackles, and the flourishing of a cowhide over their heads, when it is patent that the public opinion of

Europe would no longer permit the nigger-driver to apply those engines of torture to their limbs.

A lady sympathiser with the "Expiring Anaconda"—if I may be permitted to cull a beauteous trope from Yankeeland —recently distinguished herself in a very funny manner in Venice. A pork-pie hat on her head, and a parasol in her hand, she was taking a walk in the Merceria dell' Orologio, when she espied at a street-corner one of those wicked little placards headed, "*Vogliamo Vittorio Emmanuele, &c. &c. &c.*" This was too much for her Austriacantism, and incontinent she proceeded to an overt act of suppression. With the ferrule of her parasol she essayed to dig the obnoxious placard from the wall; nay, if report speaks true, she enlisted her fair finger-nails, protected, let us hope, by gloves, in the good work. A nice employment for a lady; but politics, although the fact may have escaped the notice of Mr. J. S. Mill, have an almost infallible tendency towards unsexing the better sex. A crowd of idlers gathered round the zealous sympathiser. Grunts and groans were heard; and the vulgar little boys became pointedly personal, as vulgar little boys are apt to do everywhere. To them speedily entered an Austrian officer, who, in lieu of advising the lady to go home, aided her, with the pummel of his sword-hilt, to erase the terrible little bill, and the pair then withdrew, amidst much hooting and hissing.

All this is nonsensical enough; but carried to excess may bring about some very ugly complications. The blame in the matter lies, I cannot help thinking, at the Austrian door, or at least at that of the diplomatists at Vienna. Venice should have been evacuated at least three weeks ago. The surrender by Austria has long been a *fait accompli*. The necessity of pecuniary compensation was admitted by Italy as one of the bases of the armistice, and the mere question of amount would have been as well settled subsequently as prior to the evacuation. Were the Venetians men of marble or snow, they might have managed to suppress their real feelings, and to disguise their real wishes until the last Austrian "pyroscaphe" had cleared out from Malamocco; but as they happen only to be made of flesh and blood, elements which, at a certain temperature, are apt to melt and boil, I cannot but regard the continued system of tacit provocation resulting from the Austrian presence here as a very perilous experiment. No good ever came of tying down the safety-valves of high-pressure engines with whipcord. I have seen more than one boiler burst through the employment of those means.

XIV.

THE SURRENDER OF VENICE.

October 18.

At six o'clock this morning the Austrian dominion in Venice ended, so far as human prescience can foresee, for ever. The last bands of German soldiers who, by a blundering policy, had been permitted to linger in the barracks and the public buildings, and whose continued presence was a source of legitimate irritation to the Venetians, packed up their needments and slunk away during the night of the 16th. I do not remember to have witnessed a spectacle more melancholy, and at the same time more suggestive, than that which I saw about midnight yesterday under the colonnade of St. Mark's Place. A young Austrian officer—a captain—had got his route. There was a war-steamer waiting for him somewhere, to take him to the land of the Teuton; but he did not know exactly where she lay. He was wandering in a pitiably desultory manner about the *sotto portici*, two orderlies following him in obsequious but uncertain obedience; one bearing on his brawny shoulders the captain's portmanteau, the other laden with his shako, his holsters, and his sword-case. The poor young gentleman was evidently lost in Venice. He no longer recognised the capital whose inhabitants he had so long trampled under foot. In vain, by dint of his eye-glass did he strive to discern one friendly face of whose possessor he might ask the way to a place where he could take oars and go away for good.

"Retributive justice, O Captain," I thought; and I daresay that my thoughts were echoed, unconsciously, by a good many Venetians. "Retributive justice! The poisoned chalice is at last commended to your own lips! Within these last few days the handwriting has come out on the wall, and the fingers of a man's hand have written, as in sand, that the Medes and Persians are at Mestre, waiting to cross the railway-bridge which you vainly threatened to blow up with gunpowder, and that your kingdom is given to another."

I know that there is nothing meaner or shabbier than to exult over a fallen enemy. I know that the Austrians have many good and estimable points. I know that it is through the default of their own stupid and headstrong Government that they have lost the fairest province upon which God's sun ever shone; and yet I confess that I did not feel at all sorry when I saw the Austrian captain wandering about like a strayed puppy under the *sotto portici*. My thoughts carried me back just four months, minus three days. I remembered that on the 14th of June 1866, I had to bend the neck and hinge the knee to the Archduke Albert for permission to leave Venetia, and was repulsed from the outer rooms of the Austrian *Hauptmann*, his aide-de-camp, who was wolfing beef and cabbage at Verona, at eight o'clock in the morning. He told me to "wait down-stairs," did he? until he chose to consider my petition to be allowed to quit the "Austrian Empire." Aha! it is the aide-de-camp, now, who has to "wait down-stairs" in the cold, and is of less account than the meanest creature on the Canareggio. This is, I am aware, very unchristian and very uncharitable; but it is human nature; and if you will be good enough to multiply by five thousand the feelings of annoyance I suffered through a temporary slight in the citadel of Verona last June, and add to the product a long-accumulated score of hatred and disgust, you may form some idea of the sentiment entertained by the Venetians for the now ousted Government by which they have been, for so many years, bullied, outraged, and oppressed.

I was at Florian's until very late, and at the Specchi until later, and at Quadri's, and, indeed, wherever there was a chance of seeing Venetian life on the Eve of Liberation; but up to the time I went to bed, which was at a most unholy hour, there were Austrian officers about. Wrapped in their gray gaberdines, their *lorgnons* faithful to their mild blue eyes, their sabres still clanking, their spurs still jingling on the pavement, their white teeth, blonde whiskers, and fresh complexions still gleaming in the gas, they continued, until the night was very old, to vindicate their claim to be the best "set-up," most soldier-like, and most gentlemanly-looking officers in Europe. Somehow or another, between the time I retired to rest and the time I got up again, they disappeared.

There is a vague and mysterious period during the small hours, so Mr. Greenwood tells us in his beautiful *Essay without End*, during which all kinds of curious things are done—during which the Palpable fades into the Impalpable—and sick men preferably die, and infants elect to live. It must have been in this shadowy time that the Tedeschi went away, to return, I hope, no more. It was a great astonishment, a vast relief, to walk forth on to the Piazzetta in the bright October sun, and find that there were no more Croats under the arcade of the Palazzo Ducale. The Cancellate, that grim range of dungeon-bars, which screened the colonnade, and behind which the Austrian drums and the Austrian banner, the hated *Schwarz-gelb*, used to rest—behind which the Austrian bayonets used to be piled—behind which the Austrian soldiers used to squat on their benches, puffing at their meerschaums, and contemplating the Imperiale e Reale Zecca opposite with a stale and accustomed look—behind which, in fine, were ranged those six-pounders whose trail was so terrific, and which were to blow the Venetians into peelings of onions if they dared to misbehave themselves—the Cancellate, those most obnoxious of iron railings, were gone. They had been torn up bodily by a suddenly enfranchised people. Gondoliers, Garibaldini, beggars even, had lent a hand to wrench those prison stockades from their sockets. Even strangers and chance visitors, yielding to an impulse of enthusiasm, had rushed forward to help unroot the ugly signs of Austrian rule.

Was there not, as historians tell us, a turbaned Turk among the fierce French patriots who assaulted the Bastille? He could have known nothing about *lettres de cachet*, or Latude, or the Man with the Iron Mask, that muslin-kerchiefed Moslem; yet, when the time came, he tucked up his sleeves, and went to work with a will to pull down that horrible old castle of the Devil.

The Cancellate were the last outward and visible signs that remained of the Austrian rule in Venice. The double eagle had disappeared some days since from the ensigns of the tobacconists. The Imperial "I" had been divorced from the Royal "R" on the façades of the Police- and Post-office, as it had been at Rovigo, at Padua, and at Vicenza. The Venetian National Guard had been suffered to stand sentry at that grand Paviglione behind the Palazzo Reale which, of old time, was only allowed to be tenanted when Majesty itself, or at least an Austrian Archduke, was resident in Venice. The Arsenal, the Mint, the Tobacco-factory, the Finances, the Monte di Pietà, had been given up. But to the guard-house under the Ducal Palace, with its unsightly Wombwell's-show-like Cancellate, the Tedeschi stuck until the very last moment. When they gave up that, they gave up everything.

At six o'clock on this instant, Friday, General Alemann, whilom military governor of this city and fortress, bade a long farewell to Venice. It was time for him, like Ferdinand in the *Tempest*, to break his staff, burn his book, and abjure his magic. A war-steamer waited for him, too; but it was a bright and beautiful morning, and he knew full well where to find her. He came from under the Piazzetta porch of the royal palace as the clock struck six, rosy, clean-shaven, alert, and smiling, in that familiar sky-blue tunic, and with that well-remembered diamond cross on his brave old breast I had seen so often in the hot, hopeless nights on the Molo, when Alemann trotted about monarch of all he surveyed, but very likely wishing most devoutly that any monarchy but the unthankful Venetian one was his to survey. Early as was the time of his embarkation the Piazzetta was thronged. There were there a motley crowd: *barcaruoli*, fishermen, bargees, blackguards—the raff and scum of Venice, indeed, mingled with the early-rising toilers.

It was a grand opportunity, a fine occasion whereon to hoot and yell and screech, and mob a deposed ruler who had no longer any bayonets at his back. I rejoice to say that as the ex-governor stepped into his gondola there arose from the ragged and rough multitude a great, hearty, honest *Evviva!* Yes, they cheered him lustily. *He* had never done them any harm, and had always striven to do them good. The valiant and loyal little old gentleman had at first only raised his cocked-hat in military punctilio, but when he heard that sounding shout of "Good-bye, and God be with you!" he took out his white handkerchief and waved it cheerily in acknowledgment of the salute. Austrian generals are but mortals after all, and who shall say that he did not afterwards convey the cambric to his eyes, to stanch the witness of "unfamiliar brine"? Good-bye, brave and trim little captain, ever ready in the forefront of the battle, but ever kind and gentle and courteous. The Venetians are good haters; but they will long keep a pleasant corner in their hearts for "Guglielmo Barone di Alemann."

The Venetian population, I opine, would not have preserved a demeanour quite so placable had any of the minor agents of Austrian tyranny ventured upon a public departure. I verily believe that they would have torn Toggenburg to pieces. That "*indegno cavaliere,*" as Masetto called Don Giovanni, was wise enough to steal away many weeks since to Verona, and thence across the Brenner into Austria. He did not care about exchanging adieux with the Veneziani. They might have been apt to remember that the Cavaliere

Toggenburg's favourite amusement was to go down to the railway-station, and gloat over the convoys of political prisoners arriving, handcuffed, from every part of Venetia, on their way to the Spielburg. I wonder what they will do with Toggenburg now. Will they find out some petty town in Styria that wants bullying, or will they give him employment at Trent or Roveredo, where, by a great stretch of imagination, he may yet fancy he is in the Veneto, and play the tyrant in the Italian language?

There have been other subordinate despots in Venice who did not so timeously retreat as did Toggenburg. Rats will desert a sinking ship, but there are always some rats who will remain until the leak assumes alarming proportions. It was difficult to make the German *polizzotti* understand that their presence had become an abomination in a free Italian town. With infinite reluctance did ex-Director Frank pack up and clear out. During the whole of this week the Italian National Guard—who have been most indefatigable in maintaining order and tranquillity—have had hard work in rescuing the Austrian gendarmes and detectives from the effects of patriotic indignation. The private policemen have been only hooted and pelted; but the crowd have on more than one occasion evinced a lively desire to have the heart's blood of the police captains and commissaries who were wont to domineer over them.

The day before yesterday one Ramponi, who had been a terrible tyrant in his time, was within an inch of being murdered. The crowd discovered him (pretty much as George Lord Jefferies was discovered looking out of the window of an ale-house at Wapping) in some obscure caffè of the Canareggio. I am sure I don't know what he was doing there. The miserable man had perhaps a monomania for espionage, and was prowling about, even after his power had departed, in the hope of "taking up" somebody. The mob were down upon him at once; he was dragged from his lurking-place, hustled, spat upon, half-stripped, and brought into dangerous propinquity with a canal, when the National Guard, arriving in force, rescued him from the horrible fate which befell the wretched Anviti, elsewhere, seven years ago, and which in all probability, but for their intervention, would have been Ramponi's on Wednesday. For safety they took him, for a while, to the nearest guard-house, and then put him on board a gondola, and transported him to the railway-station, advising him, if he valued his own skin, to leave Venice by the very next train. The man put forth a piteous plea to be allowed to see his wife and children before he left; upon which the Commandant of the National Guard observed to him that he must forego that indulgence. "You might remember, Signor Ramponi," he added, "that when you arrested the Venetians at dead of night, and put them on board the steamers which conveyed them to imprisonment or exile, you were not in the habit of asking them whether they wished to bid farewell to their wives and families."

All Venice had learnt by heart, on the 15th and 16th, the official programme put forth by the Congregazione Municipale of Venice as to the order of proceedings to be observed on this momentous Friday. The Austrians, it was stated, would have entirely evacuated the city by daybreak. The formal surrender of the keys by the Austrian General Möring to the French General Lebœuf, and by him to the Italian

General Revel, would then take place. At nine o'clock precisely, amidst a salvo of artillery, the Italian banner would be hoisted from the three tall masts in the Piazzo San Marco, which in bygone days bore the symbols of the dominion of the Most Serene Republic over Venice, Cyprus, and the Morea. At ten a corps of five thousand Italian troops, under the command of General Medici, would arrive from the mainland at the railway-terminus, and would enter the city in three different bodies and by three different routes; one body embarking in barges, and proceeding straight along the Canal Grande to the Piazzetta; another coming round, also by water, by the channel of the Zattare; the third crossing and recrossing the two iron bridges, and marching through the streets—not one of which is wider than old Cranbourn-alley —to St. Mark's.

The hoisting of the Italian standard was a brief but most impressive ceremony. From earliest dawn St. Mark's Place had been thronged; indeed, I have no doubt that many hundreds of patriots had been bivouacking at Florian's, or among the benches of the *sotto portici*, all night. I am not prepared to state that the Piazza, by nine o'clock in the morning, was full, because it is to me a matter of extreme uncertainty whether any number of human beings congregated together, short of the number who were dispersed at the Tower of Babel, would be sufficient to fill St. Mark's Place. It is like the harbour of Halifax, Nova Scotia, which is said to be big enough to hold all the navies of the world, but opening out of which is a supplementary harbour, capable of holding any number of additional navies. So has the Piazza its supplementary port in the shape of the Piazzetta. A *co-*

dino friend who was with me—that is to say, a gentleman whose sympathies lay less on the Italian than on the Austrian side of the hedge—declared that there was scarcely anybody on the Place, and that he had seen more loungers there any fine afternoon in the days of occupation, when the Austrian military bands used to play such beautiful waltzes and mazurkas. I did not care to contradict him; yet I fancied that between the Procuratie Nuove and the Procuratie Vecchie there must have been congregated at least ten thousand souls.

St. Mark's itself was all alive. The platform above the façade was black with humanity, who did everything but bestride those immortal horses of St. Mark, which came from Corinth, which have been at Byzantium, which have been at Paris, which have been at Vienna, which may go to St. Petersburg or to New York, for aught we know, before this Human Comedy is finished, but which I was pleased to look upon this morning, preserving, even in their grimmest and bronziest aspect, a jocose and Astley's-like look, and unmurmuringly performing their eternal trot. Those marvellous semi-circular fringes to St. Mark's frontage, surmounted by sculptured crockets, which Mr. Ruskin has eloquently but fantastically compared to the twisted and petrified foam of the sea, were on the present occasion obscured by adventurous climbers. The balconies and *loggie* of the ducal palace were one mass of life; and I am sorry to say that the Venetian *gamins* had been permitted to invade the tiny courtyard of the exquisite Loggetta at the foot of the Campanile, and to climb over the beautiful bronze gates, the which to see is at once to conceive the desire of committing robbery in a dwelling-house, by carrying them off to England. When I saw the ruthless feet of those young barbarians trampling upon the delicate foliage and delicious scroll-work of the unequalled *grille*, I shuddered. I earnestly wished that the shins of the desecrators might be galled most sorely by contact with the bronze; and I shall revisit the Loggetta to-morrow full of nervous apprehension as to the amount of damage inflicted on an unequalled work of art by those incipient Goths.

Nine o'clock strikes from the Torre dell' Orologio. With the last chime you see something like a fractured rainbow battling with the air. Then three great masses of colour spring up, droop, hang, raise themselves again, develop, and at last flame out broad and triumphant against the blue. It is done. A band strikes up. The multitude give a cry of joy that is almost a sob. The cannon thunders from San Giorgio Maggiore, now an Italian fortress. From the three great masts streams out the standard of twenty-five millions of human souls who are "united and equal." The cannon thunder again. At the Hôtel de la Ville General Möring has exchanged the last protocol with General Lebœuf. The Surrender of Venice is accomplished, and Italy is free "from the Alps to the Adriatic." Will it last?

After this, although the month be October, all is midsummer madness. Venice goes clean out of her mind. Venice is stark staring mad as I sit down to pen these lines. Venice will be suffering, I have no doubt, from acute mania when I take this letter to the post, and will not recover her sanity for many moons to come. I had taken the precaution to engage a two-oared gondola for the entire day, and to stipulate with the chief boatman that a very large Italian flag should be displayed at the stern. I hurried back from St. Mark's Place to the Hotel Victoria, where my bark was to be in waiting; but, during even the brief period of my absence, Venice had become transformed. Flags by hundreds, flags by thousands, flags by myriads, had cropped up and out from every housetop, from every eave, from every waterspout, from every lamp-iron, from every bourne-stone, from every railing, from every window, from every balcony, from every door, from every hole, from every corner in this city which is full of holes and corners. *La città era imbandierata;* that is to say, everybody who possessed a morsel of red, white, and green was displaying it. The *stoffe colorate,* against which that most deplorable police director Frank used to fulminate, had at last asserted themselves.

The scene on the Grand Canal was astounding. The municipality had entreated the citizens to confine the manifestation of their enthusiasm on this particular Friday to flags and streamers, and to reserve the more gorgeous and more peculiarly Venetian display of tapestry, carpets, and window-curtains hung out of the windows for the occasion of the arrival of the King of Italy; but popular enthusiasm had been deaf to the voice of the municipality, and the woven wealth that is within Venetian palaces had to a great extent run o'er. The spectacle of a "house out of windows" was performed a hundred times a minute on the Grand Canal. Out came the Brussels and the Aubussons, the Kidderminsters and the printed druggets; out came hearthrugs and damask-curtains, all mingled with wondrous tapestries of the sixteenth century—the *chefs-d'œuvre*, it may be, of the looms of Courtray and Arras. Next to the display of textile fabrics was the lavish exposure of pocket-handkerchiefs. Everybody seemed to have at least three, not to apply to their legitimate use, but to wave in a frantically patriotic manner.

I have somewhere read that when Catherine Malcolm, a horrible old woman who murdered a gentleman in the Temple in the reign of Queen Anne, was executed at the Middle Temple-gate, the crowd in Fleet-street was so great that an industrious tradesman who sold hot mutton-pies by retail walked, without stumbling, over the close-packed heads of the multitude from where is now the shop of Messrs. Butterworth, the law booksellers, to the corner of Chancery-lane, where he disposed of a hot "twopenny" to a gentleman from Lincoln's-inn, who had adventitiously hailed him. Without vouching for the historical truth of this anecdote, I am perfectly willing to take my affidavit before any sworn commissioner appointed for that purpose, that I could have walked dryfooted, at noon on this instant 18th of October, over any part of the Grand Canal between the railway-station and Santa Maria della Salute.

The great waterway was paved with boats. There were gondolas everywhere ; and the few interstices which presented themselves were filled with skiffs and barges. It was an enormous and glowing *parterre* of pleasure-boats, of banners and streamers, of gay costumes, of gondoliers in new apparel, of flowers and bright carpets. There were public gondolas and private gondolas ; there were men, there were women, there were children, there were soldiers and sailors; there were brown-cowled monks peeping from the casements of convents; there was a great kaleidoscopic jumble of life and noise, and movement and colour, and light and shade, and reflection and refraction; there was the *Tohubohu* of the Hebrews; there was a pictorial come-and-go, a mingling and a massing, a surging and weltering of chromatic caprice, there was a sea of gold and purple glory such as the Venetian painter Canaletto never imagined, such as the Venetian painter Guardi never realised, such as the Englishmen Joseph Turner and John Ruskin, with all their magic power of pen and pencil, with all their bright poetic insight, never approached, such as no human limner, no human scribe, can ever hope completely to portray.

I saw it — dulled and hardened as I have been to shows and sights all over the world — I saw it, and felt inclined to cry because I knew that I could never convey one-tenth part of the immensity of its real aspect to you in England. I see it now, clear and distinct in my mind, as the faces of those who are dead, and who come to me in my dreams; and I am ashamed of my impotence to translate into language the ideas of which my heart is full— I am ashamed to blunder over that which at its very best must be a lame and halting narrative of a sight which I shall never behold again.

In the midst of this tremendous sea of happy holiday people, laughing and shouting and embracing, came, slow and stately, half a dozen great galleys, decked with flags, brave in draperies, full from stem to stern of Italian soldiers. As the clock struck noon the guests of the day marched out of the railway-station, and down its noble staircase into the barks appointed to receive them. There is the clash of martial music. There is Garibaldi's Hymn. There is the Royal Anthem. There is the *grido di guerra.* Now comes, swan-like, a great Argo, laden with National Guards. Then follow the *Carabinieri,* the picked men, the boldest, bravest of Italians, the *bene meriti dell' armata,* the only police force perhaps in Europe who are not unpopular. Like doves from a thousand arks, the white handkerchiefs of the women in the balconies fly out to greet these good, solid men. Now come the *Bersaglieri,* bronzed and saucy-looking, but eminently serviceable. To these succeed many boats full of Italian infantry, and gondolas conveying officers of all arms in full uniform. The pace at which the flotilla moves is but a snail's one; but it is all too rapid for the spectators, who cannot dwell too long or too lovingly on the soldiers, who, to them, represent their restoration to national existence, and their deliverance from a cruel and galling servitude.

We crept ahead and got into a fresh crowd of gondolas, but eventually landing at the Molo, crossed the Piazzetta to the Clock Tower, where I was fortunate enough to have secured a front place at a first-floor window. Thence at my leisure I saw the disembarkation of the troops, their march past the Ducal Palace, and heard the frantic acclamations by which they were greeted by the crowd. And then, I am constrained to say, it being close on four o'clock in the afternoon—we had been three hours and a half coming from the terminus to the Molo—and remembering that the post for England went out at eight, I left the Venetians together in their glory, and, diving dexterously through a labyrinth of by-lanes, returned to mine inn, there to set down so much as time would allow me of what I had seen on this most memorable day.

XV.

EVE IN ST. MARK.

Venice, October 21.

Lady Holland, in her charming life of her witty father, tells us that when the Canon of St. Paul's was old and infirm, he was wont, on fine mornings, to bid his domestics "throw open the shutters and glorify the room." By which the Rev. Sydney Smith simply meant that his servants should let in the sun. Under the sun he had beheld, in his long life, much madness and folly; but he loved to look upon the luminary, and to warm his good old face in it, and to be thankful for sunshine, until the end. The sun is the patrimony of age; all, save the blind, can bask in its rays when all other wealth is spent, and even Blind Tobias can feel its warmth. "*Vieux vagabond, le soleil est à moi,*" cries Béranger's worn-out mendicant, from his ditch. So Mirabeau, writhing on his bed of death, and vainly striving to stifle agony with spiced meats and fiery wines, bade them open the window, that he might gaze upon the sun—if not the Deity Himself, at least his cousin-german. So Jean Jacques, at Ermenonville, in the evening of *his* career of miserable glory—poor, neglected, half-poisoned, may be—bade Thérèse unfasten the window-latch, that he might fill his soul for the last time with the rays of "the Master of the World; the only master who is adored without flattery, and without greed of temporal reward." For you get nothing by toadying the Sun. It is a matter of mathematical calculation, as we were once assured on illustrious authority, that he will rise to-morrow morning; and the chances are ten millions to one in favour of humanity that he will so rise. But it is a matter of certainty as mathematical that he is not to be propitiated by odes, or won to the side of gentility by corporation addresses; that he will shine with impartial munificence upon David's enemies as upon David himself; and that, if he intends to veil his face, not all the psalms, supplications, or adjurations in the world can conjure his clouds away.

There is a certain time in the afternoon, at this autumnal season, when a certain part of the basilica of St. Mark—the most gorgeous, but the darkest church in Europe—is "glorified" by the sun. Worshippers there are in St. Mark's at all hours; but at about ten minutes to five every afternoon, when the weather is fine, a number of loungers are sure to drop into the church to see the apsis behind the high altar "glorified." The contrast which they come to see is all the more striking, as by four o'clock three-fourths of the basilica have become a gloomy wilderness, through which you might wander long ere you discovered that all around you rose columns of porphyry and malachite and verd-antique, panels glowing with gold and gems, pavements dazzling in *vermiculato* and mosaic work. Lost in umbrageous dimness are the sumptuous Baptistery, the jewel-crowded chapel of the Madonna de' Mascoli, the two fanciful *pale* that flank the high altar; nay, even the famous Icone Bisantina and the stately *baldacchino* have but a pale and uncertain glimmer. From between the intercolumniations of the windows sweep down great dark shadows, so thick that they seem well-nigh palpable, and you fear to stumble over them, as though they were half-hung draperies left there by undertakers' men who were preparing to hang St. Mark's in black for the obsequies of Day, but had knocked off from work for a spell to lounge out into the Piazza and see the sunset.

I should counsel you to keep your eyes till the proper moment bent downwards or relieve them amidst the shadows. The change you are about to see will be all the stronger. As the chimes from the Torre dell' Orologio strike the three-quarters, do you, standing right in front of the rood-screen, look up boldly towards the east. As boldly as you may; but the strongest vision will but feebly withstand the astonishing spectacle you will witness. At this moment the sun is in the west, on a level with the centre of the façade added by Eugène Beauharnais to the Palazzo Reale. Using that façade as a fulcrum, the master-Archimedes sends a gigantic lever of sun-ray slanting across the entire Piazza. The ray rushes through the central window, just tips the summits of the Evangelists' statues on the rood-loft, touches the topmost grating of the altar-screen, and ends in the apsis or semicircular recess behind the altar.

I called it a lever. It is surely one which should lift the whole world up to Faith. The great recess is all at once in a blaze. Looking out of the darkness you might fancy the high altar to be on fire. Understand that this apsis is wholly covered with golden mosaic, and that in its centre is a colossal figure of the Redeemer. This golden alcove of glory, this inexhaustible treasure-chamber, this stupendous shrine glittering and trembling in its abundance of radiance, fills you at first with unspeakable awe and veneration. You do not wonder that the poor people who come here to pray, and who are crouching humbly in the tenebrous nave, muttering their orisons, should accept in this a sure and visible symbol of their salvation — that, abject, poverty-stricken, oppressed, ragged, and hungry, they should swathe their souls in those golden cerements, anointed to them, with blessed balm— that, after a toilsome day and scant pay, these weary water-carriers, and flower-girls, and gondoliers, and fishermen, should find, in the contemplation of the glorified shrine, peace, consolation, and hope. It is very edifying, subsequently, to reflect that the glorification of the apsis is, after all, only the result of mathematical calculation — that the architects of the church knew full well that at a certain hour, at a certain time of the year, the sun would send a most mathematical ray through the great west window to the eastern extremity of the church. So they covered the eastern extremity of the church with a rich ground of gold mosaic to be lit up by the sun's rays, accordingly.

I have watched this grand sight many and many a time, early and late; for I need scarcely say that it is not always at a quarter to five P.M. that Phœbus-Archimedes chooses to use the centre of Eugène Beauharnais' façade as a fulcrum for his lever. I have watched the apsis turn into golden glory in the darkest days of Venice, when the oppressor's hand was upon her throat with a clutch which, in human likelihood, would never be relaxed—when nearly all hope of her deliverance and her resuscitation had been abandoned by a generation worn out and heartsick with continued disappointment. The great door of St. Mark's, leading to the vestibule where the storyof the Creation and the Fall, and the Deluge are told, in mosaic, with such quaint yet touching *naïveté*, is always open. To keep the radiating heat out in summer and the radiating cold out in winter, a mighty veil hangs before the sumptuous tabernacle. Towards sunset this curtain is drawn aside and looped up, to admit some cheerfulness into a church which always stands in need of daylight. Often and often, standing beneath the great cross pendent from the central cupola, and which on festival days becomes a cross of a thousand lamps—often and often, waiting for the sun's time to come and for the apsis to be "glorified," have I turned my face towards the great entrance-portal, and looked far through the vestibule across St. Mark's Place, all blank and deserted, like some vast, calm, shipless sea which had been turned to stone.

St. Mark's, given up to utter emptiness, is more oppressive in its loneliness than the Crystal Palace on a wet Sunday afternoon when there are no shareholders about—than even the reading-room of the British Museum when the last bookworm has been politely persuaded to depart, and the last hardworked attendant has wheeled the last truckload of books along the gilded galleries. And I have seen St. Mark's in broad daylight *quite empty.* This has generally been the time when the Austrian band had finished playing—when the hotel-bells had summoned the few foreign visitors to the *tables-d'hôte,* and when the fewer Venetians who chose to walk abroad had retired to sip lemonade and murmur discontent in the *sotto portici* of the Procuratie, and in Florian's or the Specchi's shady groves. They hang secular veils between the columns before the *caffès* to keep out extreme heat and extreme cold, as they do at St. Mark's, and these draperies have contributed still further to increase the desolation of the Place.

Once I remember seeing a solitary poodle with the whole of the Piazza San Marco to himself. I saw a kindred bow-wow once in the middle of the Admiralty-square, at St. Petersburg, by moonlight. The Russian dog squatted down on his haunches, and, lifting his head towards the moon, howled at it dismally. The Venetian poodle trotted about the deserted stones of St. Mark's, worn to glassy smoothness by so many millions of human footsteps. He trotted to the three tall masts which stood all of a row in front of St. Mark's, bannerless. He sniffed at Alessandro Leopardi's bronze bases, as though to inquire what had become of the three gonfalons of the Republic—of Venice, Cyprus, and the Morea. He did not howl, or seem to lament that, like Ichabod, his glory had departed. He fell, instead, into a merry mood, and happening to remember that he had a tail, began an exciting chase after that caudal appendage, gambolling in unseemly and unpatriotic gyrations, as though all were going as merrily as a marriage-bell—as though Marino Faliero's head had never rolled upon the scaffold, and the Two Foscari had never lived—as though the Most Serene Republic had never come to grief and shame, and the Austrian eagle, cruellest of birds, had not clawed out the eyes of the Lion of St. Mark. An inconsequent poodle; but he had the whole of the Piazza to himself.

Now yesterday I looked through the great entrance-portal, and all was changed. The vast expanse was full of human movement. It was as though a whole federation of ant-hills had spumed forth their teeming commonwealths upon one vast marble slab. I emerged into the Place, and I strove to look upon the strange and unaccustomed spectacle, first from the enthusiastic, next from the morose point of view. Regarding it from the first, the sight was glorious. It made one's heart leap for joy. Gone, for ever, were the Austrian sentries from before the Zecca and the royal palace. Gone were the detestable patrols, whose bayonets were continually, morally speaking, prying over your shoulders, or poking into your loins. There were no more gray-coated, bandy-legged Croats, sulking or grinning behind the hideous bars of the Cancellate, like hyænas in their dens. That aggressive standard of black and yellow was furled for ever. Those two murderous field-pieces had ceased to point menacingly across the Piazzetta. They had been unlimbered for good, and packed, with other rubbishing marine-stores, on board an Austrian Lloyd's bound for Trieste. The two monstrous gilt eagles that used to flap their domineering wings from twin pedestals in the palace-garden had taken away their four ugly heads to other eyries. The Austrian military band had uttered their last toot, and migrated to more congenial orchestras. There were no more white-tunicked or sky-blue-coated Tedeschi to loll over the tables at Quadri's, or promenade up and down the Piazza with their much-bedizened *Frauen*, eyeing the Venetians, half with a scowl of hatred, half with a sneer of supercilious contempt. There were no more skulking gendarmes, with murderous-looking cutlasses stuck in their rusty belts, like those of the *bravi* in the *Promessi Sposi*.

In their place I saw, for the first time in Venice, the real Italian people, enjoying themselves to their heart's content. Soldiers walking arm-in-arm with gondoliers; Garibaldini in their red shirts, followed by cheering and applauding groups; National Guards, belonging mostly to the club and shop-keeping class, and who, a fortnight since, would have no more presumed to handle a musket and bayonet than to climb the three tall masts under the nose of an Austrian patrol, and hoist the Italian tricolor there. In their place I saw dozens of organ-grinders playing Garibaldi's Hymn; booksellers' shops full of the portraits of the King, the Princes, and Garibaldi; legions of ballad-singers, yelling patriotic lyrics; and from every window a kaleidoscopic display of the national colours. Among the people nine out of every ten men you met had the tricolor arranged as a cockade for their caps or a rosette for their button-holes; the women had scarves and neckbows of the three hues; the children wore frocks and petticoats of red, white, and green; and almost every adult, gentle or simple, wore in his hat, or pinned to his breast, a little piece of white cardboard, bearing the monosyllable "SI," and signifying that his electoral mind was firmly made up, and that on Sunday next, when the solemn vote or *plebiscitum* will be taken, he intended to return to the elaborate question, "Are you desirous that Venetia should be united to the kingdom of Italy under the rule of Victor Emmanuel the Second?" one conclusive and sonorous "YES."

So much for the enthusiastic side of the picture. Remembering, as I did, that I had known Venice as an old curiosity-shop, as a museum of antiquities, as a barrack-yard governed only by the bayonet and the stick, as a city in a state of siege, as a dungeon, as a tomb, I felt very much inclined to fling up *my* cap and burst forth in a series of ecstatic *evvivas* for Victor Emmanuel, for United Italy, for Giuseppe Garibaldi, for *la bella famiglia*, which is an Italian equivalent for "our noble selves," for the Lion of St. Mark, St. Theodore, St. Zuliano, San Moïsè, and all our Venetian Saints. The aspect of so many newspapers, where once newspapers were all but entirely prohibited, filled me, in particular, with feelings of the liveliest gratification. It was a sight for sore eyes to see the ragged little newsboys running about barefoot, their wallet of intelligence, damp from the press, under their arms, and screeching out the names of the hundred and one newspapers which, in a deluge of typography, have fallen on Venice. There is *Daniele Manin* number one, and a rival *Daniele Manin* number two. There is the *Conte Cavour*, the *Pungolo*, the *Perseveranza*, the *Opinione*, the *Sole*, the *Sciolo*, the *Gazzetta del Popolo*, and the *Unione;* and in particular there is the *Gazzetta di Venezia*, once the terrible *Gazzetta Ufficiale*, but which is now bereft of the effigy of the double-headed eagle, and which the little newsboys, who are arch wags, cry about as *senza gallina*—without the cock-a-doodle-doo—or as *La Paolona Pentita*, la Paolona being the traditional Scarlet Woman whose repentance once equally amused and scandalised Venice.

It was as well that I did not fling up my cap, and that I did not break forth into *evvivas*. I recollected that it was no affair at all of mine; and five minutes afterwards I met an English friend, moving in the very first circles, and of a decidedly *codino* way of thinking—that is to say, in his political sympathies, Tory to the backbone. He pointed out to me that Venice was entirely spoilt; that it had become quite a vulgar and uproarious place; that the most beautiful architectural monuments were defaced by placards and handbills; that now the volunteer force was disbanded it had become as ridiculous as it was offensive for the Garibaldini to walk about Venice in their red shirts; that the Italian regular officers gave themselves too many airs, and were not half so gentlemanly in appearance as the Austrians; that Florian's and Quadri's were now thronged all day by the merest rabble; that the *plebiscitum* was a sorry farce, seeing that everybody who dared to give a negative vote would infallibly be mobbed, and probably murdered; that very few English visitors had arrived; that fewer wealthy Italian families were expected; that all the enthusiasm of which the Venetians were capable had been expended on the entry of the troops; and that the visit of the King—if it ever took place, the which he considered to be exceedingly improbable—would be a miserable *fiasco.* My *codino* friend was good enough to add, as with a melancholy grasp of the hand he bade me farewell, that none of the hotels of Venice were more than half full; that the misery and destitution among the poor of the Canareggio was hourly on the increase; and that the cholera was more virulent than ever in the narrow and crowded *calli* of the Guidecca.

This was the picture painted from the morose point of view. But, from what I have seen with my own eyes, and heard with my own ears, I prefer to elect the tableau painted from the standpoint of enthusiasm as the genuine one. For the present, at least.

XVI.

THE PLEBISCITUM.

Venice, October 24.

THE *plebiscitum*, by means of which the Venetian people were to make their political wishes at once and for ever known, took place on Sunday and Monday last. The electoral lists in the city of Venice itself contained the names of about forty thousand voters; and some thirty-six thousand presented themselves at the polling-places. The votes have yet to be formally examined by scrutineers appointed for the purpose, and some days must elapse before the result is officially made known; but it is generally stated in Venice that among the whole thirty-six thousand suffrages recorded there were only half-a-dozen "noes." As in London club elections a candidate may always reckon upon at least one nervous, or stupid, or sleepy member, who (otherwise very well affected towards the aspirant) will blackball him by mistake, so it is extremely probable that the six "noes" spoken of above were popped into the box through absence of mind or imperfect comprehension, on the part of the voters, of the difference existing between a negative and an affirmative. At Verona, I have heard, but one solitary "no" was given. At Vicenza and Padua there was a unanimous "yes."

Everybody knows that in all these towns, as in Venice, there is a considerable number of persons who would have dearly liked to answer "no" to the question propounded to them, and who are strongly, and I daresay conscientiously, adverse to the union of Venetia to the kingdom of Italy. These persons have probably abstained from voting altogether. Where universal suffrage prevails, the people have a curious intuitive faculty for discovering electors who intend to vote the wrong way; and when the division to be taken is one as between liberty and despotism, and nine hundred and ninety-nine persons out of every thousand have made up their minds to vote the "liberty ticket," the part played by the supporters of despotism becomes a very invidious, not to say a slightly dangerous one. Had I been a *Codino*, or a *Papalino*, or an *Austriacante*, or in some way or another an opponent of the House of Savoy—had I wished to see Venetia erected into an independent republic under a new Doge, or into a separate kingdom under the rule of a Hapsburg, or a Hohenzollern, or a Coburg, or a Bourbon—it does not much matter whom—I should decidedly have kept away from the electoral colleges last Sunday and Monday. I should have known perfectly well that neither my vote, nor that of five hundred politicians of my way of thinking—did such a number exist—would have sufficed to turn the scale against the enormous majority on the other side; that my negative protest would have no moral weight; and that it was as well on the whole to keep my political sympathies to myself until calmer times arrived. Mawworm may have liked to be despised, but, in general, quiet and sensible folks are chary of courting public derision and execration.

I do not think that the populace congregated round the voting-places on Sunday would have at once proceeded to tear a notorious *Codino* to pieces, or would even have gone so far as to make him eat his printed "no," after the manner of Irish peasants in the case of obnoxious process-servers, and then enable him to wash down his meal by throwing him into the nearest canal; but things in general might not have gone pleasantly. An American writer has regarded the disinclination entertained by the majority of mankind to being kicked downstairs as a convincing proof of the Immortality of the Soul, and the constant aspirations of humanity towards Higher Things. Be this as it may, there are very few of us who much like being hooted or groaned at, or pelted, when we are only conscious of doing our duty, and when we have got our Sunday clothes on. It is all very well to be stoical, and to disdain the vile rabble; but, taking one thing with the other, dead cats and rotten eggs are not so nice as showers of roses and triple salvoes of huzzahs. Ask the Right Honourable Benjamin Disraeli. Ask the Right Honourable Robert Lowe. Ask anybody who on Monday evening has had a piece of plate presented to him at a public dinner at the Freemason's, and on Tuesday morning has had to face a ruffianly mob in Clerkenwell-green.

The conviction, however, that it was humanly impossible, just now, to mend the matter, must have been the strongest incentive which kept those disaffected to the new state of things away from the poll-booths. There is nothing to be gained, and there is everything to be lost, by overt opposition to Italian unity. This the *Codini* know full well.

This, perhaps, his Eminence the Cardinal Archbishop, Patriarch of Venice, knows better than any other sympathiser with the bygone rulers of Venice. Monsignor Trevisinato, who, as a Venetian born and one sprung from the ranks of the people, and as a prelate distinguished by unfeigned piety, extensive charity, and vast learning,—especially in the Oriental languages,—has every claim to be regarded with esteem and veneration by his flock, but who is, for political reasons, most cordially hated,—has just put forth a Pastoral, a copy of which, in a neat ebony frame, and protected by a screen of wirework, is visible to the faithful on one of the door-jambs of the vestibule of St. Mark's, and is the subject of much satirical comment on the part of the gondoliers and fishermen who are generally to be found lounging about the sacred precincts. His Eminence has made a copious collection of very good set phrases in choice Italian; and the gist of his pastoral is that, for the greater glory of Heaven and the advantage of the Church, it is desirable for everybody to preserve a peaceable demeanour, cultivate a quiet mind, and, forgetting all bygone differences, acquiesce in the union of Venetia to the constitutional monarchy of Victor Emmanuel II. Apart from the set phrases and the choice Italian, the Cardinalitian discourse means little more than that the best must be made of a bad job. However, the Patriarch may now say, "*Liberavi animam meam.*" His pastoral may be accepted as at once a confession, a recantation, and an assurance that politically he is what is termed, in American parlance, "sound on the goose;" and when Victor Emmanuel comes to Venice, Cardinal Trevisinato may, with a very good grace, receive the King of Italy under the great *baldacchino* of St. Mark, authorise the customary *Te Deum*, and solemnise the customary high mass.

"I was the last man in England," said George III. to the first American Minister who came to the Court of St. James's, "to acquiesce in American independence; but I will also be the last to do aught to injure the liberties of the United States." It is to be hoped that the Patriarch of Venice may eventually fall into a frame of mind as honest and as Christianlike as that of George III. It is sufficiently hard, however, in one's old age, to have to go into an entirely new set of harness, and to pull from the collar where hitherto one has been accustomed to pull from the loins. The Patriarch owes his mitre, and his red hat to boot, to his steady Austriacantism. He has been fed upon good Viennese sauerkraut from his youth upwards. It is pitiable to see him now, condemned to a diet of Savoy cabbage.

He is the successor, although not the immediate one, of that Patriarch of Venice who, in 1849, was mainly instrumental in bringing about the capitulation which led to the reoccupation of Venice by the Austrians. The Venetians, although suffering, and having suffered for months, under the triple scourge of a famine, a pestilence, and a bombardment, were not in the least desirous to surrender. It was their desire to fight until the last Venetian should die in the last canal of the Guidecca. The Cardinal, however, as a man of peace, his paternal heart bleeding at the spectacle of the misery he saw around him, so managed matters as, by dexterous counsel and soft persuasion, to pave the way for surrender and the return of the Tedeschi. Before they returned, however, the Venetian people gutted the patriarchal palace, threw half the furniture into the canal, and burnt the rest. The Patriarch died soon after the reinstallation of the Austrians, and Monsignor Trevisinato, then only an archpriest, had to deliver a funeral oration over his remains. This oration was spoken in the Basilica, and in the presence of two Austrian archdukes. The preacher was so eloquent, alluded so touchingly to the onslaught on the late Patriarch's palace, and the holocaust made of his chairs and tables; he said so many beautiful, orthodox, and truly conservative things concerning the evils of revolutionary passions and the deplorable effects of mob violence; in a word, he contrived, by implication, so fervently to laud the advantages of the Austrian domination in Venetia, that the archducal heart was touched. Both Erzherzogs, indeed, were moved to tears; and the ingenious archpriest was so strongly recommended at Vienna, that he was soon afterwards made bishop of some unimportant place. He was next proposed to the Pope for the Archbishopric of Udine, the sure and safe stepping-stone to the more sumptuous see of Venice. Then came the patriarchate, and ultimately the *cappello rosso;* and, if his Eminence takes care, he may find himself some day in the chair of St. Peter—if, indeed, St. Peter, whose circumstances are becoming every day more embarrassed, have any chair left by the time Cardinal Trevisinato is haply deemed worthy to sit in it.

He is not the first Church dignitary who has obtained the highest prizes in his profession by preaching a clever funeral sermon. Dubois, it is true, owed his scarlet to his impudence and the Duchess of Kendal. Alberoni got his through knowing how to dress cauliflowers with Parmesan cheese. Ganganelli rose by merit, Borgia by profligacy, and Aquapendente by accident; but, as a rule, the funeral sermon may be hailed as a *moyen de parvenir. De mortuis nil nisi bonum:* let the aspirant for ecclesiastical preferment bear that axiom well in mind, and the odds are twenty to one that the living will give him something worth having.

The Venetians have pretty good memories, and they are not likely to forget their Patriarch's antecedents. He has never, however, been actively mischievous; and as it was his great good luck to be neither an Austrian general nor a commissary of police, the dislike he has inspired has been more passive than active. For the rest, the good man only wanted to get on in the world; and he got on. His revenues are large, and he gives away a good deal to the poor. The Venetians chose rather to remember that he was old and charitable, and a capital Sanscrit scholar, than that he was a creature of the stranger and an adherent of tyranny. There has, then, been little desire to mob, to denounce, or even to insult him. Some wags have, from time to time, played a harmless practical joke on his Eminence; but there has always been a vast fund of drollery latent in the Italian character—witness the waggeries of the *Decamerone*—and the Venetians are perhaps, next to the Neapolitans, the funniest people in all Italy.

For example, when the cession of Venetia by Austria began first to be talked about last July, and provisions of the *stoffe colorate*, so fiercely denounced by the now obsolete Director Frank, were laid in, with a view to future banner-displays, it was rumoured that the Cardinal Patriarch had suddenly become imbued with popular sympathies, and was having a tricoloured flag made. It was ascertained, on inquiry, that the flag was actually in course of manufacture, and was a very grand affair indeed, of silk and gold fringe. When a sufficient time for completion had elapsed, a facetious person went to the maker, and, professing to be the bearer of a message from the Patriarch, demanded his Eminence's flag. The maker, suspecting nothing, gave it up. The facetious but fraudulent messenger went away, and from that day to this the splendid standard of silk and bullion has never been seen. It may have been displayed last Friday from the window of some hovel on the Canareggio, but from any balcony of the patriarchal palace it certainly did not flaunt.

Nothing discouraged, and foreseeing that the children of Belial must eventually prevail, Monsignor Trevisinato had another flag made—nay, three flags, and even four or five; and on the momentous morning of emancipation his lacqueys were ready to make his whole palace brave in tricoloured bunting. But the Venetians were determined that their *codino* Patriarch should *not* sympathise with the cause of Italian unity. A highly-respectable deputation of *barcaruoli* and *macellaji* waited, at nine o'clock A.M., on the Patriarch, and respectfully but firmly desired him to take his flags in. His Eminence's major-domo pleaded the fervent patriotism of his master; but the deputation intimated that it was rather late in the day, and that they preferred that he should keep his patriotism to himself. Little good is to be obtained from arguing with a deputation—least of all when it is composed of boatmen and butchers. The signs of patriotism disappeared, and, on the day of the entry of the Italian troops into Venice, the only house undecorated with the Italian colours was the palace of the Patriarch of Venice.

I have dwelt at some length on matters ecclesiastical for the reason that my readers may be desirous to learn what is the precise "attitude" of the Venetian clergy, in view of the astonishing change of public things which has come down upon them very much after the manner of a cart-load of bricks. I remember that Mr. Dickens, in his *American Notes*, mentions an inquisitive Yankee, who, occupying the next state-room to him on board a steamer, was very uneasy in his mind at the undemonstrative course of conduct pursued by his illustrious fellow-traveller. "Boz keeps himself very quiet, my dear," he was heard, through the bulkhead, to observe to his wife. The truth was that Boz had a bilious headache, and was lying down in his berth. The black Boz in Venice is keeping, just now, very quiet indeed. The black panther is couchant—not rampant. So have I seen the real panther at the Jardin des Plantes, curled up in a corner of his den, lazily blinking in the sunshine, and disdaining to roar, to glare, or to spring, when the naughty little *gamins* threw nutshells at him. Could he be the real panther of Java who bounds through the air, and makes a man into a mummy in one squeeze and one crunch? Yes, he is the same old Beast, only the day is warm, and the times are dull, and he does not exactly see what good might come out of tearing up the planks of the den or dashing his head against those iron bars. He waits. A bright time may come when he may crunch bones, and suck marrow, and eat Man again. This is about the attitude of the priesthood. They are quiescent. They crouch in the corner of the cage. They fear the popular beast-tamer, with his gutta-percha whip or his stronger crowbar. They wait.

In common, I hope, with most Englishmen born and bred in an atmosphere of respectable sectarian prejudice, I have been much shocked to see that Venice has gotten her liberty, that the Austrians have gone away, that the Italian banner has been hoisted, and that the Italian troops have piled arms on St. Mark's Place, without a single *Te Deum*, without the tingle of a single bell or the smoke of a single censer, or the flare of a single taper, or the apparition of a single stole, alb, or dalmatic. What has become of the Church of Rome in the Italian peninsula? Where is it? Who believes in it? Who asks for it? Who looks for the priest to bless the work, to utter a prayer over the newly-unfurled banner of freedom? Certainly not the Italians.

If you really wish to know where Rome's friends are, you must inquire at Munich or at Madrid, in the Graben, or of the beadle of St. Germain l'Auxerrois. You must ask at Baltimore, or at Brompton. Were you to address yourself to the majority of people in Italy, you would be told that the Church of Rome did not lodge there. This is the naked, unpalatable, and incontestable truth. In the hearts of most Italians—save some ignorant peasants, some savage brigands, some half-imbecile old women, and some sour men in shovel-hats—the Romish idolatry is DEAD. It is as dead as any dog that ever hung. It is dead notwithstanding the existence of some clerical journals—notwithstanding the performance of the usual incantations in the all-but-deserted churches—notwithstanding the fact that there are here and there half-demented people who tell their beads, who make votive offerings of silver ears and noses in gratitude for their recovery from deafness or polypus, and make pilgrimages, with peas in their shoes, to the shrine of St. Bosfursus, or rub their bellies with a portrait of St. Joachim to keep away the cholera morbus. You may buy these same portraits in the city of Venice itself. They are printed on thick flannel. Everybody knows that friction with woollen stuff is an excellent stomachic; but I am inclined to think that the effigy of Mr. Stead, the Perfect Cure, would be quite as efficacious as that of St. Joseph on the strip of flannel. The fraudulent intent is, however, delicious. *Aide toi*—with a flannel belly-band; *et le ciel t'aidera*—with the portrait of St. Joseph.

There are Italian-born and Italian-speaking people who continue to place faith in these mummeries; but they do not constitute the nation. The nation has utterly and entirely repudiated Papistry—Paganism's eldest daughter. They have done with the barbarous swindling system altogether. I do not believe that Voltairianism, Straussism, Hegelism, Renanism, or any other particular "ism," is making much way in Italy. The people have simply abandoned one religion because they have discovered it to be wicked, mischievous, and useless; and they are looking out for another. I hope they may find a good one.

XVII.

VENICE RESTORED.

November 1.

THE Fenice opened last night with Verdi's opera of *Un Ballo in Maschera.* The historian regrets to have to record the fact that the entire performance was a *fiasco* of a most extensive nature. The catastrophe is, for numerous reasons, to be deplored. The chief one certainly is that the Fenice has been closed for a period of eight years; that its long-continued surcease was inseparably connected with the gloomy memories of the Austrian rule in Venice; and that its re-opening was looked upon on all sides as a symbol that the dark and bitter days were past, and as a harbinger of a brighter era in store. La Fenice once reopened, Venice was forthwith to become gay, prosperous, and happy. True to its name, the Adriatic Phœnix was to arise from its ashes, and shine very brightly indeed, for the edification of the lovers of Italy in general, and of the lyrico-dramatic art in particular. The importance, moreover, of the operatic element in bringing about that Venetian *rinascimento* or new birth which we all so ardently desire, should not by any means be underrated.

In England operas and theatres are mere accessories and adjuncts of civilisation; and in the opinion of very many worthy people we should be much better off were we to abolish operas and theatres in block, and, following the counsel of the sour old Puritan poet, "turn the minstrels out of doors, with all their rascal company." But among the Latin races generally, and especially among Italians, the stage is an institution, a power, a hierarchy, a component part of the *Res Publica*. The forum must ever have the theatre close to it. The theatres of Venice are as replete with historic associations as its Procuratie or its palaces. The Fenice, the San Benedetto, the San Samuele, even the puppet theatre of San Moïsè can all show a highly-respectable antiquity, have all a glorious and varied record, all claim their part in the *fasti* of the Most Serene Republic—are all joints, as it were, in the immortal tail of the Lion of St. Mark. The Carnival of Venice, without the theatres, would have been shorn of two-thirds of its attractions. *Regate* and *ridotti* were all very well in their way; but the *veglioni*, or theatrical masked balls, were the most favourite haunts of the dissipated patricians, and the scarcely less dissipated clergy and burgesses, whom the scandalous but graphic pencil of Casanova has drawn in undying *chiaro scuro*. During the seventeenth and eighteenth centuries Venice, as a nursery for lyric art, was more renowned than either Rome or Naples or Milan.

The boundless wealth and the inexhaustible good-nature of the Venetians led them to crowd their beautiful city with charitable institutions. If we wish to see orphan asylums now in their fullest plenitude—even to redundance sometimes—we must turn to England, or to the United States; but, two hundred years ago, the Queen of the Adriatic was the most bounteous nursing-mother to the fatherless and the destitute to be found the whole world over. The Conservatorio di Musica is a Venetian invention, and in its origin was a purely eleemosynary one, and the musical conservatories of Venice flourished generations before similar establishments were dreamt of in other parts of the Continent.

Venice had at one time so many little children under her charge, that, like the old woman who lived in a shoe, she did not know what to do with them. To give them broth without bread, and, whipping them all round, dismiss them to rest, was not part of her scheme. In other words, she was at no time so bigoted to the Roman Catholic faith as to be content with giving a semi-monastic training to her infinite orphans. The demands of her army and navy were not onerous enough to cause her to regard her orphan asylums as nurseries for future heroes; and it may be hinted that the Most Serene, being likewise infinitely sagacious, much preferred, as a rule, Slavonic or Teutonic mercenaries, for soldiers and sailors, to her own children. The mercenaries' lives were of less value—and they fought better. Eminent as Venice was in arts and manufactures, the beaver-dam-like structure of the city, and the difficulty of greatly extending it, made a discreet restriction of the number of skilled artisans a matter of public policy. It was not deemed wise to bring up all the *protégés* of the State as painters, or carvers, or glass-blowers, or velvet-weavers, or mosaic-workers. What then was to be done with them? The Most Serene determined, in its wisdom, that they should all be taught music—vocal if they had any voices, instrumental if they had hands; both if they had one and the other. At least, they argued, he who can play on the fiddle need never starve. The Most Serene went even further. They solved the problem which in this nineteenth century is puzzling us so sorely. They found a suitable and remunerative employment for women. The female orphans were taught to play on the fiddle; yea, even on the piccolo and on the bass viol.

The good old professor who comes to me every morning and endeavours to indoctrinate me in the beauties of Italian poetry tells me that when he was young almost every girl in Venice could play on the violoncello. In these genteel days, he adds with a sigh, the possession of such an accomplishment by the *damigelle* of Venice would be deemed "shocking." It is, in truth, difficult to reconcile with your notions of feminine refinement the idea of the adored one of your heart sitting on a three-legged stool, and sawing away at the double bass. Why not? In England we talk a vast deal of stuff about feminine delicacy as applied to occupations by means of which women might earn their bread. We are selfish and brutal enough to allow women to work as barmaids in public-houses, drawing pots of beer and serving noggins of gin to drunken costermongers; but what an outcry there would be if we had female waiters at the Clarendon or Mivart's, or a few lady-clerks at the Post Office and Somerset House!

It is about a year since I was coming from Manchester to London with a professed philanthropist, economist, social-science-congressman, and so forth, who was pluming himself mightily on the efforts he had made to persuade the guardians of some union in the North to "train" their young pauper girls as nurses. "There is an intuitive delicacy and sympathy," et cetera, et cetera, et cetera, "it is an employment at once so Christian and so eminently suitable," et cetera, et cetera, et cetera, he was maundering on, when I took the liberty of interrupting him. "Good God, sir," I said, "what right have you to condemn fresh young girls of fourteen and fifteen—healthful, cheerful, hopeful, feeling their life in every limb, to a hideous treadmill-existence among ulcers and poultices and pills and sleeping-draughts, and the bandages which tie up the jaws of death? Who are you, that you should presume to settle the future of your young pauper girl? Suppose she wants to fall in love and be married—whom is she to marry? The workhouse porter or the parish undertaker? Suppose she wants to paint in water-colours, or to write stanzas in the *ottava rima*, or to drive a cab? Why don't you go and ask Lady Clara Vere de Vere if she would like to poultice scald heads or stick plasters on sore shins all the days of her life?" But this has nothing to do, I apprehend, with the progress of lyric art in Italy and last night's *fiasco* at La Fenice.

My professor, I suppose, was born long after the collapse of the Most Serene, and the prevalence of big fiddling among the young ladies of his acquaintance may have been but the dim continuance of an esteemed tradition. Music, however, vocal and instrumental, had been at one time taught universally and systematically to the children of the poor, both boys and girls. Almost every Italian is a musician born, to begin with—that is to say, he or she has an ear, and sympathy, and taste. Proficiency in the practice of music served to relieve weakly boys from the drudgery of mechanical labour—to enfranchise girls from the abhorrent bondage of the needle.

The demand for such proficients was quite equal to the supply, although the Italian operas of London, New York,

San Francisco, and St. Petersburg were as yet uncreate. Italy could take as many good performers, male and female, as the conservatories of Venice could furnish. Poverty and oppression had not then made the Italians a nation of shabby niggards. They were a hospitable people. They lived largely. They feasted frequently, and on as sumptuous a scale as is represented in the vasty canvases of Tintoretto and Veronese. The works of the great Venetian masters are full of lutes, hautboys, sackbuts, and all kinds of psaltery. You never see the wedding guest but you hear the loud bassoon. They were good players themselves, as the great Dutchmen were. When Gerard Douw has finished touching up his pots and pans, he takes up his Stradivarius and discourses sweetly upon it. The bass viol has an honoured place by the easel of Palmavecchio. Giorgione clashes the cymbals, and Titian pinches the chords of the harp. Simple Catholic men, they carry their love for music up to the very heavens. They show us saints and martyrs sounding the French horn, and angels performing on the big drum. In those bright orchestral days, what a charivari there must have been from the Alps to the Adriatic, and from the Lago Maggiore to the Gulf of Sorrento! Every great noble had a band of "musicianers" in his train. Not a lord but had his chamber singers. Not a lady but had her lute-boy. Not a municipal solemnity but needed some braying and banging of metallic harmony.

The Church had stomach for a whole mine of music; nor in the Venetian fanes were female voices banished from the mass, as, from the pathetic Latin lament of the Maestro Rossini to the Pope, we learn that they now are throughout the Peninsula. Choristers were eagerly sought for by the priests of a religion which, when it ceases to appeal to the senses, falls at once before the cruel logic of reason; nay, so incessant was the demand for shrill treble voices that there arose, prompted by the Devil, that hideous *manufacture* of *soprani* of which Velluti was the last-known type in England. "*Faites-moi cesser, promptement, ces êtres là!*" Napoleon wrote sternly to his viceroy Beauharnais at Milan; and the manufacture of *soprani* ceased for ever.

Apart from the Church-needs, and those of banquets and festivals, and pomps and vanities without end, there were concerts and oratorios and theatres all hungering and thirsting for "musicianers." These were largely recruited from the Conservatories of Venice. They, however, and the Most Serene Republic herself, came to a sorry, shameful end. The Austrians, it must be admitted, brought with them into Venetia the best military bands that had ever been heard in Italy; but, their waltzes and mazurkas in St. Mark's Place notwithstanding, they contrived to strangle, suffocate, and sit down upon the musical profession in their unjustly-acquired kingdom. The Scala at Milan, it is true, they never succeeded in destroying. The Conservatory of the capital of Lombardy continued to flourish as a musical university, whither repaired students from all parts of Europe; but music in Venice the Tedeschi utterly ruined. I daresay they had not the slightest intention of doing the Venetians any such evil turn. It was not their fault. It was their system, it was politics, it was fatality, which was to blame. Still, in any case, sure enough was it that the Conservatorij of Venice went out, one after the other, like exhausted tapers, and that the decay of La Fenice and the San Benedetto kept pace with the decay of commerce and navigation—of arts and arms—of cultivated society and material prosperity—of everything, in fact, which could be blighted and withered by an unbending military despotism and a pig-headed bureaucracy.

The Fenice struggled for a time, flickered, burnt up again for a brief season when Maximilian was viceroy, then sank into the socket and utter darkness. No sooner was the cession of Venetia to Italy talked about last July than the Venetians began to talk about reopening La Fenice. The resuscitation of the famous old house was looked upon as a natural and inevitable consequence of the emancipation of the city. An army of upholsterers and painters began quietly to rub up the gilding, clean the ceiling, refurnish the boxes, and mend the holes in the stage, at about the same time that the middle classes began to enrol themselves in the National Guard and exercise with wooden muskets in the halls of deserted palaces, and the Venetian ladies began to hem tricoloured flags and stitch cockades together. The preparations for the Feast of Liberty went on concurrently. Then the Austrians vanished for good, and it was announced that the Fenice would be opened on the thirty-first of October. Some people thought it would be more loyal and decorous to wait for the arrival of King Victor Emmanuel, and solemnly inaugurate the new era with a gala performance, and the Fenice lighted *a giorno;* but the Venetians were impatient to look upon their beloved opera-house once more, and the date of the thirty-first was adhered to.

I heard, for a full fortnight, almost as much bragging and

boasting about the *primo tenore* and the *prime donne*, and the band and the chorus, and the new scenery, dresses, and decorations, which we were to see by the thirty-first, as before the war we used to hear about what *nostri prodi* meant to do in the Quadrilateral, and *nostre camicie rosse* in the Tyrol. The Italians are as fond of the use of the first person plural as are the Spaniards with their incessant "*nosotros*." When an Italian cannot possibly do anything without extraneous assistance, he is sure to scream "*Faremo da noi.*" Hope rose to a most exciting point, and was kept at fever heat by the announcement that the management of the Fenice had been confided by the committee of noble proprietors—the same patriotic patricians who so sternly refused to open the house at the invitation of the tyrant Toggenburg, backed as his offer was by the offer of fifty thousand florins by way of subvention—to the experienced hands of the *impresario* of La Scala at Milan. We were to have a first-rate troupe, a tenor *hors ligne*, a ballet recruited at once from Mahomet's paradise of houris and from the Reale Scuola di Danza, and a *prima donna assoluta* who should recall the last operatic glories of Venice prior to '59, when the great Alboni could be heard for a *zwanziger*. The magical name even of the incomparable Adelina Patti was whispered abroad; and the *cognoscenti* trembled with ecstatic expectation.

One night, very late, a gondola arrived at the Hotel Victoria; a vast quantity of luggage, a lady of a certain age, and another of an uncertain age, the former being the mamma of the latter, were discharged therefrom; and the shrill tones of a female voice were heard in the marble halls inquiring,

"*La prima mima? Dov' è la prima mima?*" It was the *seconda mima*, the second pet of the ballet, who had arrived, and to whom the first *mima* had given rendezvous at the Victoria. I call her age uncertain, because in stature she did not appear to be much over nine, whereas in agility she was nineteen, and in facial expression ninety. The next day came the *primo tenore*, who was stout, and a sufferer from the toothache, they said. He retired to his apartments and rang the bell up till one in the morning, demanding mint, tea, chloroform, laudanum, onion-peel, creosote, tobacco, cloves, cotton-wool, and other remedies for his ailment. We were joined, however, at the *table-d'hôte* by the *prima donna*, who was thickly swathed in shawls, and the tip of whose nose—which was about the only part of her person visible—did not look quite so young as it might have done. The footlights, however, make a wonderful difference in these play-acting folks; and it is certain that their profession is a very trying one for the complexion.

We next heard that they were rehearsing at the Fenice, and that the *Ballo in Maschera* would be produced on the appointed night, on a scale of splendour and artistic completeness yet unheard of in Venetian annals. Boxes and stall-tickets were, of course, at a premium; at least, foreigners were industriously told that admittance could be obtained scarcely for love or for money; and several worthy *forestieri* of my acquaintance were only too glad to disburse sums varying from twelve to twenty-five francs a-head for tickets entitling them only to standing-room. I may here mention, *en passant*, and with many apologies for being so rude, that the only one genuine thing connected with the Italian opera in Italy is the opera itself. *That* cannot be adulterated, sophisticated, tricked, cooked, and doctored; but, apart from the actual production of the gifted composer, everything else is an ingenious, artistic, and shameless swindle. In England, our most shining abilities in the way of swindling are ordinarily devoted to the buying and selling of horses, and the promotion of joint-stock companies. In Italy, Jeremy Diddler becomes an operatic manager; Robert Macaire writes theatrical critiques, and extorts black-mail from the artists he criticises; Jack Sheppard turns music-publisher; and Jonathan Wild does a neat little business as box book-keeper, with Blueskin as assistant ticket-agent.

Having been myself, on innumerable occasions, bitten in regard to the purchase of tickets for first nights, and with a keen remembrance of having paid about two hundred and fifty per cent above cost price to see the *Africaine* in the principal theatres in Europe, I made no efforts to secure stalls or front rows for the thirty-first. I waited to see whether anything would turn up. Sure enough something did. A revolution of Fortune's wheel brought me an invitation on the part of the committee of shareholders to witness the *prova generale*, or full-dress rehearsal of the opera, which was to take place on the evening of the twenty-ninth. I esteemed this favour the more highly as I was told that only the committee and a select number of the Venetian aristocracy were to be present, and that persons of the journalistic profession were specially to be "non-recipients of invites," to quote the delicate phrase employed by American reporters to signify that they haven't been asked to supper. The press taboo, however, did not prevent my next neighbour from being the sprightly correspondent in Venice of the Milan *Perseveranza*, an accomplished musician, but a terribly bitter critic, and an honest one, which is saying much when criticism is mentioned.

I found the old Fenice not very much changed. It had been, like an antique silver salver, diligently rubbed up with whitening and wash-leather, but that was all; and its tasteful, albeit somewhat old-fashioned, decorations were perhaps no worse for having had so little done to them. I should be loth to assume that the genius and skill in those decorative arts in which Italy once excelled have abandoned her for ever; but I must confess that since I have been in this country I have seen little or nothing in the way of public decoration to remind me that I was in a land once rendered illustrious by the performances of Bramante and Palladio, Donato and Sansovino.

The architectural remains of Venice are magnificent, but they all belong to the remote past. They are, in the strictest sense, funeral baked meats, and, to tell truth, do somewhat coldly furnish forth the marriage table. A trifle of colour, in the way of a *potage*, or a *hors d'œuvre chaud*, would be most welcome. The old gilding, the old scrolls and wreaths, the old girandoles, the old medallions of poets and composers, the old ceiling in tempera, showing the nine Muses, the Graces, the Hours, the Seasons, and the Passions, all with scarcely a rag on, balancing themselves in the ethereal blue, had been carefully bread-crumbed and sedulously polished; and a few books of gold-leaf had been bestowed on the tarnished frames of the mirrors in the royal box; and those plates of glass which were hopelessly cracked had been replaced by new ones. Perhaps a gross of glass drops had been added to the chandelier, and some of the stalls had been re-covered.

There is, however, a rich and subdued harmony about the interior of the Fenice not surpassed by any other theatre I have seen; and the paucity of fresh adornment was, therefore, a thing more to be rejoiced over than lamented. It unfortunately happened that what was really new was not good, but in the very worst possible taste. I could have borne with an old act-drop, however faded and *rococo*. It might have been a drop a hundred years old for aught I cared; for a hundred years ago the names of the scene-painters at the Fenice were Canaletto and Guardi. I don't think we should grumble at home if at Drury Lane Mr. Chatterton gave us now and then some odds and ends from his scene-room, painted, thirty years ago, by Clarkson Stanfield and David Roberts. The management of the Fenice presented the audience with a tawdry curtain of blue cotton-velvet, powdered with tawdrier stars in gilt-foil paper. This was bad to begin with, but worse remained before. Over the royal box there had been nailed up a most unsightly trophy, composed of tricoloured flags of the commonest bunting, with the royal crown, escutcheon, and cross of Savoy in the middle. The part which should have been gold was of the coarsest Dutch metal; and the cross of Savoy was of a silver so strident, glaring, and burnished-tin-like in tone, that it utterly destroyed the effect of the time-mellowed old gilding round it, and could suggest only one possible companion. "*Sale e Tabacchi,*" whispered the Milanese critic. It was indeed, for all the world, the image of the garish heraldic signboard hung up in front of the Government salt-and tobacco-shops.

There chanced to sit by us the scenic artist of the Fenice, and I took the liberty, as an old apprentice of the distemper-painting craft, to hint to him that just the merest coat of "size" washed over the silver cross would "kill" its tin-pot brightness, and make it harmonise tolerably with the half-dead gold around. He acknowledged that the effect was bad; but explained that it was to be amended, and that to-morrow the cross would be of gold instead of silver. I ventured to hint, again, that there was such a thing as accuracy in heraldic blazonry, and that the cross of Savoy was a cross argent, which must blazonically be translated either by silver or by pure white. He shrugged his shoulders. The committee of proprietors had ordered that it should be *tutto oro;* and—"*cosa volete?*" he concluded. It is "*cosa volete?*" indeed. I think the public had a right to expect the committee of proprietors to spend a few thousand more francs on the redecoration of La Fenice. In this case the plea of poverty, so industriously brought forward when Italian stinginess is censured, will not avail. Among the proprietors of the Fenice are a number of Venetian noblemen, with fortunes such as English peers of the realm would not be ashamed to own.

Soon after eight the rehearsal began. The band played in tune and time, and with expression. The chorus was excellent. The scenery was old, and good; the dresses were new, and bad. I must make one exception, however, as regards the costume of the young lady who played the page, and who, with her black hair dressed like a boy's, and her pretty form arrayed in a silver-laced velvet doublet, pink-silk hose, and the most ravishing pair of sky-blue satin smallclothes ever beheld since the days when our grandfathers went mad over Madame Catalani in pantaloons, quite made me oblivious, for a season, of the unpleasing fact that she could neither act nor sing. "Were I Nostradamus," muttered the critic at my side, "I would predict that yonder page will be hissed off the stage the night after to-morrow." He subsequently remarked that were he Duns Scotus he would prophesy a similar fate as in store for a cadaverous baritone in black velvet, a point-lace collar, and jack-boots *à la* Subway or Thames-Embankment fashion. I am no judge of music, otherwise it might have occurred to me too, that I was Cassandra or Doctor Cumming, and that it was my mission to foretell the utter discomfiture on the night of the thirty-first of the stout tenor with the toothache, and the *prima donna* whose nose, as visible through her shawls, had not looked quite so young as it might have done.

I saw the rehearsal through, and went away, grateful for my entertainment, but full of the most melancholy forebodings; only the remembrance that there was to be a ballet somewhat reassured me. The *prova* of the choregraphic performance did not take place until the evening of the thirtieth, and we had the advantage of beholding the *prima ballerina* in person, and in the ordinary walking-dress of private life, taking her place in the stalls, and assisting as a privileged spectator at the rehearsal of the *Ballo in Maschera*. I like to see ballet-dancers in long clothes. I like to see the Sylphide eating a pork-chop, and Giselle walking down Regent-street, very nervous at the crossing by the

Piccadilly Circus lest her ankles should be seen by the profane. I like to see Esmeralda reading the *Family Herald,* and La Jolie Fille de Gand nursing her first baby. Take my word for it, my young friend from the university—you who are so anxious to see "fast" life and to go "behind the scenes"—that the pets of the ballet, all over the world, are a great deal better than you ordinarily give them credit for being.

More than twenty years have passed since I earned my livelihood in a London theatre, and enjoyed a familiar acquaintance with at least five-and-thirty pets of the ballet. Pleasant memories do I preserve of the threehalfpennyworths of toffy and almond-rock, and the bottles of ginger-beer—some even would accept the modest half-pint of porter—to which I have treated, after treasury-time on Saturday, those hard-working, honest-minded, much-belied girls. There was a Sylphide who used to mend my socks. I have lent Esmeralda Mrs. Inchbald's *Simple Story;* and I am glad to know now a Giselle who keeps a lodging-house in Camden Town, and does extremely well; and a Jolie Fille de Gand who has married a master carpenter, and has eight children.

Our *prima ballerina* at the Fenice was the observed of all observers. No sooner did she glide—I mean, did she float—I would say, was she wafted—at any rate, did she gracefully sail, into the stalls, than I quite forgot the bare existence of the young person in the pink-silk hose and the sky-blue satin unwhisperables. This was the most charming little creature that eyes ever feasted on. Her curly poll, her diamonds, her little pork-pie hat, her little roguish *chiffonnée* face, her zouave jacket, her doll's-gloves, her Liliputian bronze boots, visible for one brief moment as she tripped down the aisle between the seats, made up an *ensemble* at once peerless, perfect—and perilous. Good Doctor Johnson told Garrick why he would no more come behind the scenes. This *prima ballerina* was clearly a Scylla, a Charybdis, a Siren, like unto those dangerous young women of the sea whom the heathen man did stop his ears against. She was accompanied by two females of mouldy aspect. I did not ask her name; I did not want to know her name; but, I thought, as I left the Fenice, and crossing the great stone bridge and losing my way, as a matter of course did not find it again till I brought up suddenly, long after midnight, in the Merceria San Salvador—"There is no fear of their hissing *you*, little one, any way."

The long-expected thirty-first arrived, and the Fenice was opened. The house was not at any time during the evening more than half-full. The foreigners in Venice had been cosened into paying exorbitant prices for their seats, but the Venetians had obtained their tickets at the ordinary tariff, and not a tithe of what may be considered good society in Venice was present at the Fenice at all. A sufficient number of *cognoscenti* were, however, in evidence to deliver an authoritative verdict that the entire performance was atrociously bad, and, from the beginning of the second scene, to "goose" it most thoroughly. The whole auditorium, indeed, reeked with the odour of sage and onions. The "goose" was complete. All the predictions of my Milanese friends were verified. When the young lady in the sky-blue satin inexpressibles had recited two bars, the pittites began to blow into latch-keys and to whistle profane airs—that is to say, that nobody would listen to the stout tenor with the toothache. As for the baritone, they made light of the pallor of his countenance and turned his jack-boots into derision. It was discovered that the *prima donna* was fifty-five years of age—I will not be so ungallant as to mention her name—and that she had been "goosed" at the San Samuele in the year '48. After this the cause of *Un Ballo in Maschera* was hopeless.

It is not at any time an inviting opera. Homer sometimes nods; and I think that were the opinion of Mr. Artemus Ward asked in this matter, it would be to the effect that Signor Verdi had gone out for a walk and got some Bourbon in his hair when he wrote *Un Ballo*. The poverty of the music is rendered even more apparent by the absolute wretchedness of the *libretto*. The story of *Un Ballo* is, in reality, that of MM. Scribe and Auber's *Gustavus III.*; but as, in despotic countries it would never do to have a royal personage assassinated by Count Ankerström, the scene is changed to "*America nel secolo XVII.*," and Gustavus becomes a "*Governatore di Boston,*" and the weird woman who foretells his assassination an Indian sorceress. The general result is bald, crass, concrete absurdity. It is just the kind of piece—apart from its musical merits, which are considerable, but unequal—to be "goosed;" and goosed it accordingly was.

The disturbance towards the end of the first act had grown so tumultuous—there was such a storm of *fischietti*, of screeching, hooting, yelling, stamping, and roaring "*Fuori! fuori!*"—that "Doldrum the manager," or whatever the *impresario's* name may be, had, in his opera-hat and opera-tights, to advance to the footlights, and submit the terms of a compromise.

He proposed that the first act should be allowed to conclude; next that the National Hymn should be sung; then that the ballet should be given; and, finally, that the remainder of *Un Ballo in Maschera* should be presented. The audience demurred to the totality of these terms. They were willing to hear the hymn, and see the ballet, but they would not hear any more opera; and when the dolorous man in jack-boots essayed once more a piteous stave, he was met with such a universal howl of "*Basta! Basta!*" "Enough! enough!" that the blue cotton-velvet curtain dropped, as though of its own volition, on the painful scene, and the *suggeritore* or prompter ducked his head, as though to evade the storm of orange-peel, or potatoes, or halfpence, or some other form of annihilation which might probably be directed to his dress by the outraged amateurs of Venice. Nobody threw anything, however. There was no need to call in the police. The people, so far as the present historian is concerned, were, towards eleven P.M., "left hooting;" but I am told by more persistent spectators, who did not leave the theatre until one in the morning, that after the hymn had been sung and the ballet danced—and I am delighted to say that not one sibillation assailed my Siren-sylphide with the curly poll—the fag-end of *Un Ballo in Maschera* did, in a most disjointed and draggled manner, wriggle itself, in the midst of fearful opprobrium and scorn, to an unhonoured close.

Such was the great *fiasco* of the Fenice on the 31st

October 1866. I think they had better have kept the theatre closed for another eight years than have opened it in this shabby fashion, and with this worn-out troupe; and if the management intend to give Victor Emmanuel, on the grand gala-night when he goes to the theatre in state, a repetition of the *Ballo in Maschera*, it will certainly be a pretty dish to set before a king.

XVIII.

ENTRY OF THE KING OF ITALY INTO VENICE.

November 7.

It is done. The grand show is over. *L' Italia è fatta, se non compiuta.* Such were the words addressed by the King of Italy to the deputation who waited on him at the end of last week, to invite his Majesty to visit his newly-acquired city of Venice; and few can question the logical correctness of the royal reply. Italy is indeed "made," although she lacks, to produce completeness, the trifling addition of the Capitol of Rome. But she has become a great fact notwithstanding. The Peninsula, once cynically defined by the sneering statesman, as a "geographical expression," is now one of the great Powers of Europe, with a population of twenty-five million souls. The land which was once only the resort of tourists and *dilettanti*—"potted for the antiquary," as Mr. Ford would say—is now a living, breathing commonwealth, enjoying all the advantages and labouring under all the difficulties which are the lot of communities which, although strong, are young, and must learn to work in order that they may prosper.

There are those, and I have been of them, who are never tired of girding at the idea of Italian unity, but who choose to forget that it is only since the day before yesterday that the atoms of the Italian structure fortuitously came together. There are those who sneer at the Italian people because they are mendacious, parsimonious, and inhospitable; but these critics forget that centuries of slavery are sure to produce the first of the vices of slavery, untruth, and that the people who have been so long accustomed to see their little all wrested from them in ruinous imposts and forced loans, are reluctant to give, voluntarily, that which was habitually extorted from them by force. There are those who decry the Italians, as a nation, because they are somewhat over-given to barking, and bite little, if at all—because, in the day of battle, their soldiers ordinarily run away, and their ships sheer off: but we are bound, I think, under any circumstances, to remember that what great, noble, and heroic qualities they may have originally possessed have been systematically suffocated and strangled by succeeding generations of tyrants and barbarians; that their bad qualities—of which the name is surely legion—must be put down to the account of the Gauls, the Franks, the Huns, the Vandals, the Goths, the Visigoths, and the Ostrogoths; whereas their good qualities, the which, at present, a double-million magnifier is needed to discern, will doubtless be developed to colossal proportions under a constitutional government and an equitable administration.

Meanwhile it is done. "Italy," as I heard an American gentleman, under the influence of patriotic sympathy and cunningly concocted maraschino punch, declare last night at Florian's, "Italy is free from the Andes to the Himalayas, and the Austrian holocaust no longer indoctrinates the city of the Quadroons." He omitted to state that the home of Venice was in the setting sun, but I daresay he meant it. Discourses, however far more ornately rhetorical than the Pogram oration, might have been tolerated last night in "the city of the Quadroons," or lagoons. Venice went mad about nine o'clock P.M., and continued in a state of acute but joyous delirium all night long. The waiters at Florian's, if they had the barest idea of knowing their customers, flatly refused to take money, and, saying, "Excellency, pay next week," darted off wildly to execute the orders of utter strangers. Distinctions of rank disappeared. Political animosities were drowned in the flowing bowl. I was asked to dinner, at two in the morning, by a Black Republican from Massachusetts. A person with ill-made trousers, and with an Irish accent, asked me for my autograph. All kinds of subversive things took place; all kinds of ultra-democratic rumours were current. A report ran that Earl Russell was witnessing the performance of *Punch* on the Riva de' Schiavoni, and that Mr. Austin Henry Layard was tossing up "heads I win" with a vendor of hot chestnuts in the Spadaria. I saw myself a British peer of the realm whispering soft nothings to a *fioraja* at the corner of the Frezzeria. I will not mention his lordship's name, as I have not yet lost the hope of being invited, some of these days, to pass a week at —— House.

In a word, the city was insane. The hotels, which were full on Monday, ran over on the Tuesday. The *tables-d'hôte* became mere scrambles for scraps of food. Bedrooms were let by the square foot, and beds by the inch, and at their weight in gold. An estimable English lady, a widow, but affable, left us this morning for Milan. "I wanted to see the King's entry," she remarked piteously, "and I am an old traveller, and can bear a great deal; but I cannot sleep until next Tuesday in a bath-room. That is where I passed last night. At Danieli's they offered me a mantelpiece, and at the Europa a dust-bin. I shall go." The sterner sex, however, could afford to laugh at the paucity of sleeping accommodation. Florian's, Quadri's, Suttil's, the Specchi never intended to close; and if the worst came to the worst, they could bivouac on the steps of St. Mark, or between the columns on the Molo. I do believe that very many respectable persons so passed the night on the 6th of November. There was some fear, however, of catching cold. A pretty sharp sirocco of the previous day had been followed by one of those warm, moist, muggy evenings peculiar to Venice. It is moist and muggy only in the shade. Where any rays of light fall, the pavement is as dry as a bone; but wherever there is a shadow the stones are covered by a greasy, humid film, perilous to the footsteps, and distilling bronchitis and diphtheria. This is the real choke-damp of Venice. Neophytes to the place ignorantly imagine that the vicinage of so many canals must be injurious to health. This is not necessarily the case. The canals are full of sea-water, and salt moisture rarely gives cold. It is the deadly clamminess of the after-damp, brought on to the stones by the sirocco, which is to be dreaded. I sincerely trust that the persons who were compelled thus to sleep *à la belle étoile* did not find themselves any the worse for their *al fresco* slumber this morning.

Sleeping or waking, however, the madness of St. Mark's knew no surcease last night. Faces that had not been seen at Venice for years appeared, to be familiarly greeted. Political prisoners long held under Austrian bolts, and long believed to be dead, started up as in a premature resurrection. Old cliques were formed again, old flirtations renewed. The natural talent for improvisation innate in most Italians asserted itself under the oddest circumstances. Venerable females were discovered uttering incoherent rhapsodies, of which the gist was the unity of Italy, on out-of-the-way bridges; and staid old gentlemen of three-score-and-ten snapped their fingers and cut six on their way homewards. The bonds of etiquette were loosened; but those of decorum and good-nature relaxed nothing of their stringency. I heard at an early period of the evening that an Austrian soldier—there are still a few lingering here—had been mobbed in the Merceria; but I learnt subsequently that the supposed Tedesco was only an organ-grinder, who, by mere force of habit, had proceeded to grind the Austrian anthem after Garibaldi's Hymn. There have been really one or two of these mobbing cases, quite cowardly and unjustifiable lately, and the much-beset Croats have been timeously rescued by the National Guard; but I much doubt whether, last night, any Venetian, even to the lowest and roughest of the population, would have thought it worth his while to insult the shadow of his ancient enemy. Everybody was too happy. The King was coming on Wednesday morning. That announcement was sufficient to cause all differences to be forgotten, and all hands to be clasped in amity.

To see a city overjoyed—to gaze upon a multitude unanimous in making merry, and from whom there escapes one gigantic chorus of "So say all of us"—does not often fall to the lot of the contemporary historian. I will venture to surmise, however, that the people in Venice who were not glad on the night of the 6th of November could have been counted, if not on one's digits, at least on the fingers and the toes combined. And who shall say that in the stillness of the night, when deep sleep falleth upon men, there were not men who, although poor and miserable, were full of joy at the thought of that coming to pass which the decrees of Fate, or their sins, or their infirmities forbade them to witness? Who shall say that there were not last night in Venice blind men who beat their hands together for glee, and cripples who struck their crutches against the wall and wagged their stumps in exultation, and beggars who rose up exultant from their lairs of rags and shavings—ay, and captives, even, in the dungeon-cell, doomed ever to rattle their fetters and stare at that intolerable iron door which only opens to admit the gaoler or the chaplain — who felt a thrill of gladness at the thought that to-morrow was to bring about the making of Italy, and the coming-in of Italy's chosen king?

The only fear was for the weather. That sirocco—that warm and muggy film on the marbles of the Broglio and the Procuratie—made the weather-wise anxious. The King of Italy has not the best reputation in the world for bringing sunshine with him. Theodore Hook said of Charles X. that he reigned as long as he could, and then mizzled; but Victor Emmanuel, with sad frequency, not only reigns, but pours. Turin is perhaps, with the exception of Rouen and Manchester, the wettest city in Europe; and the sovereigns of the House of Savoy seem to have transplanted the pluvial influences of their quondam capital to Florence, Naples, and whatever other town they have yet honoured by their presence.

The evil predictions of Tuesday evening were partially, but happily not entirely, verified on Wednesday morning. The day was raw and cold, and the whole city was enveloped in a villanous white fog. It was a Scotch mist aggravated by a Dutch haze. Venice was all at once metamorphosed into Rotterdam, and became absolutely vulgar. I almost fancied that I smelt about the smaller canals that odour of cheese, schnapps, and red-herrings so inalienable from the water-ways of the Batavian republic. Certainly, this Venice, pictorially speaking, had been painted by Vandervelde or Backhuysen, and not by Turner. St. Mark's Place was wrapped in a fleecy blanket, out of which the cathedral blinked, with its great semicircular façades, like some monstrous mouse-trap in triplicate. There were plenty of flags streaming from the windows; but the three colours had, under the foggy blight, a dull and spiritless look. They accorded only too well with the *habitués* you met at Florian's and the Specchi, dipping their milk-bread into their morning coffee, or kindling their after-breakfast cigar, and who all wore an unmistakable air of having been up all night.

This was about half-past eight in the morning; at half-past nine I prepared for the labours of the day by installing myself, in company with a number of railway-rugs, shawls, wrappers, and comforters, in a two-oared gondola. A fur-cap, a pair of sealskin gloves, and a case-bottle containing something comfortable, would not, under the unpleasantly sharp meteorological circumstances, have been amiss. Who would have imagined that this was "beautiful Venice, city of sunshine"? Her "light colonnades" were all wreathed in opaque vapour, and the "pride of the sea" was decidedly of the most muddled complexion.

I may mention that at this conjuncture I fell into a very mixed condition of mind. The local colour had set in dead against the attainment of any intellectual consistency. At first I fancied that I was going to the Derby, and that my barouche and four was waiting for me at Mr. Newman's livery-stables in Regent-street. The number of aristocratic equipages about at such an early hour rather favoured this impression; but then, I remembered, people go to the Derby in carriages, not in canoes, and there is an appreciable difference between your civil, waggish gondolier and your postilion in his blue jacket, leathers, and fluffy white hat, with his unalterable persuasion that Cheam gate is preferable to Ewell, and his incorrigible propensity to become prematurely intoxicated. *How* does your post-boy get tipsy? You are aware of his weakness, and are armed in triple mail against it. You don't allow him to get down. He cannot have any supernatural means of access to the Fortnum and Mason's hamper—which, besides, is strapped behind the barouche. You are certain, from narrow ocular inspection, that he does not carry a private flask. Yet who has not known post-boys who, starting from Jermyn-street, St. James's, as sober as judges, have become, and without stirring from their saddles, before they reach Clapham-common, as drunk as lords?

Dismissing the Epsom-race theory, I tried to persuade myself for a season that I was bound for the Oxford and

Cambridge boat-race; but, not being run down by a penny steamer ere I reached the Foscari Palace, or bullied by the Thames Police as I passed under the Rialto, I changed the venue, and imagined that I was waiting in the Mall of St. James's Park to see her Majesty pass to open Parliament. This idea was soon scattered to the winds by the absence of the Life Guards Blue. Amphibious as Venice may be, she has not yet "called out the cavalry" or organised a corps of horse-marines, and the office of riding-master to the Doge of Venice is still a sinecure.

Ten o'clock had barely struck, however, before I found out very unmistakably in what place my lines were cast. This was indeed Venice, but Venice restored—Venice revivified—Venice herself again. To salute the great triumph of the nineteenth century, she had gone back three hundred years. The gorgeous fantastic costumes and usages of the old Republic of Venice had come back again, but to usher in a tangible and beneficial rule, and not to sanction the mummery of a chief magistrate's throwing a ring into the sea. It was not the Doge who was about to wed the Adriatic, but the King of Italy who was about to marry Venice. There, however—strange anachronism!—off the steps of the railway-terminus lay the Bucentaur of 1866. Not the original Bucentaur. That hapless caravel, first scraped bare of its gold leaf by the French, then converted into a floating prison, fell at last a prey to an accidental fire.

It is best not to inquire too narrowly into what has become of the grand pieces of furniture, aquatic and otherwise, which once embellished Venice. In the last days of its decline, the Most Serene Republic sold by auction, at eightpence-halfpenny the square yard, tapestries which had been designed by Rafaelle, and woven at Arras. The rarest pictures of Titian and Tintoretto have found their way to the marine-store shops of the Ghetto. Not a month since, the Austrians were selling in the Royal Palace to the vilest brokers, and for a few florins, sumptuous hangings and gorgeous cornices which had cost thousands of ducats. Not a fortnight since, the porter at one of the Venice hotels bought as a speculation, for forty pounds, a lot of gondolas, among which was the identical one, all shimmering with faded gilding, which served for the state entry into Venice, in 1811, of Napoleon I. and Maria Louisa.

The municipality had done their best to replace the original Bucentaur. There has been built at the Arsenal, within the last few weeks, a most glorious galley, for the reception of Italy's chosen monarch. I will not attempt to describe in detail its architectural proportions or particular style of decoration; let it suffice to say that it is a kind of radiant vision of carving and gilding, silk, embroidery, crimson velvet, and bullion tassels, with a towering gonfalon of white silk edged with blue, and displaying in the centre the escutcheon of the House of Savoy, at the prow. Surmount the deck with eighteen lusty rowers clad in cloth of gold, with a canopy of satin, velvet, and gold for the King to stand under, and you may gain some faint idea of "la Lancia Reale." If further aid to the imagination be needed, please to picture the Lord Mayor's barge in the old days, when the Corporation were the conservators of the Thames, and the water procession from Blackfriars to Westminster used to delight the long-shore population; or, best of all, turn up the good old passage in *Antony and Cleopatra* and read:

> "The barge he sat in, like a burnish'd throne,
> Burn'd on the water: the poop was beaten gold;
> Purple the sails, and so perfumed that
> The winds were lovesick with them; the oars were silver,
> Which to the tune of flutes kept stroke, and made
> The water which they beat to follow faster."

You will see that I have taken the liberty of substituting "he" for "she;" and indeed I cannot, with any illusive propriety, follow the quotation further; for the robust and somewhat pugnacious-looking Majesty of Italy is anything but twin-brother to the "Serpent of old Nile;" nor of him could I venture to say that

> "It beggar'd all description; she did lie
> In her pavilion—cloth of gold of tissue—
> O'erpicturing that Venus where we see
> The fancy outwork nature."

And yet, abating the fact that, later in the day, a portly jolly-looking gentleman in military uniform was fain to serve for Egypt's beauteous dusky queen, the wonderful word-picture conjured up by Shakespeare was more than realised on the Canalazzo. There were the "gentlewomen like the Nereids;" but they were in a hundred gondolas, instead of one. There were the "pretty dimpled boys like smiling Cupids;" but they were carved in wood or cast in plaster, and blazed in Dutch metal. There was the "seeming mermaid steering at the helm;" but he was a stout Venetian *barcarolo* arrayed in fancy costume. There was the "silken tackle;" there was the "strange invisible perfume that hit the sense of the adjacent wharves;" there, in short, was one of those marvellous processions of decorated boats which the French, with their lordly contempt for zoological propriety, would merely term a cavalcade, but for which I can find no other likeness than that of an immense mob of aquatic splendour.

I had been told some days before that, brilliant as was the spectacle on the occasion of the Austrian evacuation and the arrival of the Italian troops, there had been reserved for the entry of Victor Emmanuel some novelties in the way of decoration which would literally astound me. I was curious to know what these novelties might be. Everything in the way of hanging out flags, carpets, and tapestries seemed to have been done on the 19th; and it was certainly difficult to imagine anything in the way of an increase of popular enthusiasm. But I did not yet know what Venice could do. I know now. I have seen to-day the full extent of her capacity for a nautic show. Along the whole of the Grand Canal, from Santa Maria della Salute to the Second Iron Bridge, there was one enormous concourse of magnificent equipages.

The old sumptuary laws of the Republic, which, in order to check mischievous emulation among the wealthy, imposed a uniform covering of funereal sable on all gondolas, had been summarily ignored, and the reins had been thrown on the neck of decorative extravagance. The Municipality, the Chamber of Commerce, the Congregations of the different districts, set the example in boating splendour, and the Venetian aristocracy boldly followed the lead. There were galleys blazoned in gold, and galleys whose timbers shone with silver. White-satin canopies hung in air; crimson-velvet draperies floated on the water. There were oars as splendid as the sceptre of the King of Thule. There were "Bissones," and "Peotes," and barks, with all manner of strange names and of all manner of strange shapes, bristling with scrolls and scutcheons, rustling with brocade and satin, spangled and festooned and bannered, and crowned at helm and prow with garlands of fresh flowers.

The supernumeraries of a hundred Drury-lane spectacles, the madcap revellers of a hundred Parisian masked balls, seemed to have been enlisted for the day as gondoliers. Here was an eight-oar manned by Albanian Greeks, in snowy camise and shaggy capote and scarlet tarbouche. Here was a caïque full of Turks, in baggy galligaskins of silver lama and turbans of crimson twisted with gold. Now came a sombre yet splendid barque, all black and gold; the rowers in short pourpoints, red-trunk hose, and with cock's-feathers in their bonnets, and looking very much like so many animated *cartes-de-visite* of Mr. Charles Kean as Mephistopheles in *Faust and Marguerite*. Gondoliers dressed like the Gevartius of Vandyke, gondoliers attired like the halberdiers of Hans Holbein, gondoliers dressed like the alguaçils of Velasquez, and mingled in incongruous yet picturesque chaos with men-o'-war's men in their snowy frocks and shiny hats, and those amphibious flunkeys whom a portion of the Venetian nobility will persist in allowing to infest their gondolas, clad in plush breeches, laced hats, and big-buttoned swallow-tailed coats; all these, with the boats full of staff-officers, cavalry-officers, infantry-officers, and Garibaldians in every conceivable variety of cocked-hat, helmet, shako, kepi, plume, tuft, ribbon, and cockade; all these, with the multitudinous vessels, from heavy market-barges to tiny skiffs and dingies, crammed by sight-seers, foreign tourists, and the common, ragged, merry, and overjoyed Venetian people; all these, with every inch of quay thronged by humanity—the Rialto groaning under the weight of life—with the Grimani, the Pesaro, the Contarini, the Foscari, the Vendramini, the Grassi, the Balbi, the Ca' d'Oro, the Fondaco de' Turchi, and the very governmental pawn-shop itself, crowded by ladies and gentlemen, waving their handkerchiefs; all these, in fine, with the jostling and the squeezing on the land, and the "*Evvivas,*" and the "*per Dios,*" and the jests of the gondoliers, and the gabble of voices on the water, as of a million ducks, made up a whole that only needed, to attain the summit of spectacular perfection, one little thing—to wit, the blessed sun. But the sun was surly, and kept himself to himself most persistently.

It was twenty minutes past eleven when the booming of cannon announced the arrival of the King of Italy at the railway-terminus. My gondola had taken up a capital position, about five hundred yards above the Rialto, and I had not long to wait ere the royal galley hove majestically in sight.

A regular military escort was, of course, quite out of the question. What better escort could the King of Italy have than his own people? He came along, then, hemmed and girt about by a tumultuous throng of boats, in the midst of one overwhelming surging tide of frantic people, shouting and laughing and weeping, and crying God bless him! till the good royal gentleman in uniform under the canopy of crimson and gold might have had every excuse to weep a little himself, and be thankful that he had lived to see such a day. "*Quelle chance!*" a Frenchman by me said. Yes; the luck has indeed been tremendous.

It is the will of the Almighty Disposer of events that our joys shall be, as a rule, transitory, and that few of us shall know complete bliss here below. "The circles of our felicities," says the good Knight of Norwich, "make but short arches." To some is given the full span, the immense ellipse which bridges the whole of life with fortune. Supremely happy, surely, he yonder, under those velvet hangings! Supremely happy, at least for this day, and in this hour! Gazing for the first time in his life on this incomparably beautiful city, on this priceless appanage to his empire, which has fallen into his mouth like a ripe nectarine shaken from an espalier, Victor Emmanuel of Savoy must have known that Venice had to-day but one voice, a voice to shout his praise—but one heart, a heart that beat for him—but one wish, a wish that he and his race might reign over Italy in peace and prosperity, and do that which was fair and true, like the good French King who sat under the oak at Vincennes to mete out justice, and dry the widow's tears, and take care that the orphan should enjoy his father's goods after his father's days.

And if, as I firmly believe, there is infinite happiness in beholding the happiness of others, surely we, the countless thousands on whom no crowns had fallen, but whose crosses perhaps had been lighter than even that burly man's, were warranted in waving our hats and shouting, "*Evviva Vittorio Emmanuele!*" until we were hoarse. For he is a King, after all, worth shouting for. Not a very bright genius, perhaps; not a great general; not a crafty counsellor; but a plain, simple-minded gentleman, who keeps his promises and tells no lies.

Indescribable enthusiasm attended the King throughout his entire passage. The royal galley was less rowed than allowed to drift down the Grand Canal with the tide, which was at ebb; and at a few minutes after one Victor Emmanuel the Second, by the grace of God and the national will King of Italy, landed at the Piazzetta. His Majesty, who looked in admirable health and spirits, was accompanied by his royal cousin, Prince Eugene of Savoy-Carignan, who has been Regent of the kingdom since last June, and by his two sons, the Princes Humbert and Amadeus of Savoy. The National Guard, who to-day mounted for the first time their uniforms, and looked remarkably smart in their gray tunics and scarlet epaulettes, were drawn up on the Molo to receive his Majesty, and formed a double line along the Piazzetta, and by the Loggetta to the cathedral of St. Mark. Bare-headed and smiling, and with a firm quick step, the most popular, the most accessible, and the most unassuming King in Europe walked by his cousin's side, followed by his sons and a brilliant staff, to the cathedral, where a solemn *Te Deum* was to be performed; the Cardinal Patriarch of Venice officiating. The arcades of the Ducal Palace were crammed; the windows of the Library of St. Mark and the Zecca were blocked with faces; every point of espial in the Piazza was occupied; the roof of the Loggetta was tiled with human heads; only the huge Campanile was half hidden by mist, and veiled his towering head in vapour; while in the back-ground seawards the Italian war-ships, all dressed in colours and their yards manned, loomed spectrally through the haze like so many Flying Dutchmen. There was nothing spectral about the cannon, however, or about the shouting of the multitude, who disputed with each other in rival peals of thunder until Victor Emmanuel set foot within the portal of St. Mark's.

XIX.

PASSING THROUGH FLORENCE.

November 24th.

A Conservative critic once undertook to prove—and did prove to his own entire satisfaction, if not to that of his readers—that the great work of Lord Macaulay was anything but that which it professed to be. He was willing to grant it a romance, a fable, an epic poem, a collection of memoirs, a budget of anecdotes, a repertory of statistics, a dictionary of dates, a bundle of sonnets, or a grand Christmas pantomime; but it could not be considered, so the sage Aristarchus held, a History of England. The world did not agree with Aristarchus; still his snarl remains, to be taken for what it is worth. Did I ever venture upon criticising works and things immensely above my comprehension, I should be sorely tempted to take up, with regard to the interesting city to which I am paying a flying visit, the line of argument adopted by the Conservative caviller. I might say that Florence is one of the most charming towns I have ever seen, that the beauty of its site can scarcely be rivalled, and that its treasures of art are inexhaustible. I might call it a glorious museum, an unequalled picture-gallery, a refined and cultivated place, a fashionable resort, a picturesque lounge; in short, I might call it everything but that which it calls itself, and that which the solemn decree of the National Legislature has declared it to be—the Capital of Italy.

No; it does *not* look like a capital; and not all the foreigners who are resident or are visitors here; not all the presence of King, Court, Parliament, and diplomatic body; not all the efforts of the pushing and energetic Milanese, Piedmontese, and Swiss shopkeepers, who have removed their wares hither from Turin,—will ever give to Florence a real metropolitan aspect.

You cannot create capitals, any more than you can establish religions, by Act of Parliament. Attempts in that direction have been made over and over again, but the result has generally been a more or less humiliating failure; witness Washington and Ottawa. When Napoleon I. chose to create the kingdom of Westphalia for his brother Jerome, he, unconsciously imitating Mr. Haller in *The Stranger*, "fixed on Cassel for his abode;" but all the cooks, aides-de-camp, play-actors, milliners, chamberlains, and ballet-girls, imported wholesale from Paris, failed to make Cassel a capital, and it remained, until the kingdom of Westphalia itself tumbled to pieces, a dismal, "one-horse" town, pretentious but contemptible. Time was, in our own country, when an adventurous spirit, now by fame forgotten, but once probably well known in the building trade, declared defiantly that Southend should be the Queen of Watering-places. He built it; he advertised it; he puffed it; he ran steamers; he cajoled railways; he beckoned to lodging-house keepers to come and extort; he offered gratuitous board and lodging to those interesting members of the insect world without whose presence no watering-place is complete; he positively induced shrimps to frequent Southend, and was suspected of emptying a ton of salt into the water every morning to take off its brackishness; but the thing wouldn't do. Southend was not arbitrarily to be invested with a robe of brine and a diadem of seaweed, and she continues to sit solitary and seedy on the sandhills, while Margate and Ramsgate laugh Ha, ha! in derision, and even Broadstairs genteelly simpers, and Herne Bay sardonically sneers at the claims of her sandy sister.

Agamemnon was strong, so was Samson, likewise Belzoni. The power of human volition is tremendous. Faith will remove mountains, and continuous drippings from wet umbrellas wear out the Duke of York's steps; but there are some tasks which baffle proud man, and induce a painful conviction of his impotence. He cannot propound a universal theorem; and he never could make Hungerford Market popular. He has been unable to solve the problem of aerial navigation, and he has not yet succeeded in turning her Majesty's Theatre into a paying concern. He may make a poet of Tupper, and a painter of Raphael Mengs; he may tunnel the Alps, and bridge the Straits of Dover; he may induce the British working-man to drink Bordeaux instead of beer, and banish the pernicious custom of smoking from railway-carriages; he may abolish crinoline and inland custom-houses; pull down Holywell-street, finish the Record Office, and make cabmen and grand-hotel managers civil; he may revive the use of embroidered copes in Westminster Abbey, and turn the beadle of St. Clement's Danes into a thurifer, or an acolyte, or a protospathairos; but he will never, so far as human likelihood is concerned, make the real capital of Italy at Florence.

It is a country town; it always has been a country town,

and a country town it will continue, until the whole of this orb reverts to the original Proprietor, and all is country, without any towns at all. Of the myriads of travelling Britons who have been here, and kept diaries, and printed them, and gone into ecstasies about the Venus and the Faun, the Flora and the Madonna della Seggiola, I do not know if there have yet been any who have been stricken with the amazing likeness existing between Florence and a very memorable, but purely provincial, English city—I mean Oxford. At first sight the resemblance may not be striking, and the analogy may be imperfect. Florence may vie with Rome as the studio, and surpass her as the workshop of Italy; but Galileo's manuscripts and the bibliomania of Magliabecchi notwithstanding, *Firenze la bella* must yield the palm of deep erudition and varied lore to Pisa, Bologna, and Padua. You see no capped-and-gowned undergraduates in the Via de Tornabuoni or the Cerretani. No dons awe you in the Signoria or the Piazza Granduca. No proctors in velvet sleeves prowl about accompanied by watchful bulldogs. The Arno is certainly not the Isis; for the hue of the last-named stream is blue, and of the first a muddy yellow. A violent effort of the imagination would be needed to transform the verdant labyrinths of the Cascine into Christ-Church Meadows; and the Tuscan boatmen are a weak and puny race, who, although they might, like all other Italians, bear away the bell for blasphemy, would soon be vanquished, if strength of lung could carry the day, by the bargees of Iffley Lock.

Nor is the architecture of Florence very Oxonian. You seek in vain for venerable piles of florid Gothic, or for vast façades in the Palladian style. Apart from the Duomo, with its towering Campanile, exteriorly a gigantic and most astounding josshouse of variegated marble, which, were the thing practicable, should be at once put under a glass-case, and packed off to Paris for the Exhibition of '67, and which inside is as bare and cold-looking as the old Dutch church in Austinfriars; apart from this, and the Baptistery, the Florentine churches are singularly mean and shabby in outward appearance. In domestic structures, Florence has its own peculiar style of architecture, and that certainly does not remind the tourist of Oxford. It rather suggests to him thoughts of the Old Bailey. The Medici, the Strozzi, the Gherardeschi, the Buonarotti, are names familiar as Guelph or Ghibelline in the annals of Florence; but I fancy there must be some erasures in the Florentine *libro d'oro*, and that the hiatus might properly be filled up with the name of a Jonas. Assuredly the palaces of the old nobility here look very much as though they had been originally intended as residences of the Governor of Newgate, with private apartments for the Governor's guests on each side. The illustrious Strozzi dwell, for example, in a veritable gaol—a colossal pile of granite boulders and barred casements, with a narrow portal uncomfortably suggestive of the debtors' door. I do not know whether the lady of the actual possessor of the palace and title gives "Wednesday evenings" in London West-end fashion; but the mediæval Strozzi, to judge from the style of his habitation, must have been very punctual with his Monday mornings—"hang at eight and breakfast at nine," with Il Signore Calcraft as chief butler.

Ferrara is the most murderous town I have yet seen in Italy, and Bologna the most funereal. It strikes me that in those middle ages, of which we talk so much and know so little, that it was at Ferrara you were preferably poisoned. At Bologna they buried you, and your assassin was brought to Florence to be fully committed, tried, and executed. To carry out the Newgate-cum-Horsemonger-lane illusion in the Florentine palaces, the walls are adorned, at a height of about five feet from the ground, with a series of enormous iron rings, pendent to links, and secured by strong staples to the stone. You are informed that these rings were used in the middle ages for securing horses by the bridle, while their cavaliers transacted business with the nobles within. This may or may not be true; but I imagine that animals of a superior race to the equine have been of old time tethered to these grim rings. The Florentines seem very proud of them; and I notice in a new palace, closely resembling Whitecross-street Prison whitewashed, which is in course of erection close to the Strozzi, that copies of the time-honoured Newgate bracelets have been let into the walls.

There is another marked peculiarity of Florentine architecture which I may briefly notice—the extraordinary projecting eaves of the houses in the older streets. With their preposterous eaves and tiny windows the houses look like exaggerated pigeon-cotes. Florence has always been renowned as a great place for gossip and *cancans*. May not that term of "eavesdropper," which has for so long a period bitterly perplexed the learned and chatty correspondents of *Notes and Queries*, spring from the overhanging eaves of Florence, and the necessarily incessant droppings therefrom?

But if there are no undergraduates, no dons, no bulldogs, no town-and-gown rows, how comes it, then, that Florence scarcely ever fails to remind an Englishman of Oxford? For this reason, I take it, that its pure provincialism—which is provincial to the pettiest of Little Peddlingtonism, and countrified to almost rusticity—is oddly intermingled with the flashy splendour and meretricious bustle of the most expensive town life. By the side of palaces, museums, and churches are little hucksters'-stalls and poor chandlery-shops; and then come the establishments of tradesmen selling the most sumptuous jewelry, the grandest haberdashery and millinery, the rarest books and engravings, the most brilliant and elaborate nicknacks, at prices which even in Oxford would be thought extortionate. I am not aware whether "tick," either as a word or an institution, has yet become naturalised in Florence; but the tariff adopted by the Florentine jewellers, tailors, and milliners is certainly suggestive of the largest ledgers and the longest credit. Thoroughly Oxonian, also, is the admixture in the streets of individuals whom you know must belong to the cream of the country, with the stolid, listless, narrow-minded *bourgeoisie* of a country town.

Here, in fact, as in Oxford, extremes meet. You have the social steam at its highest pressure, and a considerable quantity of the tepidest water. You have a bottle of Moët's champagne just uncorked and flying all abroad in the face of the smallest of small beer. The carriages and pair of the aristocracy, with splendidly-harnessed horses, and coachmen in spun-glass wigs, the fours-in-hand, the tandems and the breaks of Florentine "fast men," the broughams of senators, the basket-phaetons and wicked little black ponies of the Anonymous Estate on their way to the Cascine are jostled, in beggarly by-lanes, by bullock-drays and mules laden with forage, and humble donkey-carts containing the stock-in-trade of travelling tinkers.

Florence is Oxford during Commemoration, and all the big-wigs and *gros bonnets* of the land are holding festival here; but you know that the Long Vacation is coming—you know that there are very many weeks in every year when not a big-wig is to be seen in the deserted streets; when the flashy tradesmen are unable from month's end to month's end to swindle a customer; when the petty hucksters'-stalls and the little chandlery-shops will reassert their legitimate influence; when the principal event in each week will be market-day; when the hotels will become inns, the *ristoratores* farmers' ordinaries, and the caffès taprooms; when his worship the Mayor—they call him a "Gonfaloniere" here—will be the greatest personage in the place; and when, in fine, Florence will revert to that which it is really entitled to be called—a town replete with the most exquisite monuments of painting and sculpture, but always a provincial of the provincials. Blaise Pascal might have written his letters from the Boboli gardens; but you can't make it a capital, try your hardest. As well might Dulwich claim equal rank with Piccadilly because it possesses Alleyn's college and Sir Francis Bourgeois's gallery.

XX.

THE ROAD TO ROME.

December 1.

"EVERY road," we are told, leads "to Rome;" and, as is generally the case, a good sound substructure of sense and truth underlies the proverb. When Rome was the mistress and the metropolis of the world, the channels of communication with her were necessarily innumerable. From the uttermost limits of the empire, he who wished to appeal unto Cæsar, found posts, and relays, and a beaten track to conduct him to Cæsar's judgment-seat. There were P. and O.'s two thousand years ago, little dreamt of in your philosophy; and who shall say that, in its time, some Antioch, Corinth, and Rome Chariot and Galley Transit Company (Unlimited) did not convert as many talents of silver into ducks and drakes as that stupendous Kentish undertaking has done whose line and whose branches were to go everywhere—and have gone everywhere, even unto the land which is called Smash?

The Barbarians who overthrew the Cæsars did their best likewise to demolish all trace of the roads which led to Rome; and the assiduity of rapine and desolation with which they grubbed up the fertile Campagna, grinding its flourishing cities to powder, and rooting up their very foundations, as though themselves had been pigs hunting truffles, till the whole became one bare waste, is much to be commended. The Barbarians have been succeeded by many generations of highly-civilised invaders, who, clad it may be in chain-mail, in Milan steel, and eke in military garb of modern cut, have done their best to ruin Rome and to obliterate the highways leading to it. The City of Eternity, however, is inextinguishable. She is not to be wiped out. The Seven Hills have been of the hydra kind. As fast as one was laid waste another grew into life again, and the definitive brand which is to sear Rome out for ever has not yet been found. Still is Rome a metropolis and a puissance, and a marvel of marvels; and still are there more roads leading to Rome than to any other Italian city.

If you have any doubts on this head I beg to refer you to *Bradshaw*. Vast as are his resources as a constructor of skeleton through-routes, he can only point out two ways of journeying to Jerusalem, *viâ* Paris and *viâ* Trieste. But turn to Rome, and you will find no fewer than five skeletons placed at your command by the obliging myth who is to be heard of—care of Mr. W. J. Adams, at 59 Fleet-street, E.C. You may travel to Rome from London by Paris, Marseilles, and Civita Vecchia; or by Marseilles, Nice, Genoa, Pisa, Florence, and Chiusi; or by Macon, St. Michel, Mont Cenis, and Turin; or by Switzerland, coming over any one of the seven Alpine passes you choose to Milan; or, finally, by Vienna, Trieste, and Ancona. This is indeed, viatorially, an *embarras de richesses*.

Let it be assumed, however, that purposing for Rome you happen on the 29th of November, in a given year, to be, not in London, but in Florence. This was my case the day before yesterday. I sought counsel of *Bradshaw*, but his skeletons, albeit beautiful in anatomical articulation, were wanting, somehow, in sinew, and muscle, and adipose membrane.

I knew that there were a great many roads leading from Florence to Rome, but I experienced very great difficulty in ascertaining which was the shortest and the best. I was told that I could go by way of Leghorn, by way of Ancona, by way of Nunziatella, by way of Civita Vecchia, but that in one case I must be prepared for seven hours' diligence-travelling, in another for nine, and in a third for twelve of that torture. As for reaching Rome without staying somewhere on the road for a whole night, it was out of the question.

There was no trustworthy information on the subject to be obtained in Florence. Either the Florentines do not know much, or else they are singularly uncommunicative. The entire energies of the hotel-keepers are seemingly absorbed by the task of making out extortionate bills against their guests; and if they have any leisure, they employ it in milking paving-stones and skinning fleas for the hide and fat.* I asked people who had been resident for years in Florence, but as a

* Meanness, shabbiness, and stinginess, in the capital of the kingdom of Italy, have grown to be more than an art; they have attained the proportions of a science. I thought I had already seen some samples of pretty close shaving in North Italy; but when, going to a fashionable stationer's in Florence to purchase some photographs, I saw a tremendous dandy, with a watch-chain as big as Queen Guinevere's girdle, ask for *one envelope*, tender a sou—one halfpenny—in payment, and receive *four centesimi* in change, I saw that I had gotten among a race whose close-fistedness was colossal. Florence is nearly the only city where you meet the *centesimo*, the fifth part of the halfpenny, in active currency. Even the Spaniards are ashamed of anything under four reals. The Florentines have a sliding scale of parsimony worthy of Elwes the miser, who burnt rushlights on weekdays and halfpenny dips on Sunday, and one short six on Christmas-day. Thus, at Doney's, the most aristocratic *caffè* in Florence, if you ask for *caffè ordinario*, they bring you a very washy decoction, with white sugar in dust; but if you pay an extra halfpenny, you can have *caffè apposto*, which is slightly stronger, and accompanied by sugar in small lumps; and, finally, by ordering the mighty *caffè expresso*, you are entitled to a positively palatable cup of coffee and four big lumps of sugar. According to Sir Pitt Crawley's charwoman in *Vanity Fair*, "it's only baronets as cares for fardens;" but to

rule they shrugged their shoulders, and observed that really there were so many roads leading to Rome, that they scarcely knew which one to recommend as the best. I remembered that there is a Murray's *Handbook to Central Italy*, but the volume I purchased for twelve *franchi* fifty *centesimi* at the first English bookseller's in Florence turned out to be "Murray" for the year 1864. As we are close upon 1867, and at least three different routes have been opened during the last three years, I did not take much by my motion in regard to Albemarle-street. The information given was excellent; but as in its Roman section it chiefly referred to the tariff for post-horses between Florence and Rome, and the best way of mollifying the Custom-house officers at the Porta del Popolo, when you were travelling in your own carriage, it was scarcely of a nature to afford relief in my particular case.

At the inns, as I have remarked, they will tell you nothing that they cannot charge for in the bill. It is for that reason, I conjecture, that they don't give you any *menu* at the *table-d'hôte* of the Albergo di Nuova York, and that there is not a clock to be seen in any part of the house. "Naething for naething" is a locution proverbial in North Britain. Translate that discreet dictum into the Lingua Toscana, and you have the sum of Florentine social philosophy. On the other hand, there is always a tribe of *valets-de-place*

---

this thrifty class must be added the descendants of the Medici and the Strozzi. It would appear that the Florentines are anxious to make up for the extravagance of Lorenzo the Magnificent, and for the last three centuries have been striving, by pinching and paring, to repair the deficit in Tuscan finances caused by the prodigality of that expensive person. They have quite a microscopic vision for economics; and at the *caffès* at night, if a waiter sees that one side of the room is deserted by guests, he forthwith turns off the gas in that part.

hanging about, burning to show and tell you everything—from Ghiberti's gates to the time of day; from the tombs of the Medici to the hours of the departure and arrival of the railway-trains. It is scarcely worth while perhaps to pay five francs to obtain instructions which, in the majority of cases, are incorrect, for the mind of the *valet-de-place* is sadly given to incoherence, and you must not be at all surprised to learn from him that the Madonna della Seggiola was painted at twelve forty-five, or that the express for Leghorn started at the end of the seventeenth century.

The situation of affairs was growing very embarrassing, when I fortunately heard from some English friends that they purposed starting next morning for Rome, by railway as far as Ellera, thence by carriage to Perugia and Foligno, halting at the first-named place to sleep, and at the last catching the train from Ancona to Rome. This was encouraging. They had heard from another English family that the journey was to be accomplished in thirty hours, including a good night's rest at Perugia.

In no guide-book that I have yet seen is this road—the best and most interesting which offers itself to the traveller—distinctly and contemporaneously laid down, that is to say, with due notice of the latest railway developments. The plain truth is that our guides and handbooks, professing to come down to the exact month or year printed on their title-pages, are, with melancholy frequency, whole months, and sometimes whole years, behindhand. In the November *Bradshaw*, for instance, we are twice directed to page 167 for the trains between Rome and Corese—the line I came by yesterday—but there is not the slightest mention of either Rome or Corese at page 167, or anywhere else that I can discover. It is also rather too bad, after all that Bismark and the needle-gun (burn them both!) have done towards revolutionising North Germany, to be told by *Bradshaw*, four months subsequent to the conclusion of peace, that "Hanover-on-the-Leine is the residence of the King of Hanover," and that "Frankfort-on-the-Maine is a free town, seat of the German Diet, and garrisoned by 5000 troops, Austrians, Bavarians, and Prussians." I caused a new *Bradshaw* for November to be sent out to me from England regardless of expense, in view of the political changes on the Continent. You may imagine my dismay when I discovered that a *Bradshaw* for last July would have served my turn quite as well.*

Having settled to go to Rome *viâ* Perugia and Foligno, I inquired at the Albergo di Nuova York at what hour the train started, and was informed by the porter that it left at noon precisely. So, being wofully encumbered with baggage, I duly found myself at the terminus at half-past eleven, and then learnt that it was the Leghorn train which started at noon, and that the Ellera one did not leave until a quarter to one. There is no use in being angry under such circum-

* In *Bradshaw's Continental Railway Guide* for November 1866, it is stated—article "Rome," p. 391—that the journey from Rome to Florence, passing by Nemi, Terni, Spoleto, Foligno, Assisi, Perugia, Lake of Thrasymene, Arezzo, &c., "is at present performed in two days, the railway not being completed." The statement would be slightly more serviceable to travellers were it accompanied by information as to how far the rail is completed, where it begins, and where it ends. In this present month of November, the purchasers of *Bradshaw* may fairly expect to be told that from Florence to Ellera the direct Roman Railway *is* complete; that there then occurs a break which may be tided over in three hours, by diligence or private carriage, to Ponte San Giovanni; and that thence to Rome the railway communication is uninterrupted. I hope (in 1869) all this has been made right.

stances. If hotel servants tell you fibs or give you wrong counsel, it is the fault of the Grand Dukes, with their wicked Austrian connections and sympathies. If the landlord swindles you, it is the fault of Attila, Genseric, Theodoric and Frederic Barbarossa. If for four successive days there is no fish at dinner, the Normans and the Longobardi are to blame. If the ways of Florence are Chinese in their pettiness, and Abderitan in their slowness, it is the fault of the Ostrogoths and the Visigoths. "*C'est la faute de Rousseau; c'est la faute de Voltaire*," as the Jesuit preacher remarked of the vine-disease, the cattle-plague, the cholera, and trichinosis in pork-sausages.

The railway-terminus at Florence, after the sumptuous structures one sees at Turin, Genoa, and Milan, is a very mild and provincial kind of affair indeed, as quiet and tame as a station, say on some remote branch in North Devon, constructed solely at the instigation of the sharp solicitor of a company, to spite the solicitor of a rival line. There is a cheerful central hall, with very many doors opening out of it on either side, and with flourishing inscriptions denoting the departments into which they are supposed to lead; but, on trying them, I found most of these portals fast locked. The "departments," I am afraid, are akin to the Barmecide bottles one sees in some doctors' shops, and the dummy cigar-boxes laid in by tobacconists just starting in business. Let me whisper, however, that the waiting-room "accommodation" for the public at the central railway-terminus of the capital of Italy is as infamous as at Desenzano, and would be most fitly found in connection with a village in Dahomé. I can scarcely imagine that the Grand Dukes, or the Austrians, or the Visigoths are responsible for this. May not the inconceivably lazy, slovenly, and filthy habits of the people have something to do with it?

The Roman Railway is on the narrowest of gauges, and the carriages are remarkably small, hard, and uncomfortable; but the environs of Florence are exquisitely beautiful, and the scenery in the Val d' Arno di Sopra is glorious. At Pontessieve we saw the river Sieve descending from the Apennines to empty itself into the Arno. It must have emptied itself there very completely a long time ago, or else its name of "Sieve" must be taken literally in English, for not a drop of water was there to be seen in this doubtless whilom noble stream. The Arno itself is not remarkable for a good water supply; but the municipality always contrive to maintain a decent depth, of a tolerable hue, between the Ponte Vecchio and the Ponte della Trinità, from Christmas to Easter, when aristocratic English visitors most frequently tenant the suites of apartments on the quay. The which accounts for the many ejaculations you hear of "Dear Florence!" and "that sweet Lung' Arno!" from the fair lips of members of the very first families travelling abroad.

The whole road is rife with historic and artistic associations. Close to the station of Incisa the family of Petrarch lived. Between Figline and Montevarchi have been discovered immense quantities of fossil bones, which the Italian antiquaries have conjectured to be those of the sumpter-elephants of Hannibal's army, an hypothesis scarcely admitted, I should say, by Professor Owen and Mr. Waterhouse Hawkins. The mighty Carthaginian did not presumably have mastodons and hippopotami attached to his military train; and relics of both have been found in the plain of Arezzo. Tigers and freshwater testacea have also cropped up in a fossil state. At San Giovanni the painter Masaccio was born. Arezzo, once the most powerful city of the Etruscan league, was the birthplace of Mæcenas, of Petrarch, of Vasari, and almost of Michel Angelo, who was born at Caprese, in the neighbourhood—of Heliogabalus and Jack the Painter, too, for aught I know. What does it matter, when you are scampering through a country by railway? The iron has entered into the soul of the picturesque, and killed it. Cuttings and embankments, switches, sleepers, and signal-posts form the foreground of every landscape, and the middle distance and the extreme are so fleeting and shifting and unsubstantial, that the best way, perhaps, to see the country, is to pull down the blinds and shut your eyes till you reach some place where you can unpack your boxes, and, with the aid of your guide-books and photograph-albums, read up the district through which you have been passing.

I may add, too, that when I journeyed through the Val d' Arno it rained, not in torrents, but in a minute, cautious, thoroughly permeating drizzle—a Scotch mist, which had taken service, like Quentin Durward, under a foreign potentate. It rained at Arezzo, it rained at Assisi, it rained at Montevarchi; and when we reached Ellera, seven hours after our departure from Florence, it was snowing thickly, and was bitterly cold. Here there is a break in the railway, and a sufficiently steep mountain to ascend. It was horribly cold, sloppy, and snowy, and the station was of the darkest and dismalest. I shall long remember Ellera, and have marked it in my diary with the blackest of stones, for the reason that I had scarcely alighted on the platform when I lost a very choice sealskin cap, which had cost me many dollars in Canada East, and, in its time, had been much admired in skating "rinks" and sleighing trips. It could have hardly touched earth when it disappeared—snapped up, I opine, by some chilly but dishonest Ellerite. I must own that all the railway-porters ran to and fro for ten minutes with lanterns, in their zeal to find the missing article, thus clearly earning the *buona mano* which they took care shortly afterwards most pressingly to solicit; and an ancient beggar even demanded alms of me as "*Il Signore chi ha perduto la sua berretta*"—the gentleman who has lost his cap; but I did not find my sealskin for all that. I don't know of whom Ellera has been the birthplace, or what illustrious personages ever flourished there. I should say—remembering my sealskin—Sixteen-string Jack or the Artful Dodger.

A so-called diligence took us in the dark to Perugia. I am in the fashion in speaking of "so-called" institutions, for the *Osservatore Romano* always speaks of the country united under Victor Emmanuel II. as *ciò che chiamasi l'Italia* —that which calls itself Italy. The so-called was a wooden box, on a plurality of wheels, not always, so it seemed, of the same size on the same side, for we bumped terribly. Into this box they packed six ladies and gentlemen. We packed closely, like sardines, without the oil. The conductor prudently obviated the possibility of remonstrance or mutiny, by banging-to the door so closely that it could not be opened, by forcing up the window-sashes so tightly that they could not be let down, and by taking away the flight of steps which was our only means of communication with the terrestrial globe outside. Then, with not so much as the ghost of a lamp or lantern, the wheels of unequal size began to revolve, and the luggage piled upon the roof began its admired and well-known series of performances, in trying to assert its ponderosity and smash down upon our skulls, and we were off. I was not born at the time of the Black-Hole-at-Calcutta tragedy, and I have not yet, as a life convict, heavily chained, performed in a cellular van the journey between Paris and Toulon; but, next to the torture I endured when crossing the Col di Tenda last September, must be placed the agony of the drive in the "so-called" diligence between Ellera and Perugia.

We were a very merry party notwithstanding—that is to say, four of our number were Italians, who chattered continually and laughed consumedly, and, as it seemed to me, in the dark, romped. I think something of the form and texture of a lady's hat with a feather in it hit me at one stage of the journey on the nose. It may have been displaced by the jolting of the vehicle. To a like cause may be attributed divers noises, as of scuffling, in a distant corner, much giggling, decidedly feminine, and a sound resembling "applause," as the biographer of that admirable parent, Mrs. M'Stinger, in *Dombey*, would observe. We grew very friendly in the dark, and the female voice—presumably that which had giggled—asked me what was the English for *cavallo*. When I replied that it was "horse," a male voice remarked that the accentuation of the English language was very harsh. Whereupon I ventured to ask why the Florentines always pronounced *cavallo* as *havallo*, laying the harshest possible stress on the misplaced *h*, upon which the voice was mute, and, I opine, shut up. Then two gentlemen sang a duet. Then we all fell into one another's laps. Then we had an argument on the Roman question, the temporal power of the Pope, and the mission of the Commendatore Vegezzi.

So far as I was concerned, I varied these proceedings by groaning and bewailing my miserable condition; but we had, fortunately, a cheery and sanguine spirit among us, who, mentally at least—he could not see an inch before him physically—always looked to the bright side of things, and who, whenever we bumped so frightfully as to render our overturning a matter of extreme imminence, or stuck in the snow, or came to a dead halt, declared that we were at *mezza strada*, or half-way to Perugia.

I believe that the horses expired miserably at an early stage of the journey, and that for the greater portion thereof the so-called diligence was dragged by oxen; but I know that we were all turned out into the snow, at the door of a detestable little diligence-office, illumined by two tallow-candles, at ten o'clock at night, and were told that this was Perugia. The diligence was to resume its journey at half-past five the next morning for Ponte San Giovanni, the railway-station for Foligno, and until that time we were free to enjoy a game at snowballing, or to inspect the antiquities of Perugia, which are both rich and numerous. It may not be generally known that Perugia is the ancient Perosche of the Etruscans, that it was rebuilt by Augustus, that it was annexed to Napoleon the First's "so-called" Italian kingdom as chief town of the department of the Thrasymene, that here flourished the famous Braccio di Mentone Fortebraccio, the rival of Sforza, and that in the year 1524 the illustrious painter, Peter Perugino, master of Rafaelle, died here of the plague.

I am afraid that these pleasing facts did not interest me much at ten o'clock on the night of November the thirtieth. Sierra Nevada! how it snowed! It fortunately occurred to me that there was an inn at Perugia, called the Albergo della Posta, which from private information I knew to be dear, but clean and comfortable. So repudiating the icy notion of setting out at half after five in the morning in the diligence for Ponte San Giovanni, I determined to sup and sleep, and take mine ease at mine inn till ten o'clock on the first, and so hired, at a not very extravagant rate, a good travelling-carriage to convey myself and my impedimenta all the way to Foligno—a four hours' drive. I sacrificed a morsel of railway by the adoption of this plan; but, otherwise, the advantage was altogether on the private-conveyance side. The unhappy persons who were to pursue their journey at early morn would arrive at Ponte San Giovanni at half-past six, and at Foligno at eight, and then have to wait six hours and a half for the train to Rome. By leaving at ten, one had more road to traverse, but one killed time, evaded another inn, and got to Foligno in easy time to "make connections" with the train.

The Albergo della Posta proved to be all that it had been described, and more. I have seldom met with a cleaner house, so far as its guest-chambers are concerned. They are oases in the midst of a desert of dirty staircases and dirtier corridors. I never hope to pass a night in a more comfortable inn, and I think I might travel far before meeting with a more expensive one. The proprietor evidently reckons for remunerative patronage upon English people who don't care about getting up at five o'clock in the morning, and frames his measures and his bills accordingly. Perhaps he and the diligence-conductors have a private understanding. Why not? It was by means of a private understanding that my grandmother's cousin-german obtained the privilege of supplying the Crown and Anchor tavern with anchovy-sauce, and made that fortune which he so unkindly bequeathed to quite a different branch of the family.

Directly I was introduced to the proprietor of the Albergo della Posta I saw that I was in for it. He made me his lowest bow; the kind of bow which is put, under another name, in the bill. Surveying me with an eye full of deference, he proposed to wait upon us himself, and ordered his head-waiter, in a steady voice, to bring out "the plate." Upon this, I cast myself over the Tarpeian rock, crossed the Rubicon, broke my bridges, and burned my ships, and commended myself to the Saints. "You will give us," I said, "the best room in the house, and the best supper that can be obtained in Perugia." I had a good mind to write myself down "Lord Smith, Baronetto Inglese," in the travellers' book. It would not have made much difference. It is better to be hanged for breaking into the Jewel Office than for stealing an extinguisher. I was in for it. As well over boots as over shoes. The proprietor behaved in a peerless manner. Slaves of the lamp, male and female, appeared at his beck, darted hither and thither at his command, and transformed an apartment on the second-floor into a bower of bliss surpassing in splendour the "bridal chamber" on board a Yankee steamboat.

The best room in the house was engaged, I presume, by Earl Brown, or the Patriarch of Constantinople, or the General of the Jesuits, or a lucky speculator from the Pennsylvanian oil-regions; but we had the second-best. They brought us a new sofa; they laid down a fresh carpet; they heaped the hearth with blazing logs. They brought us, in a species of Roman triumph, a wash-hand jug, a tooth-glass, and a foot-bath. There was no end of towels. By asking for it we might, I daresay, have had a coal-scuttle. They sate us down to a supper fit for a Cardinal or an Apostolic Censor. There was a beefsteak so tender and so fragrantly odorous that I fancied it had been cut from a golden bull long stabled in the Vatican, and fed on myrrh, frankincense, and boiled heretics. They gave us a bottle of the very oldest Montepulciano wine—an *Est, est, est* vintage, almost equal to the Montefiascone, a dark, full wine, like melted rubies, mingled with laudanum, as rich and soft as Genoa velvet, as strong and yet as generous as he who slew the Erymanthian boar and tamed the mares of Diomed. They gave us a fat little bird, such as Brillat Savarin would have gloated upon, and longed to eat with his fingers—a deceptive little fellow, even as the marble cherubs in St. Peter's, who appear to be six inches, but are really six feet in height. He looked no bigger than a linnet, yet on his well-cushioned breast there was more than a supper for two.

In the morning the proprietor, after much stringent persuasion, was induced to make out his bill. It was delivered at the very last moment, and when the carriage was all ready packed and the postboy eager to start. Thus there was no time to dispute it. After presenting us with this document on a silver salver, the proprietor retired to his private apartments, double-locking himself in, and leaving to the head-waiter the task of fighting the matter out. You might have fancied that he was Guy Fawkes after his last pinch of powder had been laid, and prudently retiring behind the Speaker's chair, in view of a tremendous blow-up. The landlord had certainly done his utmost, but the damage on the whole was not alarming. It was something under thirty shillings, and I never grudged the outlay of one-pound-ten less in my life.

We travelled through the snow to Foligno, and at two o'clock reached the station. A few minutes afterwards the train from Ancona rumbled in, and at five-and-twenty minutes to three we started for Corese. I should have very much liked to gaze upon that famous Campagna of Rome, on the grimness of whose desolation so much eloquence has been bestowed; but *Cosa volete?* It was pitch dark by five, and the Campagna was invisible. The snow, however, gave place to rain before we crossed the Pontifical frontier, where, by a very courteous Pontifical functionary, we were deprived of our passports. The clock had just struck nine when our train came to a final halt, and an Italian gentleman who had been fidgeting about the carriage in a most excited manner for the last half-hour, and rubbing his nose against the window-panes, in a vain attempt to make out the Campagna through the darkness and the rain, clapped his hands together and cried, "*Roma! Roma! Siamo a Roma!*" This was indeed the Rome to which all roads lead; and my first experience of the Eternal City was being met by the Commissionaire from the Hôtel d'Angleterre, and asked whether

I would proceed by the omnibus or in a cab to my destination. An omnibus! Couldn't they keep a *decemjugis* or a *harmamaxa* at the terminus, for the sake of appearances? Mrs. Hemans was right. Rome is no more as she has been.

XXI.

ROMA · URBS.

"On the heights above Baccano," writes an old traveller, "the postillion stopped, and, pointing to a pinnacle which appeared between two hills, exclaimed, 'Roma!' That pinnacle was the cross of St. Peter's. The Eternal City was before us."

I suppose no man—not being a born idiot or a German bagman, next to an imbecile the most unimpressionable creature in the world, perhaps—ever beheld that cross on the dome of St. Peter's or entered Rome for the first time, without feeling his heart, in some manner or another, stirred up within him. "Moab may howl for Moab: everyone shall howl;" but you have longed, and sighed, and prayed to look upon Rome; and now your desire is come, and you are full of a happy thankfulness. The image of Rome has been set, long since, "as a seal upon thine heart, as a seal upon thine arm;" and as "many waters cannot quench love, neither can the floods drown it," so is the love for Rome intuitive, indomitable, and inextinguishable.

English grooms and flunkeys are not given, generally, to become very enthusiastic at the sight of strange cities, and I have known the British flunkey take St. Mark's Place, by moonlight, very coolly, and My Lord's *valet de chambre* bear the Kremlin with perfect equanimity. Nay, I have known a lady's-maid speak superciliously of Seville even during the *feria* week, and pronounce Constantinople to be a "nasty dirty hole." Why should not such criticisms be uttered by our domestics? They have, very probably, quite enough to do with attending to the wants, wishes, and caprices of their masters and mistresses; their education, with regard to history, antiquities, poetry, mythology, and the fine arts, has ordinarily been neglected, and they are seldom expected, on their return home, to write octavo volumes descriptive of the sights they have seen abroad. Not but that the *impressions de voyage* of a lacquey might be worth reading. Constant's *Memoirs of Napoleon* are mendacious, but eminently amusing; and who would not like to read a life of Shakespeare by his body-servant—if he ever had one, or a body to be served, or anything tangible, or palpable, or unmythical at all? I say that the usual train of menials who go abroad with our tourists are perfectly indifferent to the sights they see. There is, in most continental cities, some establishment of the nature of an English public-house. Thither the *valetaille* repair in their leisure moments to smoke and drink, and *not* to compare notes as to the monuments of the city in which they are sojourning, but to grumble at and abuse their employers, precisely as they would do at the bars of the dim little taverns which nestle in the purlieus of Grosvenor- and Belgrave-squares. With all this, I have known gentlemen's gentlemen fall into raptures about Rome, and talk quite learnedly of the Muta Sudans and the Forum of Trajan. By far the most fervent British enthusiast on things Roman occupying a humble sphere of life was a hostler. "There's heverything you can wish for in Rome," quoth he. "Hemperors and Popes, and temples and churches, and the Colosseum and the Wattican; and, bless yer, there aint a 'ossier place out. After 'Igh Park give me the Pincian 'Ill." Rome *is* "'ossy" or "horsey" in good sooth; but 'tis the English who have made it so.

Everybody is delighted to find himself in Rome. The citizen of the kingdom of Italy, because he feels within himself a grim persuasion that at no distant date the city will belong to Italy, and Victor Emmanuel will be crowned King in the Capitol. *La vieille patraque*, the Papacy, he argues, *cannot* last long. Napoleon's battalions *must* clear out of Civita Vecchia sooner or later. Mentana will be avenged. At Rome he lives in continual hopes, and rubs his hands with glee, when he proceeds southward to Naples, to think that he has contrived to smuggle a few photographs of Garibaldi into the Eternal City, or to deliver some Mazzinian message to a member of the Comitato, or in some way or another to drive a nail into the coffin of *la vieille patraque*. He looks on Rome with very different feelings from those with which patriotic Italians were wont to regard Venice in the days of captivity. They did really, at times, utterly despair of the Queen of the Adriatic ever recovering her freedom; the Austrian rule seemed so strong, so decided, so implacable. In a few hours more and more Austria could swoop down on Venetia from over the Brenner or over the Semmering. There was no doubting the sincerity of the Austrian intention to keep the tightest of holds on Venice; whereas, although the red-breeched French troops have been in the patrimony of St. Peter's, off and on, these twenty years, the Italians have never ceased from hoping—yea, and of believing—that "some day next week" was at hand when Napoleon would coolly give the Pope the go-by, pull his bayonets from beneath the tottering throne of St. Peter, and beckon to Victor Emmanuel to come up the Capitol staircase, and enter the metropolis of Italy and the world.

The fervent Catholic rejoices at Rome. It is his Mecca, his Medina, in one. Rome is to him more than Jerusalem; for in Rome he is still master, and there are no hated Greeks, no loathed schismatics to jostle him while he worships at the Holy Places. Has he not at Rome the Scala Santa, the very steps of Pilate's house? Is not the Holy Cratch, the manger-board, at Rome? Are not the Apostle's chains here? and the very prisons and the tombs of Peter and St. Paul: not in the insolent keeping of a Turkish pasha, but under the sacred guardianship of the successor of St. Peter himself? The Romanist at Rome *est dans son pays.* He is monarch of all he surveys. To M. Louis Veuillot the foul stenches and miasma of modern Rome are so many sweet perfumes —"Parfum de Rome;" whereas in the boudoirs of the Chaussée d'Antin and the parterres of Madame Prévost the austere moralist can scent only the most shocking odours. He plumes himself on Rome, for it is the only city in Europe where the shovelled hat takes precedence of the lady's bonnet; where men in petticoats have the *pas* over women in the like articles; where a snuffy old Monsignore is a greater leader of fashion than a Russian princess; or a parchment-faced vicar-general from Peru is more run after than a Japanese ambassador. It is nearly the only city where swarms of cowled-and-shaven monks are permitted to pervade the streets; and where once a year a wooden idol—the Bambino

—with twenty thousand pounds' worth of jewels on its wretched little block of a body, is held up by bishops to the adoration of twenty thousand people, in defiance of the pagan memory of Jupiter Capitolinus hard by. (When I first saw this wooden stock of a Bambino, I observed to a friend standing by me on the stairs of the Ara Cœli that, sooner than worship *that* little figure-head, I would say a mouthful of prayers to Jupiter Capitolinus, could I find any vestiges of his temple sufficient for the purpose; whereat my friend, a very high churchman, but no Romanist, was shocked.) In a word, the Romanist at Rome is in his element. If in his heart and soul he unfeignedly believes—and how shall I DARE to say that he does not?—that the good old Pope is the Vicar of &c. &c. and the Successor of &c. &c., the believer must feel, while he is in Rome, that he is sojourning in an actual earthly paradise; for he may see the supernatural Being (elected periodically, by the way, through a conspiracy on the part of several old gentlemen in scarlet petticoats, and one or more foreign ambassadors) driving out daily in a coach-and-four, or trotting about the slopes of the Pincian in a white-flannel dressing-gown and a scarlet-velvet shovel. Fancy the delight of a Moslem at being able to meet Mahomet every day, taking his drives and walks abroad; and what is the dogma of an uninterrupted succession of Infallible Popes, but a dogma of a perpetual succession of Mahomets?

The fervent Protestant glories in Rome, but darkly, furtively, and, I fear, somewhat vengefully. His worst fears are now realised; his darkest anticipations are verified; and a pretty tale he will have to tell Exeter Hall and the

Clapham tea-tables when he reaches home. Idolatry, Paganism, the Scarlet Lady, the Mystery of Iniquity: but it is needless to pursue the theme. The fervent Protestant is shocked, but he takes copious notes. He is horror-struck at the very idea of the Pope, but he is not averse to throwing himself in his way; and with the pride of conscious rectitude he relates (when he reaches Clapham) how resolutely he refused to uncover and to kneel as the idolatrous crowds around him did, when the Pope alighted from his carriage on the Pincian for his afternoon trot. Good old gentleman! I have gone down on my marrowbones when he has passed scores of times, and I hope I have had my share in the benedictions he has so liberally dispensed with his two fingers. There is something, I take it, abominably revolting in crouching down before a hewn idol—the African savage can do no more; and the Bambino is as hideous as Mumbo Jumbo: but surely there is no harm in an act of reverential courtesy to a patriarchal old priest, whose purity of life and goodness of heart are acknowledged by all the world. You kneel to a good woman, don't you? You kneel to the Queen. The Pope is king here, and so long as he can keep his Three Crowns, has a right to the customary obeisances. And finally, as the Pope himself once tersely put it to a recalcitrant heretic, the blessing of an old man cannot do anybody any harm. As for kissing his toe, that is quite another matter: although I have known many fervent Protestants (of a toady way of thinking) ready, and even eager, to perform that ceremony. To sum up, the red-hot and bilious Protestant is rather in a hurry to get away from Rome, in order that Clapham, and the columns of his favourite red-hot periodicals, shall be speedily enlightened as to the Idolatry and the Mystery of Iniquity. Abating the Bambino—which idol is to me utterly horrible and sickening—there does not seem to be much that is iniquitous about the silly mummeries and superstitions of ecclesiastical Rome. Everybody who has travelled in Spain, and especially in Mexico, must have witnessed tomfooleries ten times more preposterous and ten times more blasphemous in those countries. I spent the Holy Week of the year 1864 in Mexico City; and to this day I have never *dared*—even could I find a bookseller bold enough to publish what I wrote—to write a literal account of what goes on in *Jurves* and *Viernes Santo* in Tenostitlan.

The English Ritualist makes a joyful pilgrimage to Rome. His heart leaps up when he beholds it. He is mad to see the "functions" of Passion-week, and Easter, and Christmas, and St. Peter's-day. And after that? Well, I do thoroughly believe that it would be an excellent thing for the old-fashioned Church of England (as you, my good old friend Squaretoes, understand the doctrine and ritual of that Church) could all the ardent young Ritualists in Britain be taken to Rome in a rapid succession of Cook's tours, and be "put through" all the "functions," provided always that they took with them a *Dr. William Smith,* or an *Anthony Rich's Dictionary of Roman Antiquities* (*Muratori* or *Montfaucon* would be too cumbrous), and carefully collated all the Popish "functions" they witnessed with the descriptions of the ceremonies of Paganism. There are many grave and earnest Ritualists, no doubt—ay, and shrewd and learned men—who have visited Rome repeatedly, and whose extreme views have been rather confirmed than shaken by the investigations of each successive visit; but I incline very strongly to the belief that among the young fry of Ritualists sheer ignorance and innocent vanity are to an astonishing degree prevalent, and that they know scarcely anything about the model which they profess to copy. And not every ardent young Ritualist can go to Rome. Let them all go, I say, if it be practicable. Let them see the Real Thing—"all the Fun of the Fair"—for I do maintain that at certain periods of the year ecclesiastical Rome resembles nothing so much as a fair: waxwork shows, giants and dwarfs, gingerbread-nuts, and all. I apprehend that if all the frank, cheery, intelligent Englishmen and Englishwomen, who are not running crazy about Ritualism, were conscientiously to study *on the spot* the aspect of Ritualism's prototype, the scales would, in a vast number of instances, fall from their eyes, and they would recognise what a sorry tawdry simulacrum of rags and bones and staring paint they had been gazing at and taking for a portent.

But a truce to the *odium theologicum.* Whom else delights in Rome? Whom more than the American? And why? For the reason, I conceive, that Rome is so very, very old, and that he is so very, very new. I have studied American tourists in every country in Europe, and in every province of Italy; but I never saw them so thoroughly entertained and interested as in Rome. The ancient and the modern city have alike absorbing attractions for them. In very rare instances does the average American care anything about antiquity *per se*—any more, indeed, than does our own Mrs. Ramsbottom; yet the gray old stones of the Forum and the Colosseum seem to exercise over the Transatlantic mind an irresistible fascination. They are always poking about the tomb of Cecilia Metella, or mooning about the Catacombs, querulously anxious to know what has become of the bodies, and gladdening the hearts of the friar-guides with munificent donations; or gathering wild-flowers, and risking their necks on the summits of the arches of the Baths of Caracalla; or craning their necks to see the frescoes in the Palace of Titus; or poking at the pavement with their walking-sticks in the Thermæ of Diocletian; or vainly "guessing" at the sepulchral inscriptions in the Columbaria. They never seem tired of the statues in the Vatican and the Campidoglio. English visitors I have often seen unmistakably bored at these spectacles; and many English ladies resolutely refuse to do the antique lions of Rome after the first fortnight; but the Americans are indefatigable and insatiable. They are up early and late. They spend more money in Rome than any other foreign nation. They are the good geniuses of photographers, cameo- and bronze-dealers, statuaries, picture-copyists, and livery-stable-keepers. Their behaviour at the ecclesiastical "functions" is as the behaviour of most Protestant tourists of the Anglo-Saxon race—simply and brutally indecent. They check off the ceremonies in the Sistine by means of a *Murray* or an *Appleton's Guide-book*, and scrutinise the genuflexions of the celebrants through a double-barrelled eyeglass. During the Carnival, they have the best windows on the Corso; their equipages are the most splendid to be seen on the Pincian. Until lately, the United-States Government maintained a minister at Rome—not that there was any business to be transacted between the Papal See and the United States of America; but for the express purpose of "putting through" all Americans who wanted to see the Pope and take tea with the Cardinals. I have known Americans come straight from San Francisco to Rome, and go home again without seeing Paris or London. In addition to a numerous floating population from the States, there is in Rome a resident colony of refined, erudite, and cultivated Americans. An American, Mr. Storey, a distinguished sculptor, antiquary, and scholar, has written the best book (*Roba di Roma*) on social and picturesque life in the Eternal City that is extant. But even the floating Americans seem at home in Rome, and come back to the dear old Via Condotti and the jovial Hôtel d'Angleterre over and over again

The artist in Rome. Why, he is in Eden; for is not here the Tree of Knowledge; and may he not shake it to the last twig without sin? Everything appertaining to art is best learnt in Rome. Whatever your graphic vocation may be—are you a painter of history, of genre, of portrait, or of landscape, a sculptor, a modeller, a decorator, an architect, an engraver of gems or an engraver of metals, or a mere draughtsman of maps and plans,—you will find exemplars ready to your hand in Rome. If you seek tuition, you will find a master; if you are a master, you will find disciples. Rome is the inexhaustible milch-cow: no babe need be without a teat. She has *mammæ* for all. And moreover, in Rome, the poorest artist is somebody. The scald word "Bohemian" does not stick to ragged Dick Tinto. On the Seven Hills it is an honourable thing to be a citizen of Prague. The artists of Rome keep no state, live no grand lives, outvie one another in no vain rivalries of dress or equipage. *The artist is here, in fact, the secular priest,* and his blouse and working-cap carry, in their sphere, as much weight as in another do the shovel-hat, the shaven crown, the cowl, and the hempen girdle.

My Lord loves Rome. Our Lord, you know—his lordship who owns our land, our skies—at least, the fowls that fly in them—and will not allow us, Higgs and sons of Snell as we are, to shoot our rabbits, which, he says, are his. My Lord winters in Rome, and has wintered here any time these twenty years; you may see his sumptuous open carriage, with the bright bays, any day on the Pincian. My Lady and her ladyship's daughters love Rome quite as well; for here they find the shopping, the society, and the "scan. mag." of London, Brighton, Bath, Cheltenham, Hastings, and Tunbridge Wells.

In a word, who is NOT charmed with *Roma urbs?* The classical scholar and the lover of English black-draughts and blue-pills, the antiquary and the connoisseur in painting, the admirer of field-sports and the amateur of monastic institutions, can all find their peculiar tastes ministered to in Rome. Whether you study the bas-relief on a column from a Montfaucon's point of view, or sit yourself on the top thereof and chant doxologies for thirty years as Simon Stylites did; whether your sympathies lie in the direction of ancient sculpture, of moonlight picnics, of pound-cakes, of palimpsests, or of mulligatawny soup—they have the right sort: an oriental-club recipe, communicated by a perverted under-butler at Spielmann's restaurant—whether you like English Bath chaps, or Dunville's V.R. Whisky, or alabaster statuettes, or gilt bronzes, or Egyptian obelisks, or the Acta Sanctorum, or stewed porcupine, or photographs, or cameos,—you have only to ask for the particular dainty you require in Rome, and, so long as you have plenty of money, your wish will be gratified in a moment.

And can there be NO individuals to dislike this wonderful place? Well, I don't think the officers of the French army of occupation care much about it: and I am afraid that there are a vast number of born Romans who dislike Rome intensely, and will continue so to dislike it while the Pope is king, as well as pontiff, at the Vatican.

XXII.

A ROMAN FESTIVAL.

December 8.

To-day is the Feast of the Immaculate Conception. The shops are shut, the church-bells are ringing incessantly, and it is raining hard. The time has gone by when the Feasts of the Roman-Catholic Church were concurrent with the merry-makings of the people. A Church-holiday, originally, was surely intended to be a season when, the religious ceremonies of the occasion being duly performed, everybody proceeded to enjoy himself—when there were games and junketings, jousts and pastimes, as well as solemn rites and imposing processions—when the miracle-play was often acted in the very same fane where the mass had been sung—when banqueting-tables were spread, and good cheer was the substantial sign of the joy which, in those simple ages of Faith, filled the hearts of men who were content to believe and be thankful, and left reading and writing—perilous accomplishments at best—to their betters; that is to say, to the clergy. There is a Marriage of Cana, as we all know, at the Louvre, and another Marriage, by an early German painter, in the Berlin Gallery, in which this primitive notion of a festival is very unmistakably conveyed. The German has painted a marvellous kitchen interior, just as the Venetian has painted an equally-wonderful representation of the banqueting-board itself. You see very clearly what the feast means. It means roast-goose, wild-boar's head, fat capons, raised-pie, grapes and peaches, and nuts and oranges, and an abundance of sound Rhenish and generous Aleatico to wash the dainties down. Only the faintest reflex of these feasts, half-pious, half-convivial, is visible in modern civilisation. English people over-eat themselves, traditionally, at Christmas; and Americans consume vast quantities of roast-turkey, stewed-oysters, and "sass" on Thanksgiving-day. For the rest, the majority of Catholics have forgotten how to feast, just as the ordinary run of Protestants have forgotten how to fast. Asceticism may linger in some remote corners; and it may be that Messrs. Thresher and Glenny keep a few hair-shirts in stock for old customers; but, save from affectation, who mortifies himself on Ash Wednesday or Good Friday? To very many thousands of very good Protestants those fasts have become virtual feasts, dedicated to excursion-trains and pigeon-shooting at Hornsey Wood.

In the capital of Christianity there are few days without at least a couple of saints, and sometimes half-a-dozen, specially appointed to take care of them; but the period between Advent and Easter bristles with fasts and feasts. Last Sunday, the first in Advent, there was a Pontifical High Mass at the Sistine Chapel. The Pope and the Armenian Patriarch of Constantinople officiated, and the Host was carried processionally to the Capella Paolina. A forty-hours' exposition of the sacrament has been going on in the different churches of Rome all the week. On Tuesday was the Feast of St. Barbara. This saint is the patroness of artillerymen! As she flourished many centuries before the infernal invention of the Reverend Father Schwarz (or somebody else, who has been, for a long time, "having it hot" in the *carcer inferior* of Hades, for his benevolent invention's sake) was adapted to the destruction of humanity, it is difficult to see how St. Barbara became the protector of gunners and drivers and eighteen-pounders. Her status at the Ordnance Office seems an anachronism as glaring as the employment of heavy artillery in the celestial warfare in *Paradise Lost.*

Both inconsistencies may of course be reconciled by the use of that stick which has only one end—the miracle; but I have had the mystery of St. Barbara explained to me in another way. Before the discovery of gunpowder, her saintship looked after mines and miners, kindly settling all matters connected with ventilation and choke-damp, and chasing away the gnomes and kobolds, and other maleficent sprites, who, as is well known, haunt deserted "goafs," and prevent the working of rich veins. When gunpowder was discovered, it occurred to some bright genius that it might be made subservient to other purposes than murdering mankind. It was used in mines for blasting. The devout pitmen, previous to applying the match to a charge, naturally murmured an invocation to St. Barbara. Thus associated with nitrous explosion, the transition to big guns was obvious, and St. Barbara has ever since been the saint *par excellence* of the Special Arm of the Service. It is to be feared that she receives but scant homage at Woolwich, but at Rome she is treated with every possible honour. The guns of the castle of St. Angelo thundered forth, on the morning of the fourth, a salute to the explosive saint. I was walking in the afternoon by the Campo Vaccino towards the arch of Titus, when, close to St. Cosmo Damiano, I came upon a tolerably large crowd, and heard a series of most terrific reverberations. I found that it was only a select party of French private soldiers, who had economised their pocket-money for a blow-up on St. Barbara's-day, and were exploding a series of petards, each about the the size of a pint-pot, on the muddy waste ground.

I may add that the road from the Capitol to the Colosseum, taking in the Forum Romanum and the Campo Vaccino aforesaid, bears a very striking resemblance to Glasgow-green —assuming about two-thirds of the population of the "pawkie" city of North Britain to be dead of the cholera. It is as grimy, as filthy, as tumbledown, as forlorn, and as unpleasantly redolent of old clothes, old marine-stores, and old women, who were washerwomen once upon a time, but have long since foresworn soap, either for their own or for other's use. That the temples and palaces of the Forum and the Capitol should be dilapidated and decrepit is in the nature of things, and offers no pretext for grumbling. I do not feel inclined to echo the opinion of the American tourist who described Rome as "quite a nice place, but the public buildings much out of repair." The tumbledown structures of the Forum and Capitol I mean are the modern ones. The classical ruins *are* ruins, and behave as such. The domestic edifices all look as though they had been first half demolished by the Goths, then sacked by the Connétable de Bourbon, then gutted by Gualtiero di Monreale, and finally bombarded by General Regnault de St. Jean d'Angely in 1849.

But their dilapidation is not picturesque, and their decrepitude is not venerable. Blind Belisarius begging for an *obolus* at the Porta del Popolo is a noble ruin; but you don't care much about a nasty old man with a fine Roman mosaic of dirt tesselated into the baldness of his skull, who importunes you, under the adjuration of many saints, for two *bajocchi*, the which he presently spends on a *bicchierino* of rum, at the grog-shop round the corner. Rum in Rome! It has come to this. Rum is the favourite beverage of the lower classes in the Eternal City. No modern stimulants, however, can make either the people or their dwellings look young. They do not even pertain to the Middle Ages, from the Hallam and Victor-Hugo point of view. They have nothing to do with the interesting antiquity of the Republican or the Imperial epochs. They are simply nastily old, grubbily antique, scandalously ruinous, like the ragfair shanties of Glasgow, or the filthy Towers of Babel in the Canongate at Edinburgh, or the rookeries of the Coomb in Dublin, or those abominable houses at the corner of Stamford-street, Blackfriars, or any other unsightly, noisome slums you like to mention.

On every monument of the classical past in Rome, on almost every bust and statue in the Vatican, you may find a pompous inscription setting forth that now, purged from all pagan impieties, the relic has been dedicated to the service of a purer faith, "through the munificence" of this or that Clement, Gregory, or Pius. How dearly should I like to see, on the places where the modern Romans vegetate, here and there a brass-plate, or a marble-tablet, or even a simply-painted wooden board, proclaiming that in such or such a year this pigstye had been reformed, this guilt-garden purified, that rotten mass of hovels converted into a model lodging-house, or those other hideous rookeries swept and garnished, and dedicated to St. Saponax and St. Aquarius—all "through the munificence" of the Pontifex Maximus for the time being! If Mr. Peabody, now, would only change his creed, what a capital Pope he would make! What a St. George would he be to destroy the old Roman dragon of rubbish and stinks and malaria! Surely a longer lease might be granted to the Imperial Power, if they would only wash the Santa Sede clean, and pull down some of the unutterable Gehennas that fringe the very gardens of the Vatican.

In lieu of this, at the top of the Corso, the most fashionable thoroughfare in Rome, and at the corner of a street leading directly to the Capitoline Hill, there is a public laystall of the most revolting kind, with this cool announcement nailed to the wall: "*Deposito provvisorio delle immondezze per la notte.*" I do not pretend to understand anything about the dogma of the Immaculate Conception any more than I do that of the Incarnation of Vishnu; but I have read somewhere that cleanliness is next to godliness, and that dictum might, with advantage I think, be tacked to the Thirty-nine Articles. If Pio Nono would only proclaim the dogma of immaculate cleanliness in common life as a means of salvation, he would find a great many more people willing to listen to him than, I fear, can be found in Italy just now.

Meanwhile the French artillerymen were holding their harmless festival on the Colosseum-road, to the intense delight of the Roman *gamins*, who were allowed to scramble for the petards after each explosion, and clawed and cuffed, and tumbled one another in the mud, very much as it is the fashion for little blackguard boys to do the whole world over. The artillerymen had been to church in the morning, and in full uniform, to return thanks to St. Barbara for past favours, and solicit a renewal of her kind patronage. Officers and men dined together in the evening, so that there has been one festival at least in Advent, with an accompaniment of cakes and ale. I suppose that there is not much harm in firing-off big guns and bursting pint-pots in honour of St. Barbara. The dear good lady would probably be frightened out of her wits at the sound of a pocket-pistol, and may have about as much to do with the Royal Artillery as St. Catherine has with the fireworks at Cremorne, or St. Vitus with the shocking malady which bears his name. But what does it matter, after all? Thousands of good people go every year to say their prayers at St. Martin's Church, in London. Does one in ten thousand know who St. Martin was? or care much, at this time of day?

Moreover, when you come to gunpowder, logic flies out at the window. There is inherent in humanity the desire to make from time to time a thundering noise. Before gunpowder the world could only cheer, and ring bells, and flourish trumpets: one grows hoarse with hallooing, however, and trumpeters and bell-ringers are apt to grow tired. The blazing and banging properties of gunpowder have long since secured for it the palm in creating a disturbance. There is seldom any real meaning in the explosion of gunpowder, always excepting when the Hounslow mills "go off," and a battle is perhaps the most illogical thing in existence; but we have the thundering noise, and that is what most people require. In the Miscellaneous Estimates every year in England, you will find that a sum of from twelve to fifteen hundred pounds is blown away in gunpowder in the form of salutes to royal and distinguished personages who come to or go away from Dover. Some of these royal and distinguished ones have lately been wiped out by Bismark. To fire twenty-one blank charges after a Grand Duke or an Hereditary Small German cannot do him any good; but then it does nobody any harm, save an occasional artilleryman who is blown up by a bursten gun, or has his arm broken by its recoil. But we are a wealthy nation, and can afford to throw money into the kennel. Fifteen hundred pounds a-year, for instance, would not be of the slightest service as an endowment for educational, literary, or artistic purposes. It is a fleabite, and may, as well as not, be blown away in gunpowder.

There is another Capella Papale or Pontifical High Mass to-day at the Apostolic Palace in the Vatican: mass to be sung by the Cardinal Protector of the Borghesian College, in Santa Maria Maggiore, and a sermon to be preached by an alumnus of the Pian Seminary; there is a festival at Santa Maria d' Aracœli, and at the Church of the Twelve Apostles an octave and a discourse; at twenty-three o'clock (*sic*) there will be a panegyric and a benediction in Sant' Andrea della Valle; panegyrics will also be delivered at San Francesco Ripa, at the Church of the Capuchins at the Gesù, at St. Cosmo and Damiano, at San Carlo in the Corso, at St. Maria of the Via Lata, at St. Lucia de' Ginnasi, and about a hundred more of the three-hundred-and-sixty-four churches with which Rome is blessed. At the Oratory of San Girolama della Carità there will be a musical litany to which ladies are admitted—a grateful notification, the fair sex being excluded from very many interesting *funciones* in Rome. They are not even allowed to visit the subterranean church of St. Peter's save on Whit Monday, or on presentation of a solemn petition to the Pope through the Cardinal Datario. Ladies as well as gentlemen were granted free ingress to the Sistine last Sunday, but "opera-dress" was *de rigueur:* that is to say, the gentlemen were to appear in black dress-coats, and the ladies in black dresses and black-lace veils.

I have mentioned some of the ceremonies consequent on this Feast of the Immaculate Conception, about which, one way or the other, the poor old Pope of Rome probably knows as much or as little as does one of his own Swiss Guard, and the doctrinal assertion of which, independent of the infallibility claimed for the Holy Father, is of no more weight than would be the affirmation that the form of the earth is a polyhedron, or that the normal hue of a Bengal tiger is pea-green. The manner in which the festival of the Immaculate has been celebrated—for the shades of evening have closed in since I commenced this letter—is on a par with the rationality of the dogma itself. The day has been kept in the fashion defined by Americans as "a little mixed." Thus, while the Romans of the upper classes have judiciously stayed away from the church celebrations, the most fervent worshippers of Romanist shrines to-day have been the Protestant foreigners, chiefly ladies, staying in the different hotels of the capital. Stiff silk-skirts and elaborate veils of sable hue were at a premium this morning, and the conversation at the *table-d'hôte* was all about incense and organs, stoles and dalmatics, acolytes and thurifers.

Surely there is not much to wonder at if the minds of some silly women and sillier men at home are running crazy just now on Ritualism. It is, after all, only a matter of music and millinery, which are both things very dear to the feminine mind. We may live in hope of seeing Ritualistic rectors stand on the steps of the altar in zouave jackets and Pamela bonnets, and the clerk give out a sonnet by Swinburne, as a psalm, to the music of the Guards' waltz. I see no reason to the contrary. I have heard, in a Spanish church, in Holy Week, a set of variations on the music of the *Trovatore* performed on the grand pianoforte; and to the poor peasants who formed the majority of the congregation Signor Verdi's spasmodic strophes were as soul-entrancing as though they had formed part of the music of the spheres.

It is at Rome, however, that ecclesiastical music and ecclesiastical millinery are seen in their highest perfection; it is at Rome that the frivolous and the meretricious become colossal, and Imposture rises to the sublime. The church-music at Rome is really magnificent; the grandeur of the scenery is beyond all praise—the scenic artists are, in many cases, be it remembered, Rafaelle and Michel Angelo; the decorations are superb, the dresses sumptuous, the stage-management perfect, the supernumeraries admirably drilled. The difference between the servitor in a purple gaberdine and violet stockings who on Sunday last popped hither and thither among the artificial rocks and sham columns of the Capella Paolina, lighting up the lamps, and the gentleman in a paper-cap and shirt-sleeves who kindles the gas-battens behind the set pieces in one of Mr. Beverley's spectacles at Drury Lane, is perhaps hard to discover; but the alacrity with which genteel British Protestants, who at home are never tired of girding at the Scarlet Woman of Babylon and the Mystery of Iniquity, throw themselves into the voluptuousness of church music and millinery at Rome is, to say the least, edifying. They appear to regard the Pope as a kind of show provided by the Roman hotel-keepers, and to be enjoyed by the superior classes in common with cameos, mosaics, Castellani's antique jewelry, Piale's reading-room, and the statues in the Museo Chiaramonti by moonlight. They would walk in and out of the Vatican, if they could, as they do in and out of the painters' and sculptors' studios —half as patrons, half as sneering critics. They would take stock of the benighted old gentleman's furniture, and inquire if he wears a crinoline under his white-flannel petticoat, and gaze curiously on the enormous red-silk pocket-handkerchief with which he mops up the quantity of snuff which he bestows on his venerable countenance. "*Ebbene, Signore,*" said a Roman cardinal to the philosopher John Locke, at the conclusion of one of the most awful ceremonies in Passion-week; "*che pensa ella di tutte queste coglionerie?*" Who is in more evil case, I wonder: the cynical flamen who "rails against the quality of flesh, and not believes himself," or the gaping show-hunter who mobs the Pope, and scrutinises the elevation of the Host through a double eyeglass?

To me Romanism in Rome is at once a ludicrous and a melancholy spectacle; ludicrous from the infinite tomfoolery in which the celebrants indulge, the barefaced imposture which is palmed on the credulous, the impudent plagiarisms from pagan rites which it presents — plagiarisms so close and literal that, with the assistance of a Dictionary of Antiquities, nothing is easier than to keep a register of these mummeries by double entry, the Romish ceremony in one column, and the heathen ceremony, from which it has been obviously copied, in the other. There has been meandering about Rome, for instance, all this afternoon, an exact reproduction of the procession of the *Bona Dea*, or Venus Salammbó. For the *Bona Dea* was simply substituted a gigantic figure, enthroned, of the Virgin Mary. Before and behind was an interminable train of monks and friars, priests and choir-boys, gendarmes and Papal dragoons, with innumerable banners, and two military bands.

The whole thing, as I have said, is a "little mixed." Ophicleides and drawn sabres, epaulettes and jackboots, will get mingled, somehow, with pyxes and crosses, shaven crowns and bare feet. But the entirety is but a palimpsest of the pagan, notwithstanding. This is the ludicrous side. It is ludicrous to know that while these monks are wandering with their idol about a city of a hundred-and-fifty-thousand inhabitants, the most interested sightseers are a few groups of foreign heretics, who, in their heart of hearts, know well enough that the whole thing is a Humbug, yet who suck it up greedily, as they would the sight of Blondin on the tight-rope, or the Widow Stodare with her Sphinx. It is ludicrous to know that, although the shops are shut, the *caffès* are all wide open, and full of French officers, who—all eldest children of the Church as they are—prefer to imbibe their absinthe and smoke their cigars, and let the *Bona Dea* meander by in peace. So much is ludicrous; but there is much more that is melancholy in the sight of an enormous machine falling daily out of gear, of a house whose foundations are being daily sapped, of a priesthood whose legitimate influence is hourly dwindling away from them, of a Pontiff who is staggering to and fro like a drunken man. There could not be a more significant commentary on the Feast of the Immaculate Conception in Rome than the fact that, on Thursday, the officers of the French corps of occupation, headed by General de Montebello, had their audience of leave of the Pope; that on Friday the 71st French regiment of the line steamed out of the harbour of Civita Vecchia; that on Monday another regiment goes away; and that by this day week the Pope will have to shift for himself.*

* But he could do nothing of, or by, or for himself, poor "infallible" old man, and his French patrons were fain to come back and help him.

XXIII.

THE POPE.

December 12.

THIS is the twelfth of December: the French programme is accomplished to the letter, and not a French soldier or a scrap of French bunting is to be seen anywhere in Rome. A few clerks in charge of commissariat stores, and a few *employés* of the special French department of the Roman Post-office will remain for a time to balance their books and arrange the affairs of their bureaux; but by New-year's-day the seventeen years' occupation of the Papal States by Napoleon III. will have become as entirely a thing of the past as that other occupation under Napoleon I., when the Prefect of the Tiber resided at the Quirinal—when Perugia was the *chef lieu* of the department of the Thrasymene—and when Pasquin, alluding to the desolation of the city by a severe storm, and the promulgation of divers rigorous decrees from Paris, broke out in his memorable quatrain:

> "L' altissimo là sù ci manda la tempesta,
> L' altissimo là giù ci toglia quel che resta;
> E fra li due altissimi,
> Siamo noi malissimi."

> From Jupiter above come hail and thunder,
> From Jupiter below edicts for plunder,
> And what with one and t'other Zeus,
> Poor Rome is going to the deuce.

You will pardon the freedom of the translation I have here attempted; but the Italian text, as is ordinarily the case with Peninsular humour, is even more free, and, literally rendered into English, might not be very welcome to Protestant ears.

I should be wrong, at the same time, in saying that, although the French army have thoroughly decamped, there are no more French uniforms to be seen in the streets of Rome. You can scarcely walk ten paces indeed, to-day, in any frequented thoroughfare without meeting a pale and feeble phantom of the *zou-zou*, the *piou-piou*, and the *pousse-caillou* of La Belle France. It has occurred to the Papal Government, in its wisdom, that the Romans might be kept in good order after the departure of the stern monitors who have so long watched over them, if it dressed up its own warriors in the likeness of French soldiers. Thus the Pontifical gendarmes, to the exact measurement of the angles of their cocked-hats, and the minutest inflections of the curves of their moustaches, are copied from the French model; the last real types of which left Civita Vecchia yesterday, per war-steamer for Toulon.

The Antibes legion—if sundry ill-looking scamps I have met prowling about belong to that notable corps—are got up in imitation of French chasseurs, and the sentry-boxes are occupied to-day by fusiliers of all sizes and all ages, and with the cross-keys on their shakoes, but otherwise arrayed in the blue tunics, red-worsted epaulettes, and *pantalons garance* of Gaul. The simulacrum is as commendable as a chalk-drawing from the Apollo Belvedere, and quite as unsatisfactory. These presumably valiant persons produce a lively effect, but they are evidently not the genuine article. They are sickly, shambling, slovenly-looking creatures at the best, many almost dwarfish in stature, others preternaturally lanky, and with not more than a pound and a half of real fighting-looking muscle to each half-dozen privates. They are very dirty, and the successor of the apostles has not yet provided his legionaries with pocket-handkerchiefs. Their speech is polyglot, and they stare in at the jewellers' shop-windows in a manner which may well inspire the *bigiottieri* of Rome with an intense desire to put up their shutters till the Roman question is definitively settled. The accuracy with which their uniforms have been "taken from the French" would do honour to a London playwright, but in essentials they no more resemble French soldiers than the *Game of Speculation* resembles *Mercadet.*

The Pontifical War-office, like some unscrupulous retail dealers at home, has resorted to "the untradesmanlike device of saying it is the same concern;" but Rome and Italy will hardly be taken in by the imposture. The Zouaves are a better-looking set of fellows altogether; but they are too young and too weedy. Of course the primeval stock of the Zouave were the Duke d'Aumale's *enfants perdus*, modelled on the indigenous Spahis of Algeria: for take the white burnouse off a Spahi, and you will find that he is a Zouave underneath; but the Roman specimens I have seen appear to have been more closely studied from the Transatlantic variety so familiar in the Zouaves of Colonel Billy Wilson, who never could be persuaded to garrison West Point, because it was so very near Sing Sing, and who were so signally routed in their first encounter with the rebels, through the cunning of the Confederate commander, who simply caused a banner to be hoisted in front of his line bearing this inscription, "The police are coming." Billy Wilson's Zouaves needed no second warning, but stampeded at once.

The Papal Zouaves are clad in gray, with a deep-red sash round their loins, but the former hue is the prevailing one, and on the whole it has a Portland-cum-Pentonville look, and, with their very baggy knickerbockers, gives them the air of convicts "on the loose." There are a good many of them also who march wide between the legs as though they had gyves on, and the very sensible system followed of abolishing the choking leathern stock, and allowing them to go bare-necked, does not fail to induce a theory painfully suggestive of the absence of under-linen, as in the case of Sir John Falstaff's Own, or Coventry Rangers, in the whole of which distinguished regiment I believe there was but a shirt and a half, the shirt stolen from an innkeeper at Daventry, and the half-shirt a towel, worn across the shoulders after the manner of a herald's tabard. The P. Z.'s, I fear, will have some difficulty in finding linen on the hedges. Nothing seems to grow on the Campagna of Rome, except acanthus-leaves, wild-flowers, and buffaloes; and even the Cotton Supply Association would be puzzled to make shirts out of *them*.

I wonder whether the Pope's sham French gendarmes, sham Chasseurs, sham Dragoons, and sham Zouaves, will be of any avail in propping-up the Holy Father's rule over his 800,000 subjects, and averting, for any considerable length of time, that political collapse which, in the nature of things, seems inevitable? As for the Roman-Catholic religion and its priests, *non ragioniam di lor*. It may take a hundred, and it may take a thousand, it may take even two thousand years to extirpate ignorance, credulity, and superstition from the minds of humanity; and so long as ignorance, credulity, and superstition last, the Roman-Catholic religion will endure, and spiritually flourish. But the temporal power is a thing whose decay can be more visibly gauged, and the time of whose demolition can be more easily calculated. It is not a question of centuries; it may not be a question of days or months; but it is assuredly one to be determined within a very few years. There is nothing particularly mischievous, or wicked, or fraudulent about it, as there *is* about the Romish idolatry, which, in proportion to its wickedness and falsity, is likely to last the longer.

The little tinpot supremacy of the Pope as a king is not a much greater nuisance than many which, within the memory of men still living, we bore for years, but which we were at last irritated into sweeping away. Highway robbery, Dead-body snatching, Algerine piracy, Gretna-green marriages, Sanctuary at Holyrood, the Rules of the Bench, West-Indian slavery, the Laws of Mortmain and Deodand, French passports and personal search at the Custom-houses, the Duke of Athol's rights as a king in the Isle of Man, Climbing-boys, the Sound-dues, Eighteenpenny inland postage, the Palace Court, Smithfield Market, Intramural interments, Joseph Ady, and the Corn-laws: one need not be more than a middle-aged man to remember all those plagues. I don't think the Roman shoe pinches the Roman people more tightly than any of the inflictions I have set down above. I have lived abroad under more than one despotic government, with slaves to wait upon me, no free press, no representative institutions, no inviolability of correspondence, and spies dogging my every footstep; yet I have found existence exceedingly tolerable, and, so long as the bankers didn't break, had quite a nice time.

Many years have elapsed since Lord John Russell denounced the Government of the Pope as the very worst in Europe, and, save in a few insignificant particulars, it has not changed since the period of his lordship's denunciation. A comparison of Roman institutions with the governments of other European countries must lead us, in 1866, to very nearly the same conclusion. The Government of the States of the Church is worse even than that of Greece, whose last king, when he was kicked out, did not at least claim immunity on the score of being the Vicar of Heaven and a supernatural personage—worse even than that of Turkey, where there are at least religious toleration and commercial freedom. But, for all its intrinsic badness, one is puzzled at first to tell in what precise manner Rome is misgoverned, or the Romans themselves oppressed and ground down. There are few, if any, Protestant natives here, so that the impudent bigotry which, in the face of Roman-Catholic emancipation in England, forbids the celebration of Protestant worship within the walls of Rome, cannot press very hardly on the inhabitants. The Roman police, so far as I know, are not in the habit of opening letters at the post-office, or of paying domiciliary visits, or of arresting persons on the most frivolous pretences, or of dragging people out of their beds in order to beat them with sticks; a practice long followed, and up to a very recent date, both by the Austrian and the Russian police. There are certainly no political criminals in the casemates of St. Angelo.* There are as certainly no captives for conscience' sake in the dungeons of the Inquisition, there are no political convicts in the *bagni* of Civita Vecchia—at least, none that I have heard of—save brigands, whose claim to be considered politicians is at least questionable. I have heard some horrible stories against the Papal sbirri, but beyond a fondness for doing nothing, and for cheating anybody out of ten *bajocchi* when they have a chance, I don't suppose they are worse than other policemen elsewhere.

Of what, then, have the Romans to complain? Wherein lies the gravamen of their doleance? What is the grinding oppression under which they suffer? Their taxation is not so heavy as it is in free Italy. The Papal tobacco, I again hasten to own, is infinitely superior to the Italian, and at the Debito Regio, in the Piazza Mignanelli, you may purchase genuine havanas, specially imported by the Government of the Holy Father for the delectation of his faithful children. As a snuff-taker the Pontiff has a fellow-feeling for the smoker. King Victor Emmanuel unfortunately has an unrefined taste as regards tobacco. The coarsest of weeds are deemed good enough by his Majesty, and his realm is consequently poisoned with bad cigars.

I am aware that a tableau of the actual condition of Rome can be painted in colours far darker than those with which I have set my palette. From Florence, from Milan, from Turin, from Paris, you will receive probably very different accounts of what is going on in the Eternal City. There is an influential journal, for example, called *Il Patriota*, and

* There are *now* (1869).

published at Parma. The Roman correspondent of this interesting sheet writes, under the date of the 6th of December, that Rome is in a state of siege; that cannon are posted, "*al di quà e al di là*," here and there along the Tiber; that so soon as the bells for the *Ave Maria* are heard the streets are deserted; that nightly wayfarers are poniarded, or stripped and robbed, by the "brigands" with whom the city is swarming, and who are under the immediate protection of the Papal Government; that the Presidents of the different *Rioni* or districts have *carte blanche* from head-quarters, and arrest whom they please in order to satisfy private vengeance; that the gendarmerie stop passengers in the streets, and insult them; *that the prisons of the Holy Office are full of poveri infelici accused of heresy or blasphemy, who undergo the most frightful tortures;* that other enormities are rife, the which the pen refuses to transcribe; that malversation, vendette, rapes, arrests, robbery, and murder are the order of the day; and so forth. The correspondent of the Parmesan paper winds up by informing his readers that the *Sanfedisti,* who committed such atrocities in the Romagna and the Marches in '49, are enrolled in a "secret military legion," and will in due course of time be let loose on the shopkeepers. The *Osservatore Romano* has quietly republished the letter of the Roman correspondent of the Parma *Patriota,* heading it with the suggestive title, "*Nuove bugie e vecchi bugiardi*"—"New lies from old liars." It need scarcely be said that there is not one word of truth in the Parmesan chronicle. Rome is just as quiet as Camberwell. Until very late at night the streets are filled with people; carriages full of fashionable ladies drive about with impunity.

There are no cannon visible "*al di quà*" or "*al di là*," on the Tiber's banks; and the cells of the Holy Office are in all probability as empty as the Parmesan gentleman's head. This is but a very mild sample of the prodigious lies which are told every day in the columns of the Italian press.

I will believe that, were a *plebiscitum* called for *while* the Pope remains at Rome, the result, although the majority might be for union with Italy under Victor Emmanuel, would show a very respectable proportion of voters for the maintenance of the actual order of things. Mind, everybody must vote. The thirteen thousand priests and monks, the seminaries and the pupils of the Propaganda, the three thousand beadles, vergers, sacristans, bell-ringers, gutter-scrapers, holy-water-bottle fillers, and lamplighters and candle-snuffers of St. Peter's—the beadles, &c. of the other three-hundred-and-sixty-three churches and basilicas of Rome, the cardinals and the cardinals' coachmen and footmen, and that wonderful dragoon—the image of our own City marshal—who rides before the Pope, waving a drawn sword, after the manner of the late Mr. Gomersal in the Astleian spectacle of the *Battle of Waterloo*. The Swiss halberdiers must vote, and the Noble Guard, and the Trasteverini who yet grovel before the empty tomb which Pius IX. has caused to be constructed for himself, and groups of whom are always to be found in St. Peter's, kissing away what remains of the toe of the saint. The shopkeepers who sell mosaics and Byzantines, and gilt bronzes, and verd antique, and malachite, and copies of old pictures, the hotel-keepers, the lottery-office-keepers, and the *valets de place*, should also be admitted to the suffrage; and the result would, I am sure, be a highly-respectable list of people in Rome who wanted to keep the Pope in and the Italians out. As for the ladies, if female votes were allowed, and only the old women, in any European capital, Protestant or Catholic, you choose to mention, were polled, the majority would be for the Pope, and he would remain at the Vatican *in sæcula sæculorum.*

But neither priests, nor friars, nor flunkeys, nor shopkeepers, nor old women, nor his rabble-rout of Dutch-Irish Zouaves and Antibes Legionaries will set the temporal power on its legs again. There will not, I hope, be another Castelfidardo or another Perugia;* but the Papacy for all that will "slide," and, temporally, be effaced. The real, the sole complaint of the Roman people is, not that they are massacred, or starved, or locked up and tortured by the Inquisition, but that they are subject to a Government which belongs, not to the nineteenth, but to the fourteenth century. The Pope is a dear good old gentleman, but he is five hundred years old —he goes himself sometimes so far as to say that he is close upon two thousand—and really, at his age, he should be spared the clatter and the worry of modern politics. The Romans do not want him to go away from Rome. They are willing to make him happy and comfortable there all the days of his life; but they desire to see him adopt a policy, and surround himself with counsellors befitting the coming year 1867.

* There has been Mentana (1869).

XXIV.

ROME AND THE ROMANS.

Of course, during the fortnight preceding the departure of the French troops from Rome, you heard at least fourteen different rumours—mostly from the inventive city of Paris, or the scarcely less imaginative Florence—setting forth how the Ultramontane party had succeeded in persuading the Pope to run away from Rome so soon as the French evacuation was completed. Certainly, in the majority of instances, the wish was father to the thought, and the Italian papers, in particular, show great anxiety to prove that the departure of the Holy Father from Rome would be an act of virtual abdication. There are some notable historical precedents in support of this view. In the British Museum may be seen a copy of the *London Gazette* for a certain day in the month of November 1688, in which the Lords of the Council calmly announce that, "his Majesty having withdrawn himself," they hold the throne of England to be vacant. James II. did subsequently more formally abdicate; but the "withdrawal" noticed in the *Gazette* was undeniably the real false step which shook the crown off his head.

Were the Pope to depart, suddenly and secretly from his capital, to be next heard of at Malta, at Munich, or at Madrid, it might need no very nice discrimination between *de jure* and *de facto* rights, and no very minute hairsplitting between sovereigns *in esse* and *in posse*, to arrive at the conclusion that there was nobody to sit down in the chair of St. Peter—that is, in the ordinary locality provided for sedentary accommodation. Ultramontanism denies this, and asserts that the Pope was as much a temporal prince at Avignon—when the Tribune Rienzi was fighting the Colonna and the Orsini at Rome—or at Fontainebleau—under the lock and key of Napoleon, while the Eternal City was not only garrisoned by French troops, but formally incorporated with the French Empire under the name of the Department of the Tiber—or as at any other period of his history when he sat enthroned in high state in the Vatican, surrounded by Swiss halberdiers and noble guards, and sending his *monsignori* to govern the Legations.

The worth of an assertion—like anything else—is, according to *Hudibras*, "just so much as it will bring;" and the Ultramontane assertion does *not* bring conviction to the mind. The Pope was *not* sovereign of Rome when he lived at Avignon, because it was as much as his life was worth to have shown himself in Rome among the turbulent barons. He was *not* sovereign of Rome when Napoleon immured him in the splendid durance of Fontainebleau, simply because he had been forced into a postchaise, and hurried from Italy to France under an escort of gendarmes, while the son of his captor had been solemnly created king of the city which he claimed as his appanage.

These are not, of course, the views of Ultramontanism. Their views are summed up in the doctrine of Divine right. Those views are very distinctly expressed on the portal of a monumental tomb in the crypt of St. Peter's, where we are told in sounding Latin, that *James the Third, Charles the Third, and Henry the Ninth, Kings of Great Britain, France, and Ireland*, are interred. We know very well that there never were any such kings, and that in that stately sepulchre continue to moulder only the bones of two Pretenders, the elder and the younger, and of Henry Stuart, sometime Cardinal of York. Ultramontanism, to do it justice, is seldom inconsistent. To Ultramontanism the Count de Chambord is still Henry the Fifth, Leopold is still Grand Duke of Tuscany, Francesco King of Naples, and Juan de Borbon King of Spain;* and not a fortnight since I read in an ultra-Catholic paper a flaming panegyric on the lately-deceased miscreant—a miscreant as mad as he was sanguinary—Don Pedro of Portugal.

But will the Pope go away, either definitively or only for a short time, until he can see what turn affairs are likely to take? You may think it now rather late in the day to discuss such a question, but at Rome, as I have already had occasion to point out, much less seems to be known, and to all outward appearance much less seems to be cared about that twin-brother in abstruseness and obscurity to the Schleswig-Holstein difficulty, the Roman question, than is known and cared in France, in Italy, or even in Protestant England. The Romans are not such gossips as the Florentines or the Venetians. *Caffè* life is here almost a nullity. The erst-famous Caffè Greco—done to death by every tourist who has professed to describe artist life in Rome—is the dullest and most deserted of places; the falling-off in its prosperity being attributed to the new proprietor's raising the tariff for a cup

* Don Juan, I believe, has since abdicated his pretensions, and the present pretender is an even more obscure personage (1869).

of coffee from one penny to threehalfpence. There is no Florian's, no Doney's, no Piazza della Scala, at Rome, where the scan. mag. of the day is retailed hot and hot, like the parallelograms of juicy meat at the Beefsteak Club.

One does not resort to the Forum to hear what is going on. One goes to the Forum to see the ruins and be fleeced by the custodes thereof on a sliding-scale of extortion, varying from five *bajocchi* for a Corinthian column damaged, to three *paoli* for a statue. Triumphal arches are gratuitous. The Corso is the Bond-street of Rome, and at all hours pretty well thronged; but it is far too narrow for even two quidnuncs to hold each other by the button and gossip for five minutes. And strong as is the love in humanity for gossip, that enjoyment can scarcely be cultivated in the middle of the road at the risk of being run over by the sanguine-hued equipage of an Eminence, or an English mail-phaeton rattling towards the Pincian hill. There are very few people indeed to be seen at any time on the Piazza del Popolo, which has an odd family likeness to Highgate-archway, set down at the entrance to Cumberland-market, Kentish Town; and as for the Piazza di Spagna, and the Via Condotti, and the Via Babuino, about the last article procurable in any of those thoroughfares is Roman political intelligence.

It is the English quarter, it is the district of the vast hotels where the *Forestieri Inglesi* are taken in and done for —comfortably done for, generously done for, I grant, but at a deuce of a price. If you want Crosse and Blackwell's pickles, Brown and Polson's corn-flour, Mappin's razors, Elkington's plate, Atkinson's perfumery, Savory and Moore's drugs, Guinness's stout, Parkins and Gotto's stationery, or

Allsopp's pale ale, come by all means to the Spagna, the Condotti, or the Babuino. If a young lady wishes to hire a riding-habit or a side-saddle for the next meet of the Roman Hunt she will find everything she requires in the English quarter. Go into Piale or Spithöver's reading-rooms, and you will hear all about the workmen's demonstration at Beaufort House, and the Bishop of London's Charge, but nothing about Ultramontanism or the Roman question. If you want Roman mosaics or Revalenta Arabica, Byzantine jewelry or Daffy's elixir, antique cameos or Cockle's pills, a reduced copy of Trajan's Column in gilt bronze, or photographs of the Campidoglio nearly as big as the Campidoglio itself, and at prices to match, I cannot recommend you to a better place than the Via Condotti.

They sell beautiful English nail-brushes in the Via Babuino, likewise Harvey's sauce and Warren's blacking, and some of the nicest darning-needles I was ever sent out to purchase. The newest English novels, published under the auspices of the Baron von Tauchnitz, can be obtained at the libraries, where there is such an unrestricted supply of English literature, that I have begun to entertain grave doubts as to the existence of the *Index Expurgatorius*, and have thought of asking for the *Jesuit in the Family* or the *Dairyman's Daughter*. I daresay that these and many other anti-Babylonish works are to be procured in the English quarter. They may be prohibited, but I have not yet met anyone who has failed in bringing to Rome anything on which he had set his mind. You either obtain a *lascia passare* from your banker, in which case your luggage is not examined at all, or you get judiciously close to the pontifical *doganiere* who is about to examine your first portmanteau at the Custom-house, and recite in his ear that sweet passage from the late Professor Wilson's *Isle of Palms* which has reference to the virtues of palm-oil, and concludes, if I mistake not, with a paraphrase of the classical saying, that he gives twice who gives quickly, and without making any fuss about the gift. With all this, I should not advise you to enter the Pontifical States with a full-length portrait of the Scarlet Lady of Babylon worked in Berlin-wool as a railway-rug, or with a photograph of Garibaldi, a bust of Mazzini, a freemason's apron, a copy of the *Unità Italiana*, and a six-chamber revolver lying loose in the tray of your trunk. You should be chary, too, of airing your Italian by volunteering to tell the first Roman citizen you meet on the railway, after crossing the frontier, that "*Il Papa il non possumus rester ici perchè il est cattivo uomo, et Rome madre de toutti les abominations*," than which I have heard some observations not in *much* worse taste from my countrymen and countrywomen travelling abroad.

Florence is a curious specimen enough of that which one may term international "half-and-half." English boarding-houses elbow the Italian *locandas;* English bakers sell you captain's-biscuits and pound-cakes; and Dr. Broomback's Academy for the Sons of Gentlemen is within twenty minutes' walk of the Pitti Palace. The hotels on the Swiss Lakes, where a clergyman of the Church of England is always retained, like the late Herr von Joel, "on the establishment," at a small salary, which he may considerably augment by travelling up and down the lake per steamer, and touting for patrons to the hotel—these are hybrid enough. Boulogne is a "half-and-half" place: so is Pau in the Pyrenees, so is Nice, so is Tours; but of all "half-and-half" regions in the world, commend me to that *rione* of Rome which lies between the steps of La Trinità del Monte and the Corso. There may you see, in the space of one half-hour, on a fine wintry afternoon, at least sixteen varieties of English old maids; and, I delight to add, not fewer than sixty species of English young maids, arrayed in the most ravishing cavalier hats, mainly with feathers in them, and with Balmoral boots whose heels are of the altitude of the obelisk of Rhamses, with crinolines surpassing in circumference the sweep of the Circus Maximus, and with looks as lofty as the Pyramid of Caius Cestius. On Sundays you meet them returning from the Protestant church, which is still in a kind of barn, *extra muros*, followed by plump flunkeys carrying the orthodox bag full of prayer-books. O Britain! O my country! we can't put the Church Service in the pocket of our Astracan jacket. It wouldn't hold anything bigger than a pocket-handkerchief of French cambric and *point d'Alençon*. We must have John Thomas to carry the sacred volumes, and thank Heaven that we are not as that publican.

I daresay there are English "publics" in the vicinity of the Piazza di Spagna, where John Thomas and other gentlemen in and out of livery may, when the *peine forte et dure* is over, obtain their beer. I hope to find out one of these Anglo-Roman taverns ere I have done. I fancy it a neat house, by the sign of the Cross Keys, and kept by a sturdy Briton, formerly stud-groom to the Earl of Worldsend—that great travelling milord who had the portraits of all his racehorses taken in mosaic, in revenge for being unable to purchase Gibson's tinted Venus—and whipper-in to the Roman Hunt. Meanwhile I expect every afternoon to stumble on the Cross Keys, and hear John Thomas blowing-up the landlord because his beer is Salt and Co.'s, and not Ind, Coope's, and there are no straw pipes and birdseye tobacco.

John Thomas does not often appear in plush in Rome. He usually affects a demure semi-livery—a subdued invisible green, or pepper-and-salt, with a narrow red cord down the seams of his pantaloons, and the merest phantom of a cockade in his hat. It is not the thing for English servitors to wear livery in Rome. A groom indeed may appear in full horsey costume; and I know a shop in the Babuino where they sell buckskin-breeches, and another where they specially advertise the preparation of oxalic acid, which cleans top-boots so nicely; but if we came to plush and powder and aiguillettes, the Delaplushes of Albion would find themselves signally eclipsed by the flunkeydom of Rome itself. Their costumes, you may not have heard ere this, were all designed by Rafaelle and Michel Angelo. They are certainly very sumptuous in fashion, and they all look—especially those of the Cardinals' footmen, to whom I shall have hereafter occasion to allude—as though they had been "built" at least two and a half centuries ago.

This is the prevailing air of Rome, to tell truth. Few of the babies in arms look less than two-hundred-and-fifty years old; and I have seen some, swaddled after the fashion of the Roman fasces in their ligatures, who looked two thousand. Were you ever on familiar terms with a human bas-relief, a Cupid with his wings cut off, who has tumbled into the mud, but has gotten some rags to cover his little bare back withal? That is a Roman boy. Did you ever know an animated cameo, chipped and foul and smirched, but a classical cameo for all that? That cameo is a Roman *contadina*. The Goths and the Visigoths, the Lombards and the French, have done a good deal in their way towards breaking up Rome into little bits, but they have not succeeded in effacing the personal type of the Roman people. As for their character, I do not imagine they have changed much during the last twenty centuries, and that they would not at all object to a sovereign who gave them plenty of bread and plenty of games. I have little doubt, in fact, that they are the same Roman people, or rather Roman populace, whose ways and manners were intuitively divined by a theatrical manager by the river-side, in London, who did some very capital business in Queen Elizabeth's time—a manager, it is said, who made but a poor actor, but was a dramatist of some note, and wrote the plays of *Julius Cæsar* and *Coriolanus*.

I think I have said enough to show that it is not in the Piazza di Spagna, not in the Via Condotti, not in the Via Babuino, that you will hear aught that is cogent concerning Roman politics. You might obtain a tip for the next Derby with much greater facility than you could get an inkling of the dilemmas of the Pope and the intrigues of the Sacred College. If I might venture on a suggestion for the improvement of this convenient but unpicturesque quarter of the Eternal City, it might be that in the windows of the few shops not wholly devoted to the sale of English wares, or articles most readily purchased by English people, they should write up, *Qui si parla Italiano;* just as in the Rue de la Paix, Paris, they might announce, *Ici on parle Français;* otherwise an unhappy Italian, wandering in this Anglicised faubourg, might go melancholy mad under the importunities of "half-and-half" tradesmen or spruce young English shopmen specially imported from home to jump over Roman counters.

In conclusion, let me hint that no tourist need be nervous about coming to Rome on the ground of being unable to "speak the languages." Nor, being at Rome, is he expected to do as the Romans do. He will find the Romans only too glad and proud to do as Britons do. They are also capable of conjugating the verb to "do" in all its moods and tenses, and in several senses. There is no place in Europe where a travelling Englishman can make himself more thoroughly at home than at Rome; and only imagine the advantage of having the Scarlet Lady herself, *in propriâ personâ,* over the way, as it were, to abuse and shake your head at.

XXV.

CHRISTMAS-DAY IN ROME.

Christmas! I hope you have had a merry one in England, with all my heart. There has been an immensity of eating and drinking in the British islands, I can imagine, and overflowing audiences at the London theatres and Mr. Cremer's toyshop. Mr. Boleno has been anxious to know how we all were to-morrow, and has burnt Mr. Barnes in the small of the back with a red-hot poker, and, at a later period of the evening, has favoured the audience with "Tippitywitchet." Some thousands of the inhabitants of most large English towns have kept Christmas by getting excessively drunk, and beating their wives and families; and others have done homage to "Merrie Christmas" by going, quite involuntarily, without any dinner. The subscriptions to the poor-boxes of the police-courts have been, I trust, abundant; likewise the contributions to coal, and blanket, and soup-kitchen funds for the poor. The publishers have produced unnumbered Christmas books, blazing with gold and bright colours, and the columns of the illustrated papers have broken out in the customary eruption of yule-logs, holly, mistletoe, pigs'-heads with lemons between their tusks, Christmas carols and Christmas stories, in which the adventure of a hippopotamus-hunter on the White Nile or a new theory about Shakespeare's sonnets has been connected, somehow, with Old

Father Christmas. Yes, I can picture the festive season at home, combined with the Christmas fog and the Christmas drizzle, Christmas colds and coughs, the Christmas tax-gatherer, and the Christmas bills, and the Christmas blunderbus put to your head on the 26th of December—I mean Christmas-boxes—and other tidings of comfort and joy. Christmas comes but once a year; and those who are in exile, or are sojourners among the tents of Kedar, would not wish it, I fancy, to come oftener; for Christmas away from home and friends and children—the bills and the fogs notwithstanding—is but a melancholy time, a time when you feel inclined to go to bed on Christmas-eve, and not get up again till New-year's-day.

We do not keep our Christmas in Rome in the manner to which you are traditionally accustomed in England. I passed a very un-English Christmas-day, too, last year at Berlin, although there was a seasonably hard frost on the Linden, and they gave us at the *table-d'hôte* a preparation of treacle, macaroons, and farinaceous food, which passed current as plum-pudding. The Christmas but one before that I was in America; and, although I went to Canada on purpose to have a real English dinner on the 25th, I found things rather dull than otherwise in New York, and got into terrible trouble with the Yankees for hinting that, from a holly, mistletoe, roast-beef, and miscellaneous-grocery point of view, they did not keep Christmas at all. And now I am spending Christmas among the old stones of Rome.

We had turkey *à l'Anglaise* for dinner on Tuesday—that is to say, a roast *gallinaccio*, with a mass of soft substance in the dish, resembling a Scotch haggis slightly impregnated with truffles, which was supposed to represent stuffing. There were mince-pies, too, which, to judge from their density and tenacity under the knife, might have been blocks of travertine from the pyramid of Caius Cestius; but a mince-pie is a thing to look at, and not to swallow. I never knew more than one reasonable being above the age of nine who actually ate a mince-pie, and he died without making a will. Our Christmas banquet at the Hôtel d'Angleterre, Rome, was wound up with a magnificent plum-pudding, with a cupola like San Carlo in the Corso, and a streaming cap of melted-butter. It was a wonderful pudding, and tasted very much like jugged-hare kneaded into a stiff paste with chocolate, figs, raspberry-jam, stewed prunes, and roast chestnuts. I was helped twice to this dainty, and, feeling slightly unwell next morning, took up a Tauchnitz edition of *Old Mortality*, and could perfectly sympathise with Mause Headrigg's strong aversion to plum-porridge. It is a prelatical dish, certainly; a pretentious, incongruous, deceitful jumble—like Ritualism, for instance.

Likewise, and abating a few parties given by English residents in Rome to their friends on Christmas-eve, and numerous congregations at the afternoon and evening services of the English church outside the Porta del Popolo, there was very little that could be called seasonable to English sympathies in our Roman Christmas. It was a great deal too fine, to begin with. The sky was, as usual, spotlessly blue—I think I could count on my fingers the number of clouds I have seen during four weeks' residence in Rome—and the sun shone out so brightly and sturdily that the grimy old city seemed absolutely to wink and quiver under his beams. Those abominable little closes and wynds at the top of the Corso towards the Tiber, with their perennial festoons of linen hanging on poles from all the windows—whatever can the Romans do with their skirts and petticoats after they have been washed and ironed? it is certain they never wear them—and their permanent way of vegetable rubbish, loose stones, fragments of hats, boots, and tin kettles, and dead dogs and cats: these wretched little twin brethren of Church-lane, St. Giles's, were lit up, as though in honour of Christmas, by the all-searching sun. Our water-colour painters would have felt great joy to see the golden bars of light, lying transversely on the muck-heaps, tipping the jagged stones of the staircases, and glinting across the cracked panes of the casements. There were, indeed, some charming effects of light and shade, and the view, say towards the rear of the Porta Ripetta, was highly picturesque; but I should have liked it better for an invasion in the foreground of Sir John Thwaites, assisted by Mr. Bazalgette, and followed by the halberdiers of the Metropolitan Board of Works, who, more ruthless than Robert Guiscard or the Constable de Bourbon, should destroy these closes and wynds utterly, and, from the Via della Scrofa to the Porta Ripetta, leave not one stone upon another.

The *tramontana,* which has been rather troublesome lately, forbore to blow on Christmas-day, and in the sun the weather was as warm as June in England. The *forestieri* all rushed out without their greatcoats, and the ladies without their warm shawls, which may account for the numerous cases of relaxed sore-throat of which I have since heard in polite society. I counted, however, on the Pincian, no fewer than thirty-four pairs of white pantaloons among the male Romans, which, for the 25th of December, was pretty well. At every street-corner and under every archway there were stalls heaped high and thick with fresh flowers—with heartsease, mignonette, monthly roses, violets, camelias, ferns and grasses, and wild-flowers, without number as to species, and without names so far as my powers of nomenclature extend.

Next to the environs of Seville, where everything which is not covered with oranges is covered with roses, and the Valley of Mexico, which is one parterre of flowers all the year round, must come Rome as the chosen haunt of Flora. She revels in wild-flowers among the ruins, the tombs, the chinks of the Colosseum, and even in the waste Campagna. She runs over with tame-flowers in the gardens of her villas which fringe the Seven Hills. Flowers in Rome are literally cheaper than dirt; for dirt is a dear article—it costs lives. For tenpence you may buy such a bowpot in Rome as an English duchess might think cheap at a guinea in Covent-garden; such a bowpot as might make an English sempstress, stitching in her solitary garret, calculate how many hours of toil and miles of needle and thread it would take to purchase one poor sprig of mignonette from that abounding loveliness. You are spared in Rome the detestable nuisance of the flower-girls who in Venice and Florence dog your footsteps and thrust bouquets into your button-hole whether you will or not. Every street-corner or vacant space is, as I have said, a Marché de la Madeleine, and you may spend your loose halfpence in flowers, or leave them alone, as you choose.

The only peripatetic vendor of flowers whom I have yet met in the Eternal City is a humpbacked dwarf, who on week-days haunts the outside of Piale's reading-room on the Piazza di Spagna, and is a small Birnam Wood of choice flowers. You may make poor Lancelot Gobbo's fortune for a fortnight if you give him say forty *bajocchi*—'tis but 1*s*. 7*d*. —for an armful of rainbow. On Sundays, when Piale's, in deference to the prejudices of its Protestant patrons, is closed, the dwarf changes his station to the outside of the Caffè di Roma, on the Corso, whither, it may be hinted, a considerable section of the Protestant patrons resort to read the last *Galignani*, invisible at Piale's. On the Sabbath the Gobbo does not vend flowers; he has a pair of buffalo-horns for sale, beautiful in their polish and curvilinear spikiness, with which he stands sentry, a horn in each hand, like a stunted terra-cotta figure of Plenty, bearing ossified cornucopias. With a view to Protestant patrons, he has mastered a small stock of English. "Little lady, buy flower? bu'fil." "Little gentleman, buy horn? bu'fil." Beyond this his Anglo-Saxon does not extend. You might fancy him to be of the family of Albert Smith's donkey-boy at Alexandria, with his "Giv' um sixpence; ole gentleman always giv' um sixpence." I have often purchased flowers from the dwarf, but I have not yet ventured upon a pair of buffalo-horns. Such a possession might give a subject for a postscript to the author of *What will he do with it?* What should I do with a pair of buffalo-horns? How should I pack them? how bestow them when I got my horns home? I have an idea that when I take to discounting bills at sixty per cent—which is not at all an unpractical way of winding-up a froward and turbulent youth

—I will buy a pair of buffalo-horns, and hang them up in a bleak counting-house in Thavies-inn, between a Ready Reckoner and a List of Terms in the Exchequer of Pleas. They shall be typical horns, and symbolical of hardness and smoothness, and of the ultimate impalement of my acceptors on the spikes.

I confess that the sight of the blue sky, the bright sun, and the fresh flowers rather threw me out in my reckoning, and rendered my ideas of parallels of latitude somewhat hazy. "How to have fresh roses on Christmas-day" is a recipe I cut many years ago from one of the early numbers of the pleasant *Family Herald.* Remembering that old Time is still a-flying, you gather your rosebuds while you may, and whenever you have any spare pence in your pocket, and snipping off the end of the stalk with a sharp pair of scissors, seal them carefully with red wax,—black is unlucky, —wrap them in silver paper, and put them in the top left-hand drawer in the best bedroom, punctually locking the drawer, lest Betty the housemaid's curiosity should be the means of your buds prematurely blowing and withering, as is the way with roses and housemaids. Then on Christmas morning, if you haven't lost the key and forgotten all about your hidden treasures, you unlock the drawer, release your buds from their prison of tissue paper, snip the stalks again above the sealing-wax, pop them into lukewarm water, and lo, in the course of ten minutes, your roses are all a-blowing, and you may go down to breakfast with a flower in your button-hole, as proud as a dog with two tails. This is the pleasant theory. I remember that I once tried the recipe practically. It was a dreadful spectacle which broke upon my eyes on Christmas-morning. So much stained tissue-paper, so many dried and withered leaves, and a skeleton stalk or two. That was all. Did you ever assist at the unrolling of a mummy? Did your horse ever shy at the skeleton of a cow picked clean by obscene birds in a mountain gorge by moonlight? I felt, gazing on the dead roses, as men have felt when they have come upon such sights as those.

Christmas-day was observed as a close holiday in Rome. For us heretic foreigners inn-tables were lavishly spread, but among the Romans there did not seem to be any signs of extraneous eating and drinking going on, and indeed I have been informed that although the *natale* is a church *festa* of the most solemn order, there are devout Romanists who fast on Christmas-day. They have a feast only of prayers and "functions." Secular indulgences they reserve for the *capo d' anno*, or New-year's-day.

The only evidences of banqueting I observed during the day among the natives was at a little "*osteria di vino padronale con cucina*," in the Vicola della Rocca Tarpeia, into which I took the liberty of peeping during a morning stroll. Seven wagoners in Spanish mantles, brigand-hats, and overalls of goatskins, were sitting at a square deal table—a mere rough board on tressels. In the midst of them was a bottle with a wicker base, precisely like the oil-flasks one sees at the Italian warehouses in London, but of about eight times the size familiar to English eyes, and filled with the *vino padronale*, which comes from Velletri, I believe, and is black and heady, but not bad drinking, at about three-pence a quart. To them entered a kitchen wench, unwashed, but comely, and with a fine Roman nose and eyes like sloes. She had thrown her white petticoat over her head, where it formed a most artistic coiffure; but her *jupons* not being in duplicate, and her skirt but scanty, her lower limbs rather suffered in consequence. *Il faut souffrir pour être belle.* She, from a large pipkin, with a semi-circular handle, emptied *right upon the bare deal boards of the table* a prodigious mountain of maccaroni. It must have been hot, for it smoked. I think it was dressed with cheese, for it smelt so strongly that one of the buffaloes in the wains outside coughed. I conjecture that it was also accommodated with oil, or some other fatty matter, and that some hot splashes thereof reached the floor, for I noticed one of the wagoners' dogs, sitting by, lick his lips and wag his tail approvingly. It was a strange sight, this Campagna of grease, with the oil-flask of wine towering in the midst like St. Peter's. Upon this vast mess the seven wagoners fell tooth and nail. The simile is, perchance, not strictly correct. Teeth may be *de trop.* You should never bite or chew maccaroni, but swallow each pipe whole, grease and all, as though it were so much flattery. But their nails they did use, seeing that they ate the maccaroni with their fingers. What wondrous twistings and turnings back of their heads, what play of the muscles of their throats, what straining of their eyeballs and vasty openings of their jaws, did I study as they swallowed their food. I never saw a boa-constrictor swallow a rabbit, but here were seven men gorging boa-constrictors. They swept the board clean in an astonishingly short space of time, and then, referring from time to time to the *bottiglione* of wine, they fell a-gambling for coppers. This was their way of keeping Christmas; and I hope nobody was stabbed, and that the buffaloes were not kept waiting until sundown, when, as everybody knows, the malaria begins to steal abroad. In a fashion not widely different from this, I daresay, did Roman wagoners feast two thousand years ago, long before the Sibyl of Tivoli revealed to Imperial Cæsar the vision of the Christmas-day which was to come.

XXVI.

ROMAN "SHAVES."

December 27.

SENOR FIGARO, ex-body-servant to Count Almaviva, and go-between-in-chief to Cupid, all shrewdest of shavers as he was, seems to have made a slight mistake when he fixed on Number 15, Plaza San Tomas, in the city of Seville, as the fittest abode *per un barbiere di qualità*. He should have come to Rome. He should have set up his shop at the angle of the Palazzo Braschi, near the Piazza Navona, with that famous tailor for a next-door neighbour who has given his name to a statue which for ages has consoled the Romans for the lack of a free press and comic publications. Figaro and Pasquin would have made a pair most justly formed to meet by Nature. The tailor would have undertaken the satirical department in Roman politics; the *barbiere di qualità* would have attended to the shaving. There never was probably such a city as Rome for "shaves." Literally, the consumption of razors, grindstones, strops, and soap susceptible of forming a soft lather, must be enormous. How many thousand tonsures are there to be kept smooth and shining! a tonsure is the antithesis of a grass-plat, but it needs quite as much care and attention. How many thousand clerical maxillaries are there every day to soap and scrape! And then Beadledom requires its diurnal clean shave, and Flunkeydom—for the beadles and flunkeys of Rome are as numerous as the camp-followers of a Sepoy regiment before the mutiny. Only the little boys who swing the censers, and the shrill *soprani*—doleful creatures, who are called emphatically "the Pope's singers;" I mean Mustafa and the rest—can afford to disparage the barber's shear.

So far for the literal shaving which has to be done in Rome; but it is not that precisely which I mean. The "shaves" most plentiful in Rome are of the metaphorical kind. The names of these shaves is legion. As Venice is the chief city in Europe for gossip, Florence for small scandal, Milan for libels, and Genoa for downright denunciations of public men, so is Rome the capital for "shaves"—I mean for palpable lies most plausibly related, for baseless rumours most artfully propped up, for impudent fabrications most gravely retailed. The lives of these lies are but as those of the ephemera; but they flutter their little wings bravely for a time, and they amuse a people who otherwise might find existence rather dull. So every day has its fresh shave, and the cry is, "Figaro *su* and Figaro *giù*, Figaro *quà* and Figaro *là*." *Bella città*, this Rome.

In Jerusalem the *odium theologicum* has the advantage of being kept perpetually at boiling-point by three distinct sets of Christians—the Greeks, the Latins, and the Armenians—while the Mahometan Turks preserve order, and take care that the line of sectarian difference is drawn on this side throat-cutting. In Rome there are three different classes in society who supply the *caffès* and *salons* with "shaves," wholesale and retail. There are the French "shaves," to begin with. The French, although the Imperial troops have left, form a very numerous community in Rome, and one which contrives to keep itself to itself as completely as it does in Leicester-square and Soho. The French academy at the villa Medici has its colony of *rapins;* the French drawing-masters and modellers for bronze-workers form another section; there are little French *cafés* and little French *restaurants*, and little French washerwomen, and little French milliners, of whom M. Joseph Surface, Milor Anglais, of the Piazza di Spagna, sometimes orders a bonnet; and there are quite a surprising number of French commercial travellers.

I like the Gallic bagman much; I admire his shrewdness, his tomfool jokes, his inexhaustible good-nature. I like "Anatole Roux, voyageur, Maison Proux, Doux, Choux et compagnie, Faubourg St. Denis, à Paris," whose card I have often found stuck so proudly over his number in out-of-the-way foreign inns, and sometimes thrust beneath my door, lest I should be in want of a little hair-dye, or a few artificial flowers, or a porcelain statuette of Pradier's *baigneuse*, or so. I passed an uncommonly jolly fortnight last spring, in the south of Spain, solely in the society of French bagmen; but I was not prepared for the very magisterial appearance which he puts in here. It is obvious that you cannot eat mosaic, or drink cameos, or dye your hair with porphyry and alabaster *tazze;* and as the Romans do not appear to make anything beyond the articles I have named, and their state of civilisation is not quite up to a mark which should cause them to relish *our* commodities—marine engines, threshing-machines, anchovy sauce, Balbriggan hose, tracts, and pickles—they are compelled to fall back on France for their supply of lighter luxuries, and the French bagman is consequently continually going and coming. He seems to be generally, from his accent, a native of Lyons or Marseilles. His thirst for *petits verres* is insatiable; he is powerfully scented with garlic; he smuggles his own *caporal* and *petits Bordeaux* into the Eternal City; and his constant complaint is that cards and dominoes are excluded from the Roman *caffès*. When he wants the waiter, he shouts "*Eh! la boutique!*" which he considers a humorous compromise between the French "*garçon*" and the Italian "*bottega.*" His stock of Italian does not generally go beyond "*Sì*" and "*Diavolo.*" He has a profound contempt for the ancient monuments of Rome. I heard a Zouave ask him yesterday if he had been to the Colosseum, to which replied Anatole Roux, "*Je me moque pas mal du Colisée. Ma partie c'est dans les chocolats pralinés.*" He considers St. Peter's, as an ecclesiastical edifice, to be infinitely inferior to St. Louis des Français. For the rest, when he is not a Red Republican and Socialist, he is a very good Catholic, and his "*Le Saint Père, voyez-vous, faut qu'il reste à Rome—*" with a thump on the table, and a "*fichtre!*" or a "*tronc de cheval!*" to cap it, is audible in many coffee-house arguments.

If this good fellow could only sell as many razor-strops and cakes of scented soap as he sells "shaves," he would very soon make his fortune. He is the great expositor of French fables in Rome. He always has his news direct from "*l'ambassade, voyez-vous.*" Before the expeditionary corps went away it was from the "*état major, voyez-vous,*" that he derived his "shaves." They are astounding. Anatole Roux told me, only last night, that the Empress of the French had already been three days in Rome, but, with the exception of a visit to the Baths of Caracalla by moonlight, she had not stirred from the Quirinal; in which venerable palace she was closeted for many hours every day with the Pope, his Holiness paying his visits by means of the secret passage which, as everybody knows, leads from the Quirinal to the Vatican. One might have told Anatole that the secret passage he spoke of led from the Vatican to the Castle of St. Angelo; but what does such a trifling discrepancy matter? According to Anatole, the French are coming back in force on the 1st of January. His brother-in-law at Toulon—"*qui travaille fort dans les houilles là-bas, voyez-vous*"—wrote to him last week to say that eleven French ironclads were fitting out for the new expedition to Rome. The Emperor was determined "*d'en finir avec cette sacrée question Romaine; car l'Empereur, voyez-vous*"—and here Anatole gave the customary thump on the marble table, and smothered, in a tremendous "*fichtre*" his further exposition of Imperial Cæsar's policy with regard to Rome; of which Anatole very probably knows as much Imperial Cæsar does himself.

It is quite feasible that many of these "shaves" should come from the French Embassy, or from any other of the Legations resident in Rome, for they are all more idle and more useless than even the ordinary ruck of those idle and useless institutions. I would not venture to suggest that the Minister Plenipotentiary takes bagmen into his confidence, or that the *attachés* frequent the *estaminet;* but diplomacy has its cooks and its scullions, its valets and doorkeepers, its *infima plebs* of gossips and hangers-on; and from these gentry may proceed some of the astounding stories we hear.

Next to the French "shaves" are the *Italianissimi*. They are whispered in the Corso, and murmured at the Antico Caffè Greco. They are simply the *réchauffés* of the last lies of the Florentine press. They are the wonderful legends of which I have already given you specimens, and relate mainly to brigands disguised at the hotels and lying *perdus* in the convents, cannon planted on the banks of the Tiber, midnight assassination, arrests, espionage, terrorism, and so forth. I have had very few *Italianissimo* "shaves" to record during the last few days; for the fertility even of the *Italianissimo* imagination has its limits, and Rome is so thoroughly and profoundly tranquil that the birds of ill-omen can have scarcely known what to croak about. The last *Italianissimo* "shave" is a very mild and misty one. We are to have, it appears, "next February" a tremendous outbreak. The flower of the Roman youth, it is said, have volunteered into Garibaldi's army, and subsequently have taken a short term of service in that of Victor Emmanuel. Towards the end of next carnival *la nostra prodissima gioventù* will be liberated, and will come down on the temporal power like a hundred of bricks.

These are the "shaves" of ultra-Italianism. The third class of "shavers" are the Ultramontanes. The lies these devout politicians tell are half of a hopeful, and half of an ominous nature. Now they report that the King of Italy has informed Baron Ricasoli that he intends to march on Rome immediately after Easter; now that his Majesty has been taken with pains in his stomach and in his conscience, and has implored his father confessor to make his peace with the Holy Father. They blow hot and cold, like the man in the fable. One day it is the Sultan who has suddenly bethought him that the *Sommo Pontefice* must be own brother to the Sheikh ul Islam, and has entreated Pio Nono to take up his residence at the Old Seraglio. The next it is heretic England who feels qualms of the spirit, and implores Pio Nono to come to Malta, to Brighton, to Belfast, or any other spot in the heretical dominions he may select. Mr. Gladstone's sore-throat—and I am sorry to say the eminent statesman is still an invalid—has been productive of innumerable shaves. If Mr. Cardwell goes to see the Dying Gladiator at the Capitol, there are dark and distant rumours of "English gold" and its maleficent influences. If Sir William Hutt is seen on horseback on the Pincio, he means mischief; and there is more in the purchase of a cameo bracelet by the Duke of Argyll than meets the eye.

Most of the Ultramontane "shaves," however, contrive to converge. There is one central point on which all the shovel-hats seem agreed. A "great power" is about to "interfere" in favour of the Pope. Which is the great power, and what should it interfere for, in favour of a poor old gentleman whom nobody wants to interfere with, and who ought to be thinking of a variety of things—the transitory nature of human life included?

It cannot be France. France has washed her hands of Rome for the present—washed them as Pilate did, the Ultramontanes mutter.

It cannot be Italy. There is the King's speech in evidence to prove that Italy does not mean to interfere with the Pope one way or the other; and the bitterest enemies of the Rè Galantuomo dare not insinuate that he says one thing and means another—the father-confessor "shave" notwithstanding.

It cannot be Great Britain. The great body of Englishmen are, I conjecture, wholly indifferent as to what becomes of the Pope of Rome. If there be a party in England actively desirous that he should remain at the Vatican, it would probably be found not far from Exeter Hall. Yes, I think the "place with the Greek name," including Clapham, would be sorry if the Pope fell through. There would be nothing left to platformise about.

It cannot be Spain—the bloody Popish reaction in that unhappy country notwithstanding. Spain might very well wish to set the Papacy on its legs again, and revive Torquemada and the *auto-da-fés* into the bargain; but Spain is governmentally bankrupt and a beggar, and Doña Isabel de Borbon is too much occupied with ennobling a Meneses and an Obregon to think of "interfering" in Italy.

It *must* be the United States of America. Already has the news been flashed to us from Berlin—strangest place in all Europe for such news to come from—that President Johnson has offered the Pope an asylum in America, "where he would be more independent than elsewhere." The presence of another American frigate at Civita Vecchia, and the visit of successive instalments of her officers to Rome, have strengthened this "shave" and given consistence to the lather. I am not prepared to deny its truth. I am not prepared to deny anything which has reference to the United States of America. Anything and all things are possible in that marvellous country. And I must confess that with my own eyes I saw yesterday a Yankee lieutenant at Piale's reading-rooms, purchasing a *carte-de-visite*, price eight *bajocchi*, of the Supreme Pontiff; it is within my knowledge that the purser inquired only the day before yesterday at Spithœver's the price of one of the three-sheet photographs of the Forum Romanum.

XXVII.

COSE DI ROMA.

December 29.

Pius IX. carries his seventy-four years lustily, and in the twenty-first year of his Pontificate—ominous apogee rarely exceeded by those who have sate in the chair of St. Peter—looks as though he were quite ready to begin a new lease of life and a fresh term of office, and to go through both gaily. The cause of the Vicar may be well-nigh desperate — the treasury may be at a deplorably low ebb, the investments in the Pontifical lottery for January unsatisfactory, and the coming in of Peter's Pence but slow—the negotiations with Italy may have fallen through, and the Commendatore Tonello shaken the dust off his feet at the Porta del Popolo and returned to Florence—the Papal Dragoons may be murmuring at the favouritism shown to the Papal Zouaves, while the Antibes Legionaries are grumbling because the Papal Gendarmes had new buckskin breeches and topboots served out to them on Christmas-day—the Palatine Guard, who are mainly composed of the *bourgeoisie* of Rome, may have displayed a melancholy reluctance to get under arms at the Vatican, and several members of the Guardia Nobile resigned their commissions; all of which are among the latest "shaves" current in Rome. But still Pio Nono keeps a cheerful countenance and an unruffled mien; and in the joyous serenity of his bearing goes far to vindicate the *refrain* of the old student's song, "The Pope he leads a happy life."

To tell truth, the Supreme Pontiff, considering his innumerable woes, and the excruciating anguish which, according to the Ultramontane press and the French episcopate, the wickedness of the "Italian revolution" has caused him, looks uncommonly jolly. He is emphatically what gushing young ladies call a "dear old duck." A happy, beaming, shining face is his, for all the wrinkles which time has placed there; his eye, although the lids droop a little, is bright and cheery; and his mouth, though his molars must be growing few and far between, still preserves its peculiarly winning and benevolent smile. It is not a strong face, not a clever face, and certainly not a wise one; but its every lineament is full of amenity, mansuetude, and *bonhomie.* It is a face which does you good to look at—contrasting so strongly, as it does, with the sallow, cadaverous, skulking, eavesdropping, area-sneaking, hang-dog physiognomies which one so frequently meets under shovel-hats. The Roman-Catholic clergy are, no doubt, as a body, learned, virtuous, and pious; yet it needs no Lavater, no Gall or Spurzheim, to discern that their looks belie them, and that out of Ireland—where the priest is generally a hale, comely, cheerful-looking gentleman—your Romish ecclesiastic, facially at least, has the air not only of having gone into the Church, but of having just broken into one with a view to the communion-plate.

Thursday was the Pope's birthday; the shops were closed, and all the bells of the three-hundred-and-sixty-four churches rang quadruple peals, which, by courtesy, might be termed merry, but which must have been slightly instrumental in swelling the Roman bills of mortality for that particular day. English hospital-nurses are sometimes accused—I know not with what truth—of pulling the pillows from under the heads of moribunds who, like Charles II., are "an unconscionable time in dying." The process is known as "easing them off." But I think I would back the three-hundred-and-sixty-four peals of church-bells in Rome to ease obstinate patients off more effectually.

If the bells failed, I think I would try the barrel-organs, which swarm in Rome, and are ground at the unholiest of hours. I do not know if Mr. Bass, M.P., has ever visited Rome, and put up in the Via Bocca di Leone; but if he would be good enough to winter here, I imagine that his experience of organ-grinding agony would make him slightly charitable towards that minor phase of the torture we endure in England. I don't know exactly what is the matter with the Roman organs; but there is apparently some derangement in their viscera or some fracture of the brass small-tooth combs whereon the tunes are set, which produces the most extraordinary jumble of sacred and secular music I have ever listened to. The organist begins to grind "Adeste Fideles," and it suddenly gets mixed up with the "Guards' Waltz;" while I have never heard "Dixie's Land" without the "Dead March in Saul," or an air to that effect, being interspersed with it—cacophony being worse confounded by a series of screeches such as those once given by the macaws in the Pantheon conservatory, when they smelt the sandwiches eaten for lunch underneath the counter by the young-lady attendants in the wax-flower department.

After all, this disastrous jangling of organs is not so very inconsistent with the actual aspect of affairs. The lay element jars quite as discordantly with the ecclesiastical in all things Roman. You shall not walk a furlong anywhere in this city of incongruities without seeing the jarring and hearing the jangling. Enter St. Peter's; watch the crowd of devotees kissing the toe of the graven image in the marble chair; listen to the mass; bend your knee when the bell rings and the Host is elevated; then emerge—it is to be hoped, subdued and edified—and if you look from the loggie of the great vestibule, just before you come to the equestrian statue of Constantine, you will see a paved courtyard, two of whose sides are formed by the very walls of St. Peter's. On the opposite side is a guard-house; and in that court the recruits of the Zouave corps are being instructed in the bayonet exercise. I saw this sight myself, after mass, five days ago. An idle choir-boy, peeping from a window in the Basilica while the most awful mystery of the Romish faith was being celebrated—and a good many idle choristers, and idle priests too, may be noted at every solemn "function"—might have watched the Pope's mercenaries being taught the art of running people through the bowels. Something must be wrong somewhere. Someone must have blundered at some time. Either the Mass, or murder, must be a mistake.

I said I would back the bells, and failing them the barrel-organs. But there is another way in Rome by means of which nervous people may be driven mad, and sick people "eased off." Commend me to the *pifferari*. These are the bagpipers from the Apennines, who make a descent on Rome during the four weeks of Advent, ostensibly for the purpose of serenading the Virgin; really for that of cadging for coppers. They are villanous-looking fellows, whose costume is picturesque in photography, but revolting in an age which prefers untattered coats and clean shirts to particoloured rags and mangy goatskin breeches. I suppose that when the brigands dance with their *care spose* they engage a gang of *pifferari* to pipe to them. Some of these people are said to earn a living, out of Advent, by standing as models to the artists, and not to be mountaineers at all. Equally libellous assertions are made with regard to the Highland bagpipers, who shiver in kilts in the back-streets of London. But you have seen these Roman *pifferari*, mobbed by the boys, mocked by the cabmen, and moved on by the police, in London also. You know the horrible din they elicit from their bags, and the wild and grotesque capers they cut. Their real object, both in Italy and in England, is the same—the extraction of pence from the public; but I was not aware until I came to Rome that blasting on the bagpipes and dancing in the gutter until *bajocchi* are wrapped in paper and flung out of the window, had anything to do with Advent and the Virgin Mary. These *pifferari* are, indeed, the Roman "waits." They begin to blow at five o'clock in the morning, preferably choosing for their performances the neighbourhood of hotels frequented by heretics. I did my best, on the morning of Christmas-eve, to invest one of the serenaders with the order of the Cold Pig; but it is difficult to get a good aim with the contents of a water-jug at 5 A.M.

The Pope took an airing yesterday on the Pincian Hill. The Pontiff usually turns out in very handsome state, in a glass coach brave in gilding, and six black horses with streaming manes and tails, with crimson-leather trappings covered with gilt bosses. The reins are of gold-cord, and in the midst of a great hammer-cloth of crimson and gold, and silken tags and squabs, and fringes and tassels—an imposing structure, and in itself no mean rival of the Pontifical *sedia gestatoria*—sits the Pope's coachman, a dumpling-faced, rosy-cheeked, blue-gilled, bright-eyed, pottle-stomached charioteer, obviously full of maccaroni, polenta, risotto, wine of Orvieto, and other good things; yet with a devout twinkle in his eyes, and a *Deo-gratias* smack on his lips. There is a touch at once of the toastmaster, the beadle, the Friar of Orders Gray, and the late Mr. Brackenbury, of the "Age" stage-coach, about him. A combined halo of the old India House, the London Tavern, the Bull-and-Mouth coaching-office, and the crypt of Canterbury Cathedral, surrounds him. Perhaps the elder Mr. Weller, with a rosary in his pocket-book among the extra whiplashes and samples of corn, and a breviary bound up with his *Little Warbler*, might most fittingly sit for a portrait of the Pope's coachman.

I wonder what he thinks of the Roman question, and whether he has ever heard of Garibaldi. His berth is not quite so easy a one as that of the beefy creature in a cauliflower-wig who conducts her Britannic Majesty's eight cream-colours; but still the Pontifical *scuderia* must be one of the most comfortable of loose-boxes. Good wages, a kind master, a commanding position, and any amount of indulgences and absolution; for of course when the Pope dies his coachman drives him straight up to heaven, and St. Peter opens the celestial gates with a crash to let the grand equipage in. This high servitor is most sumptuously clad. I need scarcely say that he wears a cocked-hat. Indeed, as I have previously noticed, the Romish Church seems to hold that out of a cocked-hat, or at least a shovel one, there is no salvation. They put almost babes and sucklings here into shovels, and highly preposterous do the puny students look, straggling to their classes in hats like unto that of Don Basilio in the *Barbiere*, and loose tags hanging from their shoulders, as though they were leading-strings abandoned by careless nurses. The Pope's coachman's hat is not triangularly cocked, after the "Egham, Staines, and Windsor" pattern, but is the real, blocked, built-up fore-and-aft hat, such as we are familiar with on that frightful effigy of F.M. the Duke of Wellington, K.G., at Hyde Park-corner. He wears crimson-silk stockings, and the buckles of his shoes are gilt. His coat, waistcoat, and continuations are of the superb fabric known as "imperial velvet:" a rich velluted design, embossed on a damask ground. It is said to be worth five guineas a yard; but, for all its splendour, the wearer has an odd appearance of being made up of window-curtains and flock paper-hangings, fresh from Jackson and Graham's.

This is the Pope's "turn-out:"—sometimes there are eight instead of six horses. Three, four, five, or six footmen, cloaked, sworded, cocked-hatted, and aiguilletted—I am not certain how many there are, but there seem to be a great number of them—hang on behind, by crimson straps, to a splash-board elaborately carved and gilt, but much too small for even two flunkeys. A person in military uniform, but of civilian aspect, and mounted on a large horse, precedes the *cortége*, wildly waving a drawn sword above his head, to let Christendom know that the Pope is coming. Dragoons, clanking their sword-scabbards against their stirrup-irons, bring up the rear. The entire spectacle leaves you with a mingled impression of Cardinal Wolsey's procession to Tod-place, and the Sheriffs of London and Westminster going to chop fagots and count hobnails at Westminster. Christian archæologists and Oriental scholars will tell you that it was precisely in this fashion the Vicar's Master entered Jerusalem eighteen hundred years ago.

The liberated Roman people, in 1849, made a bonfire of most of these rattletraps. They did not hang a single cardinal, or do any harm to the Pope's coachman, but they burnt the Pontifical and cardinalitian paraphernalia wherever they could find them. To save the few remaining equipages from destruction the Republican Government, it is said, used them for the conveyance of the sick to the hospitals. Then the people respected them. But the vitality of pomps and vanities is most strange to mark. Human folly is the real Phœnix, perpetually rising from its ashes. I daresay, could the Court of Star Chamber be reëstablished to-morrow, stars would begin to glisten on the ceiling of some room in Sir Charles Barry's house, dozens of applications would be sent in for the office of Sworn Tormentor, and the means would soon be found for putting Mr. Bright in the boots and Mr. Beales in the Scavenger's Daughter. Given a Legitimist Government in France to-morrow, and the tricolor would turn pale, and lilies crop up through the eagles of their own accord. "Vive Henri Quatre!" and La Belle Gabrielle would silence "Partant pour la Syrie," and somebody would be sure to discover the Sainte Ampoule in a *bric-à-brac* shop on the Quai Voltaire.

The bonfires of 1849 burnt his Government out of Rome, and his Holiness away to Gaeta; but the times changed, and the Pontifical "properties" made their appearance again, looking as fresh — or rather as hopelessly antiquated — as ever. The tumbrils and ambulances of St. Jean d'Angely brought back something else besides cartridges, and shells, and kegs of powder. They were full of mitres and crosiers, censers and holy-water-pots, cocked-hats and shovel-hats, "Imperial velvet breeches," and scarlet petticoats, and all the tomfool vestments which a clique of demented and conceited young clergymen at home imagine that the great Protestant people of England will permit their churches to be decorated with. The Phœnix rose from its ashes. There is nothing in the Papal pride and circumstance of to-day to remind you of the grinding to powder of the idol eighteen years ago. The Calf is himself again, high on a porphyry pedestal, and glistening with fresh gold-leaf. The Ultramontanes exult over this, and tell you that it is a proof of the invulnerability of their Church, built upon a rock, and against which the Infernal gates are not to prevail. Ah! bah! how old is rouge? For how many thousand years have women been painting their faces? In the Etruscan Museum at the Vatican they will show you the pins with which they used to crimp their hair twenty centuries ago. Half Livy's books may be lost and Aristotle come down to us maimed and *manchot*, but the tailor's pattern-book is left high and dry, and the milliner's bandbox trips safely over the Niagara of ages. I grant the Romish Church its candles, vestments, and other properties intact. It is only its foundations in that Rock on which it falsely claims to be built which are rotten.

When you meet the Pope in his carriage, you are expected, if you are driving, to alight; if you are on foot, the proper thing is to kneel down. When the crowd of equipages is very dense, as on the Pincio about four o'clock, or when the ground is wet and greasy, as it was yesterday all over Rome, neither of the acts of veneration mentioned above is very easy of accomplishment; and directly the man waving the drawn sword above his head is visible in the distance, the prudent show as much alacrity in getting out of the Pope's way as the Spanish bishops do in ordering their coachmen to drive on faster when they hear the tinkling bell announcing the passage of the Host throughout the streets. "*Es Dios que pasa!*" the multitude cry, and the *señor obispo* must alight from his coach to admit the priest with his pyx. The good-natured Pope, however, does not seem desirous of causing inconvenience to his subjects. After a turn or two on the Pincian, he generally alights and walks. He has his reward in the throng of people of all classes who fall at once on their knees and ask his blessing. Gentle and simple, Roman princes and Zouaves, gendarmes and nurserymaids, old beggars and countesses in crinoline, grooms and stablemen, and little children, sink at once on their marrowbones, and crave the benediction always gladly accorded. Pio Nono wore his ordinary dressing-gown of fine white flannel, and a great shovel-hat of scarlet velvet. Altogether, he looked amazingly well and sprightly. His voice is still as clear as a bell, and he sang mass capitally last Tuesday in St. Peter's. Let us wish him a merry Christmas and a happy New Year, and better counsellors than those cadaverous parties in shovels, with their sallow faces and gallows looks, who troop after him, whispering behind their bony hands.

XXVIII.

NEW YEAR IN ROME.

January 1.

Pio Nono, in the evening of his age, seems as fond of hard work, and as capable of performing it, as was the good old Duke of Wellington, who, almost up to the last moment of his career, continued to prove to an exigent generation that he did not consider his numerous posts, with their corresponding emoluments, to be sinecures, but took as good care of the Tower as of the Trinity House, of Oxford as of Walmer, of the Horse Guards as of the 33d Foot, of the Ancient Concerts as of the House of Lords; while as constable, commander-in-chief, field-marshal, elder brother, and chancellor, he was alike efficient. The official costumes which our late field-marshal was bound from time to time to wear would have half-stocked the wardrobe of a waxwork-show. The attributes of Pio Nono are equally Protean. He has to be as many things, and to wear as many dresses, as the Duke. He is a prince, a pontiff, the eldest of brethren, the grandest of constables, and a supernatural personage into the bargain; and it is really marvellous to mark how blithely he discharges his multifarious functions, and how bravely he bears up under the fatigue of dressing and undressing half-a-dozen times a-day. Mr. Charles Mathews's *travestissements* in *Patter versus Clatter* are trifling compared with the mutation of the Pontifical toilette at Christmas-time.

But, to adhere to our first parallel, we may be again vividly reminded of the Great Duke when we see the Pontifex Maximus, unbroken by all his labours, taking his daily "constitutional" on the Pincian. Did not the Hero of Waterloo take *his* "constitutional" on Constitution-hill? The Duke, it is true, rode on horseback; whereas the Pope is either driven or walks—it is only in the gardens of the Vatican that he can indulge in occasional horse-exercise; but as the Duke, towards the end, used to sway a little in his saddle, so does the Pope—whose legs are, of course, the only shaky things about him—sway a little in his gait, and require to be propped up from time to time by servitors, who watch him as carefully as Duke Arthur's groom watched his Grace. The Duke was wont to wear white trousers when taking exercise. Pio Nono wears a white dressing-gown. Everybody used to bow to the Duke, and he invariably touched his hat, even to the meanest salutant. Almost everybody kneels to the Pope when he is out walking, and he invariably blesses the genuflectant. The Duke saluted you with two buckskin-covered fingers; the Pope blesses you with two ungloved digits. Can any parallel be closer—except, perhaps, that one which mentions that there is a river in Macedon and a river in Monmouth?

I have said that the Pope works very hard. Let us examine a little of the work he has had to go through this Christmas. I leave the negotiations with the Commendatore Tonello—of which we hear nothing new—and the settlement of the financial difficulties of the State, including the January lottery and the new silver coinage, which has made monetary confusion worse confounded—I leave these entirely out of the question. It is the hard labour of the Pope-priest, and not that of the Pope-king, of which I would wish to give heretics an idea. I observe that the Poet Swinburne—who, I should say, will go far, if his admirers give him rope enough—has alluded in his song of "Revolution" to the halcyon time when "the galley bench" is to "creak with a Pope." Already, I fancy, the *sedia gestatoria* "creaks" with an overworked old gentleman, whose daily life is, physically and morally, more onerous than that of the particoloured persons in steel bracelets, who eat polenta and skulk about, scowling at the sentries, in the dockyard at Civita Vecchia.

Take yesterday, the 31st of December, for example. It was, to begin with, the Feast of Pope St. Silvester, who consecrated the church of St. John Lateran, and baptised Constantine the Great. The Pope heard mass in his honour, in his own private apartments, at early morn. At half-past two in the Apostolic chapel of the Vatican, the first vespers of circumcision were sung, the Pope presiding. Six candles were lit on the altar and in the chancel. The Pontifical throne was hung with white draperies, flowered with gold. The *retablo* of the altar was decorated with tapestry representing the circumcision, and the arms of Clement XIII. The altar itself bore the sumptuous garniture of mother-of-pearl, the gift of Benedict XIV. The cardinals paid their obeisance to the Pope. Their eminencies wore the scarlet cassock, the scarlet *cappa* or cape, and the petticoat—I do not know its vestimentary name—of rich point-lace. The choir sang the motett, *Dies Sanctificatus*, of Palestrina. The first and third psalms were sung in the Palestrinan, in the Gregorian, and in *faux bourdon*. At the *Magnificat*, the Pope himself incensed the altar, chanted the orison, and blessed the congregation.

At four o'clock in the afternoon his Holiness, in semi-state, went to the church of the Gesù, to return thanks to Heaven for all mercies received during the year just elapsed. The spectacle was very grand indeed, and the crowd both inside and outside the church immense. This is the principal church of the Jesuits, and one of the most richly decorated in Rome. It is near the northern foot of the Capitol, and in one of the most stifling and poverty-stricken quarters of the city. The interior is one mass of precious marbles, lapis lazuli, and verde-antique, glowing frescoes, and rich carvings. Here, also, there is an image of the Virgin, called the Madonna della Strada, which works miracles; and in the adjacent convent-house sit the General of the Jesuits and his army of R.R.P.'s, hatching vain empires over the minds of men. The artistic glories of the Gesù were half-hidden yesterday by the tawdry scene-painting accessories with which the priesthood insist on spoiling, at great church festivals, the noble proportions and stately decorations of their temples. They do not even spare St. Peter's, which, this Christmas, has been profaned by the most barbarous and tasteless "properties." At a rough guess, I should say that there were at least five hundred wax-candles in the Gesù yesterday, in chandeliers of a dozen tapers each, suspended from the roof of the nave and cupola. The altar, surmounted by its enormous globe of lapis lazuli, long supposed to be the largest monolith of that kind in the world, but now discovered to be made up of several pieces, was one blinding blaze of light. The Sacred College, the Episcopate, the Corps Diplomatique, a host of priests of every grade in the sacerdotal hierarchy, and a vast number of military officers, were present. The Pope did not stay more than twenty minutes. His Holiness entered the church through the sacristy, and knelt bare-headed at a *prie dieu*, before the sacrament, which was exposed on the altar. The Cardinal Deacon, wearing his "pluvial," and kneeling on the steps of the altar, at the epistolar side, then chanted the *Te Deum* to a musical and choral accompaniment. At the second verse of the *Tantum Ergo* the Pope "incensed" the sacrament. The benediction was given by the Cardinal Deacon, and then the magnificent gathering broke up.

At the same hour, at the church of the Ara Cœli, the Senator and Conservators of Rome, preceded by the corps of *Sapeurs Pompiers*, were likewise present at a *Te Deum*. It is at first difficult to discover any connection between the Senator of Rome—an office once held, to his destruction, by Cola di Rienzi—and the semi-military force, with helmets and hatchets, whose duty it is to "run with the machine" and put out fires. On closer examination, however, it would appear that the Senator stands in lieu of the Roman Consul of antiquity. He is a Roman Prince, and his principal privilege appears to be to allow foreigners, duly provided with certificates of respectability from their respective consuls, to ascend the tower of the Capitol, whence a very fine view of Rome is to be obtained; but, otherwise, he exercises about as much power as does the Lord Mayor of London's sword-bearer. The names of the Senators are, indeed, inscribed on certain marble tablets affixed side by side to the classical *Fasti Consulares* in the Conservatorial Palace. On this assumption the *Sapeurs Pompiers* might be supposed to represent the Lictors of old Rome. I think that on gala-days it would be as well to dress them up in tunics and sandals, and give them fasces to carry. They would not look one whit more absurd than the Pope's Swiss Guards, who, to doublets and trunk-hose of the time of Francis I., add Prussian helmets and gray greatcoats *à la Russe.* Certainly firemen with fasces would not be a more incongruous combination than the sounding initials S.P.Q.R. with municipal placards on the walls of Rome fixing the price of beef—*Seconda qualità di carne di manzo: coscia piena, fracoscio, spalla e coscia vuota, esclusa la polpa di stinco, ogni libra soldi* 9. In the name of the Prophet, figs! The S.P.Q.R. are only eloquent to the effect that second-class beef is worth fourpence-halfpenny a pound.

I mentioned that the crowd both inside and outside the Gesù was immense. In the interior the sanctity of the edifice and the solemnity of the occasion forbade, of course, any demonstrations of popular feeling at the entrance of the Pope. The Romans are not yet so far advanced as the Venetians, who cheered their King and hooted their Patriarchs in St. Mark's. Neither sanctity nor solemnity, however, deterred a large number of foreigners, presumably Protestants, and I am afraid mostly of the Anglo-Saxon race, from behaving in the Gesù with extreme indecorum. This was not the first time, perhaps, in Rome, when it was necessary to remind strangers that a church is neither a volunteer review nor the Oxford Music Hall, and that pushing, jostling, stamping on the bystanders' toes, or digging elbows into their chests, the whole accompanied by very free-and-easy remarks in the

English tongue, are not exactly the best means of persuading foreigners that we are Christians, or indeed that we have any religion at all.

It may be as well to state, once for all, that these shameful scenes have been repeated in every church in Rome, from St. Peter's and the Sistine to the little church of San Tommaso degl' Inglesi, any time since December 24th; and that on St. Peter's-day and in Holy-week there will be even more crowding, more impropriety, and more irreverence displayed. The Papal authorities have done their best on these grand occasions to preserve decorum and exclude the *canaille* by enacting that only persons in evening-dress, and ladies in black, with black veils, shall be admitted to the precincts of the altar; but it is precisely the people in evening-dress—I say nothing, of course, about the ladies—who behave themselves in the worst possible manner. The frock, the proverb tells us, does not make the monk, and a tail-coat and white "choker" fail sometimes to make a gentleman. Swiss Guards and gentlemen-ushers are posted all about the churches on gala-days to see that none save in the prescribed costume are admitted to the reserved spaces; and a halberdier will occasionally feel you about the hips, after the manner of a searcher at a dockyard-gate who is inquisitive about tobacco, to assure himself that you have not linked or pinned-up your frock-coat into the similitude of a swallow-tail. These sumptuary laws, however, have not had the desired effect; and there is ten times better conduct observed in the body of the church, in the darkened aisles, and remote chapels, where the people who are ordinarily termed *canaille* are to be found thick clustered. These good souls have only come into the church to pray; and they drop down on their keees quietly, and keep on praying till the ceremony is over.

Outside the Gesù, when the Pope reëntered his carriage, there was a real demonstration of popular sentiment, and were I writing for the *Poughkeepsie Seer* or the *Communipaw Chronicle* I should say that his Holiness was "ovated considerable." The multitude on the steps in the Piazza di Gesù and in the adjacent streets was very dense, and composed, apparently, of every class of the population. In addition to working-men and women, and even cloudier plebeians, and a fair sprinkling of Zouaves and Antibes Legionaries off duty, there was a considerable number of well-dressed Italians, both ladies and gentlemen. The cheering when the Pope made his appearance was very loud, very general, and seemed very sincere. It was certainly louder than when Pio Nono went before Christmas to the SS. Apostoli, when the presence of an official *claque*, and of fuglemen connected with the police, was manifest enough. Such a *claque* may have been on the spot yesterday at the Gesù.

Is there a country in Europe, excepting only our own happy and favoured land, where the services of such hired applauders are not occasionally required? Even in free Italy, even in recently-liberated Venetia, I have heard of strong-lunged gentlemen employed by the Questura to shout "*Viva il Rè!*" at the rate of five *lire* a-day. Who gave the cue at the Gesù it is not easy to say; but the populace took it up *con amore*, and the loud and renewed shouts of "*Viva Pio Nono!*" "*Viva il Papa Rè!*" must have been infinitely grateful to the venerable Pontiff, whose trembling fingers were blessing his loving subjects right and left. The Pope is said to covet martyrdom; but surely popularity is a more comfortable thing. The cries of "Long live the Pope-king!" audible to all, but which will, doubtless, be denied by the veracious Italian press, are considered here, by the ultra-clerical party, to be extremely significant, and evidential indeed of the triumph of their cause. The crisis, they say, is over. The worst is past. Satan is beaten down under the Pontifical feet, and the "Italian Revolution" may run away and hide itself, howling, in the Cave of Despair. Understand, they point out, that it was the Pope, not only as Pontiff, but as King, who was cheered so lustily yesterday. That is to say, if we read the signs of the times through Ultramontane spectacles, the Roman people are thoroughly satisfied with their present form of government; they admire the Swiss Guards and the foreign mercenaries; they do not want their streets paved or their postage-stamps perforated; they would rather not have representative institutions and a free press.

The most philosophical conclusion, perhaps, at which one can arrive is, that these popular demonstrations do not mean much one way or the other. It cannot be too often repeated that there are great numbers of persons in Rome who like the Pope and the Papacy; who even love the first and admire the latter. These persons are not all clerical. The lay element is sufficiently marked among them. There are old people, simple people, dull people, credulous people, people who are governed by women, people who do not care about thinking for themselves, people who are young and enthusiastic *pro*, as there are other youngsters enthusiastic *contra*. Let us remember the crucial test of the quack who answered the question as to how he got so many patients by pointing from the window and asking his interlocutor how many of the people he saw passing he thought to be fools.. I do not say that it is foolish to venerate the Pope, or the Grand Lama of Thibet, or the King of Corea; but I do say that there are people whose likings and dislikings are in one direction, while those of others point a contrary way. The people who like the Pope as King were about the Gesù on Monday, and cheered him to the echo. Those who did not like him either stayed away, or looked on and held their tongues. But the question of the Temporal Power is, I take it, no more affected by such a demonstration than is that of modern costume by people who like going to fancy-balls dressed up as Madame de Pompadour or Ivan the Terrible.

To attend church for a couple of hours in the morning and for twenty minutes in the afternoon may not appear to be such very hard work; but it is the continual dressing and and undressing which would tell on most elderly persons. At the early vespers the Pope wore the *falda*, the alb, the cordon, the stole, the white pluvial embroidered with gold, and a mitre of cloth-of-gold. He came to the Gesù in his white robe, with a purple *rochet* over it, and a velvet skull-cap. In the sacristy they dressed him in the *sottana*, the *mozetta* of red velvet, trimmed with ermine, and the scarlet stole embroidered with gold. This kind of thing has been going on for a week. On Christmas-eve his Holiness officiated at the Sistine, seated on a splendid throne erected on the gospel-side of the altar. In addition to the vestments I have enumerated above, he wore the amice. He incensed the altar, and was incensed in turn by the cardinals. This was the day on which the sacred manger-board from the stable at Bethlehem was exhibited to the veneration of the faithful, in the church of Santa Maria Maggiore. It is enclosed in a crystal casket, framed in silver, and surmounted by a little silver Bambino couchant on golden straw. At the Basilica of St. John Lateran was exhibited the "acherotype" image of the Saviour.

The Pope this year was not present at the midnight mass, and omitted his customary visit by torchlight to Sta. Maria Maggiore; but he sang mass in St. Peter's on Christmas-day. Previously the veil of the Virgin and the mantle of St. Joseph had been exhibited at the early or "Aurora" mass at Sta. Anastasia; while at the church of the Agonisants were shown the swaddling-clothes of the Saviour. At Sta. Maria Maggiore and at St. Peter's some of the stones from the stable and some of the straw on which the Divine Infant was laid are exhibited. St. Mark's Church also possesses some straw; and at the Santa Croce di Gerusalemme they exhibit *some of the hair of the Infant Jesus.** At Sta. Maria in Trastevere can be shown, close to the high altar, only the place from which once issued a miraculous fountain of oil. It is not at all unlikely, bearing in mind the geological conditions of the Roman soil, that a real oil-well, not at all miraculous, did flow hereabouts at some time or another. *These things are;* and there are people who believe in them.

At the pontifical high mass the Pope joined the sacred college in the chapel of the Pietà in St. Peter's, wearing, in addition to the dress I have described, the girdle with golden acorns and a *rochet* of lace. Then a procession was formed

* "*Fêtes de Noël et de l'Epiphanie à Rome.*" Par le Chanoine X. Barbier de Montault. Rome, Joseph Spithoïver. 1865.

of collegiate procurators in black cassocks and capes, apostolic preachers of the Capuchin order, in cowl and sandals; confessors of the apostolic palace; *bussolanti*, or ushers, in violet cassocks and scarlet capes; the apostolic jeweller in a court-dress and with a sword by his side; the secret chaplains, carrying the precious tiaras and mitres.

There are four pontifical tiaras or triple crowns; one the gift of Napoleon I. to Pius VII. It weighs eight pounds avoirdupois, and is worth ten thousand pounds sterling; the second dating from the pontificate of Gregory XVI., and worth only four hundred pounds; the third presented by the Palatine guard to Pio Nono, and estimated at the value of nine hundred pounds; the fourth, the grandest and richest of all, being a present made to the Pope in 1854 by Queen Isabella of Spain, and valued at 535,000 francs, or over twenty-one thousand pounds English. It contains no fewer than eighteen thousand diamonds; and, let me see, what is the actual market-price of Spanish bonds?

After the chaplains came the *aides-de-chambre*, the consistorial advocates, the singers of the Papal chapel in their white cottas, the Referendaries, the clerks of the apostolic chamber, the auditors of the Rota, the master of the Sacred Hospital, the voters of the Signature, the apostolic sub-deacons, the abbots of the monastic orders, the commander of the Order of the Holy Ghost *in Saxia*, the bishops, archbishops, primates, and patriarchs, the cardinals according to their rank as cardinal-deacons, priests, and bishops, in scarlet, but wearing white dalmatics and mitres of snowy damask, and each followed by his "caudatary" or trainbearer, with a sling of gauze round his neck to hold up his eminence's mitre when his eminence takes it off, and his groom of the chambers in court-dress, a rapier by his side, and a short black coat over his left shoulder. To these succeeded the conservators and the senator of Rome, in togas of cloth-of-gold turned up with scarlet silk; then Monsignore the Governor of Rome, in a violet tippet trimmed with ermine; then the prefect of the ceremonies; then the staff-officers of the Guardia Nobile and the Swiss Guard; and, finally, the Pope, in a white alb and pluvial broidered in gold, carried on his portable throne by twelve *palefrenieri* in scarlet damask, between the two gigantic fans of ostrich mingled with peacock feathers, under a floating baldaquin of white silk, of which the poles were borne by eight Referendary prelates, and escorted by the Swiss Guard in head-pieces, back- and breast-plates of burnished steel, with their swords drawn, mace-bearers with silver maces following, and the Pope's physician, his body-servant, and another detachment of Swiss Guards bringing up the rear.

The Pope was dressed and undressed during the different ceremonies of the mass at least half-a-dozen times. They put on his good old head a variety of things; they led him up to his throne and down from his throne; and they smoked him with frankincense and benzoin. At the end the presbytery offered him a purse of white *moire*, containing thirty golden Juliuses, each of the value of five *scudi*, *pro missa bene cantata*, for so well singing of his mass. Certainly his Holiness deserved thirty pounds and more for all this fatigue. It is the custom for the Pope, after thanking the priesthood of St. Peter's, to present that purse to the cardinal-deacon, who, in his turn, presents it to his "caudatary," or tail-bearer. This functionary is expected to carry it to the chapter—the original donors—from whom he receives only twenty-five pauls, or thirteen francs and a half, a composition which can be regarded only as shabby in the extreme.

If you are sent for to sing at the Imperial Court of Russia, you receive next day, in lieu of money-payment, some ornament in diamonds. If you are fond of diamonds, you may keep the gewgaws and exhibit them on your return as a proof of the warm affection in which you were held by the Czar of All the Russias; but if you prefer ready-money, you may take your diamonds to the Treasury of the Hermitage and receive so many roubles for your brooch or your snuff-box, abating a discount of fifteen per cent. I think that on Boxing-day a system at least corresponding in liberality to the Russian might be adopted in Rome; but I honestly confess that were I a Cardinal's caudatary I should regard the purse of white *moire* as legitimate *backshish*, and "stick to" the thirty golden Juliuses.

XXIX.

OLD CHRISTMAS-DAY.

YESTERDAY was the vigil of the Epiphany; and to-day is old Christmas-day. You are aware that in the Oriental Churches the sixth of January continues to be celebrated as the Feast of the Nativity, and that even among Western Christians the tradition which fixes Christmas-day on the 25th of December was for three or four centuries a matter of sharp discussion. The authority of St. Augustine and St. Chrysostom seems to have been the weightiest in favour of the 25th; but the learned and lucid Abbé Martigny, in the superb *Dictionary of Christian Antiquities*, recently published by Hachette—a work fully worthy to rank with the classical dictionaries of Mr. Anthony Rich and Dr. William Smith—candidly admits that many Fathers of the Church were of the opinion that our Saviour's birthday was neither on the 25th of the old year nor on the 6th of the new. A variety of dates have been suggested by these non-content fathers, whose testimony has been collated by St. Clement of Alexandria, and they range between the 19th of April and the 20th of May. Tillemont has written a whole folio on this long-controverted point; but the 25th of December is still, I apprehend, an all-sufficing Christmas-day to the majority of Christians. When the symbol celebrated relates to Eternity, it seems to me puerile to be very particular about Time.

I venture to refer to such matters, in such a place, not for the reason that I see the columns of English newspapers filled, day after day, with letters and articles about confession, absolution, and the divine legation of priests, their vestments and the mysteries of their ritual, but because it is impossible to live the life of Rome, and mark what is going on around, without reflecting that the solemnisation of festivals which we have grown used to pass by with indifference when we meet them in our Letts's *Diaries*, side by side with the dividends that are due at the Bank, the beginning of partridge-shooting, the end of the long vacation, and the birthday of the Princess Mary of Teck, is the daily business of thousands of ecclesiastical persons in this city, and the object of the piety and veneration of many more thousands of laymen. Temporal power, clerical misgovernment, ignorance, fraud, and hypocrisy must all be dismissed from our consideration when we reflect that this is indeed a city of the Levites; that the Pope, whether he be the Vicar of Heaven or not, is still invested with all the attributes of Aaron the High Priest; that St. Peter's and the Sistine fill as large and as intimate a place in the transactions of common life here as Solomon's Temple did in old Jerusalem, even to the introduction of a few doves and a few money-changers in the purlieus of the sacred places; and that all these people we see going about in seemingly masquerading-dresses—old men in scarlet petticoats and lace-tippets, monsignori in purple stockings, college-students in shovel-hats and flowing cassocks, monks with shaven crowns and sandalled feet, penitents with ghastly cowls and crosses on their breasts, nuns with rosaries, relics, medals, and knotted cords at their girdles nearly as heavy as a galley-slave's chain, beadles, vergers, choir-boys, and candle-snuffers—have all a direct and special connection with the performance of the capital rites of a most Ancient Faith.

If we take Rome, and what is done at Rome, in good faith, it is impossible to deny the logical position which I heard laid down the other day by a preaching friar, that this world must either be devoted to the service of God or of man, and that it is better that it should be devoted to God; and arguing upon this position, the Papal Government is clearly justified in neglecting to pave its streets, perforate its postage-stamps, ventilate its houses, and wash its popularition. At least, it keeps God's house in good order. St. Peter's is being continually beautified, swept, and garnished. Not one of the fourscore lamps round the Apostles' tomb is ever suffered to become extinguished, and not one mass, vesper, vigil, or orison in honour of any one of the innumerable saints, virgins, or martyrs who crowd the Roman Calendar is ever omitted.

I repeat that it is impossible to spend Christmas in Rome without mentioning—and that, too, very frequently—the tribe of ceremonies—or "functions," as the Romans call them—which are stuck, set, embroidered, and hung all about one simple pathetic Fact, which is narrated, without any kind of gewgaw adornment, in the New Testament. That board from the Manger at Bethlehem, be it genuine or be it spurious, which is shown as a sight at Santa Maria Maggiore, is a significant illustration of what Christmas has become. A dark, dim, decayed morsel of something—wood, or tinder, or bone, you do not know which—lies in a crystal casket, with a gorgeously-chased frame, and surmounted, as I told you, by a silver doll lying upon golden straw. But I have no desire to describe these shows in detail. Hitherto I have been content with barely enumerating them; but to pass them by in utter silence would give cause to the inference that I looked upon Rome as a place chiefly remarkable for curious jewelry, copies of old pictures, indifferent modern statues, a show of aristocratic equipages on the Pincian almost equalling, and certainly closely rivalling, our own show in Hyde Park; a number of crumbling ruins, highly interesting to the antiquary; and an infinity of vile smells.

There are in Rome just now, however, a number of my countrymen who appear to take a warmer and closer interest in the intricacies of the Romish ritual than I do. I am not alluding to the ordinary sightseers and tourists, English or American, who regard the Supreme Pontiff, the Sacred College, the Dominican and Capuchin friars, the masses, vespers, and vigils, the churches, statues, and pictures, the ruins and the statuary, the Columbaria and the Catacombs, simply and purely as so many shows and spectacles gotten up as part of the attractions of the winter season in Rome, and provided exclusively for their, the sightseers', gratification. I think these good people would get up an indignation-meeting if the Pope were to decline giving an audience to Protestants, or if his Holiness passed a sumptuary law enacting that the Cardinals were henceforth to go clad in gray serge, or that the frescoes in the Sistine Chapel were to be covered up; and I don't think they would grumble very sorely if the midnight

Pastorella at St. Peter's or the *Te Deum* at the Gesù were charged for at the hotels in the bill, at the rate of a *scudo* a-head.

The amateurs of spectacular Christianity I mean are a group of young English gentlemen, presumably from the Universities of Oxford and Cambridge, who are walking about the streets of Rome in costumes ten times more preposterous and absurd than those worn in London by the gawky young acolytes of St. Philip Neri, who used to be "guyed" by the boys, when the Oratory was in King William-street, Strand. I observe that the statement made in the *Saturday Review* as to the grotesque exhibition of sucking Ritualists in the streets of Oxford was, at the time, indignantly denied; but I can vouch for the corporeal appearance in the streets of Rome of a clique of brainless young Britons clad in grotesque imitation of Jesuit priests. They cut their hair very short; but I do not know if they have yet assumed the tonsure, and gone to Figaro for a Roman "shave." They wear long-skirted coats that are all but cassocks, and "M.B." waistcoats that are all but amices. Their hats are growing broad about their brim, but are not as yet perfect shovels. They are "otherwise clean shaven," and walk in pairs with a demure and cat-like mien. They are the great admirers and critics of the sacerdotal incantations in the churches. They check off the genuflexions on their fingers; they know to a wick how many candles are lit, and cunningly interpret and comment upon the numberless mummeries and millineries.

If these boys want to "go over to Rome" for good and all, let them go. We have all known more than one young gentleman who has gone over, and is sorry for it, and wants to come back to Ridley-and-Latimer land, but dares not for very shame. If Ritualism has such fascinating charms for the hobbledehoys in the "M.B." waistcoats, let them do it thoroughly, and become Papists; but it is rather inconsistent, it is slightly incongruous, to meet them at night in the *caffès* and in the smoking-rooms of the hotels tossing off their *petits verres*, and pulling at their short-pipes—I hope only on flesh-days—and gossiping about the "functions" of the morning as though they were talking about boating, or steeplechasing, or Van John, or some other recreation dear to the youthful university mind.

The vigil which commences the octave of the Epiphany was observed yesterday by the celebration of Vespers at the Vatican, the Pope being present, and the tapestry behind the altar representing the Adoration of the Magi. Vespers were also sung by the boys of the Propaganda at their college, near the Piazza di Spagna. It may not be generally known that this world-famous seminary, whose very name has so terrible a sound to Protestant ears, is dedicated to the three Magian kings, Caspar, Melchior, and Balthasar. At the church of St. Andrea della Valle, at the same hour, there was actually above the high altar a waxwork-show, consisting of *personnaggi in cera* the size of life, richly dressed and ornamented by the munificence of the Banker-Prince, whom Mr. Thackeray used to call Polonia, but who was very well known to bearers of letters of credit as Prince Torlonia, Duke of Brancaleone, and Rothschild of Italy. It was at a ball given by his Highness, you remember, that Mrs. Rebecca Crawley, *née* Sharpe, met, for the last time but one in this life, the Marquis of Steyne; once afterwards she met him on

Monte Pincio, when he was driving with Madame Belladonna, and when his valet followed Becky and warned her that the air of Rome was not good for her. The waxwork-show represents the Adoration of the Magi. Magi were also shown as large as life, in lieu of the ordinary shepherds, in the scenes representing the Stable at the Ara Cœli and St. Francesco a Ripa.

This morning, being the Epiphany, a salute of fourteen guns was fired from the Castle of St. Angelo, and the pontifical colours were hoisted. At half-past ten there was a Papal chapel at the Vatican, and the Pope attended high mass, with the triple crown on his head. An indulgence was conceded to all persons present of thirty years and thirty "*quarantines.*" I confess that I do not know what the last means, or whether it has reference to purgatory or the cholera. The missal used by the cardinal singing mass was the splendid volume illumined by Biondini for Clement XII. At the church of St. Athanasius mass was sung by the Bishop of the United Greeks, and consecrated bread was distributed to the faithful. At half-past three o'clock this afternoon Vespers will be sung at the church of the Ara Cœli by the Franciscan friars, and subsequently the SANTO BAMBINO will be carried processionally from the church to the top of the great staircase, where it is usually shown to the assembled multitude, who are then blessed by the officiating bishop.

I bought a photograph of this Bambino, warranted from the original, at Piale's, for eight *bajocchi*. It is an image grossly chopped rather than carved by a Franciscan monk in Syria, some time during the sixteenth century. Its swaddling-clothes are one network of diamonds and other precious stones. On its head is a magnificent crown. One of its feet is made of pure gold, and is submitted, at stated periods, to be kissed by the faithful. Inside one of the toes are relics of the Virgin Mary. To sick persons who desire a visit from the Bambino, it is brought in a close carriage by two monks. Respecting the miracles it works with the sick, including that of frightening them to death by its hideous appearance, I advise you to read Mr. Charles Dickens's *Pictures from Italy*. I dare not repeat what he further says about the Bambino. He wrote his book more than twenty years ago, and the world has grown since then wonderfully straitlaced. Of course the reverend fathers of the Oratory will maintain that the Bambino is only a symbol, and that the ignorant thousands who fall down before it are not really worshipping a wooden doll. I refer, in this regard, the reverend fathers of the Oratory to the refrain of an old English poem, called "The Soul's Errand." If they say that to adore the Bambino is not idolatry, they LIE.

Epiphany is kept in yet another fashion in Rome—a fashion much more human, and not nearly so wicked, although troublesome enough to persons of nervous temperament. It is the great Roman holiday for children; and the rising generation of Rome, from sundown on Saturday to sunrise on Monday, are privileged to run about the streets blowing on penny trumpets, beating upon drums, clashing upon gongs, squeaking like Punch, whistling, hurdy-gurdy grinding, and otherwise making the air hideous. I have not yet heard the Ethiopian bones and banjo, but almost every other kind of psaltery has been audible. Down by the Piazza Navona last night, and in the densely-populated districts round the Pantheon, there were numbers of illuminated booths and stalls heaped with toys, which faintly reminded me of the New-year's *baraques* on the Paris boulevards, and the Christmas fair round the old Schloss at Berlin. I saw some children in paper cocked-hats, and some with false noses, and a few with torches. Abating the incessant squeaking and the drubbing of parchment, which noises were incessant, the festivity seemed tame and spiritless enough. The real holiday shows are in the churches, and there the audience is immense, and very nearly as free in their comments as at a theatre. Good luck to the children, anyhow, however. I conceive that the original design of the Saturnalia at the Epiphany was to console them for the annual whipping inflicted by devout Roman parents on their offspring on Innocents' Day, in order that the memory of the fourteen thousand babies slaughtered by the cruel Herod of Jewry might never be erased from their minds.

XXX.

ROMAN NOTES.

It might be worth the while of London archæologists to inquire whether in the narrow little lane which, until lately, existed in the immediate neighbourhood of our metropolitan cathedral—I say until recently, for there is no knowing how many lanes, or streets, or whole districts, even, have been swept away since I was last in England—and called "Paul's Chain," there was ever a chapel dedicated to the great Apostle of the Gentiles, in which the fetters wherewith he was bound were exhibited to the veneration of the pious. The place was surely not called Paul's Chain for nothing; but it is to be feared that the Reformation, or the even more iconoclastic deluge of Puritanism, made short work both of the images and the relics accumulated during long ages of faith. Rome, however, yet teems with such memorials. The Catacombs, it is true, have long since been emptied of human remains; but every church is an anatomical museum; every altar has a coffer beneath it full of jewelled skulls and saintly bladebones, set in pearls and diamonds. In Rome there is still exhibited the Scala Santa—the identical flight of steps once forming the grand staircase of Pontius Pilate's house, which was brought hither from the Holy Land by the Empress Helena, and by ascending which on your knees to the chapel called the Sancta Sanctorum, and repeating a certain number of *aves* and *paternosters* during the process, you may gain, for each of the twenty-eight steps composing the staircase, no less than nine years of indulgence. Twenty-eight times nine: the total is but two hundred and fifty-two, which, deducted from say five million years of purgatory, sounds at first but insignificant, but is, after all, something to the good.

But to return to St. Paul's Chain, or rather Paul's Chains—they are tangible objects in Rome, contrasting it very strongly with heretical England, where the shadowy names of so many things have been preserved, but where their substance has long since been disregarded, or contemned, or lost. Take Candlemas, for instance. It is probable that at home the average receipts of Price's Patent Candle Company are not increased by a single shilling on the second of February, and that the beeswax market is not in the slightest degree ruffled by the occurrence of the festival of the Purification of the Virgin. Still we keep the name of Candlemas in our calendars, knowing not why, and caring still less. Very different is the case in Rome. A hundred shrines will be begirt next Saturday by the "holy shine" of tapers innumerable, and for some days the grand architecture of St. Peter's has been disfigured with tawdry upholstery and gew-gaw drapery in anticipation of the solemn "function" of another day, when the Pope will sit in state over against the Baldacchino, and bless long-sixes by the ton weight. It must be admitted in favour of the Romanists that they are consistent; that they forget nothing, and neglect nothing in the outward forms and shows bequeathed to them by immemorial tradition; and precisely as the pageant was under Gregory the Great, so it is under Pius IX.

St. Paul has no church within Rome proper, and the absence of such a fane in a city with which his name, though without any historical evidence, is so indissolubly connected, has given rise to many curious conjectures. Among the common people an absurd legend is current to the effect that St. Peter and St. Paul quarrelled about a pair of shoes; and this grotesque story may have some dim reference to our proverb about "robbing Peter to pay Paul." At all events, the popular belief is that the two Apostles were not on good terms, and that the absence even from intramural Rome of any church specially dedicated to St. Paul is to be attributed to the affair of the shoes. There must have been a Pauline party in Rome, however, from the earliest times, and outside the walls the Doctor Gentium has no reason to complain of the lukewarmness of his devotees. He has a church about four miles out of Rome, called "San Paolo alle tre Fontane," erected on the spot where he is said to have been decapitated. The dungeon in which he was confined, and the marble pillar which served as a heading-block, are still shown. His severed head, on striking the earth, is said to have rebounded three times, and from each of the spots it touched a fountain miraculously sprang.

But the little Church of the Three Fountains is a mere oratory compared with the gigantic basilica of "San Paolo fuori le Mura," or St. Paul's without the walls, which, St. Peter's excepted, is the most splendid church in Rome, or in the whole world. The old basilica, built by Valentinian II. and Theodosius on the site of a still more ancient edifice erected by Constantine in the fourth century, over the catacomb of Lucina, a noble Roman matron and Christian convert, was almost entirely destroyed by fire in 1823. A few columns and rare mosaics escaped the flames; but the present basilica must be regarded as almost wholly new. Its exterior is, in common with so many Roman churches, exceedingly ugly and cumbrous; a factory turned into a workhouse, and then occupied as a barrack, would give the closest idea of its appearance. The interior is of almost unexampled splendour, and is so dazzling with gold and silver and precious marbles, with frescoes and sculptures, carved woodwork and mosaics, that, remembering that the completion of this vast creation is due to the piety and munificence of the reigning Pontiff, some incredulity naturally arises in the mind of the foreign spectator as to the truth of the many doleful stories he has heard of the poverty of the Papal exchequer.

Something like a million sterling must have been spent in the erection and embellishment of this most gorgeous temple; and, calling to mind on how many other public works of an ecclesiastical nature in Rome Pio Nono has lavished his treasures, one is puzzled to discover where all the money could have come from. Marble, it is true, is cheap in the Roman States, artistic handicraftsmen are plentiful, and do not look for splendid remuneration from any but the *forestieri*. If they do so look for it, they certainly do not get it. If excellence has departed, if Rafaelles and Berninis are no longer to be secured, efficient mediocrity at least abounds; and there are vast numbers of Roman artists who can cut marble and polish it, carve wood and gild it, and cover canvas and stucco with brilliant colours laid over designs which, if not original, are cleverly adapted from the great masterpieces of the Renaissance. The modern school of Roman art—and indeed of Italian art in general—is perhaps the most contemptible in Europe; and since the death of Canova, the only painters and sculptors who have made Rome illustrious as an art-city have been the foreigners Thorwaldsen, Overbeck, Gibson, Lehmann, and Story; but the Eternal City can yet boast of a host of copyists and adapters and translators, servile it is true but faithful, and not devoid of that tasteful grace which is inborn in every Italian, however corrupt and however ignorant he may be in other respects. So all that the copyists and adapters in stone or in stucco could do for St. Paul has been done, and the result is almost inconceivably superb. The mosaic manufactory at the Vatican, which may be defined as the Woolwich-cum-Enfield of the Church militant, has also been most prodigal in its supply of tesselatory art; and any number of niches and vaultings have been covered with any number of million squares of coloured glass and *pietra dura*—apostles by the score, popes by the string, angels by the legion, and martyrs by the army.

With all this, however, the consumption of hard *scudi* must have been tremendous; and it may be accepted as an axiom that you cannot build a basilica on credit, or with paper money which has no forced circulation. The Pope has no private fortune. The cardinals derive their public salaries from the monopolies on snuff, cigars, wine, salt-fish, and similar articles of common use granted them by his Holiness to keep up their state withal, and I have not heard of any actual member of the Sacred College who has contributed a single *bajocco* to the restoration of St. Paul's. The taxes do not bring in much more than will suffice to pay for the jack-boots and buckskins of the Pontifical gendarmery, and all that the Custom-house and the gambling lotteries can produce is wanted for the maintenance of the Swiss Guard and the other mediæval hangers-on of the court of the *Servus Servorum Dei.*

Whence, then, the *scudi* which have been spent upon St. Paul's? It is a mystery, like so many other things in Rome. Large sums have been bestowed from time to time towards the work by Catholic sovereigns and princes. Mehemet Ali gave the gorgeous columns of oriental alabaster which support the *baldacchino;* even schismatic Russia contributed huge blocks of malachite and vast slabs of lapis lazuli for the sides of the altar; and that English lady-convert, who is said to give five thousand pounds a-year, being the half of her fortune, in frank almoign to the Pope, may have done somethnig note-worthy towards the decoration of the confessional of St. Timothy—for in death, as in life, the Disciple is close to the Apostle. But all these, and the Peter's pence so industriously collected all over Catholic Christendom, fail to account for a tithe of the enormous sums which have been squandered here. Perhaps the Pope has a long stocking somewhere. Perhaps the gold to buy the marble and pay the masons, and painters, and carvers flowed as miraculously as the water from the Three Fountains. But what a pity it is that some proportion of the wealth swallowed up here—say twenty per cent of the gross amount—was not laid out in repairing the filthy road which leads to the glorious edifice, or in propping-up the tottering old Porta San Paolo, or in washing and clothing the deplorable creatures who crawl about the sumptuous basilica, airing their foul rags in the ruddy light from the stained-glass windows, or clinging to the skirts of the foreign sightseers at the gates, brandishing their stumps, and showing their sores as though they were crosses of honour, and yelping in the name of the Madonna and the Saints for three *bajocchi*.

The high altar of St. Paul's was burnt to a cinder in the fire of 1823, and it is now no longer stated, even by the Romanists, that the body of the Apostle, whose remains are said to have been transferred here from the Vatican in the third century, is to be found in the new basilica. As a compensation for the loss of the actual relics of the saint, his chains are exhibited. Friday last was the festival of the conversion of the Apostle; and after High Mass the faithful were invited to adore the holy fetters. There seemed to be about half-a-dozen links, making up a length of about eighteen inches. These were held in a white napkin by a priest, who carried them round to the kneeling worshippers, extending the napkin and its rusty contents to be kissed by each in turn, and carefully wiping the links before he submitted them to a fresh salutation. There were a great many women among those who adored the Apostle's bonds, and a considerable number of poor country-people, to whom the splendour of the churches, and the multiplicity of the pageants may well serve as a consolation in adversity, and in some measure compensate for the squalor and destitution of their own homes. A whole company of Pontifical Zouaves marched in about two o'clock, and, kneeling, kissed the chains with military precision. The Pope also came to the basilica in the course of the afternoon, staying, however, but a very few minutes. For the rest, there were no Italians of the class conventionally termed respectable to be seen in the place. The ecclesiastical sights of Rome seem to be patronised exclusively by beggars and shepherds, English and American tourists.

January 18.

Christmas and the New Year are seasons when men's hearts are ordinarily open to the influences of charity; and it is remarkably cheering to observe how very charitable the organs of the clerical party in Rome have lately become towards their neighbours. Their charity does not begin, in accordance with the wise maxim to that intent, at home. Charity seldom does. We are usually more prone to weep over the sorrows of Cochin China than over those of Somers Town, and the spiritual destitution of a native of Antannarivo is, as a rule, more affecting than the corporeal needs of a denizen of Duck-lane. If Roman charity began at home, it might almost end there, from sheer weariness, so much misery might it find to relieve. I am well-nigh tired of telling, and you must be quite tired of hearing, that the poorer inhabitants of this city of sumptuous basilicas and stately palaces, and in which there are probably more wax-candles burnt and more footmen in livery employed than in any city of Christendom, are lodged far worse and fed far more poorly than any Irish cotter's swine. You must be beginning to find it rather stale information that the streets of Rome swarm with beggars, some in extreme old age, others so young as to be scarcely able to toddle; some cripples, others frightfully-afflicted creatures exhibiting revolting sores; but all clamorous for alms.

The charity of the cassocks and shovel-hats might find plenty of room for exercise among these deplorable wretches. In their scrupulous courtesy to foreigners, however, the Romans prefer to leave the relief of such miserables to the foreign visitors, whom the attractions of the jewellers' shops and the photographs bring in the worst of weather to the Piazza di Spagna. The natives, so at least I am inclined to think from close observation, seldom if ever give anything to the street-beggars whom they allow to prey on the strangers within their gates. Blessings they may bestow upon them, but the pence they distribute are as few as those which they confer on the waiters at the caffès. If they have any spare *bajocchi* and feel liberal, they reserve their elemosina to fling them out of window to the screeching and organ-torturing vagabonds who seem to sing expressly false, and to grind purposely-injured instruments. In England foolish people bid these nuisances to go away, but I fancy the Romans pay them because the discord is grateful to their ears. I think they like cacophony, as that Sultan of Turkey did who only derived pleasure from the performances of his brass-band when his musicians were tuning up their instruments. "Mashallah! let the dogs play that tune again," cried the Sultan to his Italian bandmaster. And I can aver, that not only in Rome, but in Italy generally, the land of song, you may hear in the course of one day, either inside a theatre, or in the streets outside it, more execrably bad music than you will hear in England—whose people are supposed by foreigners to have no ear and no taste for music at all—in the course of a whole year.

The beggars, therefore, thrive on the *forestieri*—a simple race born to be shorn, and who are apt to be either touched with compassion, or worried into parting with their small change when they are pertinaciously followed — say from Spillmann's restaurant to the Piazza Colonna—by wailing children with blue noses and bare feet, or decrepit old women, taking the Madonna and all the saints to witness that they have not tasted food for four days. The born Roman can command, when solicited for alms, a stare of such utter stoniness, and a look of such superbly stolid indifference, that you might imagine him deaf and blind to the wretchedness yelping and whining at his feet or his elbow. I do not believe that they thus pass on through real hardness of heart. I think that there is a tolerably general average of hard and soft hearts, as of hard and soft red-herrings, all the world over; and that no set of people anywhere, always excepting workhouse guardians and Marshal Narvaez, are much better or much worse than any other set of people. The Romans turn a deaf ear to the street-beggars, probably because from their youth upwards they have known them to be arrant impostors, or at least persons whose destitution is the fault and shame of a neglectful Government. I have no doubt that they have their own objects of charity, to whom they are seasonably benevolent.

For instance, since the octave of the Epiphany commenced, all the church-doors have been beset by posses of semi-ecclesiastical mendicants, with red crosses on their cassocks, who hold in their hands tin-boxes with slits in the lids, and carefully padlocked by their superiors, the which they rattle in a monotonous manner. They seem to do rather a good business, especially among the women, who in all countries (bless them!) are bountiful to everybody save cab-men. *Those* they screw down frightfully. The "collectors," if I may call them by that polite name, at the church-doors, seek subscriptions for a variety of purposes: sometimes *per nostre povere monache* (for our poor nuns); sometimes for the repair of churches and convents; sometimes on the simple plea of the "octave of the Epiphany," which leaves a conveniently-broad margin, and reminds one of the joint-stock company promoted during the South-Sea mania, with a capital of a million sterling, "for an object hereafter to be named;" and sometimes for the conversion of England to the Catholic faith. I had the honour, too, lately, at St. Andrea della Valle, of subscribing three *bajocchi* towards the fund for the canonisation of the "*Benedetto e beato Labu,*" who is to be raised to the celestial peerage, if his friends can find money enough, next June. I have not the slightest idea of who this saint elect was, or what he did; but it was worth three *bajocchi* to know that even a saint cannot be made without ready-cash. I suppose the fees of the *Avvocato del Diavolo* are pretty heavy.

All this almsgiving, however, is not by any means the kind of charity to which I desire to call your attention. I allude to the great outburst of commiseration in Rome for the dreadful sufferings of the people of constitutional Italy. "*La Fame in Italia*" is the sensation heading of an article in the chief Ultramontane organ in Rome, in which a most distressing picture is drawn of the state of things brought about by the "revolution" in the unhappy region which has been emancipated from the rule of Austrian bayonets, Bourbon *sbirri*, and Tuscan and Modenese Grand Dukes. "Hunger in Italy"—the Indian famine is trifling in comparison with the dearth of revolutionised Italy. There are thirty thousand people in Venice looking to public charity for their daily bread. In the island of Sardinia—in which, if I mistake not, the "revolution" cannot be chargeable with much mischief, seeing that the island has been an appanage of the House of Savoy almost ever since it ceased to be the prey of the Arab corsairs, and the Sardinians are as devout Catholics as any in Italy; but perhaps it is placed under the "revolution" ban for the reason that Garibaldi's islet is only a few hours' distance from La Maddalena—in the island of Sardinia the necessaries of life are almost entirely wanting. Whole families are perishing for want of food. The laws are contemned, the authorities powerless. In the neighbourhood of Cagliari the unfortunate islanders have been living for months on *crows and myrtle-boughs*—a curious diet, somewhat analogous to a course of magpies and stumps. It is not more curious, however, than that of the shovel-hats in Rome, whose only nutriment, as all men are aware, consists of cloves and olive-branches. As for the kingdom of Naples, it is notorious that beggary, famine, and brigandage are rampant there; and nothing can be more miserable and more lawless than the condition of the island of Sicily, including the city of Palermo. The clerical critics forget to mention how many Neapolitan brigands have received material aid from the Papal Government and from the Papal *protégé*, the abject Bombicella; nor do they dwell on the ugly fact that the chief promoters of the disorders which lately called for stern measures of repression in Palermo were brutish and profligate monks—own brothers to the hulking friars who infest the Roman streets, and compete with the brass-badged mendicants for the crusts and the coppers. When to hunger, brigandage, and lawlessness, you add such things as impiety, atheism, immorality, debt, taxes, and a constantly-increasing deficit in the revenue, the condition of the revolutionised Peninsula may be faintly imagined. "This is the end," the Ultramontane Jeremiah concludes, "of all the golden dreams and the seductive illusions of the unhappy Italian people. This is the end of the magnificent promises made to them; and this would be the fate of the happy and contented Roman people if they submitted to be 'regenerated and redeemed' by the revolution." If to this were added a little personal abuse of King Victor Emmanuel, we might almost fancy that we were listening to Sir George Bowyer.

This in all conscience is bad enough; but worse remains behind. The poverty and embarrassments of Italy, we are warned, together with the prevailing wickedness and irreligion of the "Piedmontese party," are breeding in the public mind a state of despondency verging on despair. While loyal and pious Rome skips like the little hills for joy, the Italians, so the shovel-hats declare, are going melancholy mad. Witness the number of suicides which have lately occurred in revolutionary Italy, even in the highest ranks of society! Witness the lamentable act of self-destruction committed by the Commendatore Giambattista Cassinis, Senator of the kingdom, at Turin! The responsibility of this unfortunate event must be laid at the door of the Italian revolution. It is very impertinent for me to venture to prompt the accomplished scribes of Ultramontanism, but it might be as well to suggest that their agreeable comments on the death of an eminent Italian statesman are incomplete without a repetition of the old lie so dear to the Ultramontane heart—that Calvin died cursing, that Voltaire choked himself with his bed-curtains, like the python at the "Zoo" with his blanket, and that Rousseau took poison, all because they were so wicked.

The people of Turin, it appears, are getting up a subscription for a statue to the late M. Cassinis, and Ultramontane wit—which very much resembles that of an elephant in black knee-shorts and shoe-buckles—is making very merry at the expense of the Turinese on this head, stating that henceforth revolutionised Italy must be called, not the "land of the dead," as M. Lamartine described it, but the land of monuments. Cavour, La Farina, Massimo d'Azeglio, the brothers Bandiera, Moro, Farini, Fano, have all had, or are to have, their statues. Who next among the "coryphées of the revolution"? the clericals ask. Putting up a statue to anybody, human or divine, living or dead, is perhaps a stupid thing, which had much better be left alone; but humanity can no more desist from the practice than it can from scribbling its name on the pedestal when the statue is put up. But the clumsy pleasantry directed against the erection of monuments to Italy's great men comes with a very ill grace from Rome, the city *par excellence* of dolls, pagods, fetishes, and Pontifical guys—the city in three of whose churches yesterday I saw a waxwork-show, with decorations by theatrical scene-painters, and dresses apparently from

Nathan's, but which Mr. Artemus Ward would have scorned to exhibit to that hypercritical audience at Utica, who "caved in" the head of Judas Iscariot—the city of stone cherubs with swollen cheeks, and bloated angels with their draperies distended by rude Boreas, displaying their biceps and sartorius muscles on public bridges—the city of impossible saints perched on the peaks of pediments, and apocryphal martyrs standing on one leg.

But although the clerical mourners over the sufferings of Victor Emmanuel's subjects are so exceedingly virtuous, there are still cakes and ale in Rome. The ginger might be a trifle hotter in the mouth; but it is still ginger, and not gall and wormwood. When we had entered on the Carnival we were very agreeably reminded of the fact by the opening of the theatres. The edict of the Pontifical police authorising the commencement of "*il divertimento del teatro,*" was one of the most amusing documents I ever read. I perused it in a placard pasted on an old wall; they do not post upon the hoardings here, seeing that they never build new houses, and when an old one tumbles down they call it a ruin, and inscribe on the prostrate chimney-pot "Munificentia Pii IX. Pont. Max."—side by side with the latest fulmination of the Congregation of the Index, condemning two or three French works in history and science, and that S.P.Q.R. notification I told you about which fixes the price of leg of beef and scrag of mutton.

The regulations of the Pope's police on the subject of theatres are far more rigorous than the unwritten laws of our Lord Chamberlain and his licenser. The audience are not permitted to applaud "immoderately," or to encore any song, dance, speech, or scene. They are not to "yell" (*gridare*). They are not to employ whistles (*fischietti*). They are not to call for any actor or actress, or speak to any musician—a stern taboo this on any irreverent manifestation of a "Play up, Catgut!" nature. They are not to wear any unseemly garments, or to throw any bouquets, or to buy or sell any photographs in the building. I wish that among these prohibitions there were one forbidding Italians who think they can sing—and they all think they can—from humming all the airs in the opera, not by any means in a *sotto-voce* tone, in accompaniment to the singers on the stage; and it would be certainly desirable if the management were brought to understand that an opera is, after all, a performance possessing some dramatic as well as lyrical interest; that there are operas—such as *Norma*, *Lucrezia Borgia*, and the *Sonnambula*—as exciting in the curiosity they awaken as any tragedy of Alfieri or any comedy of Goldoni; and, if, understanding this, they were restrained from interpolating between the first and second acts of the opera a long and wearisome ballet.

Anything longer and anything duller than a Roman ballet it is impossible to conceive. It is literally a pantomime—that is to say, a pantomime without any fun. They give moral ballets at the Apollo Theatre here—I don't mean that the coryphées are compelled by the Cardinal Vicar to appear in Turkish trousers of green gauze reaching to the ankle, as in the Bourbon times at Naples—but ballets with a story, ballets with a purpose, ballets full of good and evil spirits, lost children, pious cottagers, benevolent countesses, and venerable hermits in gowns of glazed calico and beards of whitened tow, who rush about the stage in a demented manner, prophesying their old heads off, in dumb-show. There is a ballet called the *Giotta d' Adesberga* given at the Apollo just now, which is like one of Mrs. Barbauld's stories dramatised by a lunatic and performed by the scholars of the Deaf and Dumb Asylum. Now, morality is an excellent thing; but morality in short skirts, and didactic reflections on one leg, and sententious maxims combined with the double-shuffle, are rather provocative of merriment than of edification.

They play some odd tricks with the operas too, and the titles and recitatives are made to undergo strange metamorphoses. *Norma*, to avoid the impropriety of a priestess of any faith forgetting herself, becomes a peasant-girl in *La Foresta d'Irminsul*, and *Giovanna di Guzman* stands sponsor to the *Sicilian Vespers*. But why don't they give the wicked operas in their entirety, but with a sound Pontifical moral at the end? Don Basilio in the *Barbiere*, after singing *La Callunnia*, might doff his shovel and deliver a good set speech against revolution; the Commendatore in *Don Giovanni* might say some very stinging things about the profligacy of certain revolutionary princes; and the occasion of Masaniello's death might be improved by the recitation behind the scenes, and to the accompaniment of red-fire, of a homily pointing the obvious moral, that seafaring men who foment revolution invariably go raving mad and bring about an eruption of Mount Vesuvius. If poor Masaniello's body were brought across the stage on a stretcher, in a red-shirt and a pork-pie hat, to the music of Garibaldi's Hymn, the moral effect would be tremendous: more tremendous, perhaps, than the moralists would like to risk.

XXXI.

THE STREETS OF ROME.

January 21.

MUCH sympathy, which would have been better bestowed elsewhere, has been thrown away in bewailing the almost entire disappearance of the streets of ancient Rome. In the first place, persons are apt to forget that, although temples and basilicas, solidly constructed, may endure for a couple of thousand years, and, abating earthquakes, sieges, and the barbarians—to say nothing of princes who strip from old monuments the building-materials for new palaces—may show, at the end of twenty centuries, as few symptoms of decay as the Maison Carrée at Nismes, or the Amphitheatre at Verona, or the Temple of Vesta, here ordinary dwelling-houses are more fragile in their construction, are preserved with greater difficulty, and burnt down with greater facility. There may have been Chancery-suits, too, under the old Roman civil law, which proved as efficacious in ruining house-property as any great case of Jarndyce *versus* Jarndyce among us. Cheops built, and Praxiteles sculptured, for Eternity; but the mass of houses in the mass of streets in this world are but little cockboats launched on the broad river of Time, and doomed, *in* time, to be swamped or run down by bigger barks. Round about old cathedrals, it is true, the old, old dwelling-houses of our ancestors are curiously tenacious of vitality; and, in spite of all the efforts of the Houses-of-Parliament Commission and Baron Haussmann, some generations may yet elapse before the antique hovels which cling to the purlieus of Westminster Abbey and Notre Dame de Paris disappear: but these are but barnacles sticking to the keels of very old ships; elsewhere, new brooms are being continually made, and the sweeping away of old houses is incessant. The change they suffer, although thorough, is imperceptible, just as a certain school of physiologists tell us that once in every seven years or so, although we think that we have the same heart, lungs, liver, skin, and hair, we get a bran-new set of those organs and tissues. The Poultry, by Cheapside, is abstractedly the same narrow Poultry which Sir Christopher Wren, to his own sore discomfort, was forced to lay down, after the great Fire of London, on the lines of a still older street; yet I question if, the chapel excepted, there are half-a-dozen houses in the Poultry that are a hundred years old.

I have met a great many travellers professing an expectation to find the streets of Rome with precisely the same configuration, containing the same houses, and presenting the same characteristics, as they may have done under the Twelve Cæsars. They require their inn or their greengrocer's-shop to be in exact accordance with the canons of Vitruvius. They look for the *atrium*, the *impluvium*, and the *alæ*. They want statues of the Lares and Penates in the peristyle, fresco arabesques in the *cubicula*, "*Cave canem*" on the door-jamb, and "*Salve*" on a slab of mosaic to serve as a door-mat; and if they don't find these things, they cry out that Rome is very much fallen indeed; and I have heard fast young gentlemen from the universities declare over their cheroots and punch—they make punch with *white rum* at the Caffè di Roma, and, just tomahawked or dashed with maraschino, after the recipe of the Right Honourable Benjamin Disraeli: it is very good, and might convert Mr. Spurgeon to Romanism—I have heard these fortunate youths, moderns of the moderns, declare Rome to be a "sell," and, as a relic of antiquity, not half so interesting as Chester.

I suppose one might just as well expect to find the old Roman *domus* in modern Rome as to meet ladies and gentlemen arrayed in the *toga*, or the *peplum*, or the *tunicopallium*, followed by their slaves, and surrounded by their freedmen and clients, passing to and fro in the Forum, praying in the Temple of Saturn, or making their way to the games in the Circus Maximus. We know that such sights, out of the Carnival, are impossible. We know that the Papal Zouaves are no Prætorians, and that the Pontifical gendarmes carry no *fasces*; and if we thirst for anachronism, the Swiss guards in their masquerading canary-bird dress, the dirty shavelings, and the infinite people in shovel-hats, should be quite old enough to satisfy the most ardent member of the Royal Society of Antiquaries. Still, even those who expect little, and are in consequence rarely disappointed, those who have taken the portraits of many cities and dissected many schemes of civilisation, are unable to suppress something akin to a sigh of regret when they find the *tabula rasa* which has been made of old Rome—when they discover that the ruins of the City of the Cæsars are all but isolated from the City of the Pontiffs—when they behold the streets of modern Rome and find them so very like modern Clare-market and modern Whitechapel, only much dirtier, and not quite so felonious.

Lord Lytton is responsible for much of the sadness thus engendered by the destruction of fondly-cherished illusions. The *Last Days of Pompeii* sent everybody, in person or in imagination, to that wonderful place. The novel so exquisitely and so truthfully portrays the city, that the houses of Glaucus and Pansa, the theatre, and the gladiators' wine-shop, have become as indelibly impressed on the readers' minds as the forms of the dead Pompeians on the hot ashes with which they were stifled. Bulwer has made Pompeii his own; the *Last Days* are the best possible guide-book to the disinterred city; and after a visit to Naples, or that which is next best, and in some respects preferable—after careful study of the Pompeian Court at the Crystal Palace—we come to Rome and are surprised at not finding "PANSA ÆD." in red letters over the first private house in the Corso, and feel ourselves aggrieved when, being asked out to dinner, the repast is not "after the manner of the ancients," with a wild-boar stuffed with chestnuts and honey, and a sow's bosom served with *garum* to follow—all to be taken on the *triclinium,* with youths from the Isles of Greece to warble soft melodies in praise of Venus Aphrodite, and slaves to crown us with flowers while we quaff the Falernian.

I have purposely exaggerated the feeling which I assume many visitors to Rome have experienced; but I am convinced that some such state of mind is very common, and that very few cultivated persons conclude their first day's wandering in the streets of Rome without a sensation of bitter disappointment. Was it for this that they came so far—to see imitation French soldiers in red breeches, and dragoons in helmets with horse-tails after the pattern of the Cuirassiers of the Imperial Guard; to meet everywhere Jouvin's gloves, *chocolat de santé*, and the eau-de-Cologne of Jean Marie Farina; to be told that Mr. Lowe sells Bengal chutnee and family Souchong, and that Mr. William Brown gives the highest exchange for English bank-notes and sovereigns? They may not exactly exclaim that Rome is a "sell," but still they are gravely disappointed. If you wish to see a real Roman house, and—substituting the cloak, the mantilla, and the burnouse for the *toga*, the *redimiculum*, and the *bardocucullus*—to see people attired after the manner of those of antiquity, you must go to Andalusia or to Algeria; there the *patio* admirably figures the *impluvium*, and the hot, vehement, blood-thirsty throng in the bull-ring—I have seen eight thousand people shrieking with exultation over one lamentable horse with his bowels hanging out—completely satisfies the imaginative craving to know what a gala-day at the Colosseum could have been like.

But in modern Rome, Papistry has taken up Paganism, swallowed it, welded it into its own components, and made it bone of its bone and flesh of its flesh. Apart from the huge ruins of the Forum, the Baths, and the Tombs, the Pope's paw is upon everything Roman. If you stumble on an ancient column, it has a saint flaming at the top. If you light on an ancient inscription, it winds-up with some more freshly-cut reminder that the munificence of Somebody "Pont. Opt. Max." has permitted it to escape destruction. The mitre and the shovel-hat have quite extinguished the *pileum*. The cupids and genii have gone down before the Madonnas at the street-corners, with their environment of dumpling clouds and more dumpling cherubs. Very often do you see the grim, grimy columns and entablature of a pagan temple chained up, as it were, in the tasteless structure of a Romanist church, which clings to the old marbles and sculpture, strangling them with its flexible claws, like Victor Hugo's devil-fish in the *Toilers of the Sea*. Over this absorption Romanists exult, and many devout persons, no doubt, thought it a wicked thing for Cardinal Mai to have scraped away St. Augustine's Commentary on the Psalms from the parchment, and exposed Cicero's Republic, the oldest Latin manuscript extant, which lay beneath.

For my part, while I deplore the havoc that has been made of so many antique temples, basilicas, palaces, fountains, baths, aqueducts, columns, and statues, I do not see the slightest cause for regret in the evanishment of the streets and dwelling-houses of classical Rome. The excavations of Pompeii show us with microscopic distinctness what those streets were like; and it is plain that—all their frescoed arabesques, mosaics, encaustics, bronzes, alabaster, and *rosso antico* notwithstanding—the Pompeians must have lived miserably. It is plain that their streets were narrower than the meanest alleys in the meanest Moorish town; that their houses were badly lit and badly ventilated; and that they had every need to frequent such huge baths, such enormous theatres, and such a wide forum or gossiping-place, in view of the wretched little hutches in which they were cooped-up at home. Many an English squire's hounds are more amply kennelled than would have been the guests who accepted the hospitality of the patrician whose villa is to be visited every day at Sydenham. Things at Rome were doubtless all on a grander scale than in the neighbourhood of Vesuvius, yet this is a case in which we are surely entitled to reason from analogy. Pompeii was probably to Rome as Tunbridge Wells was to London, and we certainly look for comfort and even elegance on the Pantiles.* The civilisation of old Rome was, it cannot be doubted, grand and sumptuous; but the old Romans were, for all that, I suspect, a nasty, dirty set of people, who had need to go to the bath so often, seeing what pigsties they wallowed in elsewhere, and who wore their togas until—like the Russian peasants, who send their hats to the village oven to be baked, and thus freed from insect life—they were compelled to send them to the fuller's to be made decent again. Depend upon it, bad as modern Rome is, badly built, badly paved, and but half-lit with gas, ancient Rome was even more intolerable.

Let us not, therefore, beat our breasts and utter the wail of woe because Alaric, Genseric, and others, from the fourth to the sixth century, successively performed with Rome the admired feat which in later days was so notably repeated by Field-Marshal Turenne, by Field-Marshal Tilly, and by Generals Sherman and Sheridan, and other famous conquerors, including Genghis Khan and Timour the Tartar, and which is known as knocking a city into a "cocked-hat;" or because Belisarius gutted the inside of Rome to strengthen the walls outside it; or because Robert Guiscard and his Normans burnt Rome from the Antonine column to the Fla-

* According to Horace the inns, even at a short distance from Rome, were most miserable.

minian gate, and laid waste the Esquiline hill; or because the Savellis and the Frangipanis, the Contis and the Caetanis, barbarians within, completed the havoc of the barbarians without; or because there was an inundation in 1345 which only left the summits of the Seven Hills above water, and an earthquake in 1349, and the Constable de Bourbon in 1527, who was worse than all the Goths and their compounds put together, and another inundation in 1530, with a long succession of Popes before and after, who despoiled and stripped every monument of antiquity to build or to ornament their own churches. "Fust cum smut in the corn," said the New Englander, recounting his experiences as a farmer, "and then cum the Hessian fly, and the next year cum the caterpillars, and they capped the climax of my catastrophe." Popery capped the climax of the catastrophe of Rome. It has left only one of the shabbiest modern cities to be found on the earth's surface; but the shabbiness and dirtiness of Rome are things that can be mended, when greater enlightenment and a better government shall prevail.

The best way to inspect the streets of Rome, if you wish to study as well as see them, is to break your pocket-compass and burn your maps and guide-books, as Prospero did his conjuring-apparatus, and, forgetting that such things as *ciceroni* at a *scudo* and a half a-day ever existed, take Chance for a Mentor, and lose yourself. This I contrived to do very effectually the day before yesterday. I have just turned up, and propose to commit an account of my wanderings to paper. I must have halted, now and again, on the way, and brought-up at *caffès* and reading-rooms to rest, and I must have slept, and I think I dined-out yesterday; but walking the streets has been my principal occupation during the last six-and-thirty hours, and I have the satisfaction now of knowing that I have worn a new pair of boots into a most comfortable state of slipshodedness, inflated my lungs with a variety of gases—some of them, I am willing to believe, unfamiliar to British chemists—and acquired an amount of Roman experience which may prove in the future, I trust, not wholly unserviceable.

I did not victual for the campaign, for the Roman larder is admirably supplied, and there is more to eat and drink procurable in the streets of Rome than in any other city in Italy. The Romans eat very odd things, it is true, and some that scrupulous people in England might term nasty —such as frogs, lizards, and hedgehogs; but at least their markets are full, and even the smallest wineshop, or *spaccio da vino*, has its *cucina*, or kitchen, attached to it. I did not provide myself with defensive weapons for the excursion, as nervous tourists still do when they take a trip to Tivoli: first because I had no pontifical license to carry arms, and next because I thoroughly disbelieve in the alarming stories current at the *table-d'hôtes* and in the smoking-rooms about brigands, *Sanfedisti*, infuriated Dutch Zouaves who stab inoffensive persons unable to provide them with Schiedam, bloodthirsty Antibes legionaries promenading the back-streets, and bayoneting civilians of heretical appearance as they emerge from the *botteghe oscure* where they have been beating down old-curiosity vendors, and felonious Trasteverini, who sharpen their knives upon stone statues of the Madonna, sprinkle their life-preservers with holy-water, and go out robbing and murdering so soon as the vesper-bell has finished ringing.

I daresay there are back-streets in Rome which are not safe, during the small hours, for people who persist in wearing eighteen-carat gold watch-guards outside their greatcoats, who won't wear gloves, and will wear diamond-rings on all the fingers of both hands, and who toss for napoleons under every lamp; but then I daresay the back-streets of Belgravia—or the front ones either, for that matter—would not be much safer to such wayfarers, say between midnight and two in the morning. There are rogues in Rome, as in every other great city; but pedestrians who are neither foolhardy nor tipsy may penetrate into all quarters of the city without the slightest danger, at all reasonable hours. I have heard, on good authority, that the civil governor of Rome, arguing from the reports of the different presidents of the Rioni, or districts, and their police-commissaries, has declared that at no time during his experience has the city been so thoroughly tranquil and well-behaved, both as regards political demonstrations and crimes of violence.

I write this, both with a view to correct the false impressions which may be current in England, springing from the barefaced falsehoods told in the Italian newspapers—falsehoods greedily caught up by the opposition newspapers in Paris—and to reassure some kind friends of my own in England, who have been writing to me letters of condolence on my alarmingly-perilous position in a city infested with bandits, and so soon to be given over to rapine and massacre. We have not yet come to that charming state of things which is chronic in Mexico, where you go to church armed to the teeth, and return from a whist-party with a revolver in one hand and a bowie-knife in the other, walking in the middle of the road, lest an assassin should be lurking under an archway. We have not even come to realise the state of affairs prevalent in London—which I have heard called the metropolis of the world—many of whose most frequented thoroughfares are impassable, to decent people, not only after dark, not only at dusk, but often at broad daylight, from the gangs of costermonger "roughs," of blackguard boys and girls, of pickpockets, sharpers, and cadgers, and of common courtesans, who are suffered by a badly-organised police, and an incredibly lax and incompetent municipal government, to infest them. I will say nothing about the state of the suburban London roads at night, save to hint that I would much rather stroll along the Via Appia than Haverstock-hill after ten P.M. I might possibly meet a fox among the tombs; but I should prefer *that* to a garotter among the trim villa residences.

Unarmed then, unfurnished with provender, and with very little money even in my purse—for foreigners who walk about in Rome are very apt to come home with no gold and silver, but with a large stock of Roman scarves, cameos, and photographs, all picked up, of course, as bargains—I journeyed forth towards my unknown destination. The world was all before me where to choose as I emerged from the Hôtel d'Angleterre. Five minutes' careless strolling either to the north, the south, the east, or the west would bring about, I knew well, the consummation I had in view—that of not knowing where I was; but I was ambitious, and wished to lose myself thoroughly, and at as great a distance from my habitation as was possible. So I took a cab, and bade the man drive me to the post-office.

The public conveyances of Rome, I may remark once for all, are generally uncovered, little, light, one-horse calèches, not unlike the St.-Petersburg droschkies—not the droschkies on which you sit astride and pull the isvostchik's ears as you wish him to turn to the right or left, but those in which your legs are spread out before you in the normal manner. The Roman *calescini* are passably clean, not at all uncomfortable, and very cheap, that is to say, a drive to any part of the city within the walls need not cost more than eightpence. For two-horse carriages you pay a *lira* and a half for a "*course,*" and forty *bajocchi,* or one-and-sevenpence, for an hour. For excursions *extra muros* there is no settled tariff; a bargain must be made; and as foreigners are the principal patrons for drives beyond the gates, they must expect to be cheated. If you object to this, I should advise you to hire a carriage, not from the public stand, but from the hotel in which you are staying. In that case you will not be cheated, but simply overcharged. The price of a carriage for an entire day—and which is a really handsome turn-out, with two fiery horses, and a most aristocratic-looking driver in semi-livery—is five-and-twenty francs. You may engage it for half a day; but in the computations of Roman hotel-keepers the day has no first half, the long and the short of which is that if you require a *remise* for a drive on the Pincian Hill in the afternoon, or to take you to the theatre in the evening, you pay half-a-guinea for it; but if you merely want a drive among the ruins after breakfast, you pay a guinea.

Save when the claims of gentility assert themselves, and I elect to live for an hour-and-a-half at the rate of two thousand five hundred a-year, I prefer the hack *calescino* at eightpence the *course*. It is very cool and pleasant, and you can see everybody, and everybody can see you, as it was with Brothers the Prophet and the Devil in Tottenham-court-road. As you are usually alone, too, in this vehicle—for it is not genteel to offer a lady one-horse exercise—the *calescino* has something triumphal about it; and, by "making believe" a great deal, as Dick Swiveller's Marchioness did when she put the orange-peel into water and made believe it was wine, you may bring yourself to believe that you are a Conqueror by the name of Cæsar, and proceeding along the Via Sacra in your chariot; Zenobia, Queen of Palmyra, trudging before you a captive, with muddy sandals and shackles on her finely-proportioned limbs, and a host of elephants following you, laden with the spoils of your campaigns. You propose in the evening to paint yourself a bright scarlet, and to sacrifice several of your prisoners to the gods. What scenes in the circus you will have to-morrow with the elephants, and the lions and tigers, and Christians, and other wild-animals! Ah, what does that servile person standing on the splashboard of your triumphal chariot venture to whisper in your ear? That you are mortal. What impertinence! Are there no lictors to take him up, or at least cry, "Whip behind"?

That I was mortal I was reminded, and in a very curious manner, not ten minutes after I had entered my *currus triumphalis* at fifteen *bajocchi* the course. In the maze of narrow streets which hem in the Post-office we got mixed up with a funeral. It was a delightfully fine and warm afternoon, and anything more grotesquely ghastly than this funeral I never saw under a bright sun and a blue sky anywhere. It was a walking funeral. The coffin was a great painted ark, bedizened with rosettes of tinsel and foil-paper, and hung with festoons of paper-flowers and shreds of coloured calico. It looked as though Jack-in-the-Green had gone the way of all flesh which is grass, and was to be buried in professional costume, with my Lord and my Lady as chief mourners; and I am sure that the 19th of December in Rome was very like the 1st of May in less-favoured climates. This ark was borne on painted poles, apparently distrained from barbers' shops, on the shoulders of half-a-dozen lads in long red gowns, beneath which their dirty boots "stole in and out" in anything but the mouse-like manner of the little feet of the bride in Sir John Suckling's ballad; and they swayed to and fro with their burden, and staggered along, now and then halting to trim their bark and adjust their balance, in a fashion which was, to say the least, unseemly. In a surplice, which had evidently not been washed since last Easter, and which was disgracefully ragged, came along a thurifer, with a great crucifix on the top of a pole. There was an old priest in spectacles, and a young priest with many pimples on his face, walking leisurely along, and crooning forth, in that dull, listless, heartless chant which, to heretics, is the most distasteful and irritating of all things in the Romish rite, the Office for the Dead. The old priest had something the matter with his knee-shorts, which compelled him every two minutes or so to stop and hitch them up; and the young priest, at the imminent risk of getting a crick in his neck, was staring at the occupants of the very tall houses on either side the street, droning out his chant meanwhile, and yawning occasionally, as though he found the Office for the Dead rather a bore than otherwise, which I daresay he did. There was a sprinkling of choristers carrying candles, and choristers swinging censers; but the most extraordinary part of the *cortége* was that which brought up its rear.

A mob—for I can give them no other name—of hulking fellows came clumping along, their features and all but the dim outline of their limbs concealed under most hideous robes and hoods of bright green-baize, with white-calico crosses sewn on to the breast. Their cowls, drawn over their faces, with two holes for their eyes to peer through, looked inexpressibly horrible. I have met more than one Trappist monk, and in Spain I have seen the Confraternity of the Passion, who carry images about and wear disguises of fine white flannel; but this rabble-rout of green-baize maskers in Rome staggered me. If anything could add to the incongruity of their aspect, it was this: that the robes of many were too short for them, and that beneath the green-baize vestments I noticed one pair of shepherd's-plaid pantaloons, and one of corduroy. They were howling, in a most drearily-demented manner, some litany or penitential psalm of their own, which completely failed to harmonise with the Office for the Dead going on ahead.

I asked the driver who these people were, and he informed me that they belonged to one of the innumerable Confraternities of the Dead, who in Rome appear to be a kind of amateur undertakers. According to the driver, they were great rogues; and he even hinted that as soon as they got possession of a corpse their principal endeavour was to extract as many *pauls* as they could out of the bereaved relations: but this, I hope, is not the case. It is certain that they attend condemned criminals to the scaffold quite gratuitously; and the intense horror of death and puerile terror even of the sick-room, which prompt so many Italians to abandon the sick and dying to the priest and the hired attendants, render the intervention of these confraternities necessary. Somebody finds a shroud; a coffin is easily hired for the occasion; and the priests and hooded people do all the rest. Funerals must be very cheaply conducted in this country; and, abstractedly, there is nothing purer and nobler than the voluntary penance to which these green-baize persons devote themselves in the performance of offices generally found so revolting. Practically, perhaps, it would be better to employ regular undertakers than these howling amateurs. Foreigners are always told that many of the proudest Roman nobles are members of these confraternities, and that the eyes you see blearing through the slits in a hood may belong to a Colonna, an Orsini, or a Pamfili-Doria; but I scarcely imagine that the green-baize guild numbers many patricians in its ranks. I had a taste of their quality ere long.

I have said that we were mixed up with this funeral. The painted coffin and its carriers, the priests, the cross-bearer, and the choristers, all became inextricably entangled with my *calescino* and its horse, with a string of peasants bearing sacks of charcoal, with a dray piled with pumpkins and drawn by two of the savage buffalo-looking oxen of the Campagna, with a knot of Dutch Zouaves rather the worse

—or the better—for their visit to the adjacent *spaccio di vino,* and with a *contadino* on horseback, who, cloaked up to the eyes, and with his shaggy overalls of goatskin, his high-peaked saddle, and huge rowelled spurs, wanted only a coachwheel-hat and a lasso wound round the cantle of his saddle to make him the twin-brother of a Mexican *guerillero.* You may add to these several priests off duty, and with shovel-hats, quite broad enough of themselves to block-up a street of ordinary width; a select party of young gentlemen returning from some theological day-school, and clad for the occasion in salmon-coloured bed-gowns, also with shovel-hats—nothing religious can be done in Rome without a shovel-hat, and even the Pope wears one, of a bright crimson, like a cardinal's turned up, during the performance of certain rites—a sprinkling of monks, some barefooted and some clumsily shod, who, in infinitely-varied stages of dirt and imperfect shaving, are always hopping about Rome, like pigeons, taking what they can pick up; and innumerable monks without hoods and shaven crowns, but with brass-badges on their breasts licensing them "*a domandare in Roma,*" and who were professional beggars.

These, with the children wriggling about under and between the legs of the adults, like eels, and a poor mule, seemingly belonging to Nobody, and who had gotten his eye knocked out, and was wandering about in a dumbly-distraught manner, the blood trickling from his orbless socket, very pitiable to view—these, with a tribe of furious dogs, and a number of old women, clawing each other's heads on the doorsteps, and, more furious than the dogs, the Confraternity of Death howling their banshee serenade, made up a picture of modern Roman life for which I was quite unprepared. For all its frequentation by the *forestieri*, the grass grows between the stones on the Via Condotti and the Piazza di Spagna; but here there was life and animation and bustle of quite a turbulent order. It was life and animation, however, quite two centuries and a half old, and struck me, as I sat in a hack-cab on the 22d of December 1866, as being life and animation not precisely real and vital, but of a spasmodic and galvanised description.

A heretic of heretics, I was nevertheless taught in my youth to uncover my head whenever a corpse passed by. We owe, at least, that reverence to the Unknown King. And if Death had not been there, the Cross at least was. So I took off my hat, an action not imitated by my driver, so soon as the procession straggled into view, and I have to record that in Catholic Rome I got well laughed at for my pains. There is, perhaps, not much harm either in uncovering when in a public picture-gallery you stand before a picture of the Crucifixion, or the Mother and Child; but I have always been stared at and grinned at if I have paid that slight mark of respect to that which I do not Understand, but which I Revere.

The Confraternity of Death are much to be commended for their pious zeal; but I am afraid that the familiarity with the Office for the Dead and other sacred things has engendered something like contempt for that and other sacred things. At all events, they and the coffin-carriers *and the cross-bearer* indulged in a regular slanging-match with the driver of my *calescino* and the conductor of the dray laden with pumpkins. My driver gave them quite as good as they brought, and the result was the usual torrent of blasphemous Billingsgate, in the comprehension of which six-months' commerce with *gondolieri* and *vetturini* has rendered me a tolerable proficient. There is a richness and fulness, a copiousness of scurrility, in the Roman allusions to the principal persons mentioned in the Scriptures, which I have not yet heard equalled. The attendant priests did not in any way reprehend this scandalous scene, but "bullyragged" the driver themselves in good set terms—quite free, however, I hasten to admit, from blasphemy. At last, the dray being enabled to move on, my *calescino* got round the corner of the next street, and then the boys in red gowns began to carry the corpse, and the choristers began to swing their censers, and the old priest began to hitch-up his knee-shorts, and the young priest began to stare up at the windows, and the men in green-baize began to set up a renewed yowl, so dismal, that you might have fancied them the very Dogs, and not the Confraternity, of Death. Then I got down near the Post-office, asked if there were any letters, found there were none, and, plunging into the next half-dozen streets, forthwith lost myself.

There is something about funerals irresistibly encouraging to pugnacity. What a row there is whenever an Irishman is buried! What bloodshed followed the funeral of General Lamarque! What a frightful riot was that which attended the funeral of Queen Caroline! How the yeomen of the guard, if Horace Walpole is to be believed, fought for the wax-candles at the funeral of George II.! In modern English society, which is so very genteel, our funeral combativeness is of a subdued and decorous kind; but bad blood and set teeth have been manifest ere now on the way to Kensal-green. We disparage the cake and wine in undertones, grumble at the gloves, and mutter things sometimes not wholly complimentary to our dear brother departed.. I have had myself before now words with a man in a mourning-coach. I once saw two gentlemen—Irishmen by name, and sailors by profession—get out of a "brougham hearse" in the middle of Russell-square and fight, the undertaker waiting for the purpose, and an admiring circle of partisans in hatbands and scarves cheering the combatants on from their cab-windows; but the slanging-match in Rome the day before yesterday, the blasphemy, the Billingsgate, the tawdry coffin, the dirty surplices, the howling mummers in green-baize, and the Cross above all, like the mast of a wrecked ship visible above a stormy sea, made up a spectacle which will never be effaced from my mind.

If New York has been called a city of one street, modern Rome may with equal justice, or injustice, as your architectural taste or prejudices lead you to assume, be described as a city of no streets at all. Of course such sweeping criticisms applied to a metropolis once numbering a million of inhabitants, and now about two hundred thousand,* must

* The population of Rome in 1863, when the last census was taken, was computed, exclusive of strangers and the French garrison, at 201,161. In 1800 the total number of inhabitants was only 153,000; but in 1813, at the conclusion of Napoleon's rule, it had sunk to 117,000. Since that period it has been constantly on the increase, and in 1854 it was 178,042. The calculations as to the population of ancient Rome are, as a rule, the wildest guesses. Some antiquaries put it down at two, and some go as high as three-and-a-half millions. Topographical engineers, taking the extent of the lines of circumvallation as standpoints, declare that there could never have been more than a million of people in Rome. To have done with statistics, I may mention that the ecclesiastical population is composed of fifteen hundred priests, nearly four hundred seminary pupils destined for

to some extent necessarily partake of the nature of paradoxes. In New York, Fifth Avenue and all the other avenues, Eighth-street and all the other streets up to Ninety-first-street—if there be such a thoroughfare—the Bowery and Chatham, Wall and William, and the remainder of the streets in the old Dutch quarter of the island of Manhattan, have a clear right, municipally, statistically, and politico-economically, to be termed streets. They are built and numbered, and paved and populated, in due accordance with street-law. Yet, in the opinion of many, who, like Mercier and De Balzac in Paris, or Mr. Peter Cunningham and Mr. John Timbs in London, hold that a street is nothing without social characteristics and historical associations, New York has only one street, and that one is Broadway. In modern Rome, the paradox is even more sustainable. Broadway is at least a main thoroughfare, a grand artery leading from the heart to the head of the city, a High-street, indeed a trunk-road from which innumerable smaller thoroughfares branch off; but there is nothing arterial about the Corso of Rome. It is simply a very long, narrow, and dirty lane, with many turnings, by patiently threading which you may possibly get from the Piazza del Popolo into a network of filthy alleys which debouch on the Forum. It is not the highway of Roman commerce. The best Roman shops are not in the

---

the priesthood, two thousand five hundred monks and friars, two thousand nuns, and two thousand beadles, sacristans, custodes, bell-ringers, choristers, and other persons of the church-rat order. In this summary of the civilian army of the Pontiff I have not been quite so minute as the German statist who began his table with "Popes, two; cardinals, thirty-six;" adding, in a foot-note, "By the other Pope I mean the General of the Jesuits." His "other" Holiness is usually known in Rome as "the Black Pope," in contradistinction to Pio Nono, whose habitual attire is white flannel.

Corso; and were it not that it is the most convenient passage for carriages going to the Pincian Hill, it would be no more the main street of Rome than Holborn is the main street of London, or the Rue St. Lazare the main street of Paris.

I have, in a preceding page, mentioned the Via Condotti, which is the principal resort of foreigners, and the chief emporium of the exquisite nicknacks manufactured by the Romans for the delectation of foreigners and the impoverishment of their purses. The Via Babuino might also, by a great stretch of courtesy and the imagination, be termed a street; so might that of the Fontanella Borghese; so—a very large margin being allowed to the admission—might the Vie di Ripetta and della Scrofa. But none of these are streets, in the rigid acceptance of the word as used by civilised beings in the nineteenth century. The would-be dandy of the Regency had a garment made of Saxony broadcloth with silk linings, which probably cost him half-a-dozen guineas; but when he showed it to Brummell, expecting laudatory remarks, the Beau took the collar between his finger and thumb, and asked the abashed neophyte of fashion whether he called "that thing a coat." So is it with streets. We don't call Pentonville-hill a street, nor, the Board of Works notwithstanding, do we confer streetal dignity on Hanway-yard, or on that infirm and incult gap in which the Garrick Club have built their new house. Vigo-lane is not a street, and never will be. It will take another half-century to make New Oxford and Victoria genuine streets; and even King William-street, Strand, though more than thirty years old, is still in an incipient and embryotic state, wanting the real *cachet* and *imprimatur* of street vitality.

I have premised so much lest there might be persons yet untravelled, but studious of topography, who, on reading this, should produce a monstrous map of Rome from the pocket of a guide-book, flourish it before me, and ask what I meant when such a viatorial labyrinth had been laid down by the copperplate engraver; or lest members of the more felicitous classes, who have spent a winter in Rome, should, half-astonished and half-indignant, want to know what I was driving at. "No streets in Rome?" they might say: "why, we have been nearly run over half-a-dozen times in the Via dell' Angelo Custode. We have bought West-India pickles and Durham mustard in the Via Babuino. We have lost our way in the Via Capo-le-case, and have seen the horse-races in the Via del Corso."

With all this I respectfully submit that there are no streets in Rome; and I would say to the felicitous beings who *have* wintered there, "Ladies and gentlemen, you lived on the Piazza di Spagna, or the Piazza del Popolo, or the Bocca di Leone; and every morning and evening a carriage came to take you to the Capitol, or the Forum, the Quirinal, the Vatican, the Lateran, the Appian Way, or the Pincian. Do you remember those long dreary drives through by-lanes full of hovels and pigsties, full of dirt and beggars and foul smells? Surely you could not call those slums streets! In the afternoon, perhaps, you took a little gentle exercise, or did a little shopping within five hundred yards of your abode; and in a short time you would find out the principal places for the sale of cameos and mosaics, black draughts, blue pills, photographs, alabaster tazze, French bonnets, and sham Etruscan vases. But within how small a compass were those shops! You deal at perhaps twenty, and there should be at least twenty thousand in this huge city."

One of the chief advantages of a paradox is, that it may be qualified, modified, and taken with as many verbal and mental reservations as an oath by a Jesuit. There are few, if any, streets in Rome which are paved, well lit, handsome, commodious, or even commonly decent. There are few, if any, in which three friends can walk arm-in-arm, or in which Materfamilias can sail along surrounded by her olive-branches. In the Corso, for instance, the foot-pavement is so narrow, that if a lady halt for a moment to look into a shop she is in imminent danger of being jostled into the kennel by a Zouave, or a Monsignore, or a barefooted friar, or an Antibes legionary, or a "trasteverino" with a basket of charcoal on his back. As for the Condotto, there is not one inch of foot-pavement in it. Streets, indeed, where people can lounge, or even walk with convenience, are nearly altogether lacking; but on the other hand, there are some scores of Roman streets not less than three-hundred-and-fifty years old. Not that they are picturesque in their architecture, like the streets of Frankfort, Heidelberg, or Vienna; their three centuries and a half only represent an accumulation of dirt, discomfort, rags, and foul smells.

If you will only consent to give the nineteenth century the go-by—and I own that it is so continually forced down our throats, both from printed column and from spouting platform, as to have become a very close imitation of a bore,—and will consent to become thoroughly mediæval, you may take your fill of streets in Rome, and form a sufficiently accurate notion of the misery and wretchedness which the non-felicitous classes suffered during those same middle ages. Those ages have been unjustly decried, the sentimental devotees of the past inform us. There are people who wish, or profess to wish, for their reëdification. The amiable Tory poet, Lord John Manners, has put on record a couplet which, although not so well known as the famous "old nobility" one, is even more expressive of his lordship's views in regard to social progress. In the sweet volume of lyrics which he published in conjunction with the gentleman who afterwards turned Papist, and died Superior of the Oratory at Brompton, his lordship indulges in soft aspirations for the return of the halcyon time when "the humbler classes once again" shall "*feel the kind pressure of the social chain.*"

Walk about the streets of Rome, and you will see how the "humbler classes" felt "the kind pressure of the social chain," with a vengeance, during the middle ages. To that kind pressure, in France, in England, and in Germany, were due the plague, the sweating fever, the falling sickness, and the black death which used to swoop down on the kindly-chained ones periodically, and, where Alaric, Attila, and Totila had slain only their thousands, would lay their millions low. To the few remaining links of that "kind chain" which still rust and fester at home, we owe Bethnal-green and Spitalfields, and chronic cholera and typhus. Rome has felt the "kind pressure" so long as to have grown accustomed to it, and there are many Ultramontanes, I daresay, who assert that the Romans prefer their backward state of life to the feverish progress of the non-Catholic nations.

Would you tell me, if you please, why it is that the most orthodox Catholic cities always stink so intolerably? It is the odour of sanctity, I suppose. Many of the saints smelt more powerfully than pleasantly, and were additionally venerated for that reason. I will mention Seville, Cordova, Toledo, Toulouse, and Vienna. All those cities are orthodox, and in all of them the stench is unendurable. The streets of Rome, the houses of Rome—to the very palaces and museums—reek with such horrible odours that you are very soon led to conjecture that the ever-quoted malaria from the Pontine Marshes has been made responsible for a great deal of which it is quite innocent, and that one of the chief predisposing causes of the Roman fever is the inconceivable filthiness of the people and their dwellings.*

But it is heterodox, of course, to ascribe the stagnating filth of Rome, and the diseases bred from it, to the ignorance, stupidity, and bigotry of a government of old women; by which I mean priests. It is heterodox, of course, to point out that the cause of true religion could scarcely suffer if the Government of his Holiness the Pope would condescend to such trifles of administrative reform as to pave the streets,

* There are medical authorities, I know, who maintain a contrary opinion, and who ascribe the unhealthiness of Rome to the desolation of the circumjacent Campagna, the diminution of the population there, and the number of deserted villas, in whose wildernesses of abandoned garden a kind of choke-damp is bred. According to these sages, whenever a large number of persons have been crowded into a confined space in Rome, as in the Ghetto and the densely-thronged quarter about the Capitoline Hill, the salubrity of the situation has been apparent, in spite of the dirty habits of the people. Now, were this statement accepted unreservedly, it would be one of the most powerful arguments ever adduced against soap, small-tooth combs, fresh water, and abundant ventilation. Similar arguments were often heard in England when it was proposed to clear out St. Giles's and abolish Smithfield Market; but I am happy to remember that they did not prevail.

light them better, drain them, perforate their postage-stamps, and hint to the *employés* at their post-office that there is no need for them, in the month of December, to take a siesta from twelve to two P.M., and at four shut up the office altogether. Catholic Unity, the Faith, the Immaculate, and the Vicar of &c. &c., would all doubtless be imperilled if an attempt were made to cleanse the Augean stables in which the humbler Romans have been weltering any time since the middle ages, and in which they are likely to welter till this antiquated Papal machine tumbles to pieces—not from any overt violence, I hope, but of its own accord—and something new and serviceable, more in accordance with the requirements of a civilised age, is built up in its place.

These fetid pigsties, these abominable dens, were the kind of places people lived and died in during the middle ages, all the while such splendid churches and palaces were being built, such glorious pictures painted, such beautiful missals illuminated, such exquisite bas-reliefs carved in marble and oak and ivory, such delicate tapestries worked, such rich armoried glass stained, such brave goblets and tankards chiselled, such gallant suits of armour and trenchant swords and keen poniards hammered. All the while the "humbler classes" lived like dogs, were beaten like dogs, hanged like dogs, bought and sold like dogs, and died at last, dog-like, in such kennels. There are the very stalls where they bought their poor scraps of meat, their bunches of vegetables, their loaves of coarse sour bread. There are the very taverns where their wine was sold at a mean price to them, and where, getting hysterical at last with acid drink upon half-empty stomachs, they dug one another in the ribs with knives, as they do to this day. There are the same casements stuffed with foul rags, the same black and crazy staircases, from which peep old and weazened faces, or faces young and wan, or faces bleared by passion and poverty or the greed of other men's goods; or at which sprawl and squall, cascading at last to the kennel below, ragged, frowzy, elf-like children, many of them maimed by neglect, many of them scarred and seamed frightfully, more by the hot cinders of the braziers with which they have been allowed to play than by that other children's scourge, smallpox, and most of them, up to eight years of age, more than three parts naked.

I have not yet seen the "humbler classes" in Naples and Sicily, but up to this writing I have seen nothing so forlorn and so revolting, so miserable and so degraded, as the "humbler classes" of Rome. You man in the shovel-hat, who talk so unctuously about the Virgin Mary—you who have set up at every street-corner a painted idol, with a lamp before it—you who fill the minds of your penitents with all kinds of lying legends about the saints and their miracles—are you, too, so blind, so ignorant, so stupid, as not to see that in the lives of these deplorable creatures, fluttering in rags, wallowing in dirt—in these mothers, who from sheer lethargic carelessness suffer their babes to become hump-backed and bow-legged—in these slouching, unkempt men and lads—in these swarms of beggars, now cringing and now clamorous—in these homes, unfit for human beings, and scarcely fit for hogs, there is one constant, dull denial both of the Mother and the Son of God—there is one standing negative to the tremendous assertions of Romanism in the Basilica hard by? The filthiest streets of Rome are in the Borgo, and the Borgo is composed of the streets immediately surrounding St. Peter's. "*Tu es Petrus,*" runs the great inscription in mosaic round the drum of the dome, in letters every one of them as tall as a Life Guardsman—"*Tu es Petrus, et super hanc petram ædificabo ecclesiam meam;*" but underneath the rock of the Church priestcraft has built up a dunghill.

One loses patience altogether with the splendour of the Roman church, when we contrast that splendour with the squalor by which it is environed. At least, among us heretics, consigned by the Romanists to eternal torment, the church goes hand in hand with the trim school-house, full of clean and rosy children, with the hospital, the asylum, and the reformatory. But here there is but one step from Rafaelle's pictures and Bernini's statues to Beggar's Bush and the Cadger's Arms. Bramante's and Fontana's great façades only screen the nest of hovels behind; and all the loathsome losels of the Roman Alsatia wash their rags in fountains adorned with saints and angels. The very steps of St. Peter's, the very corridors of the Vatican, to within the shadow of the halberts of the Swiss guard, are beset by beggars. But is not mendicancy itself orthodox? Did not many of the saints themselves beg? And has not a life of sloth, uncleanliness, and mendicity, otherwise known as "holy meditation," been expressly pointed out by many Fathers of the Church as the direct road to salvation?

There are streets in Rome whose names are more poignant in their suggestiveness than the fiercest satire of Juvenal. The Vicolo Gesù-Maria is close to the Via degl'

Incurabili. The Street of the Guardian Angel is the most abandoned place you ever saw out of St. Giles's; the Street of Paradise is a poor imitation of Saffron-hill; and the Street of Death skirts the wall of a grand palace. All the saints have streets named after them; all the articles of religion, all its mysteries, and most of the non-apostolic personages in the New Testament, have their streets, with an occasional Triton, or Dolphin, or Nereid to make up; and now and then plain truth peeps out to the discomfiture of fiction, as in the "Street of the Old Shoes" and the "Street of the Dark Shops." But, amidst all these rankling hovels, among all the garbage, amidst all these tatters and tatterdemalions, the three-hundred-and-sixty-four churches and basilicas of Rome rear their sumptuous heads; without, all sculpture and ornate architectural ornament—within, all glowing fresco and radiant mosaic, gilding and embroidery, gold and silver plate. For my part I think it would be much less sacrilegious to sell every Rafaelle and Domenichino to the dealers in the Ghetto—to scrape every particle of gold-leaf off the statues of the Virgin, as the French did at Puebla—to melt down all the silver candlesticks, and despoil the very shrine on the altar of its gems, and apply the ready-money thus obtained to building a few model lodging-houses and a few baths and washhouses, than to allow Rome to seethe and rot in the corruption of neglect and abandonment, while the monuments of a preposterous idolatry blazed all around in gold and jewels.

XXXII.

A DAY WITH THE ROMAN HOUNDS.

"A southerly wind and a cloudy sky proclaim a hunting-morning," to which I may venture to add that "You all knew Tom Moody, the whipper-in, well." It will be perceived by these quotations from the once-popular anthology of the cover-side, now degraded, I am sorry to say, to a very dog's-eared condition in the "fourpenny box" at the bookstalls, that my intent, on the present occasion, is a sporting one; that I purpose rhetorically to array myself in scarlet, and to substitute top-boots for the classical *cothurnus*, and that the burden of my song throughout this letter will be "Yoicks!" "My name is Nimrod, and on the Esquiline hills my father kept his hounds, a noble pack, until—not being a frugal swain—my sire outran the constable, sold his dogs, and went to them himself." To have done with circumlocution, I aspire to give you an account of the great meet of the Roman Hunt as it occurred one day in the month of December 1866.

If a "southerly wind" be essential to the proclamation of a hunting-morning, the sons of Nimrod in Rome on that day must have had every reason to be satisfied. The sirocco, which is a southerner, with a dash of the easterly, like a Carolinian who has married a lady from Massachusetts, put in a very lively appearance throughout the forenoon. The

Roman sirocco is no arid and suffocating blast, such as that awful wind in Algeria which comes scouring in from the Sahara like a *goum* of wild Bedouins, its burnouse laden with impalpable sand, which pierces the lungs of the consumptive even as a sharp scimitar. When the sirocco blows in Algeria the people hasten to close their doors and windows, stopping up the very chimneys and keyholes, and remain in their back-parlours, trembling, till the flying pillar of hot dust has passed away. But when the Roman sirocco blows we open our casements, and invite the gentle gale to fan our cheeks and ventilate our apartments. It is a soft, mild, caressing wind, more resembling warm milk in a volatilised state than anything else. In summer the sirocco is said to be both debilitating and oppressive; but a fortnight before Christmas, and with the knowledge that your friends in England are being choked with fog, drenched in Fleet-street mist, or rendered despondent in the morning by the appearance of ice in the water-jug, the balmy south-easter is inexpressibly grateful and refreshing. At least ten thousand times a year we are informed by didactic journalists that there were people who wept for Nero—not such a very bad fellow, perhaps, after all: a kind of Mr. Sothern fallen into evil ways and gone mad, but a great actor always—and I am determined that there shall be at least one bard to sing the praises of that much-calumniated wind, the sirocco. For the world is growing very stale and jejune, and paradox has ever a salt flavour.

With the "southerly wind" came, however, no "cloudy sky." The cerulean vault might have been taken down bodily—since this is the city of miracles—and used to crown those enormous slabs of Russian lapis lazuli in the Baldacchino covering the sepulchre, where, outside the walls at Rome, *they say* the Apostle of the Gentiles is buried. St. Peter and St. Paul! It is not more shocking and irreverent perhaps to breathe those tremendous names in a newspaper-article than to have them huckstered about to you by *custodes* and *valets-de-place* at so many *bajocchi* a piece. "Down dere part of St. Paul be buried; rest of him in de oder church;" or "*A gauche, Excellence, sont les ossements de St. Pierre, apôtre et martyr.*" Mr. Kingsley, in his time, was shocked at the gross familiarity with which the sacred names of the colleges at Cambridge were bandied about by unreflecting under-graduates; but Romish and Cambridge ears grow, I suppose, in time alike hardened. The Ten Commandments here are so much fresco or encaustic; and the Passion is done in mosaic at so many *scudi* per foot. The Trinity has become a trade. Miriam cures wounds, and Pharaoh is sold for balsam.

Yes; the sky was bluer than any ultramarine that Winsor and Newton could sell at a guinea an ounce; and, save one little fleecy speck of vapour, wandering like a lost lamb in the fields of Elysium, it was without a cloud. The weather-wise declared the fleecy speck to be a sign that ere noon had passed the southerly wind would shift to the north and the sirocco become a tramontana, which is a very rude and blustering gale, harsh and penetrating, cracking the lips and reddening the nose, and playing old gooseberry with the ladies' crinolines and the ampler skirts of the Roman clergy. The sun shone bright and strong, to the infinite glee of the *forestieri*, but far too brightly and strongly for the Romans, who, in common with other Italians, have a deep-seated reluctance to exposing themselves to the rays of Phœbus. They never walk on the sunny side of the street if they can help it, and the only possible objection that can be taken to the hotels of Rome, which are exceptionally clean, comfortable, and well-managed, is that most of their rooms are as dark as Sir Walter Raleigh's bedroom in the Tower of London. "Murray" tells us of a Roman saying, that "none but Englishmen and dogs walk in the sunshine." * It is very odd how cosmopolitan are these proverbial sayings. Not nine months since I was told at Madrid, that nobody save "*un perro o un Frances*"—a dog or a Frenchman—walked on the sunny side of the Puerta del Sol. There were numerous Romans, however, yesterday in the Campagna, who were fain to be as dog-like as Englishmen, and not only to walk, but to ride, for a good many hours in the full blaze of the lord of the unerring bow, as Lord Byron calls the Apollo, whose bow must have erred sometimes, seeing that it is now hopelessly broken. You cannot ride to hounds with an umbrella, or take a stone wall in a brougham; at least, I fancy that Nimrod and the *Sporting Magazine* would not approve of such proceedings.

The Roman Hunt is an institution of respectable antiquity, and probably owes its origin to the great influx of aristocratic English to the Papal capital which took place

* The Roman doctors would not seem to be quite so strongly prejudiced against solar influences as their patients are, for the faculty in Rome have their own proverbial saying, to the effect that, in rooms where the sun does not enter, the physician invariably must. It is after all a question of season. There are months in the year, in Italy as in Spain, when the sun from a benefactor turns to an intolerable despot. In the hotels in Seville you pay for rooms without sun double the price charged for apartments *al sol;* and at a bull-fight *un paloo à la sombra*, or box in the shade, costs twice as much as one in the sun.

after the fall of Napoleon, and after Sir Thomas Lawrence's pencil and the munificence of George the Fourth to the Cardinal of York had made the Pope fashionable, and a winter in Rome the very genteelest of things to do. It is curious to mark the infinite ramifications stricken into the English mind, all springing from the common trunk of our hatred to the First Bonaparte. If Napoleon had used the Pope well, his Holiness would have probably remained the reviled and despised "Bishop of Rome;" but the French Emperor maltreated the Sovereign Pontiff, kidnapped and imprisoned him; so genial society in England forthwith "took him up," and he became the "dear good Pope" whom Belgravian ladies talk so ecstatically about.

The Roman Hunt fell into abeyance for a period of seven years. The suspension was due partly to the troubles of 1849, from which Roman society has never entirely recovered, and never will recover, until the fount and origin of the evil —the temporal power—is removed, and partly to the painful impression made on the mind of the benevolent Pio Nono by the numerous and sometimes fatal accidents which had taken place in the hunting-field. The truth was, that the English gentlemen who joined the Hunt imagined that they could do in the Campagna all that they had been in the habit of doing with the Quorn and the Pytchley, and that the Roman patricians who so blithely assumed the scarlet and buckskins—as the costume *de' veri cacciatori Inglesi*—tried, incited by noble emulation, to do all that the veterans of Melton Mowbray attempted, and more. The consequence was that, with melancholy frequency, the noble sportsman's horse would shy at the stump of a Corinthian column, or shy him neck and crop into the profundities of a sepulchral monument; and it was obviously more classical than convenient to crack your skull by contact with the broken bust of a defunct Prætor, and be carried to the hospital on a bronze door.

Since 1864 the Hunt has been reëstablished, and with the full concurrence of the Pontifical authorities—a special proviso, however, being added to the permission given by the kind-hearted old Pope, to the effect that the noble sportsmen should be accompanied by a mounted corps of Pioneers, consisting of one *contadino* on horseback, equipped with an axe and a pick, to cut down hedges that were too tall, and knock down stone walls that were too stiff to leap. The Hunt is placed under the management of a committee of Roman noblemen—I think Prince Odescalchi and Prince Colonna are alternately Masters—and consists of at least one hundred members, or *azionisti*, each paying a hundred-and-fifty francs a-year, and engaging to keep up their subscriptions for at least three years. Strangers may become annual members, and those staying but a short time in Rome are always welcome at the meet. I need not say that nine-tenths of the foreigners who thus avail themselves of the privilege are our own countrymen. Now and then a "fast" Yankee, an illustration of the Paris Jockey Club, or a Russian prince, makes his appearance in the field; but the Anglo-Saxon element is by far the predominant one; and the scene, apart from its wondrous associations of the buried past, is a thoroughly English one—that is to say, genial, good-natured, and jolly, with just a spice of the national eccentricity—which foreigners mistake for madness—and just a leaven of the national stuckupishness—which foreigners have no name for, but which they laugh at. I do believe there are English people who would give themselves airs in Charon's boats, as young Bibo did, till the stern ferryman hit him over the pate with his oar to teach him humility, and who would use smelling-bottles and eyeglasses in the very dock before Rhadamanthus' judgment-seat. I have seen "stuckupishness" at the top of the Alps and at the bottom of the Catacombs, and I saw it yesterday in full bloom at the Roman Hunt.

The meet for Thursday, which was to be the most brilliant of the season, was announced to take place at the Tomb of Cecilia Metella; but the actual rendezvous was on a rising knoll in the Campagna—very likely the crest of a partially-sunk tumulus, about a mile farther on, to the left of the Appian Way. The Tomb of Cecilia Metella, and the left-hand side of the Appian Way! What a trysting-place for foxhounds! Well, they must meet somewhere; and, given the favourable nature of the locality, we need not inquire too minutely into its history. The Duke of Wellington kept a pack of hounds in the Peninsula, and the Great Captain's short, sharp "Ha! ha!" was often heard as he galloped over the green slopes of Andalusia. Boabdil and Muley Abbas did not interfere with Jowler and Boxer, and Tom Moody, a colour-sergeant on ordinary days, was the whipper-in. The oldest and the dearest friend I ever had was a great huntsman, and emigrated to South America to re-make the fortune which he had lost at home. He went to Valparaiso, and did well—principally, I believe, in coal-mines—and I met a Scotchman at Cadiz who told me that he had known him well in Chili, that his old passion for the chase had revived, and that he kept a pack of hounds, all to himself, at the remote *hacienda* where he dwelt, often without seeing a European face from year's end to year's end, and went out hunting by himself, monarch of all he surveyed, like a top-booted Robinson Crusoe. Not a stranger rendezvous this, among the sierras and pampas and copper-coloured Indians, than here, among the tombs, with Numa Pompilius looking over the wall, and Professor Niebuhr denying him round the corner, while the voice of the late Sir George Cornewall Lewis is heard in high dispute with Mutius Scævola from the adjacent sepulchres. Associations, *à la longue*, are but adventitious. They may crop up everywhere. The bluff Leicestershire squire, the sturdy Yorkshire farmer, have their gatherings among associations as old and as interesting—now by a Roman encampment, now by a Danish colony—now by where Druids worshipped the mistletoe, and roasted people in wickerwork cages—now by where Canute rebuked his courtiers, or Hardicanute got drunk, or Boadicea was scourged, or crookbacked Richard fell in fight with Richmond.

I had made up a party, and filled a barouche and pair, and, at half-past ten, started from our hostelry in the Via Bocca di Leone for the tomb of Cecilia Metella. It is, perhaps, unnecessary for me to hint to you that your rambling interlocutor is not a hunting-man, and that he prefers to witness such things as battles, fox-hunts, and, if possible, shipwrecks, on four wheels, to joining in them on four legs—that is to say, on horseback. *A chacun son métier:* and it is not mine to follow the flying fox. The late Mr. John Leech and the yet extant Mr. Anthony Trollope have done quite enough to vindicate the individualism of literature and art in the hunting-field. I saw a Saturday Reviewer at the meet on Thursday, and I am right sorry that he did not catch a fall, for I am not one of those who profess to love my enemies. My enemy I should like to have, in handcuffs and without a hat, at high noon, in the middle of the Great Desert. I would then read him my printed opinions of him (which are highly sarcastic and, I think, clever), and refresh him from time to time with anchovy sandwiches and boiling Worcestershire sauce.

No, I do not hunt. I remember once staying in a country-house whose hospitable owner pressed me very much to "ride to hounds," and offered me something which he called a "mount;" and I am afraid that, under the influence of *capillaire* and seltzer-water, late at night in the smoking-room, I promised to "show" at the meet the next morning. I remember that I received important letters soon after sunrise, and went to London by the 8.40 train. Is there any harm in admitting that you never hunted anything bigger than a flea or a guinea? I hope not. Yet there are some people who grow quite savage, and sneer at you viciously, because you do not appreciate the delight of galloping after a wretched vermin at the risk of breaking your neck, or because you do not understand the slang of the hunting-field. How stupid are these sneers! Can we all of us do everything? Suppose I ask Nimrod what a *mezzotinto* scraper is; or how he would use the *roulette* in half-tones; and what is the best way of laying a soft ground, or knocking up a plate which has been overbitten? Suppose I ask Tom Moody how, on a given horizontal, he would construct an equilateral triangle, or how he would inscribe, in a given parallelogram, the ellipse known as the "gardener's oval"? Ten to one he would know nothing at all about these things.

Please, then, my noble sportsmen, don't sneer at me because, until dinner-time on Wednesday night, I did not know what the "fox's pad" was. Why should I? I never saw a fox unstuffed in my life; but, sportsmen, did you ever see a dolphin, or a shark, or a brigand, or a wild Indian? Life is short, and art is long; the study of English technology rivals that of the Oriental languages in abstruseness. I had heard of the fox's brush; but this is how I came to hear of his "pad"—the which, I apprehend, is his foot. "He brought home the fox's pad, did the captain," quoth a young Englishman at the *table-d'hôte,* "and he gave it to the cook to dry on the top of the oven, and, by Jove, sir, the fellow fried it and sent it up the next morning for breakfast, with chopped parsley. You may smell it in the kitchen now." I asked, deferentially, what the fox's pad might be, not knowing exactly whether it was something to eat or something to sit down upon, and being enlightened, experienced considerable gratification. The English tongue is certainly a most copious one, and its wealth of synonyms is inexhaustible. The foot of a fox is his "pad," and that of a dog his "paw." The head of a wild-boar is his "hood," and the tail of a hare his "scut," and the stomach of a horse is his "barrel."

We drove over the slippery flagstones of modern Rome amidst a wilderness of old churches, old pictures, old beggars, old women, and old clothes, and through the old Porta San Sebastiano and the older arch of Drusus, on to the Appian Way. It is certainly not wider than that back-lane which leads from Walham-green to Hammersmith, but it is the most interesting road in the world. To reach it, by the route we took, you must pass the gigantic Baths of Caracalla, and the still more gigantic, but more dilapidated, Palace of the Cæsars, which the Emperor of the French is so busily excavating, but which, for all the quotations from Livy he has stuck up as sign-posts, will scarcely become anything more than a shapeless mass of ruins—a Titanic brick-kiln, sent into a state of distraction by a colossal earthquake.

You must pass the tombs of the Scipios, and those of the Pompeys—the Columbaria, so called from their pigeon-house conformation, where baked Romans are potted down in such very circumscribed spaces, that the practicability of being burnt on a fourpenny-piece, and having your ashes collected on a postage-stamp, and being buried in a portemonnaie, at once occurs to you. The first time I visited the Columbaria the custode took out of a jar—originally, so it seemed, intended for Bengal chutnee—a handful of little bits of black stuff, and told me *that* was a Roman senator. Yes; and it might have been Cleopatra, or Marc Antony, or Alexander, or the Lady of Shalott, or the costermonger's baby burnt to death in the back-garret in Bethnal-green last Monday was a fortnight. We pack very closely, and give very little trouble when we are in a jar, calcined and powdered fine, that is certain. They might make a good pigment for house-painters out of a senator, and consular ashes might be useful in bleaching linen.

Lord save us! what infinite pains these Roman magnificoes were at, not only in these pigeon-cotes, but for miles and miles along the Appian Way, to have elbow-room in their tombs for their stuckupishness, and to let the remotest posterity know what grand folks they were! What myriads of alphabets were there not graven to record their styles and their titles, and the years of their births and their deaths. Not one in a thousand of the inscriptions is perfect; by not one in ten thousand is aught conveyed beyond a hollow noise that has no meaning. Now and then the sound is vocable, and has stress, as in the solemn warning, "Touch me not, O mortals; revere the manes of the dead;" or as in the exquisitely pathetic apostrophe, in which the bereaved mother endearingly implores the "kind fever, the good fever, the holy fever," which has taken two of her children, to spare the two that remain. But time and the barbarians have been as good as the fever, and neither children nor grown-up people, nor the manes of the dead, nor slave nor senator, have been respected; and this Appian Way is but a chaos of charnel-houses, with the Pope's highway running through it, along which post-chaises and hackney-carriages drive.

Do you know the bone-grubbing purlieus of Kensal-green, or the great *Croquemort* promenade on the way to Montmartre or Père la Chaise, or Stonecutter's-row in the Euston-road, or Greenwood Cemetery in New York? Take all the tombs and statues, tear up the vaults, lay bare the catacombs, break them up into fragments large and fragments small, play at nine-pins with them, half hide them in the earth, let grass cover and weeds choke them; grow the acanthus on the Corinthian capital, and let the thistle riot over the cornice—"down with the nose, down with it flat, take the bridge quite away"—from legions of bodiless heads, and shear the arms and legs from legions of headless marble bodies. Let this be a valley of dry bones, of petrified Chelsea and Greenwich pensioners. Turn the whole chaos loose in the building-yard of a Lucas or a Cubitt, after a long strike, or a longer lock-out. Shoot the rubbish of ages there; sprinkle with dust and innumerable brickbats, and serve hot, with trailing vines, and a bright sun, and a blue sky for sauce. This is the Appian Way.

Never was there such an eloquent rebuke to the pride, and vanity, and ambition of man. You may put the Pontifex Maximus in your snuff-box, and carry away a vestal virgin in your waistcoat-pocket. Those tremendous Romans here attempted to set up a lasting text of the sublime and the stupendous; and lo! Time sits on a broken tombstone, and reads a lecture on the Infinitely Little. The poorest Paris *gamin* shovelled last week into the *fosse commune*, the wretchedest pauper whom the board can worry and the nurse bully no longer, and whom the parish undertaker has nailed-up between four deal-boards and carried off to the paupers' burying-ground, is of as much account as the Roman Prince who had five-hundred slaves, and a thousand clients, and a fortune of four millions sterling.

The Via Appia is thronged with beggars. I will not say infested; for here they do not seem out of place. They are in perfect consonance with the decaying scene, with the decaying Church, with the general "mitycheesiness," so to speak, and twenty-centuries-old aspect of everything around. A Carden here might be prodigal of *bajocchi;* a Marquis Townshend, even, induced to bestow a *paul* upon a poor widow with a callow brood of brats. There is a very hideous creature on the Appian Way, a mendicant, who has a sliding-scale of ailments at his command, and who, in proportion to your liberality, will get more and more frightfully afflicted. A gratuitous view may be obtained of him; but he is then simply a spiteful idiot, with bandy-legs and St. Anthony's fire in his face. For two *bajocchi* he will have St. Vitus's dance; for three, his right side will be paralysed; for five, he will have an epileptic fit and foam at the mouth.

The *Papalini* tell us that Rome is full of charitable institutions, where every conceivable human ill is ministered to by "*nostri poveri monachi*"—by those charming monks and nuns whose convents the wicked and atheistical Government are so ruthlessly suppressing. Could not the Pontifical almoners find a corner in one of their admirable hospitals for this deplorable object on the Via Appia?

Signs of the Hunt began to appear as soon as we were clear of the arch of the Drusus. Outside the walls there was a great muster of ladies' and gentlemen's steeds; for the slippery flags of the Roman streets are terribly trying to horses shod for hunting, and prudent Nimrods prefer to mount *extra muros*. Many even drive to cover in dogcarts, *chars-à-banc*, or barouches. There were half-a-dozen English ladies, at least, who did not vault—vaulting is, I believe, the term—on to their crutch-saddles until they were well clear of the walls; but the spectacle then became charmingly equestrian, and the Appian Way was brightened by a most vivacious cavalcade. Gracefully-cut jackets, more graceful English faces, plumed hats, flying skirts, cambric handkerchiefs in the pocket of the saddle, daintily-varnished boots, tiny gauntleted hands, whips with amber, and coral, and bucksfoot handles—nay, even the famous "ladies' riding-trousers, chamois leather with black feet," were visible among the tombs. The gentlemen made an equally gallant show. With some, the modest pepper-and-salt shooting-jacket, with doeskin pantaloons and high boots, were deemed sufficiently "down the road;" but a goodly proportion of the noble sportsmen had evidently left England with malice prepense as regards the Roman Hunt. They may have aired their "pink" at Pau, in the Pyrenees; but the full bloom of their Nimrodism had been reserved for the Campagna.

The ladies tell me that there is not a prettier sight to be seen the whole world over than a gentleman in full fox-hunting dress. *I* think that the prettiest specimen of humanity possible to view is a lady riding in Rotten-row on a fine May morning; but, I daresay, were I a lady, that the cynosure of my eyes would be a slim figure in a well-fitting swallow-tail of brightest vermilion, with a shiny chimney-pot hat, a blue birdseye scarf with a horseshoe pin, buckskins fitting like a glove, and top-boots shining like a mirror. The present generation of hunting-men run slim, and have a tendency to moustaches, not innocent of *pommade Hongroise.* Indeed, about many of the dandies of the Roman Hunt there hung a mysterious odour of Truefitt's and Pratt's, the Raleigh Club, and M. Francatelli's *cabinets particuliers.* Yea, even of the Treasury and the Foreign Office, Whitehall.

The Roman Hunt is a highly-select one, principally because the Campagna is rather a long way off for a tenant farmer or a sporting publican, and Mr. Soapy Sponge thinks twice before taking a second-class return-ticket to Marseilles and Civita Vecchia. I did not see Mr. Sponge at the cover-side by Cecilia Metella's Tomb. I did not see Mr. Jorrocks.

Squire Western was absent; but Sophy Western was there, and young Tom Jones—third paid secretary of her Majesty's Legation, Ecbatana—making desperate love to her behind a sarcophagus. I did not see any of the burly, bloated fox-hunters, their scarlet coats smirched by innumerable spills, and stained purple, besides, by after-hunting orgies, with whom we grow so familiar in Luke Clennel's pictures; mighty hunters before the Lord, riding over five-barred gates all day, and keeping it up to all sorts of hours at night, always cracking t'other bottle, always drinking the "King, God bless him!" with nine times nine, over flowing bowls of punch, waving foxes' brushes over their heads the while in a distracted manner. A tipsy, swearing, Test-and-Corporation-Act-supporting, collar-bone-breaking generation they were, scouting the bare idea of railways, and holding the Elgin marbles in but slight estimation. They drank deep, but they did not smoke, and were far from the frivolous vices of the age of sham science and soda-water. And they won Salamanca and Waterloo, clearly.

There was no meet at Cecilia Metella's Tomb, and the fox, who must have read the announcement of the rendezvous in the *Osservatore Romano* of Tuesday, was doubtless bitterly disappointed. For, if there be any truth in the good old British theory that the fox likes being hunted, we may expect Reynard to be as punctual as anyone else in keeping his hunting-appointments. Moreover, the meet was to come off at eleven, and it was now a quarter to twelve. Appealed to, to reconcile this discrepancy, the driver of the barouche pointed to the extreme distance of the Campagna with his whip, and declared that "*i cani e tutta la caccia*" were "*un po' avanti*"—a little farther on. So he drove us for another mile and a half along the Appian Way—always among the tombs; but still no meet in sight appeared.

I was sorry, for the sake of Cecilia Metella, with whom I had already formed an acquaintance, and whom I much admire. What a noble old ruin is the mausoleum of Crassus' wife! Battered by the barbarians, converted into a castle, besieged and retaken half-a-dozen times by the more barbarous Roman barons, stripped of its sumptuous shell of marble by the lime-burners; rifled by Clement XII., to furnish artificial rocks for his monstrous fountain of Trevi; and at last so utterly given up to abandonment and neglect that its original intent was lost, and it was known only to the country-people as *La Torre del capò di Bove*, or Bull's-head Tower, from the white marble bas-reliefs on the frieze, in which festoons alternate with bulls' heads—the tomb of Cecilia Metella is still one of the most perfect vestiges that remain of ancient Rome, and with the Pantheon and the Temple of Vesta induces the most definite idea of the beauty, the strength, and the magnificence of the structures of this wonderful city. Clements, and Bonifaces, and Robert Guiscard, and the Constable de Bourbon have done their best to devastate it; but still "the stern round tower of other days," with its garland of eternity, its two thousand years of ivy, stands "firm as a fortress with its fence of stone," and frowns haughtily upon the Campagna, like an indomitable woman.

There is nothing inside the tomb but bats, and, at night, I suppose, an owl or two; but I could fancy the fox sitting at the bottom on his haunches, and murmuring that it was really very rude of the gentlemen of the Hunt to keep him waiting so long, and that if they meant hunting, they had better look sharp about it. Foxes have feelings as well as other people, which should not lightly be trifled with. We came on the meet at last, to the left-hand side, as I have already mentioned, of the Appian Way. The sight we saw fully atoned for the delay we had experienced in reaching it. There were the hounds—thirteen couple and a half, I think, they told me—the half being a young dog of piecrust-and-creamy hue, who would wag his tail at the wrong time, and was continually incurring personal chastisement on that account. There were the English gentlemen-riders, and the English lady-riders, and a very fair muster of noble Romans, some of whom appeared in true British scarlet and top-boots, while others favoured us with jackets and jockey-caps of black velvet, and varnished boots reaching mid-thigh. The show of horseflesh was capital; and as regards the noble sportsmen who had not brought their own hunters with them, but were content to hire them at the rate of forty francs for the day, the exhibition reflected the highest credit on Mr. Jarrett, who appears to be the Quartermaine of Roman livery-stable-keepers, and whose little son, in the quietest and prettiest of hunting-gear, and mounted on a very strong horse, distinguished himself greatly during the day, and took some of the stiffest leaps attainable.

There was a tent at the trysting-place, and external symptoms, in the shape of hampers of champagne, that something good was going on inside. Not being a subscriber to the Roman Hunt, I could not of course push my inquiries in this direction further. There was a great muster of private carriages—many of the most *recherché* equipages you meet on the Pincian, with their most *recherché* occupants, were indeed present—while the "ruck" was made up of yard-barouches, such as our own. The familiar sounds of one's mother-tongue were continually audible; and an occasional "melodious twang" with "I guess," or "O, my!" or "Yes, sir," to give it zest, led to the conclusion that the American as well as the British element was "on hand." After some twenty minutes' giggling and gossipping, and mutual inspection through eyeglasses, the huntsmen, the hounds, and the noble sportsmen decamped from the trysting-place, and the people who had come in carriages hastily alighted in order to follow the Hunt on foot. Then did the historian see sights!

There is a wonderfully droll Irish story of a matchmaking mamma, who is continually striving to delude subalterns in her Majesty's foot regiments into matrimony, by inciting her daughters to proceed in advance in a country walk, and "show Ensign Somebody how the turkeys walk through the long grass." That matchmaking mamma should have brought her daughters to the Campagna. Ensign Somebody would have proposed at once, had he seen Miss Jemima O'Flynn walking through the thistles. I have not the honour of Miss O'Flynn's acquaintance; but on inquiring of an English lady with whom I am on speaking terms, I elicited the fact that walking through thistles, with an occasional variation in the way of climbing a stone wall, was extremely painful to the feet, ruinous to the stockings, fatal to kid boots, and trying to the temper. In addition to the thistles, many parts of the Campagna were knee-deep in wild-flowers, most beautiful to look upon; and the deep purple of the distant Alban hills was exquisite. With all this, you don't care about having your boots cut to pieces, and your gracilis muscle lacerated by sublatent enemies of Scottish extraction.

The ladies who were best off were some very high-born Italian dames, who had adopted the last new Paris fashion for a walking-dress. Have you seen it yet in London? It is a marvellous make-up. You wear a hat, to begin with—anybody's hat—a cocked-hat, if you like, but preferably Tom Tug, the jolly young waterman's, glazed, flat-brimmed, and with a blue ribbon round it. The next thing is to go without your gown, and appear in public with your petticoat-skirt, which should be of scarlet quilted silk, like your great-grandmother's counterpane, and which reaches no lower than the tops of your boots. Your boots, by the way, are top ones, or rather Hessians without tassels. You wear a jacket, too, if I remember aright, of velvet; and to be perfectly proper and modest, you wear round your waist, not a fig-leaf, but a curious slashed-and-tagged structure, something like a bustle in duplicate, rigged fore and aft, as the sailors would say, and cut into pendent vandykes. Then, having left your crinoline at home, you borrow a very tall bamboo-cane from the fifth footman, and go out walking through the thistles. I don't think Ensign Anybody could have resisted *that* sight on Thursday. Unfortunately, most of the ladies so attired were princesses, or, at the least, duchesses, and the ensign would have had but a poor chance. O, I forgot one thing! Although it is so early in the morning, you paint your face an inch thick.

The noble sportsmen were subjected to a test of almost a crucial nature before the real business of the day began. The expanse on which the tent had been erected was separated from the wide waste of the Campagna by a long stone wall of considerable steepness—a very Irish-looking wall, and a very ugly one, to boot. There were no gates in it, and no gaps; and unless you went a quarter of a mile to the right, and struck the Appian Way, there was no dodging it. The wall, I am proud to state, was taken, in the majority of instances, "in style." The toy-hurdles they set up for the circus-riders at Franconi's could not have been cleared more deftly than was that Roman wall by at least three-fourths of the Actæons and Dianas present; and, so far as the four-footed participants were concerned, any amount of *scudi* must be put down to the account of Mr. Jarrett's stable. Now and then a horse would smell the wall, and prudently wheel away from it. One obstinate gray declined to do more than stand with his two fore-feet on the coping, and insinuatingly endeavour to wriggle his rider off his back; and one evil-tempered animal, a bright bay, fairly showed the wall a clean pair of heels, and bolted back towards the arch of Drusus.

The whole field, however, got over at last; at least, that portion who couldn't manage the leaps got *through* the wall. A mob of *contadini*, ragged, active and vociferous, started up from the adjacent tombs as though they had been ghouls, and very soon made practicable breaches in the barriers by the simple process of pulling down the loose stones; for no mortar had been used in their structure. Thus, we pedestrians, too, were enabled to "take" our stone walls and follow the Hunt, to our great internal joy, but to the increasing laceration of our tendon-Achilles. Surely on that hunting-morning the thistles must have savoured all the sweets of vengeance for the injuries inflicted on them by I know not how many generations of donkeys.

This kind of thing went on for a full hour and a half, the noble sportsmen meandering about the Campagna under the guidance of the huntsman, and the pack wagging their tails in unison, or keeping them in a state of quiescence in apparent obedience to the nod or the wink of the whipper-in. It was very pretty to see the ladies "schooling" over the walls, or when there came a hedge with too much brushwood about it, to see the corps of mounted pioneers lop away the impertinent twigs lest the Amazons should scratch their pretty faces as they swept through. There was a dash of the steeple-chase about it, and a suspicion of Mr. Sleary's circus, the audience being unrestricted in their locality. I say that it was very pretty; but by about a quarter to two I began to grow impatient to hear the hounds "give tongue"—is that the correct phraseology?—or to hear somebody cry "Yoicks!" or "Hark away!" I began to get weary, too, of the "schooling," and irritated at the corps of mounted pioneers, who was a grisly man, with a black beard, mounted on a black horse, with a black axe, and all manner of sinister-looking implements of a prevailing sable hue, slung at his saddle-bow. He looked like Herne the Hunter, who had emigrated from Windsor Forest to be nearer graves.

At about two o'clock it occurred to me that the excitement of the chase would be very much enhanced if such an article as a fox were added to it. It was very clear, as the condemned criminal remarked to the ordinary when the sheriff looked at his watch, and observed that it was growing late, that the fun couldn't begin without *him*.

An English friend volunteered the information that he had met the fox, the day before yesterday, on quite another road, and going in the direction of the Porta del Popolo, to keep an appointment, it is to be presumed, at a private henroost. For my part, I could not divest myself of the impression that the fox was still squatting snugly at the bottom of the Tomb of Cecilia Metella, lunching off a cold chicken, and repeating that it was very ungenteel behaviour on the part of the gentlemen of the Roman Hunt to keep him waiting so.

There was plenty of cover, both in the underbrush of the slopes and in the inexhaustible graves, and for another half-hour the huntsman went poking about, followed by his dogs. At every moment I expected to see a gentleman with a brush scurry out, and, indeed, I should not have been surprised had he sallied forth, with a shovel-hat and bands, and buckles in his shoes, and, looking up from his breviary, like Don Abbondio, in the *Promessi Sposi*, calmly inquired what all this clatter was about on the Feast of St. Odille, the eve of St. Nicaise, and the morrow of St. Lucia. But no fox appeared, and in default of Reynard, I was fain to admire the dashing horsemanship of Mr. Jarrett's little boy, and the equally intrepid Amazonship of a lady who stuck at nothing, and went at everything, who was capitally mounted, and did not look more than six-and-twenty, and who, I was told, was Miss Charlotte Cushman, the tragic actress. Lady Macbeth foxhunting! I was quite prepared after this to see the ghost of Cecilia Metella taking the lead, or Galla Placida flying over a five-barred gate.

They found a fox soon after this, appropriately enough, in a tomb; and here the duties of the scribe come to an end. I may well be excused from accumulating any more solecisms on matters which I do not understand. I trust, however, that the excellent newspaper, *Bell's Life*, had a correspondent in the field, and that this splendid run with the Roman Hounds will be duly chronicled. I was very glad to get back to the barouche, and return to Rome, to lunch, and send my boots, which were rather too elaborately decorated with the Order of the Thistle, to be mended. I have come to the conclusion that hunting is a very abstruse science, and that, in addition to the intense study it requires, you must be Born to it.

The Duchess of Berry, it is said, once witnessed a cricket-match gotten up by some Englishmen at Dieppe for her special delectation. After some hours' batting and bowling, in a broiling sun, she asked "when the game was going to begin." She had mistaken all the batting and bowling for mere preparation. Thus may I have made too light of all the meandering and the poking about, and have seen a fox-hunt without being aware of it. I heard in the evening that the fox, though hunted, was not killed. After a sharp run the poor little beast took refuge (always consistent) in another tomb, and they benevolently left him there to be hunted another day. At the last meet an enthusiastic English sportsman insisted that the fox should die the death, and, having some lucifer-matches in his pocket, he smoked him out of his earth, and so delivered him to the dogs and secured his "pad." I don't know what lady had the brush. In any case, I still hold the opinion that the animal I saw chevied was not the genuine one, and that the real original fox remains to this moment in the Tomb of Cecilia Metella, picking a merrythought, and observing that punctuality is the soul of business.

Some people are born to do things by contraries. I never saw a cock-fight till I went to Africa, and the only cricket-match I ever witnessed was in the Valley of Mexico. It was quite consistent with the rule of contraries that I should have to wait for a trip to Rome ere I beheld a pack of English foxhounds.

THE END.

LONDON: ROBSON AND SONS, PRINTERS, PANCRAS ROAD, N.W.